MONTGOMERY
CLIFT

A BIOGRAPHY

MONTGOMERY CLIFT

A BIOGRAPHY

PATRICIA BOSWORTH

HARCOURT BRACE JOVANOVICH

NEW YORK AND LONDON

For my husband, MEL ARRIGHI,
without whom this book could not have been written

Preface

When I first began researching this biography in 1973, I knew my focus would be a double one: I wanted to show how Montgomery Clift evolved into one of the definitive actors of the 1950s, but I also wanted to explore the inner life and tragic strivings of a man who remained an enigmatic figure even to his closest friends.

I tried to talk to every director, every actor, and many of the playwrights Monty worked with. I talked to most of his close friends. I talked to his agents, his lawyer, his doctor, his barber, his former secretary; I spent one afternoon wandering through the rooms of his elegant brownstone.

Basically, I went back to primary sources. My greatest debt is to Monty's older brother, Brooks. Brooks has saved everything that had to do with Monty—photograph albums, costumes from almost every movie, old letters—even one of the first cryptic notes Monty scribbled to his mother as a little boy, which stated: "I love you. Why not?"

Brooks helped me trace the origins of the Clift and Anderson-Blair families back five generations to Tennessee and Maryland, and helped me recreate Monty's childhood in Europe and Chicago, his years on Broadway and in Hollywood, and his last years as a semi-recluse in New York.

Brooks's recollections were supplemented by Monty's twin sister, Ethel McGinnis, who also generously lent me her letters and photographs. I am deeply indebted as well to Monty's mother, Sunny Clift, for her time and assistance.

For their interviews, letters, and constant encouragement I must thank especially Kevin McCarthy, Augusta Dabney, Jeanne Levy, Ned Smith, Lorenzo James, Robert Lewis, Bill Le Massena, and Jack Larson. They often alerted me to out-of-the-way source material.

To Paul Meyers and the staff of the Theatre Collection of New York's Lincoln Center Library of the Performing Arts and to the staffs of the New York Society Library and the Library of the Academy of Motion Picture Arts and Sciences in Los Angeles for their unstinting help, my thanks.

I would also like to thank Arthur Miller, Elia Kazan, Fred and Renée Zinnemann, Judy Balaban, Katharine Hepburn, Tennessee Williams, Maureen Stapleton, Nancy Walker, Lynn Tornabene, Irwin Shaw, Patricia Roe, Hope Lange, Ed Foote, Janet Cohn, Edie Van Cleve, Phyllis Thaxter, Morgan James, Patricia Collinge, the late Diana Lynn, Michael Kellin, Nora Ephron, Mike Maslansky, Harry Sions, Jim Goode, Francis Robinson, Herman Shumlin, Robert Parrish, Nancy Pinkerton, Rosemary Santini, Arline Cunningham, Lehman Engel, Mira Rostova, Eli Wallach, Inge Morath, Frank Taylor, Jim Bridges, Dolly Haas, Max Youngstein, Dr. Arthur Ludwig, Dr. Richard Robertiello, Mildred Newman, Fred Green, Deborah Kerr, Peter Viertel, Susan Kohner, John Weitz, John Huston, Eleanor Clift, Don Keefer, Karl Malden, François Truffaut, Myrna Loy, Bill Kenly, Joanna Ney, Irene Sharaff, Sybil Christopher, Richard Burton, Dore Schary, Kay Brown, Phyllis Jackson, Audrey Wood, Donald Windham, Sandy Campbell, Sidney Davis, Harriet Van Horne, Norris Houghton, John Fiedler, Ellen Adler, Roddy McDowall, Bruce Robertson-Dick, Burt Padell, Ben Bagley, Anne Baxter, Danny Selznick, Giuseppe Perrone, Herman Citron, William Wyler, Herb Machiz, Thornton Wilder, Isabel Wilder, Ruth Gordon, Garson Kanin, John Dartig, Ed Epstein, John Springer, Bill Werneth, Shelley Winters, James Jones, Martin Swenson, Nicola Dantine, Helmut Dantine, the late Robert Ryan, Elaine Dundy, Judy Feiffer, Guy Moneypenny, Brooke Hayward, Bill Gunn, Marie Crummere, Gladys Hill, Paul Kohner, Robert Lantz, Shirley Lantz, Helen Merrill, Merle Miller, Edward Dmytryk, Stephen Boyd, Lucy Komisar, William Marchant, Dr. Lily Ottenheimer, J. William Silverberg, M.D. And for their editorial guidance, the late Tony Godwin, Dan Okrent, Tom Stewart and Gene Stone.

And lastly a brief note on my own impressions. I met Montgomery Clift when I was a young girl. My father, the lawyer Bartley Crum, helped organize Monty's trip to Israel, and he also arranged for Monty to spend several days in the death house in San Quentin as part of his preparation for the killer he was to play in the movie *A Place in the Sun.*

I'll never forget Monty pacing back and forth across our living room, describing with accuracy and much emotion the convicts he'd met in prison.

Twenty-three years later when I began studying his performances on film, I realized that Monty's best work was always his remarkable paring down to the essentials of a character. In his movies Monty personified nonconformists and loners, who, in the midst of some violent crisis, seemed to be groping toward an understanding of themselves and the world: in so doing Monty always revealed some basic human truth.

That is the final pleasure in Montgomery Clift's acting, and it is the reason why I wanted to unravel the mysteries of his special artistry and set forth the story in a book.

Prologue

The little dinner party on May 12, 1956 at Elizabeth Taylor's home high in the hills of Coldwater Canyon was in honor of Montgomery Clift. Monty, as he was called by everyone who knew him, was Elizabeth Taylor's dearest friend.

Monty Clift was at the peak of his career in 1956. The first actor to defy Hollywood's studio system and win, he had always refused to be typecast as a conventional romantic hero. Instead, in the preceding eight years, he had chosen to play a series of complex, original, offbeat characters in such movies as *Red River, The Search, From Here to Eternity,* and *I Confess.* He had already been nominated for three Academy Awards.

Now he was starring opposite Elizabeth Taylor in a gargantuan, wide-screen, Civil War epic entitled *Raintree County,* which MGM had budgeted at $5 million. The first movie Monty and Elizabeth had made together, *A Place in the Sun,* was already being described as the emblematic film of the 1950s. They hoped *Raintree County* would be as successful.

Monty and Elizabeth talked a lot about *Raintree County* during that dinner party on May 12. They kidded each other about how gorgeous and young the cameraman, Bob Surtees, was making them look in the first rushes; they talked about how they looked on film because there didn't seem much else to say. The party wasn't going very well.

The other guests, Rock Hudson and his secretary Phyllis Gates, and the actor Kevin McCarthy wandered around the sparsely furnished living room trying to keep conversation going while Taylor's husband, Michael Wilding, lay on the not-too-clean white couch, the victim of a back spasm.

For part of the evening, Monty lounged on the floor. He had not bothered to shave, and a stubble of beard coated his cheeks; still, it was easy to see why he was called the most beautiful man in the movies.

Every so often, Elizabeth punctuated the conversation by putting another Sinatra record on the hi-fi. Monty kept jumping up to help her. He also poured the warmish rosé which the Wildings had in endless supply, but Monty refused to drink any himself. He said he was exhausted.

At eleven-thirty he excused himself politely and left, accompanied by Kevin McCarthy, who was going to drive ahead of him in his car and guide him down the canyon to Sunset Boulevard. Monty's parting words to the group were: "Kevin has to help me down that mountain or I'll drive around in circles all night."

Then Monty got into his car and, following Kevin, started driving down the steep, winding, dark road. About twenty minutes later Kevin was back, pounding on Elizabeth's front door and yelling hysterically, "Monty's been in an accident! I think he's dead!"

When Elizabeth and the others reached Monty's car at the foot of the hill, they saw the automobile crushed against a telephone pole. There was broken glass and blood everywhere. Blood spurted onto Elizabeth's silk dress as she crawled over the front seat and cradled Monty's head in her lap.

She looked down into his face, which was a bloody unrecognizable pulp. He stirred in her arms and moaned. He was alive, but his nose was broken, his jaw shattered, his cheeks severely lacerated, and his upper lip split completely in half.

Montgomery Clift survived that night and lived for ten more years, but his real death occurred as he lay bleeding and half-conscious in Elizabeth Taylor's arms. Nothing would ever be the same for him after that.

PART ONE

1

Edward Montgomery Clift was born October 17, 1920 in Omaha, Nebraska, several hours after his twin sister Roberta. "I was always the gentleman," Monty would joke years later. "I let Sister see the moon before I did."

The twins were delivered at home by an obstetrician. Their mother, Sunny, a tiny strong-willed woman of regal bearing and luminous eyes, had suffered through the delivery without anesthetic. The babies in her arms, she vowed "never again." There was already an eighteen-month-old brother, Brooks, in the nursery. Sunny had had an operation to conceive him, but she had not expected twins and privately had no idea how to handle them.

At the time of Monty's birth the Clifts were living in a comfortable three-story house full of red plush and stained-glass windows. Father Bill Clift had just become first vice-president of Omaha National Bank, so he could afford both a maid and a nurse for his burgeoning family.

Previously he had sold stocks and bonds for the National City Investment Company, traveling all over Nebraska and Kansas and working a fourteen-hour day. He and Sunny had lived in cheap boarding houses, and when times were lean Sunny had knitted sweaters and sold them to friends. Now their fortunes had turned, and Bill, who had always wanted a family, was excited about the prospect of settling down in a big house.

In a sense he hoped to recreate the atmosphere of his boyhood home in Chattanooga. As the youngest of six brothers and sisters, he had grown up in a close-knit Southern family; Bill Clift loved reminiscing about the Clifts. According to him, there had been Clifts in America since 1695, when the first Clifts came over from Essex,

England, and settled in Maryland. Seven generations of Clifts had participated with distinction in every war fought by the United States, with the exception of the Spanish-American War; a fact Bill Clift was fond of repeating.

By the 1850s most of the Clifts were living in Tennessee. Industrious patriotic folk—preachers, lawyers, and soldiers—they wanted to take advantage of this wild Southern state where there was so much opportunity. They made small fortunes in banking and road building, and they invested their money in the cotton wealth of Memphis.

In time the Clifts married into the Preston and Kefauver families. These branches still reside in Nashville.

Monty's great-grandfather, Colonel William Clift, was a squat, rugged pioneer. He owned 45,000 acres in Soddy County, Tennessee, land rich in iron ore and timber, and by the age of thirty he was a millionaire. A deeply religious Baptist, he did not believe in slavery and freed many slaves just before the firing on Fort Sumter, giving them farms on his vast property.

The rest of his family was incensed; they were anti-abolitionists and supported Jefferson Davis. As soon as the Civil War began, the Clifts divided even more when Colonel William joined the Union forces and his youngest son, Moses, became an officer in the Confederate cavalry.

For the next four years they fought on opposite sides. At one point during a skirmish, father and son captured each other, then fell into each other's arms laughing. Whenever they happened to arrive home together between battles, they would sit down at the table with their various relatives and toast each other in "a cordial and loving manner." "Family loyalty was a hallmark of the Clifts," Monty's father once recalled. He was referring to *his* father, Colonel Moses.

Shortly after Reconstruction began, Colonel Moses moved from Nashville to Chattanooga where he built a large home on McCallie Avenue and proceeded to raise his six children (two sons and a daughter by his first wife, two sons and a daughter by his second wife, Florence Parrot, a vivacious young woman from Catersville, Georgia).

The Colonel thought himself a devoted parent, although family life was formal and impudence was not tolerated. He devoted most of his time to his law practice, often working until dawn preparing briefs. He soon got the reputation for being one of the best lawyers in the state, though colleagues often described him as having a "butter heart" when confronted by people in need. When it came to arguing a case, however, no one was more passionate or articulate. He ultimately became president of the Supreme Court of Tennessee, a position he held proudly until his death.

As the youngest son, Bill Clift tried very hard to please his father by getting good grades and reciting the Old Testament from memory. He was a good-natured, placid little boy who for a while thought of becoming a preacher. When his father advised "practice the golden rule," he listened solemnly and never forgot it. He also believed, as did the Colonel, in "Our Lord and Savior who feels compassion to all humanity."

But the humanitarian sentiments of the Clift family were strictly Southern; blacks were the exception to the rule. Rumors abounded that some Clift relatives—a distant cousin in Nashville—had been involved in a lynching. Whether or not that is true, as far as the Colonel was concerned blacks were second-class citizens. "We must maintain white supremacy, but we must be just," he said. Bill Clift could never accept the idea of whites and blacks sitting comfortably together in the same room; towards the end of his life, when Monty brought his black male secretary home for Thanksgiving dinner, Bill was unable to contain his extreme agitation.

As a boy he had never had to cope with such social shocks. Life on McCallie Avenue was languid and shuttered, though the Clifts themselves were a noisy and quarrelsome bunch when left alone. The Colonel defined the lines of social distinction for his children to follow, and before Bill took out a girl, her social standing and family wealth were checked out by both his parents.

As a young man Bill dreamed of becoming a banker like his uncles, whose heroes were Jupiter Morgan and Cornelius Vanderbilt. When he told his parents of his ambition, they discouraged him by saying there were fortunes to be made in road building and in transportation; they pressed him to study engineering. Incapable of arguing with his parents and unsure of his own judgment, Bill went to Cornell in 1908 and followed their wishes.

Just before he left for Ithaca he had a photograph taken. It reveals nothing more than a round-faced young man with a serene expression, enlivened only by occasional dimples.

There are very few photographs of Monty's mother, Ethel "Sunny" Fogg, as a young woman. She was too restless to pose. Only one portrait can be found, taken when she was around eighteen. The camera recorded an aristocratic face, a slopingly beautiful face, marked by an almost unbearable sadness. The nose is patrician straight, and the huge, deep-set, staring eyes, accentuated by thick expressive dark brows, glitter as strangely and hypnotically as Monty's.

Sunny was born on September 29, 1888, in Philadelphia, Pennsylvania. The birth certificate does not give her a surname but records "Sophie and Frank Adams" as her mother and father. The attending physician, Dr. Edward E. Montgomery, took care of Sunny until she was a year old. He then arranged to have her adopted by the Charles Foggs of Germantown, who were paid a sum to take care of the infant, whose parents and origins they never knew.

Charles Fogg worked only periodically, as foreman of a steel mill in Germantown; he was an alcoholic. Most of the time he stayed at home and made life miserable for Sunny. She did not know why the neighborhood children refused to play with her; until she started school she lived a totally isolated existence. When she was eight, Mrs. Fogg told her she was an orphan and that her parents had abandoned her. From then on, whenever Sunny talked back to her, she would say she hoped she wouldn't grow up to be a bad woman like her mother.

Sunny's only escape from Fogg's taunts came when she attended church. The sermon and the rich vibrating organ music gave her some comfort. Dr. Montgomery was always present at the services, and afterwards they often chatted together. One afternoon when she was around ten, he invited her back to his home for tea and during their conversation he asked her how she was being treated by the Foggs.

Not well, she admitted, but then perhaps she deserved no better. She was not a very good girl, she said, and she had been warned that if she didn't behave she would grow up to be a bad woman like her mother. With that Dr. Montgomery took her into his arms and told her that her mother was not a bad woman, she was an aristocrat, and that she, Ethel Sunny, should be proud of her heritage; she was a thoroughbred and had fine American blood running through her veins.

Sunny was astonished. She begged the doctor to tell her who her real parents were, but he said he could not, he had been sworn to secrecy. However, he assured her that someday her natural mother would claim her as her own.

From then on Sunny lived in the hope that her parents would

acknowledge her existence: in anticipation of that event she studied very hard to become a top student. Although she still felt miserably alone and abandoned, she no longer cared when her classmates snubbed her; she was a "thoroughbred" and as such she possessed a secret pride about herself.

Throughout her adolescence, Sunny pursued her goal of self-improvement, earning straight "A's" in school and taking singing and music lessons paid for by Dr. Montgomery, who also encouraged her to speak French and to recite Shakespeare. Every effort was made to turn her into a beautifully cultivated young lady so that when her family came for her they would not be ashamed. She longed to know who her distinguished forebears were and vowed she would not rest until she did.

Sunny pressed Dr. Montgomery to tell her what he knew, and finally when she was eighteen and about to go to Cornell on scholarship, the doctor revealed the mysterious circumstances of her birth.

Her mother, Sunny discovered, was Maria Anderson of Virginia. Maria, sweet voiced and serene, was the daughter of Colonel Robert Anderson, the Union commander of Fort Sumter, whose brilliant and heroic defense of that Charleston fort in 1861 (he refused to surrender to Jefferson Davis and evacuated only after four months of intensive fighting) marked the beginning of the Civil War.

Late in life Anderson married Elizabeth Clough, whose father was a Clark of the northwest frontier Clarks. Elizabeth was an imperious snappish woman given to violent fits of rage, but her husband adored her. She and Anderson had three daughters, Sophie, Erba, and Maria. Anderson doted on his youngest daughter, Maria, nicknaming her "Bobbie," after himself.

After his death in 1880, his wife, Eliza, hysterical with grief, refused to allow her daughters out of their home in Washington, D.C.

She needed them now for constant companionship because she was afraid of being lonely. Besides, she told them cruelly, "You're all going to be old maids anyway." Despite the restrictions, Erba, the oldest, ran off and married almost immediately. The younger sisters, Maria and Sophie, stayed by their mother's side and appeared totally dominated by her.

In 1886 Maria began going out again to dances and receptions. She was then thirty years old. Somewhere, someplace she met Woodbury Blair, the dashing bachelor son of Montgomery Blair, attorney for Dred Scott and also postmaster general in Lincoln's cabinet. Maria and "Woody" fell in love.

The Blairs were as distinguished and wealthy as the Andersons, having been among the first settlers in Maryland, where they drank, dueled, raced, and were addicted to cock fighting. Their family estate, called Silversprings, was one of the great estates of Maryland. In architecture and landscape it resembled Versailles.

Despite her mother's disapproval, Maria saw Woody frequently throughout 1886 and continued to do so until Mrs. Anderson began throwing tantrums. She was furious at Woody's father because she believed he could have persuaded President Lincoln to send troops to reinforce her husband at Fort Sumter and had made no effort to do so.

Woody countered that his father was the only member of Lincoln's cabinet who *had* supported Anderson in Charleston. Mrs. Anderson called him a liar. Woody countered that she was not only out of her mind, she was as "mean tempered as Mary Lincoln." With that Mrs. Anderson banished Woody from the house and forbade her daughter ever to see him again.

Nevertheless they continued to meet secretly. Maria's sister Sophie was the only one who knew of the affair. Eventually the couple eloped somewhere in Maryland, but because of her mother's state of mind, Maria continued to live at home. She and Eliza fought constantly over Woody Blair—finally she admitted that he was her husband. Eliza promptly got the marriage annulled. She then locked Maria in her room, where she was kept a virtual prisoner.

The only time she left that room was during her pregnancy. She was pregnant with a child by Woody Blair, and she insisted on having the baby, although Eliza wanted her to have an abortion.

In the summer of 1888 Maria traveled to Philadelphia with her sister Sophie and her mother, Eliza, taking up residence at a small house at 1618 A Street. Dr. Edward Montgomery, who had served with Colonel Anderson during the Civil War, delivered the baby who was named Ethel. Later Montgomery began calling the child Sunny because of her lilting golden voice.

Immediately after the birth, the Anderson women returned to Washington, D.C., Maria whispering that she would send for her daughter as soon as she could, Eliza ordering Montgomery to put the child up for adoption. Montgomery waited almost a year before doing so, taking care of the baby himself. It was only when he was assured by Mrs. Anderson that both Woody Blair and Maria agreed to such an arrangement that he found a foster home at the Foggs'.

At that point he was sworn to secrecy as to the identity of Sunny's natural parents.

Even so, as she grew up, Dr. Montgomery wrote letter after registered letter to Maria Anderson keeping her informed as to her daughter's development. He repeatedly asked for permission to tell Sunny about her real mother and father when she came of age. All his letters were returned unopened. Because he felt so guilty about his own involvement in the matter he took it upon himself to speak frankly to Sunny.

Dr. Montgomery's revelations were profoundly shocking to the eighteen-year-old Sunny Fogg, but she did not reveal her feelings; already she was intensely self-contained. Inside she experienced frustration and misery to the fullest; she felt that what had been done to her was immoral, vicious. She had not chosen to be born into this world, but her parents, whether they liked it or not, had a responsibility to her and this included giving her her birthright.

Along with Dr. Montgomery she began writing a fresh series of letters to Maria and Sophie Anderson in Washington, D.C., telling them of her deep need to be acknowledged. She appealed to their sense of honor, their conscience—she never received an answer.

Studying her genealogy became Sunny's lifelong preoccupation, and her energy poured into it, overwhelming, secretly hysterical, engulfing, great. The study was almost a necessity; in that way she was earning the right to share her families' lives—at least vicariously.

Soon she could recite—to herself—the minutiae about her relatives and ancestors—from Larz Anderson, the diplomat under President Wilson, to the fact that Montgomery Blair had been John Brown's attorney after Harpers Ferry.

At the library she pored over photographs of the Andersons and the Blairs, and she was pleased to note that she bore a striking resemblance to both sides. The Blairs were dark, slender, fine boned, and so was she. From the Andersons she inherited large glittering wild eyes, accentuated by thick expressive brows.

Bill Clift knew nothing of Sunny's secret when he met her at Cornell in the fall of 1910. He knew only that he fell in love with her the minute he saw her. She was one of the brightest girls on campus and one of the most popular. Men circled about her, attracted by her mysterious personality, her golden voice. She dressed in carefully ironed shirtwaists that showed off her beautifully shaped breasts, and she was always moving, moving, moving to the library or the tennis courts or to chorus practice. She dazzled with her desperate blazing energy. He had never met anyone like her.

His previous sweethearts had been well-behaved decorative Southern girls who had nothing to say. Sunny was full of opinions. She told him she thought he was foolish to be an engineer if he wanted to be a banker. She was considering going into law, a highly unusual ambition for a woman in 1910.

She told him that as a child she had traveled to the steppes of Russia and eaten chocolate tortes in Vienna. Bill Clift had never even been to New York. To him Sunny Fogg seemed unbelievably worldly.

Bill Clift was so in love he never questioned her apparent lack of both background and money. What did it matter? After they had known each other a while she confided that she was an orphan. Her childhood had been horrible—blighted, she said, and now that it was over, she wished to forget it.

Naturally such remarks made Bill curious, but she would tell him no more and he didn't dare pursue the subject further, afraid she might fly into a rage. What fascinated him most was her royal manner. He would not have been surprised if she had commanded him to kiss her foot.

He wanted passionately to marry her, but there were other men around who seemed more confident than he, so he drew back. Bill Clift graduated from Cornell in 1912, and Sunny, two years behind, stayed on to finish her degree. They parted affectionately but perhaps, they thought, forever.

But Bill couldn't forget her. For the next two years he worked at a series of engineering jobs, corresponding regularly with Sunny; her letters, by their confiding nature, gave him subtle encouragement. Bit by bit she described her life's goal—to live and experience life as a thoroughbred. Bit by bit she revealed her complicated background as well as her continued efforts to reach her mother, Maria Anderson. Bill's answers were lengthy and encouraging. During her senior year at Cornell he came up to visit and they became engaged.

That summer, after graduation, they traveled excitedly to Chattanooga to meet his family. Before their arrival Sunny begged him not to say anything about her real parents—not until she was legally acknowledged. Bill promised, and the meeting so anticipated by the Clifts turned out to be disastrous. In the South it was not simply wealth that counted socially, it was family, and Sunny appeared to have neither: she was an arrogant Yankee orphan.

During her entire visit the Clifts ignored her and talked instead of Colonel Moses, who had been dead for three years. Listening to the drawling anecdotes in the stuffy Chattanooga living room, Sunny knew that she would never be accepted.

Bill's mother said as much when Sunny was unable to make anything but the vaguest statements about her foster parents back in Germantown, and finally Flo Clift told her scornfully that she would ruin her son socially and economically if she became his wife.

By the end of her stay in Chattanooga, Sunny had come to that conclusion herself. But she was bitter about it. "I was such a naive little fool," she wrote Bill later. "I thought your family would love me. How wrong I was." She wanted to break their engagement, but Bill refused to let her do it. "I want you to be my wife," he said, and held firmly to that statement even though it meant estrangement from his family.

Together they left Chattanooga and were subsequently married sometime in October of 1914. They didn't have enough money for a honeymoon—instead they went directly to the tiny hamlet of Saltillo in Mississippi, where Bill had a job building dams. Once there they rented a room from a family of deaf-mutes. "Saltillo was full of deaf-mutes," Bill told Monty later. He and Sunny slept on a mattress of corn husks, and she cooked their meals in an open fireplace. She had brought an exquisite trousseau with her, but the dresses remained in the trunk—"the conditions in Saltillo were extremely primitive," she once remarked to Monty.

The next four years were hard. Sunny wanted Bill to leave engineering and become a banker. At her insistence he took night courses in investments. Then, again at her insistence, they moved from Mississippi to Kansas and then to Omaha, Nebraska. During the First World War Bill sold more Liberty Bonds than anyone else in the Midwest. Still, he was often so broke he had to wear his overcoat indoors at work—his jacket was that threadbare.

When Sunny found herself pregnant in 1919, she told Bill she intended to raise the child and any others they might have like Anderson-Blairs—in the elegant, princely manner which they deserved. She would never allow them to be deprived of affection nor of their prestigious heritage as she had been, and now that they were to become parents she hoped Bill would join her in her efforts to claim her rightful birthright; she would not accept defeat.

She hoped Bill Clift understood how important this was; she made him promise he would never divulge her true identity to their children until the circumstances warranted.

Bill Clift agreed, but the keeping of that secret drastically affected their marriage and the lives of their children, Brooks, Roberta, and Montgomery Clift.

2

As long as she remained in Omaha Sunny was considered a beautiful if unorthodox mother. Throughout that intensely cold first winter after their birth she could be seen wheeling Monty and his twin sister in their carriage past high snowdrifts and into freezing winds. "Everybody thought I was crazy," she said, "but I built up their little constitutions. They never had so much as a sniffle."

Brooks's earliest childhood memory is of Sunny going off to a dance one evening. "Ma was wearing a sweeping full skirt and she had on a marvelous perfume. She and Pa were laughing together."

The second memory is a slightly grimmer one: the Clift family kitchen maid, a cheerful middle-aged woman, that same evening setting fire to the nursery. She then scooped up the twins and Brooks in her arms and hurtled down the stairs.

"She threw us all down on a settee and went off to call the fire department. Monty was only eight months old. He and Sister both peed on me in their excitement," Brooks recalled the following day when Emma Wilke, the nurse, red-eyed from weeping, took him into the pantry for a glass of milk. Wilke had been on her day off the night before, so she blamed herself for the fire.

Wilke was a big-shouldered, uncommunicative woman originally from Chicago, who remained with the Clifts until Brooks went off to Harvard. "No matter how broke we were, Wilke stuck by us. She absolutely worshipped Ma. Thought she was heroic."

In 1919 Sunny had hemorrhaged during her pregnancy with Brooks and was rushed to the hospital in Omaha. The only way to save the baby was to lie immobile; in spite of intense pain she lay flat on her back without moving for three weeks. Wilke, who was head nurse, took care of Sunny, marveling that she never cried out.

Shortly after that Brooks was born, a perfect, healthy baby. Wilke told the Clifts she wanted to look after him and any other children they might have. "When Ma wasn't around Wilke bossed us and told us how to dress and what to eat," Brooks said. "Monty and I hated her."

Before the twins' first birthday Flo Clift suddenly wrote from Chattanooga asking if her grandchildren could visit her. Sunny agreed, and Bill hoped at last there might be peace between his volatile wife and family. But the attempt at reconciliation failed.

After several stilted conversations over meals and walks about Chattanooga, Flo Clift attempted to pick up Monty and Sister in her arms. With that Sunny gave a ferocious animal cry and rushed at the older woman, frightening her half to death. "Sunny was like a lioness defending her cubs," Bill said later when describing the incident. He thought her reaction "adorable." His mother did not. She never saw Sunny or the children again.

While the children were still young, Sunny took them away from Nebraska in July and traveled to New England where she rented a series of large summer homes. Bill Clift stayed behind in Omaha at the bank. He tried to accept his wife's restless need to be on the move; he knew she was determined that Monty and the others absorb the American history that was part of their heritage.

During the summer of 1922 they sublet a shingled house in Great Barrington, Massachusetts. There were frequent outings to Lenox, to the graveyard at Stockbridge, and to Tanglewood, then a private estate overlooking the shimmering Lake Mahkeenak.

There are snapshots of that summer in Brooks Clift's album. One picture shows the three children standing in a cart with Wilke next to them on a country road outside Lenox. Sunny can be seen kneeling in the dirt opposite her brood. She is formally dressed in an ankle-length pleated tea gown. Her dark hair is bound back. The sun is hot on her face but she doesn't seem to notice; her attention is entirely focused on Monty, who already bears a striking resemblance to her.

Next to him, twin sister, older brother, and nurse smile fiercely back at Sunny. Only Monty is gazing in the opposite direction. He seems intent on his own thoughts, his own fantasies, and already he appears set apart and alone.

In 1924, when the twins were four, Bill Clift obtained a more lucrative position as sales manager of Ames Emerich Investment Company in Chicago. He was to originate new business for them and to buy securities in the Midwest and New York, so he began traveling continuously. He also began making a great deal of money. It was the zenith of the 1920s bull market; the future of United States industry seemed boundless.

Sunny and the children moved from Omaha to Highland Park, a wealthy Chicago suburb; the family lived in a capacious Tudor-style house filled with exquisite antiques and the finest of silver.

Although Highland Park was home base for the family, the children lived there briefly. For the next decade they were continually uprooted, traveling with their mother from New England to Bermuda and Europe and then back to the United States. Meanwhile, Bill Clift remained in Chicago, presumably making money to keep his family in the lavish style to which Sunny wished them to be accustomed.

"While we were away from home, there was never any explanation for Pa's absence," Brooks said. "We were just told he was too busy to be with us. We used to talk among ourselves about Pa. We got the feeling that he was obsessed with business and finance."

However, his letters contradict that impression. Here is part of one, dated July 20, 1925, when the family was in Great Barrington, Massachusetts:

> Dear Brooks and Monty and Sister,
> Daddy has some snapshots of you which Mother sent him and when he looks at them he gets so homesick he almost cries and sometimes he wishes he could cry just like you do when you get hurt. Daddy does not like to be away from his little ones nor from your dear mother. You know Daddy is so busy in the day time that he does not have time to think much about home, but at night when he goes home [to Highland Park]—it is not really home because he and mother are not there—so let us say when Daddy goes to his room he walks up and down and wants to see you all so much he does not know what to do with himself. He has a hard time even reading. You are all so dear to me that I do not like to have you far away. . . .

In spite of these protestations, Bill Clift rarely saw his children during this vital period of their growth. He was usually exhausted—invariably preoccupied. Privately he did not approve of the way the children—in particular his sons—were being raised, but he said nothing. Sunny's word was law. Once when Brooks ran to him begging to be allowed to part his hair differently from the twins, his father told him, "Do as your Ma says, she knows best."

Monty and the others were being raised as triplets, given identical haircuts (Dutchboy bobs), clothes, lessons, and responsibilities, regardless of age or sex. Sunny believed strongly that she was being fair and impartial, but Brooks, as the oldest, rebelled, kicking and talking back when he was told he must dress like Monty and Sister. "I wanted to be myself."

The only acknowledgment of any age difference was the fact that each child had a different kind of piggy bank. Brooks's was for quarters, Roberta's for dimes and Monty's for nickels. Every day that they were well behaved they were given the appropriate sum. "It was more difficult and less frequent for me to be good," Brooks said, "so my payola was larger."

Monty appeared the most docile, the most obedient of the three children. He did precisely as he was told. He was a quiet little boy, and he clung silently to his twin sister for comfort and protection. Only in the cartoons he drew when he was six does one see reflections of his subconscious. He sketched grotesque and remarkably accurate caricatures of his entire family. The crude balloon faces with their thick black brows and spindly legs expressed the spirit of the enigmatic Clift persona to a remarkable degree.

Two leather photo albums Sunny kept are a visual record of that period. South Egremont, Massachusetts, summer 1925. Pictures of a big white clapboard house covered with roses. In front of it the twins and Brooks frolic nude on the grass. "Naked in the Berkshires," Sunny had captioned the picture.

Yorktown Heights, New York, fall 1925. More pictures of a rambling Victorian mansion. This house was second home to the Clifts; since Bill was traveling frequently in and out of Manhattan on business, the children spent months at a time there. Snapshots in the album show Bill relaxing in his Yorktown Heights garden. There are other snapshots of Monty, Sister, and Brooks glowering under identical crewcuts.

Sometime after that in Somerset, Bermuda, the winter of 1925, the children and Sunny lived in a cottage called "Seaview" right on the ocean. There are brownish snapshots of Monty at "Seaview," looking immaculate and very serious as he learns to watercolor.

In Bermuda, Monty also learned to make soup, and he and his brother and sister took golf lessons.

Sunny did not tolerate any of her children breaking the strict

schedule she had set up for their lives. The twins and Brooks were
not allowed to vent their anger or opinions. "Ma was always right."
If they started shouting at each other she would chide them. "I've always taught you to be gentlemen and never raise your voices." And
she would invariably add that her entire life was dedicated to, and
sacrificed for, her children, so the least they could do was *behave*.
And yet Sunny was very affectionate, hugging and kissing the children, rocking them in her arms. Brooks and Monty developed the
habit early on of passionately embracing their friends. "We were a
very warm, very loving family," Sunny recalled. "There was always a
great deal of open affection."

It was in Bermuda late in 1925 that Sunny learned of her
mother's death. She had never received answers to the dozens of letters she'd written Maria Anderson over the previous decade, but still
she felt a terrible sense of loss. She immediately sent white lilies to
the grave site at West Point where Maria was to be buried next to her
father, Robert Anderson. From time to time after that Sunny visited
the grave, making sure there were always fresh flowers on the tomb-
stone.

Now she redoubled her efforts to reach the surviving members
of the Anderson family. More than ever she wanted to claim her
birthright—for her children's sake.

She enlisted her husband's aid. In his free time, Bill Clift hustled
about Washington, D.C., and Virginia talking to lawyers and genealogy experts. After much effort he made contact with Sophie Anderson, by now an eccentric old lady in precarious health and state of
mind, living alone in the Hotel Wyoming in Washington. Bill convinced Sophie she must at least answer one of her niece's letters.

Sophie and Sunny began a correspondence and the letters gave
Sunny encouragement. Elated, she began tutoring Monty and the
others relentlessly, teaching them how to read and write and spell
phonetically. They would never go to school until they went to college, she told her husband. Tutoring was part of her grand scheme to
raise them as she believed the Andersons and the Blairs had been
raised, in an isolated but classic tradition. They would be beautifully
educated but they would have to associate only with each other,
"with their own kind."

While still in Bermuda she sent away for a correspondence
course in Latin—in the evenings they conjugated verbs together; afterwards she read them Shakespeare or Dickens. Sister remembers that

when her mother recited *Prisoner of Chillon,* Monty burst into tears over the prisoner's plight. "He was terribly sensitive even then."

Sunny had already been thinking about their destinies. She wanted her children, particularly her sons, to become achievers—men of action—diplomats, lawyers, or bankers; because if they made their mark in history, they could blot out the shame of her obscure beginnings.

Monty, the linguist, the charmer, had the manners of a diplomat already; Brooks seemed headed for business. Sister, as the best student of the three, could turn into a fine historian.

Sunny never asked if her fantasies corresponded to their own. They never heard the question "what would you like to be?" Instead they listened to a barrage of continued declarations on their talents, looks, charm, thoughtfulness. Brooks said, "I took those words to mean I was worthless or such protestations wouldn't be necessary. I also thought Ma was more interested in us being successful than happy. The word happy wasn't in our vocabulary."

In the fall of 1926, Sophie Anderson summoned Sunny to Washington for an emotional confrontation at the Hotel Wyoming. Afterwards she reported to Bill Clift that "the minute I entered that hotel suite my aunt fell to her knees screaming and crying, 'You look exactly like my sister Bobbie.'"

Almost hysterical, the old lady then began berating herself for not having come forward sooner to acknowledge her niece as her kin, and she confided that she "dreaded death and seeing my Maker after what I have done to you."

Sunny demanded to know why her mother, Bobbie, had never come back to claim her in Germantown as she'd promised. Why had her letters remained unanswered, why were her appeals ignored? Sophie blamed Sunny's grandmother, Eliza Anderson, for the total breakdown in communication. According to Sophie, Eliza had kept Bobbie a virtual prisoner; she never received any mail, she had no friends, and whenever Bobbie threatened to tell the world—or at least the rest of the family—she had a daughter growing up in Germantown, Eliza would whisk her off to Europe or lock her in her room and Sophie had to guard her.

Sunny accepted her aunt's explanation of her mother's strange silence; in the next three hours the two women went over and over the blurred details of her birth and abandonment. Sophie finally admitted that Sunny had been adopted by the Foggs without her natural father's—Woodbury Blair's—knowledge or consent. "To this day he is not aware of your existence," her aunt told her.

After that meeting Sunny visited Sophie periodically in Washington, sometimes bringing Monty along. "He looks just like his grandfather, Montgomery Blair. Montgomery Blair was a twin, you know."

When Sophie met Brooks, she took a liking to him too. She began sending both brothers family heirlooms: a bracelet made out of Union Army buttons, a shaving mug with the initial "A." At one point she promised Brooks the Anderson grandfather clock. At another she told Sunny she and her sister Maria had interchangeable wills and that of course Sunny would receive everything from her mother's estate when she, Sophie, died, including the family silver and the portrait of Robert Anderson. That portrait now hangs in Brooks Clift's Washington, D.C., home, along with an oil painting of Mrs. Robert Anderson.

Every so often during their talks, Sunny would politely ask if she could please meet the rest of the Anderson family in order to be acknowledged by them. At the mention of the word "acknowledge," Sophie would fly into a rage and threaten to kill herself.

"You mustn't make a move!" she would rant. "Now is not the proper time!"

And Sunny would promise not to do anything that would make her aunt regret she had come into her life. Privately she decided that, however exacting and unreasonable Sophie's demands were, she would endeavor to comply with them.

It was difficult for her to remain so passive. In the summer of 1927, restless and unhappy, she took the children to an estate in Harmon, New York. It was unduly hot that summer, golden blazing hot, and while Brooks and Sister got sunburned and Monty ran down the road catching butterflies, Sunny took long walks by herself through the dry brittle grass and attempted to come to terms with Sophie Anderson's eccentricities.

She simply could not fathom the old lady's logic. Why wasn't this the "proper" time to be presented to her distinguished relatives? Hadn't she suffered enough? There were cousins and aunts and uncles all over Washington and Virginia and Maryland. It was tantalizing to be so close to her goal of achieving an identity, and yet, despite her aunt's acknowledgment, she still felt faceless and alone.

In the fall of 1927, the Clifts rented a house in Manhasset, L.I., and the children's tutoring continued. A Scottish carpenter named

Singleton taught them carpentry and Monty built a bed for his teddy bear.

Bill Clift came and went between "deals" in Manhattan and Chicago. The children complained they were lonely because they weren't allowed to play with other children on the block. Sunny never explained, she just forbade it. Actually, she was afraid Monty might be asked, "Who are you named after?" "Where does your mother come from?"

Early in 1928 Sunny could tolerate the situation no longer; she informed her aunt that since she couldn't see the Andersons, she would contact her father, Woodbury Blair, on her own. He was still residing at the family estate in Maryland. She would go there and confront him, she said.

If her niece did that she would throw herself out the window, Sophie screamed. When she calmed down she repeated that she was the only one who could arrange such a meeting and if Sunny would only be patient she would eventually do it.

However, before such a meeting could be arranged, Sunny must take Monty and the others abroad for two years. They must stay at the best hotels, seeing the sights and museums, being coached in tennis and tutored in French and German until they were fluent in both languages. Always they must keep to themselves while traveling—like royalty—they must never mingle, never speak to ordinary souls. After their cultural education was completed and their manners polished to a fine sheen, they could return to America.

Then, and only then, would Sophie feel they were properly prepared to meet with the Andersons and the Blairs. At that time she would give a gala party in Washington, and at this party she would introduce Sunny and Monty and Sister and Brooks as part of her family. Then they would all finally be recognized as Anderson-Blairs.

Sunny agreed instantly to the European venture, but she refused to think of the consequences until she returned to the house in Highland Park where the family was again living. Then she began to wonder what she would tell her husband.

She was not quite sure he would want her to take the children away now that they were all finally together again after almost four years of constant uprooting. She knew how much a permanent home meant to him. She loved the round-faced, balding man who was so trusting, so unfailingly generous with his money. He had worked weekends and fourteen-hour days trying to give them all the creature comforts Sunny had insisted were their right by heritage.

As soon as he came home from the office that night Sunny told Bill Clift of her decision to take Monty and the others to Europe. "My parents never argued," Brooks said. Bill agreed to the trip abroad at once. Although he was not sure about Sophie Anderson's flighty promise of recognition—she had gone thirty years without acknowledging Sunny as a legitimate member of the Anderson family—Bill Clift loved Sunny beyond reason and he wanted to make her happy.

"My father would do anything in the world to please Mother," Sister Clift said.

3

In May of 1928, Bill Clift saw his entire family, including Nurse Wilke, off to Europe on the *Ile de France*. It was the first of many luxurious crossings organized by Sunny, who was clever enough to sense that ocean travel was part of the culture of the 1920s, and who wanted her children to experience it.

After being kept in isolation from the world, Monty and the others reveled in shipboard existence. For the first time in their lives they were exposed to people—all kinds of people—and it left them in a state of stunned delight. They spoke to millionaires and sailors—to beautiful divorcées and silent screen stars like Buster Keaton. There were even some secret flirtations. (Brooks maintained he lost his virginity in a lifeboat on the *Ile*.)

The twins explored the promenade deck, and Monty imitated the couples strolling self-consciously about in their flannels and tweeds. He and Sister gorged on consommé and crackers and then bundled up in blankets, lay on deck chairs, and watched the sun sink behind the waves.

During the crossing on the *Ile,* a boy held Monty underwater in the ship's swimming pool and he almost drowned. In a desperate attempt to breathe, he burst a gland in his neck and developed a serious abscess in his ear. By the time the boat docked, Monty had a temperature of 104°.

Sunny rushed about Paris trying to obtain the best doctor in France to diagnose her son's condition. She was unimpressed by the ones she met—they weren't good enough. Imperiously, she stormed the American Embassy and demanded they give her the name of the greatest gland specialist in Europe. He turned out to be a Munich surgeon who had once treated the Kaiser. After phoning him, she and

Monty took the next train to Germany. By the time they reached the hospital, Monty was close to death.

His subsequent operation went on for hours. Brooks recalls that when the surgeon came out of the operating room around four in the morning, he had blood soaked through his uniform. "He reminded me of a butcher."

For weeks after the operation Monty was forced to lie flat in his hospital bed wearing a cast from neck to hip while the infected gland healed. At least twice during that period Sunny tried to make Brooks go in to him and say, "I love you. I love you." But he couldn't. He was terrified Monty would never leave the hospital alive.

He didn't die, but Sunny complained bitterly that the Kaiser's doctor had cut too deeply and over too wide an area, causing the long scar on Monty's neck.

Meanwhile Bill Clift wrote Monty a despairing letter from New York: "I think of you all the time. You are as dear to me as your mother and I never knew it before. I love you most dearly and how glad I will be when you are well and summer is over and you are home again."

When Monty finally recovered in late summer they returned to Paris. At that time—in 1928—the French capital was, in Janet Flanner's words, full of "obstinate gaiety." There were new plays, new ballets, operas, and costume balls almost every night, often accompanied by spectacular fireworks. The fountains gushed. And the great originals of the period, Picasso, Cocteau, Chanel, Gertrude Stein, and Dali, all pooled their talents and produced works together in an unheralded burst of creativity.

Although Sunny Clift was not part of this rarefied group, she tried to absorb what was pulsing around her. She bought the novels of Louise Vilmorin and struggled through them late at night in her room at the Hotel Crillon, where they were staying in the Woodrow Wilson suite. She insisted that the first French tutor she hired explain at once the importance of Proust's *A la recherche du temps perdu*.

After their lessons in the morning, she took the children and Wilke to the Louvre, and afterwards they strolled through the Tuileries Gardens and rolled their hoops. They went to concerts, the ballet or theater almost nightly. Monty heard the singer Yvonne Printemps that summer and he was enchanted by what he later described as "the unreal phantom quality of her voice." Afterwards he began collecting her records, and throughout his adolescence he played them over and over again in his room.

That same summer he saw the Comédie Française. "I could hear my heart thump as the curtain went up," he told Brooks. The actors on stage excited him terribly. He talked about the experience for days afterwards. They were leading an imaginary life on that gaudy set—they were involved in situations and in thoughts that were not their own—and yet they seemed totally committed. The idea of creating experience, of hiding behind another character's skin, fascinated him.

Paris awakened his passion for theater—for the worlds of make-believe. He began creating little plays in his head and he discussed them privately with Sister.

Sister had originally been christened Roberta after Bill Clift's favorite sister whom Sunny loathed. When the schism between the two families deepened, during their travels abroad, Sunny announced that hereafter her daughter would answer to the name of Ethel. The little girl agreed, although both mother and child heartily disliked the name.

Throughout his life Monty relied on Sister for comfort and advice. "Sister is the sensible twin," Nurse Wilke often said. "She sees things in black and white. Monty sees all the colors." Whatever their differences, deep subconscious longings drew them close. Their insecurities made them inseparable. By the time they were seven they were sharing every secret, every fantasy.

Sister was stronger and taller than her brother, and she was as homely as he was almost girlishly beautiful. Since they were anything but identical, both of them experienced moments of uncertainty as to which twin they were sexually. (At age forty, just before filming *The Misfits,* Monty suddenly asked his personal physician, "Did I start off as a girl in Ma's womb?")

As children, with twins' fear of loss of identity, Monty and his sister rarely were rebellious or even misbehaved. To bolster their identity and for protection, they invented a private language, which they perfected in Europe and which they used only with each other, much to Sunny's annoyance, since she hated to be left out of anything. "It took me years to translate what they were saying," Brooks recalled.

In the fall, they left Paris and traveled to Montreux, Switzerland. Sunny took them to see various points of interest, including Geneva and the medieval castle of Chillon.

Shortly after Christmas they went to Saint Moritz, where Sunny rented the top floor of the Villa Guardelei in Saint Moritz Champfer, one of the many small communities strung along the mountain valley. Outside their windows the snow was deep, and they could see the towering Alps in the distance. That winter they learned to ski, and in the evenings they sometimes had dinner with Lady Astor who gave Brooks a book inscribed, "To my boyfriend."

Brooks became a champion figure skater in Saint Moritz, and Monty, always competitive, followed close behind. Years later, when he toured with the Lunts in *There Shall Be No Night,* the entire cast went ice skating on frozen Lake Michigan, and Monty impressed everybody with his precise figure eights and dizzying corkscrew turns. "He was as graceful as Fred Astaire," an observer recalls.

While they were at Saint Moritz, Sunny hired a tutor, M. Helman, who coached the Clift children in history, English, literature, and languages. Desks were set up in one of the villa's bedrooms. There was a blackboard propped on a dresser, and on it was scrawled in chalk: "Study! 8:30 A.M." Photographs show Brooks, Monty, and Sister looking lonely but diligent, seated hunched over their notebooks. Nearby, an open window reveals the snowcapped Jungfrau.

Never a top student, Monty showed a distinct aptitude for French and German: he soon spoke both languages fluently. He was proud of the fact that he was trilingual and sprinkled his conversations with German and French phrases.

Years later Helen Merrill, a literary agent, recalled going to a party at Roddy McDowall's in New York where she and Monty discussed Thomas Mann in German. "He spoke so beautifully, so tenderly. I have never forgotten it."

In Saint Moritz the winter he was eight, Monty produced his first play. It was called *The Conversion of King Clovis*—he had concocted it from a French history book. He not only acted in it, but he helped make the crepe paper costumes and crowns for his brother and sister, who also had parts. They performed the show in their villa bedroom for Wilke, Sunny, and M. Helman, the tutor. When it was over the three adults applauded vigorously; afterwards Sunny gave notes as to how the performance could be improved.

That winter was memorable in another way. The three Clift children made friends for the first time with a jolly, young, twenty-three-year-old American geologist named Kate Billings. She had arrived at Saint Moritz fresh from two years in Africa, and she was full of vivid tales about the Gold Coast.

Kate took a liking to the shy Clift twins and to the more gregarious Brooks; she sought them out herself, and they eagerly accepted her friendship, skiing and tobagganing together until Sunny put a stop to it.

"I remember Kate and Monty and Sister and me drinking some delicious cream of pea soup Wilke had made," Brooks said. "We drank it from a thermos, sitting on the hard-packed snow, and we had such a marvelous time talking and laughing." After Kate left Saint Moritz, Brooks and Monty corresponded with her for years. "Kate was our first real contact with the outside world. We didn't want to lose her."

Although they had plenty of opportunity to meet people, passing as they did through the gilded lobbies and dining rooms of some of the finest hotels in Europe, Kate Billings was the only friend they made during their years abroad. Sunny refused to allow Monty and the others to "mingle indiscriminately." There were definite lines of social distinction to adhere to, as spelled out by Sophie Anderson. It was not just being rich that counted socially, it was family, and Kate Billings had neither. She was too ordinary; she didn't fit.

Ed Foote of the Boston Footes did. Ed's family had lived on Beacon Hill for generations. His uncle was Senator Saltonstall; his grandfather was Basil King, the rector of Christ Church, Cambridge.

Ed met the Clifts in Vevey, Switzerland, early in 1929. "Sunny struck up a conversation with my grandmother, Mrs. Basil King, and asked her all sorts of probing questions about her background, which Grandmother found amusing. She liked Sunny's fierceness, her gall." The two women became friends and had tea together almost every afternoon in Vevey.

However, young as he was (he was eight at the time), Ed Foote never got over what he called "Sunny's overweening social ambition. She gushed over us in an almost desperate way. And she kept referring to *her* distinguished relatives, her aristocratic family, but she never elaborated. I thought she was making it up."

Ed found Monty difficult to be with as well. "He was conceited and self-involved." He had already picked up his mother's air of exquisite arrogance; he walked about with a distinctly superior expression on his handsome face. He had also inherited Sunny's deep suspicion of people. He couldn't trust easily. "He was always giving me wary looks," Ed said. Still, urged on by the elderly Mr. King, the two boys played tennis together several times, after which Ed had some protracted talks with Brooks. "Brooks was a cheery, pleasant fellow, interested in a lot of things. We got along."

In the late 1940s Ed and Monty became casual friends. "Monty took to dropping by my sister's place in New York for Sunday lunch. He was delightful then, full of fun—it was right after *Red River,* so he was enormously successful—very much in demand."

Ed's last memory of Monty is an evening he spent with him and Elizabeth Taylor. "We all got totally soused somewhere on the West Side—and I remember Monty shouting to Liz, 'You are the only woman I will ever love,' and Elizabeth slumped in a chair staring at him with those magnificent violet eyes and crooning, 'Baby, oh baby,' over and over again."

4

When Monty, Sister, and Brooks returned to Highland Park, Illinois, in February 1929, after nine months abroad, they were behaving, according to their father, as if "they'd forgotten America."

"In our identical reefer coats, chattering away in French, we came across as effete eccentrics," Brooks recalled. "We bowed from the waist like exiled royalty. Pa was distraught—the kids on the block left us alone. We were dying to make friends, but we didn't know how. So we made no moves and *that* looked like snobbism."

Bill Clift wanted his sons to be sent to military school at once so they could learn some discipline and get "toughened up." But instead Sunny tried putting all three children into a Highland Park public school as an experiment. It was disaster.

None of them could adjust, although Sister managed to survive with dignity because she was an excellent student. Brooks and Monty were beaten up regularly for not acting American enough. "We were tortured and ridiculed because we knew nothing about chewing gum or Babe Ruth's batting average," Brooks said. "There were terrifying bike rides back to our house. Monty and I would be pedaling like crazy and we'd be followed by a pack of kids shouting threats at us." The only reason the boys managed to escape was because they had French racing bikes that were much faster than their American counterparts.

"Ma couldn't understand why us freaks in short pants and bangs would have trouble getting along with tough American kids," Brooks said. "We begged to get long pants. We pleaded to be allowed to slick our hair back, but Ma said no."

The cruel teasing and wild bike rides continued until the children were taken out of public school and tutored again at home. But

Sunny never admitted she'd been wrong. She made everyone—including her husband—feel that no one with any brains could possibly disagree with her and still be a person of consequence.

As a result Monty and the others lived in a state of constant surprise and hurt. "But we never stopped dreaming that the situation could change. We'd know *instinctively* we were right about something —like the long pants—and yet time and time again we were forced to swallow our opinions in front of Ma and agree to her demands. We were never allowed to trust our own judgment or experience."

Monty developed mechanisms of adjustment so automatic he was unaware of the denials and deceptions these transformations required of them. "When I was a little boy I never knew the joy of being right," Monty once remarked to jazz singer Libby Holman, and she is said to have answered, "You could have been a transcendental man if it hadn't been for your mother."

By the spring of 1929, Monty was already so extraordinarily handsome, people would stare at him on the street. His features were perfect, as if carved, and his manners were described as "like those of a little prince."

He was also developing a quirky sense of humor. He loved to mimic people and he had a genuine flair for it. Sunny disliked this trait and tried to curb it. "You're being undignified," she'd say when he'd imitate Nurse Wilke's lumbering walk. "Oh Ma," Monty would retort in a precise echo of Sunny's voice. And in spite of herself she would laugh.

Sunny was focusing on him more and more. When he'd run off to get a glass of milk or search for a book, she'd call sharply, "Monty! Stay where you are. I'll get it."

It was a pattern repeated over and over, and his independent impulses, his drives, were curbed again and again.

In the fall of 1929, they returned to Saint Moritz where their cultural and scholastic schedule was intensified. Not only were they tutored in history, languages, and science, but both brothers were given piano lessons (for which they showed no aptitude). Then they traveled to Munich, and Sunny next decided Brooks could be a "fiddle prodigy." She arranged for violin lessons, and he was forced to practice till he felt "like fainting."

Their athletic instruction was accelerated too, because Sunny believed that Brooks and Monty could be, if they wished, "genius figure skaters, champion tennis players and skiers." She did not pay much attention to her daughter Ethel. "Ethel was allowed to escape into books."

They had a new tutor, a M. Quiot, who was mustached and liked to wear snug jerseys. Between classes with him the children received special instruction in body building on the lawn.

Monty excelled in these classes. He performed handstands and somersaults with the greatest of ease; he particularly loved doing stomach exercises. He found he was almost a contortionist; he could bend his body into any shape, like spaghetti. He took delight in this fact, and for the rest of his life he kept in superb physical shape, working out daily at a gym and occasionally, for friends, performing physical feats of strength and coordination.

Bill Clift, meanwhile, was traveling frantically back and forth from Chicago to New York, trying to make more financial "deals." His letters were frankly melancholy.

Every so often he would mention Marie Sermolino, an Italian woman who kept him company when he was in New York. Bill kept his friendship open so Sunny would have no need to suspect anything. "I don't think Bill ever loved Marie," said an observer, "but she seemed to be necessary to him during the lonely years when his wife was in Europe."

Eventually, when the family was reunited, Bill Clift arranged a meeting between Sunny and Marie. The two women disliked each other on sight.

October came and with it the Crash. Now Bill's letters were full of descriptions of the panic on Wall Street. By January of 1930 Sunny and the children had returned to the big Tudor mansion in Highland Park where the rooms were hung with cobwebs from so little use. Bill Clift had suffered serious business reverses and funds were short. For the next six months Monty and the others remained at Highland Park, being tutored but otherwise left by themselves to play and argue. "We went to the International Horse Show and we heard Yehudi Menuhin play at the Chicago Civic Center, but otherwise we stayed home," Brooks said.

Strapped as they were financially, there were still several trips to Washington to see Aunt Sophie. But after meeting with the twins and Brooks, the old lady pronounced the children "still rough around the edges." They could not be presented to the Andersons and Blairs yet, she said. They would have to go back to Europe for another year.

Sunny's heart sank, and she immediately reported Sophie's ultimatum to Bill Clift. He wearily told her that her aunt's foolhardy scheme had created enough problems. At the moment, with the depression gripping the country, his cash position was deplorable. Didn't she realize they had committed themselves to a life-style they could no longer afford?

But Sunny was determined to follow her aunt's outrageous demands. In spite of her husband's protests, she managed to scrape up enough money for passage on the liner *Bremen*. In June of 1930 she took Monty and the others back to Europe. This time they stayed at the Hotel Bristol in Berlin, spending part of each day during the month of June trooping through the Galerie National.

Before seeing the Passion Play at Oberammergau, they stayed overnight at the house of actor Lang Alois who had played Jesus. At breakfast, Monty couldn't stop staring at him. Then they motored along the Rhine, visiting the ornate castles and stopping off in Strasbourg where Sunny allowed the children to taste the fine goose liver (for which Monty developed a passion; he ate a goose liver sandwich the day he died).

By November their money had run out, so Sunny came back to Highland Park. She was certain the children's French and German were fluent now, but to make sure she kept them drilled in both languages throughout that winter and spring. Then, in May 1931, she hustled them all back to Europe on the liner S.S. *Leviathan*.

Immersion in classical music, in the concertos of Bach and Beethoven, seemed to be Sunny's goal that year; they spent most of that summer in Austria, attending the Salzburg Festival, touring Mozart's home, and collecting postcards. Then, outfitted in brand-new lederhosen, they went on to Garmisch, Innsbruck, and, lastly, Vienna.

"This trip seemed the most hectic," Brooks said. "Ma seemed to want to cram an awful lot in. We were constantly in and out of train stations and strange hotels. Ma wrote a lot to Pa that summer and she got letters back almost every day."

Bill Clift had good reason to write. He wanted to keep Sunny informed of his proxy battle with the TransAmerica Corporation—Bank of America's then unheard-of concept of interstate branch banking (as conceived of by A. P. Giannini). Bill invested most of his money and his company's stock in TransAmerica. With the depression, TransAmerica fizzled. Late in 1931, Bill Clift went broke.

Abruptly, Sunny and the children returned to Highland Park, and within weeks the house was sold and most of their antiques and silver auctioned. In December, as snow fell thickly on the streets of New York, they moved into a furnished room in Greenwich Village.

"Everything happened so fast to us, we were all dizzy from it," Brooks recalled. "One minute we were traveling first class on the S.S. *Leviathan* and spooning up caviar at the captain's table. The next minute we were crowded together in one room above an Italian restaurant on West Ninth Street, and Pa was sitting in a chair staring into space."

Shortly after the traumatic arrival in New York, Brooks, then twelve, took the subway up to Times Square and allowed himself to be pushed through the crowds of aimless, lost people, many of whom looked very sick or very hungry. It was New Year's Eve. "There were guys selling pencils and apples on the street corners, but nobody was buying. Lights blazed down at me from the theater marquees."

Later that night when he came back to the one-room apartment in Greenwich Village, Brooks found that Sunny had made up all the beds with silk sheets.

As far as she was concerned the harsh uprooting, the genuine poverty they were facing did not require any adjustment for her children. They were told to behave as if nothing had happened. Monty and the others were taught that adjustments weren't necessary; the worst thing they could ever do was to show any emotion.

All during the following two years—and into 1932 when 25,000 World War I veterans and their wives marched on Washington to ask President Hoover for relief—the Clifts' financial situation remained desperate. Try as he would, Bill Clift could not get work. He was able to borrow a little money from his family in Chattanooga, and Sunny pawned some valuables. Eventually she got two jobs. By day she took down medical case histories at Mt. Sinai Hospital, by night she scrubbed floors at the Forty-second Street Public Library.

She never complained. She did everything with supreme good grace. She kept the one room on West Ninth Street immaculate, and she even saw to it that the children continued their tutoring. "How she managed *that* I don't know," Brooks said.

Months passed. Unable to support his family, Bill Clift fell into a deep depression. He would come home after another unsuccessful day of job hunting and would slump on his bed, staring into space.

The only person who could reach him was Sunny, who, of course, would not allow him to give up. She sat beside him on the bed and built up his self-confidence with passionate words of praise for his honesty, his integrity, his trust in people. Gently, she urged him to keep looking for work, and he did.

Years after the depression, Bill confessed to Monty, "Your mother is the most noble creature in the world. She gave me courage when nobody else would."

Late in 1932 Bill Clift decided to change his profession. "If people aren't interested in securities they still want to protect their lives and properties," he said to Brooks. He went into the insurance business, and Sunny took on yet another job—at a literary agency or in a museum—Brooks wasn't sure which.

Of this period Brooks and Monty had no distinct memories save one—they could never forget their parents' behavior toward them. "They acted as if we were still living in Highland Park. Ma would set the table with every bit of proper silver, even in that one dingy room, and we still slept on silk sheets."

"What bothered us most was that they refused to level with us. We knew we were broke, why not admit it?" But Sunny and Bill refused to discuss anything with their family; as a result the children felt more isolated than ever.

Only once does Brooks remember his father responding openly to their crisis. It was when Sunny arrived home one night from her dual jobs so exhausted she could hardly stand. At that point Bill begged her to quit the library, and then he blurted, "Why do you push yourself so?"

With that his wife drew herself up to her full five feet. "Don't you know the difference between a thoroughbred and a plug, Bill Clift? When a plug is exhausted it gives up, but a thoroughbred goes on to win."

As an adult, Monty refused to discuss his childhood with anyone—not even his closest friends. "His family—where he came from—was shrouded in mystery," said actor Kevin McCarthy. "It was as if he had amnesia," said journalist Eleanor Harris who once tried to question him about his background for an article in *McCall's*. " 'My childhood was hobgoblin—my parents traveled a lot,' he told me, and then he shrugged. 'That's *all* I can remember.' "

But then Brooks and Sister couldn't remember much either. Once they left home and began living their own lives they blanked out much of those years—the years spent in strange, opulent hotels and rented houses throughout Europe and America.

"Psychologically we couldn't seem to take the memories," Brooks said, "so we forgot. But at the same time we were obsessed with our childhood. We'd refer to it among ourselves, but only among ourselves. Part of each of us desperately wanted to remember our past and when we couldn't it was frustrating. It caused us to weep, when we were drunk enough, when some minor detail from our past was released. Monty once said the smell of boot polish reminded him of winter when he was a boy. He could get hysterical over the smell of boot polish."

Even more than his twin sister or Brooks, Monty secretly yearned to recapture and to understand his childhood years. He was constantly attempting to relive the months in Europe and Chicago and New York before he became an actor.

After he started analysis his desire became more acute. "He'd phone me from Hollywood," said Brooks, "sometimes as late as 4:00 A.M. and he'd say 'Boof?'—that's my childhood nickname, Boof— 'what exactly happened to us in Geneva in 1929? Was that when we caught chicken pox and learned to crochet? Did I get separated from my twin in Munich? What happened to us? Oh Boof, dear, can't you remember? Were we happy then?' I couldn't answer that one and finally we'd hang up. . . ."

5

In the fall of 1932 while Bill Clift remained in New York selling insurance policies, Walter Hayward, formerly a professor of English at Amherst and now the new family tutor, drove Sunny and the three children to Florida. They were going presumably to cure Brooks's asthma, which had grown worse each year, but the prime reason for moving was financial—it was cheaper to live there. Once in Sarasota, Sunny rented a large house. The weather was balmy, and in the evenings, surrounded by Walter Hayward and her children, Sunny played the piano and sang "My Darling Clementine" in a clear, true voice.

The next months were not unpleasant; living in a new environment distracted them. For a while the twins and Brooks forgot they were still existing in a closed-off little world. During the day, when they weren't having croquet fights on the lawn, Walter taught the children the entire works of Shakespeare. Together Monty and Brooks recited speeches from *Julius Caesar* and *The Merchant of Venice* under the palm trees. "We relished it," Brooks said. "We were born hams."

Monty was twelve then. He especially took to play acting. "He had total belief in what he was doing," his brother said. "You know how kids make up stories? Monty had a marvelous gift for dramatic invention. He could tell a story, acting out all the parts, and you listened, enthralled."

Sarasota was home of the Ringling Brothers Circus; occasionally Monty would wander off and watch the various acts being put together at the circus camp. He would come home and describe what he'd seen—the lion trainer snapping his whip, the somersaulting clowns, the trapeze artists swinging back and forth into space, the boy his own age riding a galloping horse while balancing on one hand. . . .

But Sunny discouraged his circus visits. She insisted that he and the other children concentrate on their studies, as they had in Europe. The rigid schedule of tutoring continued under a brilliant Florida sky.

The children were too shy to make friends their own age. In the relaxed and casual atmosphere of Sarasota, their isolation again became almost unbearable.

Meanwhile Bill Clift wrote Monty from New York: "Your mother is the heart of the Clift family. All our hopes and ambition center around her. We love her better than all else and we are ambitious because of her. She is the very life blood of the family and without news of her I am miserable."

In Florida it became more and more apparent to Monty and the others that Sunny's ambitions for them were actually restrictive. The harder she tried to cast everyone in their assigned roles, to deny their individual needs, the more fiercely each was forced to fight for freedom and self-definition.

It was a matter of survival. They were each quivering on the brink of adolescence. At thirteen Sister was tall and shapely. All three children felt profound anxieties they could not comprehend.

Now, although their whereabouts were still relentlessly monitored by Sunny, they began escaping from the gloomy confines of their rented home in Sarasota as often as they could. These excursions were brief but delicious. Once released, they would race down the hot streets, propelled by their youthful energy and their inexplicable dreams.

The twins confided their secret little experiences only to their older brother and sometimes not even to him. Their experiences seemed inconsequential perhaps—like drinking coconut milk without permission—but it made them feel giddy.

Brooks managed to form secretly a few friendships with kids on the block. He also slept with three girls, and, in the privacy of his own bedroom (the twins shared a room), he occasionally masturbated. He eventually decided that Monty and Ethel should know what he was discovering sexually.

"One afternoon we went up to the attic and I gave them a kind of birds and bees lecture after which I tried to show them how to play with themselves. It was pretty crude and the twins were both shocked and refused to have anything to do with me for days afterwards. Maybe I was wrong to initiate them the way I did, but I sensed that what I was discovering about my body was important and I wanted to share it."

Inadvertently, Walter Hayward got Monty started as an actor. Something of a performer himself, Walter knew a stock company producer in Sarasota; he often dropped by his office hoping to be given a part.

On one of his visits that winter, he discovered his friend was putting on an amateur production of *As Husbands Go,* and he needed a handsome twelve-year-old boy for one of the leads. Walter told Sunny.

She immediately accompanied Monty to an audition. The minute he walked out on stage he looked as if he belonged there. He seemed completely at home in a theater, and he impressed the director and producer with his poise and charm. After reading just one scene, he got the part. Sunny stage-managed the show.

Rehearsals went smoothly. In the evenings Sunny cued Monty on his lines while Sister and Brother listened, fidgeting. Opening night everyone came to the theater—Nurse Wilke, the Haywards and their brood—and they broke into applause when Monty made his first entrance.

"He had this charisma about him," Brooks recalled. "He carried his own spotlight, as the saying goes. He was only thirteen, but he seemed in total control on that stage. And I could tell he was enjoying himself in that fantasy situation. His physical presence and intensity were hypnotic. You couldn't stop looking at him."

When the curtain came down Sunny did not go out front directly. Instead she sat for a moment. She realized that he was a natural actor; once trained, he would be special. For as long as she could remember she had dreamt of him becoming a diplomat or an artist. And yet, somehow wearing grease paint and emoting behind footlights was not part of her grand scheme for Edward Montgomery Clift. But everybody who saw Monty on stage in that amateur production told him he was destined to become an actor. "And maybe a star. He's that handsome. He had such ability!" Sunny recalled. "I couldn't give him that. But I never pushed him to do anything. I was simply ambitious as any mother would be who had a talented son."

As the weeks passed, Sunny, weighing the pros and cons, became convinced that her son could remain in the theater and still pursue his music and languages. True, show business was not exactly a "gentleman's" profession, but if his career developed as predicted, he would probably meet cultivated and influential people—directors, producers—who might help him get ahead in a more socially acceptable art form.

It was obvious Monty enjoyed being on stage. The experience delighted him. And acting seemed a way of channeling some of his enormous nervous energy.

As soon as the family returned to New York in the fall of 1933, they moved into an ugly brick apartment building called "The Chateau," in Jackson Heights. Brooks was sent away to Friends School in Germantown in order to prepare for Harvard; Ethel enrolled at Dalton; Monty continued to be tutored in the mornings by Walter Hayward. In the afternoons his mother would accompany him to Broadway where they would try to find auditions.

Neither of them knew how to make "rounds," so they wasted a great deal of time going in and out of offices in the Brill and Sardi buildings, hoping to meet with agents and producers. Nothing happened. After a few months somebody told Sunny to register Monty at the John Robert Powers Model Agency. She did so, thinking this might be an entrée.

Powers, who then operated out of a dilapidated brownstone on the West Side, was enthusiastic about Monty's "supreme good looks and poise." He immediately arranged for test shots to be taken. Shortly after that, Monty began getting booked to pose for Arrow shirt ads. His biggest job was an all-day shooting for Steinway pianos. The ad ran in *Liberty* magazine and showed Monty moodily seated in front of a baby grand.

Monty hated modeling with a passion—he hated spending most of his waking hours trotting in and out of photographers' studios up and down Lexington Avenue and the Murray Hill district. He found striking poses an indescribable bore, but he did make money, money which the family needed. Although Bill Clift had a decent job selling insurance, there were still mountains of debts to pay off. Sunny was working part time, too, organizing papers at the Metropolitan Museum. Even so, she usually managed to pick Monty up from his modeling chores or auditions.

She continued to feed him culture. He went almost nightly to the ballet, theater, or concerts at Carnegie Hall. How Sunny managed to afford all the tickets and the extra music lessons, the expensive clothes and shoes, nobody in the family knew, nor did they dare ask.

She lavished expensive gifts on Monty, big art books, opera records, and rented a grand piano. After the piano was delivered she drew Brooks aside (when he was home on school holiday), and she whispered, "This is your piano, don't tell Monty." She then told Monty the piano was Sister's, and to Sister she whispered the piano was for Monty.

Later the twins and Brooks compared notes on their communal gift. And after that they each decided to pretend the piano was theirs alone so Sunny wouldn't be upset. It was a kind of game she forced them to play. It divided them and it also brought them together in a peculiar, but understandable, way.

As a model, Monty was around cameras so much he eventually took up photography as a hobby. Sunny bought him some expensive equipment, and he started recording everything he saw on film. He was allowed to develop and print pictures at home. One bathroom in the apartment became his darkroom. "The tub was continually filled with negatives," his sister recalls.

Monty enjoyed photographing people's faces. "I love people's faces stretched to the limits," he would say. But he wanted to photograph nature, too. He spent whatever free time he had wandering through Central Park, clicking away at rock formations, at the silhouettes of apartment buildings poking up through the trees. Ultimately Monty's photographs were published in the *Daily News* and in photography annuals, winning several awards.

He would spend hours composing a still life before he photographed it. Even then he was dimly aware of the difference between intention and effect in art; aware of the fact that no matter how hard something is willed into creation, the result is never exactly as planned.

Later he would become obsessed by this difference and its reflection in acting as he struggled to achieve his own precise artistic intentions.

Meanwhile, he relished the specifics of photography. A photograph reflected a given moment in time, and yet the more specific it was, the more universal. Acting, at its finest, was the same.

By the summer of 1934 the Clift family separated again. Brooks went off to Chile with his father who had an engineering job to do in a friend's gold mine. Ethel was sent to camp. For most of that summer Sunny and Monty remained in Jackson Heights. But in

August they retreated to Sharon, Connecticut, where Sunny had rented a little house.

In nearby Stockbridge, Theron Bamberger was producing a comedy entitled *Fly Away Home,* by Dorothy Bennett and Irving White. Thomas Mitchell starred as a father who returns from years abroad to attend his eccentric ex-wife's wedding. In his absence his brood of children "have pushed their education to the point of anarchy."

From next-door neighbor William Harris, a Broadway producer, Sunny discovered that Bamberger needed a young actor to play one of Mitchell's snottiest sons. Sunny hustled Monty over to the Berkshire Playhouse where he auditioned and promptly won the role of Harmer Masters.

"I can't say I was that impressed with his talent," Bamberger said. "But Monty was without doubt the most poised thirteen-year-old I've ever encountered. Nothing fazed him. Opening night Mitchell was a bundle of nerves, but Monty pulled him through the first scene they had together. He was as cool as a cucumber." *Fly Away Home* was a resounding success in Stockbridge, and after the summer tryout, Monty was offered the part of Harmer Masters in the Broadway production of *Fly Away Home* at a salary of $50 a week. Sunny accepted with alacrity.

The play opened at the 48th Street Playhouse on January 16, 1935, to very nice reviews. Monty was singled out as "artless enough to be charming." Brooks Atkinson called the show a "boisterous comedy—hilarious stuff." Audiences flocked to see the production; it ran for seven months.

Monty remained with the show until it closed, never missing a performance. The theater proved to exert an irresistible attraction for him. It also served as a protection; he felt safe committed to the childlike art of play acting.

He could not understand why he felt so sure of himself caught up in an imaginary role, but it was as if all the anxiety and terror he embraced in real life melted away behind the footlights. "I had found my calling," he used to say. "God how I loved playing that loathsome brat!"

In the beginning he felt absolutely no fear in front of an audience. "My fears came later when I knew what I was doing," he laughed.

After the first few weeks of *Home*'s run, he convinced Sunny to let him stay on Broadway between matinees. On these afternoons mother and son would eat a light supper at Luigino's, an Italian restaurant on the block, and then they would return to the playhouse and walk back and forth across the dimly lit set, mouthing lines at the rows of empty seats.

Monty often had Sunny climb up to the last row in the gallery to make sure his voice could be heard. The technicalities of acting fascinated him. How precisely could a voice be "thrown" into the balcony? Why did one exit provoke applause or laughter? Some of the cast occasionally rehearsed scenes among themselves after the show opened. Monty listened to dialogue repeated over and over again. No effort seemed too great to achieve a heightened effect.

In the dressing rooms before half hour was called, a spirit of exaggeration and gossip reigned, increasing with the run. Everybody talked about everybody else—love lives, bathroom habits, and nervous breakdowns were discussed as casually as the weather. Monty shrank away from answering specific questions about his own background, a reflex action he had learned from Sunny, who ordered him never to discuss the family. Despite friendly inquiries, he remained aloof and guarded with most of the cast, and later asked Brooks if self-revelation were part of success. Whatever Brooks's response, Monty always treasured his privacy.

He was too shy to make real friends in the production, but he did get involved with some practical jokes. Towards the end of the run monotony set in; to combat it the younger actors—like Sheldon Leonard—began ad-libbing and breaking each other up on stage. Monty went further than that. He and his understudy would stand in the wings pelting the rest of the cast with grapes as they took their curtain calls. On another night he slipped ice down the leading lady's costume.

Sunny ignored the matter. She had other problems, primarily Brooks, who, at seventeen, appeared to have none of the drive and ambition she had tried to instill in him. She focused the intensity of her concern on getting Brooks into Harvard. To insure this she enrolled Brooks at the Germantown Friends School in Pennsylvania, and she arranged to have him board with the Ned Smiths, a pious Quaker family in Germantown who were friends of Gertrude Woodruff, a classmate of hers from Cornell.

Ned Smith, the Smiths' son who later became a close friend of Monty's, remembers the Clifts' arrival with Brooks in 1935. Sunny was "busy, attentive, meticulous, the perfect mother giving her son over for the winter."

For the next eight months Brooks remained with the Smiths, attended Friends School, and finally passed his entrance exams and got into Harvard.

He went to Harvard for the next four years but it was not a happy experience. "I knew I was expected not only to graduate with honors but to go on to Harvard Business School as well. I simply could not stomach that. In other words I knew I could not turn miraculously into the successful tycoon Pa had failed to become."

Brooks envied Monty. "He'd an alternative—an escape into acting. Now he no longer had to live up to the image Sunny imagined for him. He was having his troubles, too, adjusting to the outside world but he was starting to fulfill his talent on stage. And he really enjoyed what he was doing. He couldn't stop talking about Broadway."

6

The Broadway season of 1935–1936 was a glorious peak. There were fewer plays than in previous years, but the ones that were produced were of high caliber—plays like Robert Sherwood's *The Petrified Forest* with Leslie Howard and Humphrey Bogart, or *Victoria Regina* with Helen Hayes.

Stars like Alfred Lunt, Lynn Fontanne, Katharine Cornell, Orson Welles, and Burgess Meredith triumphed in a dazzling array of roles. Monty watched them all perform; he especially liked Meredith's intense underplaying in *Winterset.* Along with Welles, Meredith was considered to be a boy wonder on stage.

As soon as *Fly Away Home* closed in June of 1935, Monty was immediately cast as the "good young prince" in the Cole Porter–Moss Hart musical *Jubilee,* a takeoff on royalty led by actors Melville Cooper and Mary Boland as Monty's parents. They played "a king and queen who are just folks at heart"; the King enjoys rope tricks, the Queen has a crush on Johnny Weissmuller and Noël Coward. Not long after rehearsals began everybody was humming the song that became the hit tune of the show, the exotic "Begin the Beguine."

Monty's role was minor and in the cast of eighty, he did not stand out. Opening night in Boston, nevertheless, brought him notice and notoriety when both he and Moss Hart were threatened with kidnapping.

A police guard was posted at the stage door of the Colonial Theater, and a newspaper account of the story, passed backstage, caused a thrill of fear to ripple through the dressing rooms. The threat had been made earlier that week. According to Sunny Clift, just as she was about to board the Boston Special from Grand Central Station, she was called to a pay phone and a strange female voice warned her that if she allowed her son to open in Boston she'd be sorry.

The caller went on, "Montgomery Clift better not play the good prince in *Jubilee* or he'll have worse than a head cold," and then threatened to kidnap both him and Moss Hart if Monty remained in the production.

The F.B.I. later discovered that the threats came from an irate stage mother whose son had previously auditioned for and lost the part of the good young prince; when Monty retold the story he would add, "It just goes to show how far an ambitious parent will go for her children."

For a while after that bodyguards accompanied Hart and Monty everywhere—including the opening night party at the Ritz. As added protection during the Boston run Monty and his mother stayed at the ornate Foote mansion on Beacon Hill.

Ed Foote had not seen the Clifts since they were together years before in Switzerland, and he found Sunny as irksome and troubling as ever and Monty more insufferable. The morning after *Jubilee* opened he recalls seeing Monty in the bathroom staring lovingly at his handsome face in the mirror. "I stopped to say hello and he turned on me and said, 'My God, you're ugly.'"

Foote was then covered with acne. "I was flaming from it so I was not at my most attractive, but his remark hurt me and I burst into tears." However, no mention was made of the incident later; Foote and Monty dined together politely almost every evening for the next two weeks. "But I never forgave his cruelty—it seemed so gratuitous."

While in Boston, Sunny Clift became acquainted with another stage mother, Christina Roe. Mrs. Roe was a sometime actress whose two children, Raymond, eight, and Patricia, three, danced in the chorus of *Jubilee*. During the performances the two women sat together in the Green Room comparing notes on show business.

"My mother taught Sunny Clift the theatrical ropes," Patricia Roe said. "She gave her tips on how to make the rounds with Monty, where to find the most knowledgeable casting directors, who the best agents were."

And it was Christina who suggested Monty take elocution lessons to drop the English accent he'd developed in Europe. She recommended Minette Lange, the widow of John Lange, who'd gained fame as Flo Ziegfeld's musical conductor. Since his death, Minette had tried to support herself and her three daughters, Faith, Hope, and Charity, by giving voice lessons. While she was fairly successful, her three little girls were even more so. They worked regularly in Broadway and were the veterans of several long-running hits.

Mrs. Lange, Christina Roe, and Sunny Clift often met for tea in the Langes' Greenwich Village floor-thru where they would talk about their ambitions for their children. Sunny would tell them how she was educating Monty in a "special and privileged way." "He speaks French and German fluently," she would brag. "He's seen every great museum in Europe." Properly handled he could turn into one of the most distinctive actors of his time, precisely because he was so cultivated.

She went on to say that she was seeing to it that he led a disciplined, if somewhat rarefied, life, "a life free from too many pressures, too many strangers." It was a life befitting someone of particular breeding and disposition, it was the life of a "thoroughbred."

Christina and Minette were in awe of Sunny's determined point of view, of her elegant remoteness. Often she seemed troubled; they wished they could help. Yet she acted superior even in her suffering, and so they held back, silent.

Her anguish centered around Aunt Sophie—shortly after *Jubilee* opened on Broadway the old lady had summoned her to Washington, commanding that she move bag and baggage into the Hotel Wyoming with daughter Ethel. "You two will be my companions until I die," she announced.

When Sunny argued that she couldn't abandon her husband and two sons in New York, Sophie taunted, "Why not? Don't you want to finally be recognized by the Andersons and the Blairs?"

This time Sunny held her ground, saying that such an arrangement would be impossible. The two women quarreled violently, and at the end of the argument Sophie screamed, "Get out! Get out! Never darken my door again!"

Sunny left Washington feeling utterly betrayed. She had been a fool to believe Sophie would someday introduce her to her family; she probably hadn't any intention of doing so. Still the thought that the endless financial sacrifices, the years abroad, the self-imposed isolation had been to no avail—that her identity and the children's were still a blur—these were thoughts that were almost too painful to contemplate.

Once back in New York she channeled her energies into

Monty's career, accompanying him to auditions, singing and voice lessons, ballet class, concerts. She saw to it that Brooks remained at Harvard and that Ethel prepared for Bryn Mawr. And she continued to make concerted attempts to reach the Andersons and Blairs.

Together with Bill Clift she wrote letters, made long-distance phone calls and took train trips seeking out distant cousins in Delaware and Washington who might be sympathetic.

But the Blairs refused to see her, calling her story "hogwash." The Andersons, however, while at first incredulous, ultimately accepted, verbally and in written affidavits, that she was the abandoned daughter of Maria Anderson and Woodbury Blair.

One cousin wrote her, "You don't deserve the hell you've been subjected to." And another cousin, named Florence Hilles, who was not only related to Maria Anderson but who had been also her best friend before the First World War, told Sunny that she was overwhelmed by "the striking resemblance" to her mother. She believed Sunny's story totally and did everything she could to help her legally claim her inheritance. She said that Sophie had alluded to her on many occasions. Eventually Florence gave her everything she possessed which had belonged to the late Maria "Bobbie" Anderson. (When Sophie Anderson died she left Sunny $25,000 in her will.)

Meanwhile, of course, Monty and the others knew nothing of their mother's relentless quest for identity. They knew only that they were related to some "distinguished and powerful Americans," but, since they were told no more than that, they dismissed the information as "part of Ma's eccentricity."

It wasn't until 1948, when Brooks was scouting for scripts for David Susskind in Paris, that Bill Clift, also in the French capital, asked him to drop by his hotel to discuss "something of grave importance."

"Now you're old enough [Brooks had just turned thirty] to understand what drove Ma so."

Haltingly he described Sunny's anguished search for her true identity, her roots. He spoke in detail of the Andersons and Blairs, of Aunt Sophie and her terrible unkept promise. He spoke of the legal and emotional obstacles and of the intense disillusionment. He never used the word "illegitimate"—that would have been too shameful— but he admitted that even after thirty years of unbroken efforts Sunny was still not recognized in a court of law as a direct descendant of Colonel Robert Anderson. It was the secret tragedy of her life, he said, and she would continue to keep it locked inside herself until she was recognized.

"Everything she did for you she did because she believes you are thoroughbreds," he went on. "If only I could convince you of your mother's greatness—she is a great, great woman. She wanted you to have every advantage—and all the love she never had. She wished you none of the pain."

Later that day Brooks, "feeling shell-shocked," met Monty in a café on the Bois du Boulogne and told him what his father had said. Monty just nodded his head rapidly up and down. "He had already known this," Brooks remembers. "Presumably Pa had told him. Maybe even Ma. I never asked how he knew. He just knew."

Both brothers began talking at once. They talked until it got dark. They accepted without much comment Bill's explanation of their isolated childhood. They tried to understand Sunny's motives, but they could not forget the hours upon hours with strange tutors in European hotels, the enforced isolation because they were so "special." It was hard not to resent the mental punishment they'd been put through; at the same time, they couldn't help but respect their mother's fierce determination, her sense of pride.

Much later that same night they wandered out on the Champs Élysées, ending up in a café where they got roaring drunk. Their past faded in and out of their consciousness like newsreel clips— Vevey, Switzerland, Kate Billings, their only friend, the tutor M. Quiot on the Riviera—Brooks remembers nothing of their garbled conversations, only their explosions of hysterical laughter and Monty yelling at one point, "Oh, God, Boof, wasn't that Sophie Anderson a *shit?*"

After that evening Monty told Brooks, "I don't give a damn about my ancestors, my bloodlines," but the older he got the more he behaved like a dispossessed aristocrat; although he mingled with low-lifes and celebrated achievers, he would regard them—depending on how the mood struck him—with respect or contempt, and always with amusement.

Often, when the brothers got together, they speculated about the Andersons and the Blairs, and they marveled over their mother and how she had with her secrets and evasion almost turned them into a separate breed. "In some ways Monty and I felt illegitimate," Brooks said.

He suspected Monty probably discussed the whole business

alone with his mother. "He and Sunny had a secretive relationship which Ethel and I never intruded upon."

After Bill Clift died in 1964, Brooks finally brought up the subject of the Anderson-Blairs to Sunny and asked why she had never told him. "It would have explained so many things," he said. Perhaps, she replied bitterly, but there was no point unless she was legally acknowledged. She kept on trying until 1972. She was then eighty-four years old.

Brooks subsequently became as obsessed as his mother with his past. He began collecting everything he could find about the Andersons and the Blairs, and he started a small library about their involvement with the Civil War. He named three of his eight children after either Blairs or Andersons. One of his youngest sons is called Woody for short—after his grandfather, Woodbury Blair.

7

After *Jubilee* closed in 1936 Monty enrolled in the Dalton School along with Ethel, but he remained less than a year. "He couldn't seem to adjust to being just another pupil in class," Brooks said, "although he made one friend whose name I can't remember—a boy who was a long-distance runner."

In late June of 1937 Sunny arranged to have Monty stay with Ned Smith's sister, "Fish," and her husband, sculptor Thomas Benton, in Newport, Rhode Island. She thought it would be nice for Monty to see the famous old resort capital and to learn how to sail.

Ned Smith recalls, "My first reaction was 'what do I want that damn sissy actor around for?'" Ned had his own boat, which he sailed in all day long by himself. "I didn't want this Montgomery Clift fellow to spoil my summer."

The day of his arrival, Bill Clift drove Monty up in a 1933 green Buick (it was a car Monty later drove until it literally fell apart). "Monty got out of the car," Ned remembers, "and I'll never forget him, dressed in starched white—absolutely the most magnetic person I'd ever met. Vigorous. 'Glad to meet you!' He was ready to try anything." He was then seventeen.

Much to Smith's amazement, "We became instant friends. I don't know quite why because we were the exact opposite—Monty was gregarious, full of fun. I was a loner—taciturn, about to study engineering at M.I.T. But we enjoyed each other's company enormously."

Together they sailed up and down Narragansett Bay; they raced to the Ida Lewis Lighthouse Yacht Club and back. Smith taught Monty how to tack around the wind. They swam, took long walks on Bailey Beach and they toured the Breakers, Cornelius Vanderbilt's

Italianate villa. To watch the Fall River steamboat make its nightly run, they hiked up the steep hill at Conanicut Island.

Later Monty took pictures of Ned scowling into the sun, and a photograph he took that summer of Tom Benton's son crying in his crib won an award and was published in *Good Housekeeping*.

While he was in Newport, Monty received a phone call from Sunny every day. He always told her exactly what he was doing, and then he hung up. During the month he stayed with the Bentons, bundles of new clothes from Brooks Brothers arrived at regular intervals. "I remember how beautiful and expensive they were," Smith recalls, "and how beautifully wrapped."

Near the end of his stay when Monty and Ned were coming home from sailing one afternoon, they saw a snub-nosed, freckle-faced kid sitting on the stoop waiting for them. "He was the local plumber's son—his name was Van Johnson, and he wanted to be an actor," Smith said. "He'd heard about Monty and wanted to meet him."

Johnson introduced himself, and he and Monty started talking about Broadway. "Monty didn't seem that interested in the conversation, but as he advised him he assumed an almost theatrical air."

Not long after that Johnson went to New York and landed in the chorus of *Pal Joey*. MGM saw him, signed him to a contract. By the middle of World War II he was the number one movie star at the box office.

As soon as Monty came back to New York, he plunged again into his strenuous regime of lessons. He took ballroom dancing and learned to play the violin. Because Sunny wanted him to play the piano as well, a Miss Gladys Brady of Pelham was hired to give him lessons.

"Monty had a knowledge of music," Ned Smith said. When Ned first began visiting him in New York he heard him play. "I remember it sounded so beautiful I ran in to listen to him up close, but as soon as he saw me he stopped and jumped up from the keyboard." He didn't seem to want to share his music with anyone, and he denied to many people that he played at all.

In November of 1937, Monty started rehearsals as Lord Finch for *Yr. Obedient Husband* under John Cromwell's direction. Set in eighteenth-century London, the play by Horace Jackson was really a series of character sketches about the English gossip Richard Steele and his family and friends.

Sunny thought that Jackson's comedy might be a big career break for Monty since he was acting not only with Fredric March and Florence Eldridge, who were playing Mr. and Mrs. Steele, but with Dame May Whitty and Brenda Forbes.

However, during tryouts in Indianapolis Monty came down with the measles; while he was recuperating, director Cromwell's wife, Kay Johnson, went on in Monty's place with Cromwell feeding her the lines from the stage set fireplace.

Yr. Obedient Husband opened at the Belasco on Broadway on January 11, 1938. Critics described the show as "totally indifferent." But Johnson in the *Journal* wrote: "The best performance is Montgomery Clift's. His single scene captures some of the rattlebrained amusement and ingratiating humor that is sadly lacking in the rest of the production."

Years later, Fredric March told the *New York Times*'s Guy Flatley that "Monty had a great talent." But March also confided that he'd foolishly invested a great deal of his own money in the show. *Yr. Obedient Husband* closed in a week, during which several cast members came down with the measles.

Shortly afterwards MGM began to conduct a nationwide talent search for Tom Sawyer, and although Monty was not freckled, and certainly too elegant to go fishing barefoot, he auditioned several times for the role of the Mark Twain hero with seventeen-year-old Anne Baxter, auditioning for the role of Becky Thatcher. Miss Baxter, the granddaughter of Frank Lloyd Wright, had recently appeared on Broadway as the ingenue in *Seen But Not Heard*.

"When I met Monty he had pimples," she said. "He seemed hyperenergetic, hypersincere. We acted out scenes from the script. Once I remember we sat perched together on a desk. Later we screen-tested together but neither one of us was cast." To commiserate, Monty asked Anne Baxter to a concert at Carnegie Hall.

Almost eighteen, Monty still had few friends his own age, and with his brother and sister away at school, Sunny was now Monty's principal companion. Their relationship was turning combative, as he fought to keep from being dependent on her, resenting it when he was. She alternately indulged him with presents and reproached him bitterly whenever he tried to run free from her obsessive control.

"Mother's life was concerned with not only giving us every advantage but doing and seeing that everything was done for us," Ethel said. "We were not subject to discipline or to requirements to do for others."

"The tragic thing was, Sunny thought she did everything out of love," said Patricia Roe. "She did for him and did for him because nobody had ever done for her," but in the long run it was too much, and her anxiety, her self-consciousness, her excessive preoccupation with appearance and style engulfed him and thickened the air he breathed.

He began to feel terribly ambivalent about her. He was edgy, jumpy, and contentious, easily exasperated. Sunny continued to accompany him to auditions, canceling them if it rained. She wouldn't allow him to get his feet wet. She negotiated all contracts. On May 4, 1938, when he appeared with Barry Sullivan in the flop, *Eye On the Sparrow,* she hired a limousine to take him to and from the Vanderbilt Theater.

He saved Ethel's opening night telegram: "Darling, I adore you with fervent tenderness. I wish you fame, success, and greatest happiness. Your twin."

When he wasn't working, and despite aggravation with his mother, Monty crowded his free time with activities. He studied photography with James Abbe; he attended every art exhibit at the Metropolitan; he went to ballet, concerts, and of course the theater. He also took swimming lessons because Ethel, who was on her college swimming team, had beaten him in the backstroke. "He practiced and practiced until he could beat me," she said.

He and Ned Smith were corresponding regularly, and as often as he could Smith would come down from M.I.T. and spend the weekend at the Clifts'.

"I had first visited them in a walk-up in the Village; now they were living at 116 East 53rd in a very big apartment. Obviously their fortunes had improved."

There were deep rugs everywhere; Smith recalled Toulouse-Lautrec originals on the walls, English antiques highly polished; "everything in the finest of taste. Each window had a mechanical air purifier. . . . But it was a place where you were afraid to talk too loudly." Total silence hung over the mahogany furniture.

Bill Clift traveled back and forth from Wall Street where he was currently with the stock exchange firm of Tucker Anthony and R. R. Day. He remained opposed to Monty's involvement in the theater, but he did not discuss it with his wife. Instead he confided his worries to a client, Miss Cohn, a spinster who came to his office for investment advice. "Sunny is pushing, pushing Monty," he would tell Miss Cohn. "I'm not sure he wants to be an actor."

Father and son rarely communicated about anything, but Ned Smith recalls they did share the *New York Times*. After breakfast Mr. Clift would take the business section and Monty would take the theater section, and they would sit in the living room reading, rarely exchanging a word.

When Monty was home he spent most of his time in his room, a long narrow place at the end of the apartment. It was sunnier than the other rooms, and his bed was always cluttered with newspapers and books. He was an omnivorous reader. He also kept a journal and scribbled in it constantly at home and even at rehearsals. He carried the journal everywhere, and although he never allowed anyone to read it, he showed it to people, among them a young girl he befriended in a stock company. The girl, an apprentice, was working backstage at the little theater in Millbrook, New York, where Monty went in the summer of 1938 to appear in a show called *The Wind and the Rain* with Celeste Holm.

"The play wasn't very good," the apprentice recalled. "It ran a week, and during that time Monty became my friend. I can still see him scribbling in his journal in the wings and telling me how it was an outlet for him. 'It helps sort out confusions and demands,' he said."

The apprentice was not doing too well at her job. "I was a dreamer, I made mistakes." Monty heard that she was being fired, and went to the producer of the theater and convinced him to keep her. "Then he sat with me and we talked for a long time. I poured out my troubles to him and told him my aspirations, too. He was unbelievably sympathetic and receptive. Nobody had ever paid so much attention to me before. Monty empathized with my desire to work and have a career and he encouraged me."

The apprentice felt completely at ease with him. "It was as if I was talking to another girl. He said one thing I'll never forget. 'If you're good at what you do nobody can get at you.'"

8

Monty called 1938 a turning point in his life. He made another friend, actor Morgan James, and his name appeared above the title of a Broadway play.

Dame Nature was a rather bizarre little French comedy by André Birabeau about adolescent love—and trouble—which the Theatre Guild had decided to try out at their Westport Playhouse. The plot revolved around two high school students who become parents at fifteen. Director Worthington Minor wanted the young father in question—"André"—to look innocent and speak English like a European.

Monty was auditioning for the third and final time when Morgan James came in to read for the role of André's conspiratorial best friend Batton. James was then twenty-two and a graduate of the American Academy of Dramatic Arts, but this was his first Broadway audition so he was "scared to death" by his own admission.

Monty, seated in the Theatre Guild's waiting room with a script on his lap, smiled reassuringly at James. "Monty seemed to sense what I was going through. I was terribly frightened and he wasn't. He acted amazingly poised and I envied that. Anyhow, we introduced ourselves. He put me right at ease. We discussed the play and the parts we were up for." Later they auditioned together. "We were both cast."

During rehearsals they became friends, going out to lunch, sharing tea breaks. James, who was open and voluble, discovered that Monty's poise was something of an act. When talking with someone his own age he became self-conscious and insecure.

He alluded to his modeling days only by saying that he had

hated the work with "a passion." He referred to his years in Europe as a "blur," and he refused to discuss his family. James's early impression of Monty was that he was "a very lonely confused person inside a sleek well-groomed exterior."

At rehearsals he seemed "charming, terribly eager to please," remembered Patricia Collinge, an actress who'd translated *Dame Nature* from the original French and who also became Monty's good friend.

Early on in rehearsal Miss Collinge noticed that Monty was extremely creative. "He'd invent bits of business or character details that were sometimes offbeat or strange. I'm still reminded of Camus's phrase 'create dangerously' when I think of Monty's acting, because he was starting to make unorthodox acting choices even then.

"There is one long speech in the play when Monty as André tries to explain to his father how his loneliness and unhappiness had forced him to seek affection from an equally lonely girl.

"Monty's performance was heart-rending. It was so quiet and sincere that it seemed almost untheatrical, except underneath the controlled tone was an absolutely compelling sense of torment."

When the cast of *Dame Nature* went up to Westport for the tryout, Morgan James and Monty shared a room in a boarding house close to the playhouse. They talked between run-throughs and into the night about the play and its chances of opening on Broadway, about the Theatre Guild's financial troubles, and a lot about sex. Monty asked James questions and he fantasized about what it would be like to seduce one of the actresses in the cast.

Listening to him James decided, "Monty *was* utterly innocent and he carried his feelings of frustration and innocence on stage and actually became André, a character struggling to understand the mysteries of sex and birth.

"Monty played the scene in which fifteen-year-old André discovers he's going to be a father with delighted astonishment and some terror," Patricia Collinge recalled. "It was glorious acting."

The opening night audience at Westport singled out Monty's performance with a special burst of applause when he took his curtain call. The next day *Variety* described his characterization as "brilliantly effective."

Leland Hayward came backstage; as did playwrights Marc Connelly, Sam Raphaelson, and S. N. Behrman. Monty's success was beginning and he knew it and he bubbled with excitement. That is, until reporters asked him questions about his family. Then he withdrew. He disliked getting personal.

But sometimes after the show he would confide in James. "Monty told me he was sick and tired of being in a cocoon. He was so bright and perceptive he realized he'd been isolated from the world. He knew it was unhealthy," James remembers. "His seeming lack of life experience maddened him." James would tell him about his own life, "which I didn't think was that extraordinary," but he'd gone to various schools, made friendships. "I'd competed—been in fights—had enemies. Monty envied that. He even envied the fact that I'd attended Raymond Duncan's dance school at Carnegie Hall. Raymond was Isadora Duncan's brother; he wore a toga and had long, shoulder-length hair. Anyhow, Monty kept saying, 'Oh God, how I envy you; you've experienced so much more than I have.'"

Midway through the run of *Dame Nature,* Sunny Clift came up to Westport to see the show. She moved into Monty's room for the weekend and James moved out.

"Everybody at the Guild thought it was rather odd for an eighteen-year-old boy to share his bedroom with his mother," Pat Collinge said. "Of course, nobody said anything, but eyebrows were raised."

That weekend Miss Collinge had a chance to study Sunny at close range. They all had lunch together. "I found her bewitching and charming but a killer too. She stifled and repressed Monty by not allowing him to give vent to his enthusiasms or his deep needs. It was odd how the characters in *Dame Nature* reflected the characteristics of Monty and Sunny. In the play the mother is socially ambitious and domineering, and even when her son becomes a father she still tries to make him wear short pants and play kiddy games in the nursery—eventually, of course, André fights back."

Miss Collinge felt Sunny's power at that lunch. "If she forbade him to do something, he obeyed." That weekend Miss Collinge offered some chocolate mints at the luncheon. Monty politely refused. She learned later that he had never even tasted candy because Sunny told him candy was unhealthy for him to eat.

Towards the end of the summer, before going into rehearsal for the Broadway production of *Dame Nature,* Monty spent a few days at a dude ranch in Wyoming where his family was vacationing. The Clifts were in turmoil because Brooks was engaged in a casual affair with one of the ranch waitresses. Sunny had discovered the affair after reading a passionate exchange of letters between the two.

Inevitably there were violent quarrels and hysterical accusations.

Brooks claimed angrily that his rights of privacy had been violated, and Sunny countered with: "How could you see someone who is beneath you?" The waitress was fired later, which angered Brooks even more.

Bill Clift remained a silent witness, refusing to take sides in the matter. Monty ignored everybody and rode horseback, took long walks in the desert, and played tennis.

During the weekend he commented only once about the affair to his brother. "Our parents are full of misery, Boof." And when Brooks confided that he was in love with Ann Pearmain, Monty exclaimed, "Then, for God's sake, don't let Ma and Pa find out!" Two years later Brooks eloped with Ann.

9

The night *Dame Nature* opened at the Booth Theatre, September 25, 1938, Hitler invaded Czechoslovakia. The actors were tense on stage, and the audience seemed restless and in no mood to sit through a whimsical little play about fifteen-year-old children having babies.

During intermission Lawrence Langner, the founder of the Theatre Guild, rushed down to Times Square and watched the news of Nazi destruction and doom move in electric lights around the Times Building, saying later, "Our little French comedy died in front of our eyes."

Some critics were no help. Shortly after the opening night Ruth McKenney wrote in the *New Yorker:* "The idea of a young father trying to get a 10 percent reduction on a baby carriage via his Boy Scout card makes me look for the nearest exit." And George Jean Nathan, who had seen the play at Westport and liked it then, called the Broadway production of *Dame Nature* "oversentimentalized. . . ."

Other critics, however, admired Monty's performance. Brooks Atkinson called his acting "nicely modulated and original," and Richard Watts in the *Tribune* said, "Young Mr. Clift has an enormously difficult part and on the whole he manages excellently, although there are times when he makes the father too neurotic for comfort."

Days after the opening his name went up in lights at the Booth Theatre, and Leland Hayward, the most prestigious agent of the time, signed him up. Word spread around Broadway that Montgomery Clift's performance was special, unorthodox, and it had to be seen. So although the show only lasted for forty-eight performances, everybody in the business bought a ticket and came backstage. "I wish he'd kept a list of the visitors to his dressing room," James said. "Orson Welles, Ruth Gordon, Katharine Cornell, Guthrie McClintic, George Abbott, Elia Kazan . . ."

Countless girls dropped by his dressing room as well. There were lonely girls, attracted by his beauty and his talent, there were older women who wanted to sleep with him, and then there were the Wall Street brokers and piano players and even a few salesmen from out of town. They came backstage too, on the pretext of complimenting Monty's performance. Some of them also got around to asking him for dinner or a drink.

Monty charmed them all with his compelling gaze. "He became a terrible flirt during the run of *Dame Nature*," Pat Collinge said. "He'd sign autographs and make small talk and he had a way of looking at you with those gorgeous eyes of his and you'd feel faint."

Sometimes on matinee days Monty would arrange a rendezvous with one of his female admirers, but he rarely kept those appointments. Instead, as soon as the curtain came down he'd sneak across the darkened stage and up the aisle with the last of the departing audience. Then he'd make a dash through Shubert Alley and into Sardi's where he'd watch until the girl he was supposed to meet would finally wander out dejectedly from the Booth stage door. Monty would often make a scathing remark under his breath.

Between matinee and evening performances he preferred to go to the burlesque houses on Forty-second Street. Monty and James both loved the tacky theatricality of the shows, the cheap sex jokes, and the sweaty men in the audience with their coats on their laps. He wanted to photograph the strippers in their dressing rooms, but James wouldn't let him. Nonetheless, Monty did manage to take some photographs of strippers passing to and fro in the wings.

Sunny approved of James, probably because his father Henry James (no relation to the novelist) was an extremely successful physician and listed in the Social Register. Dr. and Mrs. James and three of their five sons lived in a well-appointed townhouse on East Seventy-fourth Street. The elder James did not approve of his son Morgan's passion for theater, "another bond between Monty and me since Mr. Clift didn't approve either. Whenever Monty would drop by for dinner, my father would denounce him as 'an actoreen'—a term he'd learned in Virginia where he grew up. It was not complimentary—my father would call him 'an actoreen' and then pretend to banish Monty and me to the kitchen with the servants. Monty thought this was hilarious."

After the theater James and Monty prowled the city, often ending up in an all-night deli. "We had great times. Once after the show we'd just finished a snack—it was around 1:00 A.M. We'd gone outside on the street and suddenly Orson Welles hove into view and began marching down Broadway reciting Shakespeare at the top of his lungs. Half the Mercury Theater was with him—Marty Gabel, Hiram Sherman, and Joseph Cotten. It was something we never forgot—Welles's rich throbbing voice bouncing off a backdrop of garbage cans, and moving taxis, and dirty transient hotels."

Once or twice during the run of *Dame Nature* James arranged a date for Monty with Diana Barrymore, who was then a pudgy and arrogant eighteen-year-old. She had just been dubbed "the personality debutante of the year," and proud of the title, she tried to live up to it. She desperately wanted more attention than her rival, Brenda Frazier.

"She was the kind of person who would haul off and slap you across the face at a party for no reason at all and then howl with laughter," James said. "She had a habit of throwing ice water on people's heads from her apartment window on Sutton Place."

Undisciplined and wild, Diana identified with her father, John Barrymore, whom she adored but whom she rarely saw. She thought that since she was a Barrymore people should bow and scrape to her. She also thought she could get away with murder. Monty thought she was outrageous. He called Diana "a circus," and he loved seeing her, but not too often.

Sunny continued to discourage Monty from dating, ostensibly because she wanted him to conserve his energy for his career. Consequently he did not date often, but in between infrequent outings with Anne Baxter or the young actress Louisa Horton he fantasized about women.

"He'd get crushes on girls," James recalls. He read about eighteen-year-old Brenda Frazier, the very rich, very pale, dark-eyed brunette currently being publicized in all the gossip columns as America's number one glamour debutante. "Brenda Frazier intrigued Monty because she seemed so remote."

In the holiday season of 1938, which the *Journal American* described as the "biggest wettest craziest merriest New Year's season since the caviar days of 29," James took Monty to Miss Frazier's coming-out party at the Ritz Carlton Hotel.

"It was very glamorous," James said. "Fifteen hundred guests jammed the main ballroom, over two hundred barrels of champagne were drunk. I thought Monty would be a big hit," James said. "He was so handsome, he had a great sense of humor. I thought he'd introduce himself to Brenda."

Miss Frazier did not arrive at her own party until almost midnight, when she whirled into the center of the dance floor to the strains of "You Must Have Been a Beautiful Baby." She also performed the kicky new step, the Lambeth Walk, with a variety of partners. Then she complained of exhaustion and a cold. Around one in the morning she wrapped herself in a tablecloth and sat drinking champagne.

James lost track of Monty in the midst of the crowds and the music. Finally he found him talking to one of the grey-haired chaperons. "There he was, the handsomest guy at the dance, acting like a wallflower! He told me he'd been so tongue-tied he'd never got up courage to ask Brenda to dance. I kidded him a lot about that."

Recalling these shared experiences, Morgan James describes Monty as "a young man set apart."

James spent the Christmas of 1938 at the Clift apartment. "It was stiff and formal, but since Monty and I had grown up in that atmosphere we paid no attention to it, we just accepted it and had a good time among ourselves."

Sunny had ordered a huge Christmas tree, decorated with real candles, that stood in the center of the living room. The tree shimmered, radiating light and heat, and dripping wax. During the evening a branch caught fire; Monty and James rushed over and pushed the tree over to stamp out the fire. Conversation ceased and then began again as if nothing had happened.

After *Dame Nature* closed Monty spent most of his free time photographing dancers in rehearsals at Gluck Sander's studio.

He was excited by the pounding rehearsal piano as he captured images of dancers at the bar or moving across the polished floor practicing steps to movements. "There's a dreamlike quality about the dance," he said, "but at the same time there's this intense emotional quality underneath."

Felicia Sorel, the imperious chain-smoking choreographer, made a great impression on Monty. When she began choreographing the musical *Everywhere I Roam* Monty asked if he could photograph her dancers at work. After rehearsals he and Miss Sorel had long discussions about the fantasy and magic inherent in good theater and how dance could elevate fantasy and make it soar.

"Monty half fell in love with Felicia," Morgan James recalled. "She had a remote quality like Brenda Frazier—she was mysterious—independent—unattainable. Monty adored her."

One afternoon in January 1939, during a rehearsal break, Felicia Sorel introduced Monty to Lehman Engel, the conductor. Engel was thirty—ten years older than Monty—and already established as a force in the Broadway musical theater. He had worked with Brecht, the Group Theater, and Orson Welles. He had an encyclopedic knowledge of opera and ballet and was an anecdotal nonstop talker. Engel and Monty immediately took to each other.

After rehearsal, accompanied by Felicia, they went out for coffee at Schrafft's on Broadway at Forty-third Street, across from the Astor Hotel. "We had a marvelous time talking theater," Engel recalls. "Monty was in an exuberant frame of mind. He knew me—what I'd accomplished—he seemed to admire my knowledge. He was taking piano then, and he was very interested in music theory."

Two weeks later when Engel was in Stamford giving a lecture on Renaissance madrigals, Monty appeared in the front row of the auditorium smiling up at him. After the lecture, they returned together to Engel's West Fourteenth Street apartment, "where we talked and talked—not only about classical music but about the roots of blues and jazz and about what social situations music came out of. . . ."

From then on, whenever their schedules permitted they saw each other. "Every time Monty phoned me I used to feel a rush of happiness," Engel said. "Monty would say, 'Mon vieux, there's an exhibit of Blake paintings in Philadelphia. Do you want to meet me at Penn Station?'"

Once, Engel recalls, they took a night boat up the Hudson River. "Another time when I'd been working hard composing for a show, Monty suggested we go to Boston for the entire weekend, 'So you can relax.'" They stayed at the Ritz Carlton Hotel. "After a marvelous big breakfast we took a walk through the Common and fed the swans. We ran into Moss and Kitty Hart; they were having a big cocktail party at the Ritz that evening and they insisted we come. I remember that they were particularly pleased to see Monty. He inspired such affection and loyalty then. He was so handsome and full of spirit, like a precocious child."

That April Monty played briefly on Broadway in a production of Karel Capek's political play *The Mother,* which starred Nazimova, the great Russian tragedienne. Brooks Atkinson called the play "more an evening of brooding than an evening of theatre." It closed in a few weeks.

Monty and Engel continued to spend a great deal of time together. They went to concerts, ballet and plays. They saw films like *Dark Victory* and *Gone With the Wind.*

Sunny Clift approved of Monty's friendship with Engel. She seemed impressed with his reputation as a conductor. "I think she found me cultivated," Engel said. Engel thought she was trying to suffocate Monty with love and ambition, but he always tried to be nice to her.

In the late spring of '39, Monty and Engel traveled to Mexico. "I'd planned to go alone but then Sunny phoned and said that Monty very much wanted to go with me, so I said of course."

They went on the *Orizaba,* the old ship from which Hart Crane had disappeared a few years earlier. Engel and Monty had planned to share a cabin with four other people, "but when we arrived at the dock I discovered that Bill Clift had rented the only suite on the boat and Sunny had filled it with candy, fruit, liquor, and books for Monty and me."

Monty had never heard of Hart Crane, so during the trip Engel filled him in on the splendidly ambiguous poet whose verses embraced the bridges and harbors of Manhattan, the tropics, jazz, and the sea. That he had been a homosexual and a drinker fascinated Monty, and that he had an ogress mother who practiced emotional blackmail on him in Cleveland made him laugh hysterically.

"Monty was highly susceptible to other people's personal dramas and tragedies," Engel said. They read much of Crane's poetry together as the boat steamed toward Mexico.

After five days the *Orizaba* reached Vera Cruz, and there the two men boarded a train that took them around gorges and mountains on the way to their destination, Cuernavaca. "We stayed at the Hotel Marik sharing a cottage next to the swimming pool. The garden was full of orchids. It was idyllic."

Later Rose and Miguel Covarrubias, the well-known Spanish caricaturist for *Vanity Fair,* joined them. They were followed by the John Garfields, who came up from Mexico City where Garfield had been promoting his latest movie, *Juarez.* He was full of contempt for his performance: "How can a boy from the Bronx play a Mexican revolutionary?"

Garfield, the hottest young star in the movies, represented an entirely new kind of screen personality: he was brooding, tough, cynical, and obsessed with himself. Engel said, "John—or Julie as he was known—let all his hangups hang out."

Monty and Garfield did not become friends. "They seemed uncomfortable together, possibly because of their different backgrounds and styles."

However, despite the differences between them, Monty accompanied the Garfields and Engel on an exhaustive sightseeing tour of Cuernavaca.

When it was over, Engel decided to stop seeing Monty for a while. "I felt our relationship couldn't be permanent. I sensed that this beautiful darling boy would always remain a child. Monty was incapable of growing up."

Engel told Monty what he felt. "He just stared at me with those glorious unblinking eyes of his without moving. He was in perfect control, but I could tell he was very upset. He didn't argue or try and change my mind. Only once he interrupted and asked, 'Aren't all actors *supposed* to be children?' We had once talked about how the greatest artists always hold on to their innocence. I don't remember what I replied. It was very painful. After that morning we never discussed it again."

Soon after, they left Cuernavaca by car for Acapulco where Monty became very ill with dysentery. Engel decided to charter a private plane to take them back to Mexico City. They took off in a rickety plane without instruments or a radio and they promptly got lost over a jungle. The flight that usually takes forty-five minutes took five hours.

In Mexico City, Monty, so gripped with pain he could hardly walk, boarded the next plane for New York. For several months afterwards he suffered from amoebic dysentery—a disease from which he never fully recovered.

Once Monty stopped seeing Engel he began to create a life separate and apart from his mother. He brought very few new friends home, hoping to keep his private involvements private. But Sunny said, "I knew right away he was addicted to little boys. It shocked me and I told him so, and I said it would weaken him artistically. His father was furious. 'How can a son of mine stoop to this?' he asked. He said I was entirely too gentle about the matter."

As time passed, Monty slept with both men and women indiscriminately in an effort to discover his sexual preference, but his conflict remained obvious—almost blatantly so, the director Edward Dmytryk recalled. " 'Oh, Jesus!' he'd say, 'look at that disgusting fag.' When I saw him at a cast party making love to that same fag actor I left the room."

"Monty was a bisexual," his brother Brooks maintains. "I met two girls he got pregnant. He was never exclusively one thing or the other; he swung back and forth. Because we'd been raised in Europe where homosexuality was more or less accepted, he never felt ashamed—until much later when he grew up. Once a secretary of Monty's asked me, 'What do you think about Monty being a fag?' and I said, 'My brother isn't a *fag*.' Monty disliked effeminacy, and he used to talk wonderingly about how some heterosexual men are so effete and some gay men so masculine."

Elizabeth Taylor told journalist Tommy Thompson that Monty showed up one night at her house with a mincing chorus boy and the next with a very proper young lady. It was as if he were saying— "Look Ma—I can—and I must—do both."

10

Monty remained weak from repeated bouts with dysentery. Sunny sent him to a variety of specialists, each having a different cure, each prescribing different pills. Monty became obsessed with his health, taking pills for aching stomach and pills to combat the diarrhea and bleeding; he carried pockets full of pills and began reading material on all kinds of drugs.

His diet became another prime concern. He could eat only raw steak and drink only milk by the quart to control his symptoms. But he still worried about gaining even a pound. He prided himself on having a lean, hard body. Even when he was feeling weak he worked out daily at Stillman's gym, practicing the breathing exercises he'd learned in France as a child to strengthen his stomach muscles.

After a recuperative mountain climbing trip to Maine with Ned Smith in August 1939, Monty won the coveted role of Clarence Day in *Life with Father,* only to be fired five days into rehearsal. Someone close to the production thought it might have had something to do with Monty's peculiar sense of comedy or his staccato way of speaking: to make his voice carry to the back of the house, he broke up sentences with short pauses. His delivery maddened author Russel Crouse, who was already concerned that his material wasn't particularly funny anyhow.

Whatever the reason, it was the first time Monty had been fired; he became depressed and impulsively called Engel, who consoled Monty by telling him that everybody gets fired at least once—he should stop brooding over it.

Monty was still upset when Leland Hayward phoned and said he was sending him *There Shall Be No Night,* a new script by Robert

Sherwood. The play, essentially a propaganda piece, reflected Sherwood's rage against the Russian invasion of Finland. Alfred Lunt was to direct the production as well as play Dr. Valkonen, an eminent and highly civilized Finnish scientist, who believes that violent resistance to an enemy solves nothing. Lynn Fontanne was to play Mrs. Valkonen, and Monty was up for the part of their son Erik who goes off to war, not for glory, but to preserve freedom.

The Lunts were then the most dazzling husband and wife in legitimate theater. For over twenty years they had been mesmerizing Broadway and London audiences with their performances in plays like *Elizabeth and Essex, Design for Living, Idiot's Delight,* and most recently the Giradoux farce, *Amphitryon 38.* Offstage the pair lived a high-keyed existence, full of mischief and glamour. Their friends included Noël Coward, S. N. Behrman, Ruth Gordon, and Alexander Woollcott.

Monty had always wanted to work with the Lunts. Every time he saw them on stage he sensed that these particular actors were strange wonderful beings who were somehow able to define their existence through the art of make-believe. The animal vitality of their performances and their gusto for acting continually amazed him.

The day of his audition for *There Shall Be No Night,* Monty was so nervous he drank three pots of strong tea; when he arrived for his appointment at the Alvin Theatre and sauntered across the stage his head was held high—"like a young prince," someone said. He was wearing a beautifully pressed grey flannel suit from Brooks Brothers, his shoes were highly polished, his hair and skin gleamed. Turning out front he gave everybody in the theater the benefit of his glittering solitary gaze and then he bowed over Lynn Fontanne's hand. "He almost clicked his heels," actor Bill Le Massena said.

Mrs. John Steinbeck, casting director for the Theatre Guild, remembers that Lunt exclaimed softly, "Look what the wind blew in!"

As soon as he began to read, the Lunts sensed Monty's creative vitality. Although his instincts were not yet totally focused and he still tended to be somewhat superficial, the natural talent bubbled out of him as he read the lines.

Yet after the reading, although the Lunts were encouraging, Monty was so convinced he had not gotten the role he had his hair cut—the worst crime an actor can commit before landing a part. The Lunts nonetheless had decided his quality was perfect for Erik, and Monty was signed immediately. There was a sense of urgency surrounding the production and the rest of the play was quickly cast with Lunt regulars Sydney Greenstreet, Thomas Gomez, Richard Whorf, William Le Massena and Phyllis Thaxter.

Monty could hardly wait for rehearsals with the Lunts to begin. In the mornings, he raced through breakfast, sometimes forgetting to say good-bye to Sunny in his haste to get out the door. He almost ran to rehearsal, down Fifth Avenue and then west past the rows of dilapidated tenements and greasy bars that bordered the Broadway theater district.

What amazed Monty more than anything during the rehearsals was Lunt's ability—when he was acting—to change readings. As the character Dr. Valkonen he could say a line in a dozen different ways, but the character's intention or objective remained the same. The essence of both the Lunts' art was not their seemingly nonchalant way with dialogue, it was what went on behind the lines, the thought processes, the specific character needs. Subtexts were always meticulously worked out, coloring each performance, making them original and provocative.

Lunt encouraged Monty to trust himself and Monty's acting began to blossom. "Monty had this glorious instinctive talent bursting out of him and Mr. Lunt recognized it and helped him focus and cultivate it," said Bill Le Massena, Monty's closest friend in the production. "He kept asking Monty questions about his part—specific questions—he helped him develop an inner life for the character by using elements of himself. Like Lunt, Monty was a natural actor, a born mimic. He never needed or wanted to hide behind a fake mustache or accent. He used his inner self."

During the out-of-town tryouts of *Night* in Providence, Boston, Baltimore, and Washington, Monty got into the habit of discussing the whys and wherefores of his role. "We sat in his dressing room before half hour," Le Massena said, "and we argued back and forth about what makes a man go to war. Was it patriotism or a need to show independence? Do men really want to be heroes?"

Monty chose as his hero Wendell Willkie, a liberal New York lawyer, who had just appeared in the news as a possible dark horse candidate in the upcoming presidential election. He liked Willkie's stubborn individualism.

"We sat and argued about whether Willkie was a liberal Republican or an old-fashioned Democrat or a combination of both," Le Massena recalls. "Monty was a furious questioner. He wanted the answer for everything. He tried to inject that sense of questioning, that weighing of ideals, into *Night* and it worked."

For a while during the out-of-town tryouts, Monty came across as a younger Alfred Lunt. He spoke in Lunt's voice and moved like him, even to standing with his back to the audience as Lunt did. The imitation eventually gave way to his own hard-edged interpretation, and, by the time *There Shall Be No Night* opened on Broadway on April 30, 1940, at the Alvin, the clever, mimicking juvenile had become young actor exhibiting his own depth and sensitivity. As Erik he received reviews that were among the best of his career.

The play got raves. "Enormously impressive," wrote Brooks Atkinson. It went on to win a third Pulitzer Prize for Robert Sherwood.

Finally settled into a run on Broadway, Monty became part of the Lunts' inner circle. He was the only actor in the company, save Sydney Greenstreet, who had immediate access to the star dressing room. Often he would drop by to chat or take photographs of Lunt sitting morosely at his lighted makeup table rubbing greasepaint across his cheeks. He ran errands for Lynn Fontanne and listened to her talk about why an actor shouldn't drink or smoke and why an actor must get plenty of sleep.

After a performance he sometimes accompanied Lunt when he went off to see a burlesque show, and every so often Monty was invited to an after-theater supper at the Lunts' elegant apartment on East Fifty-seventh Street, where Lunt, a superb cook, concocted cheese soufflés and jellied aspics for the likes of George S. Kaufman, Helen Hayes, and Alexander Woollcott. The conversation at the table sparkled. After the brandy was served, Lynn Fontanne sometimes suggested a game of Scrabble, and then Lunt usually retired to the kitchen where he washed the dishes himself. Monty joined him to dry the dishes, and over the soapsuds Lunt described his days as a cook in a Minnesota boarding house, and confided his painful self-doubts. He was a moody man, given to bouts of violent euphoria and equally violent depression. Although he knew he was one of the greatest actors America had ever produced, he was filled with anxiety about himself and his performances. "Sometimes I hate the sound of my own voice," he told Monty.

Two decades later Monty burst into tears after reading Noël Coward's explanation of Lunt's ennui in Zolotov's biography of the Lunts. "Alfred's wretchedness is genuine," he said, "it is a nervous reaction for trying so hard for perfection."

In 1940 Monty was only beginning to understand his own struggle for perfection. He and Lunt often talked about the artist's dedication to his craft until it became a habit, and about how the artist must submerge both conscious and unconscious until the craft becomes rooted deep within the personality. "Don't work for money—don't work for fame," Lunt told him. "Work to be good at what you do. It's the *quality* of the work that is important, not the salary or size of your billing.

"And if you're good at what you do, you damn well know you can be a helluva lot better. You must never stop working. There are only glimmers of perfection in acting and they are always astonishing. But creation is a mystery and the end result is only acceptance if you don't see the work behind it."

Bit by bit the Lunts came to look on Monty as the son they never had. One of Monty's most prized possessions was a photograph of the Lunts inscribed: "from your *real* mother and father." They took personal pride in his development as an actor and encouraged him to read more plays to broaden his range. When they talked about him they implied he was their best disciple and if he worked on roles like Treplef in *The Seagull,* and Hamlet, he could carry on in their tradition. Already he was an actor who had only to enter a scene to create a sense of drama.

During the run of *There Shall Be No Night,* Monty saw a great deal of Phyllis Thaxter, who understudied the maid in the play. Miss Thaxter, born in Maine, was then a slight brunette with tousled hair and a fresh, animated face. She was, in her own words, "terribly young, appallingly naive, and determined to be a great actress."

She and Monty spent hours talking about the theater, and sat with Sydney Greenstreet reading Shaw and Shakespeare. During the day they often went to see old movies at the Museum of Modern Art. "All Monty wanted to be was the best actor in the world. He worked so hard. I've never seen anyone so dedicated."

Later when Miss Thaxter replaced Dorothy McGuire as *Claudia* on Broadway, Monty gave her moral support. A half hour before curtain, he came backstage with a present, a tiny silver pin from Jensen's and his card on which he had written, "To a wonderful person." "I was shaking—absolutely terrified, and I remember he put his hands on my shoulders and said, 'Darling, darling, don't worry, everything is going to be all right.' He was tremendously sympathetic because he too suffered from awful stage fright every time he walked out on the stage."

While she was starring in *Claudia,* Phyllis Thaxter lived with the Clifts for several months. She remembers Bill as "kind and generous" and Sunny as a "tiny energetic woman trying to do everything for me —too much for me." Sunny insisted that she lie under a sunlamp for at least fifteen minutes every day, and "I agreed because somehow with Sunny it was difficult to say no."

Often Monty would come into Phyllis Thaxter's room in the mornings and crawl into bed with her, and then Sunny would appear with trays and serve them breakfast in bed. Monty told Phyllis a great deal about his family in those months. He said he thought he was descended from the Robert Andersons and Montgomery Blairs and that his mother was Woodbury Blair's illegitimate daughter.

"By an odd coincidence my uncle was the lawyer for the Blair family in Washington," Phyllis Thaxter said, "so I'd heard references about Sunny Clift from him."

Monty and Phyllis Thaxter seemed so close that a great many people assumed they would eventually marry. Sunny confided to friends that Monty and that Thaxter girl were awfully serious about each other. The Lunts encouraged them to marry the way they had and become a great acting team.

"Monty and I loved each other very much, but it was a romantic kind of love—I never went to bed with him," Miss Thaxter said. "But we finally thought—well maybe we *should* marry. It seemed like a good idea."

Then one afternoon while she was still living at the Clifts, Monty sat her down and said, " 'I've been thinking about it, darling, and I can't get married. It just wouldn't be right.' He seemed so serious and a little sad, as if he knew something I didn't. I didn't ask questions; I just said all right and we never mentioned marriage after that."

Miss Thaxter says she sensed "even in my innocence" that "he liked both men and women. He was absolutely wonderful to women. He felt tremendous empathy. But I also sensed he lived a very separate life when I didn't see him—a life I had no part of and never asked about."

Monty remained affectionate, teasing with Phyllis Thaxter, but privately uncommitted because his real passion was reserved for an aspiring actor he'd met at Klein's gym. The actor, "Josh," originally from New England, was exceedingly tall and rather stooped. "I looked old even when I was young. Monty used to tell me I was too trusting, too nice to be an actor . . . but I've never regretted the way I am."

The two men were lovers for two years. "Our affair was for me the most beautiful experience in my life," he said. "I'll never forget it. We were still sexually rather pure and innocent. We laughed a great deal, and played together. We hadn't started cruising yet, and neither one of us had ever gone to a public toilet or a bathhouse to make contact. We didn't hang out at Forty-second Street movie houses. We'd never seen a drag show, and I for one didn't know what a male hustler was."

Josh met Sunny a couple of times at the Clifts' Fifty-third Street apartment. "I didn't know whether she suspected our friendship. She didn't feel threatened by me as she might have by a woman in love with Monty."

When they were together they rarely brought up the subject of homosexuality. They had both been raised to believe that homosexuality was a form of mental illness, a psychiatric disorder.

"When we were alone it was like Monty and I were shut away from reality for a couple of hours. It was a disorienting experience. Alone we could be emotional and passionate but outside we had to hide our feelings.

"Naturally we felt guilty about what we were doing, but we couldn't help ourselves. We were violently attracted to each other and knew we had fallen in love. Sure, there was danger if someone caught us fooling around in Monty's dressing room. So usually he'd come up to the apartment I had near Columbia.

"Up until a few years ago it would have been career suicide for us to have confessed our homosexuality. Now it doesn't matter. Then it was crucial to *hide everything*. I remember Monty telling me how Lunt scolded him sometimes. Lunt adored Monty, but he was afraid he was turning gay. He never said anything direct about it, but alluded to Gielgud, and then he said, "Well, y'know Noël Coward's an exception. You can't ordinarily be a pansy in the theater and survive.' It's all changed now, thank God.

"One of the things that was starting to torture Monty back in 1940 was the fact that he had to hide his sexual feelings. He despised deception, pretense, and he felt the intolerable strain of living a lie. He was scrupulously honest with himself, and he had a tremendous sense of morality about what is right and wrong. I think that's one of the reasons he was in such conflict about his homosexuality. There was no tolerance for it back then. Gays were totally oppressed. The

Church was against it; certain psychiatrists were scathing about it, calling it an aberration."

Josh said their affair ended when he joined the Navy in 1942, "but we saw each other frequently as friends after that, even after Monty became a big star." They remained close friends until his death. "What floored me was Monty's ability to keep every single relationship separate and apart from every other relationship. I don't think any of his other friends knew about us, but then I didn't know any of his other friends—Monty was selfish about friendship. He didn't want to share, but within a friendship he could be exceedingly generous with his time and with his money. . . ."

In the spring of 1941 *There Shall Be No Night* began an eight-month tour of the United States. At the tour's beginning Monty was twenty, and in the words of Bill Le Massena, "He was conceited as hell because he was such a great beauty."

By the time the tour reached Hollywood, Monty had three offers from studios to sign long-term contracts. L. B. Mayer wanted him specifically for *Mrs. Miniver,* a movie he was planning to make about the London blitz with Greer Garson; Monty wanted to do the film, but he didn't want to sign a seven-year contract. Hollywood would have to accept him on his own terms—"I don't want to be a slave," he said.

When his parents urged him to reconsider MGM's offer of a seven-year contract starting at $750 a week with yearly options, he used the word "slavery" again. "But you'll never get another chance like this," Bill Clift warned. Monty told his father that he knew he would; for the time being he intended to remain in the theater.

The tour for *There Shall Be No Night* ended just after Pearl Harbor; President Roosevelt phoned Robert Sherwood to tell him *Night* was much too controversial politically to run in wartime. The show closed abruptly on the road.

After *There Shall Be No Night* Monty became increasingly obsessive about his development as an actor. He took more dance lessons. He was coached by a singer. "He could never carry a tune, but my God, did he believe in the lyrics!" Nancy Walker said. He would spend weeks before rehearsals working out every nuance of a characterization. In the margins of his scripts, he made copious notes in his handsome but almost illegible scrawl. What seemed so spontaneous and effervescent in a performance such as that in the film *The Search* was actually the result of hours and hours of work.

As a tribute to Lunt (who had learned how to tap-dance, sing, and play the piano for various productions) Monty deliberately set out to master something new for each of his subsequent roles. It could be as small but as telling a detail as the limp he developed for *The Searching Wind*. He usually did not talk about his choices, but before he played the priest in *I Confess,* he memorized the entire Latin mass. He spent weeks boxing as he prepared for the role of Prewitt in *From Here to Eternity*. He also learned to play the bugle. And as the punch-drunk cowboy in *The Misfits* he almost broke his back learning how to ride a bronc in Reno. He was thrown repeatedly, but he said, "It helped my characterization."

Invariably he gave Lunt credit for his development as an actor. "Alfred taught me how to select," he said. "Acting is an accumulation of subtle details. And the details of Alfred Lunt's performances were like the observations of a great novelist—like Samuel Butler or Marcel Proust."

In March 1942, while Monty was recovering from a particularly unpleasant bout with recurrent dysentery, director Robert Lewis asked him to act in an experimental production of Ramon Naya's award-winning play, *Mexican Mural.*

The play, a series of sketches set during a Vera Cruz carnival, dramatized religious superstition and the poverty and desperation of the Mexican people. Lewis offered Monty the part of a young boy unable to endure the squalor of his environment. Monty agreed at once partly because Lewis had earlier directed William Saroyan's *My Heart's in the Highlands,* an impressive and stylish production, but also because Lewis, at twenty-six, was a founding member of the Group Theater, which had nourished some of the most controversial talents of the 1930s, not the least of whom was acting coach Lee Strasberg.

To Monty it was important that the Group had produced leftist plays of social significance such as Clifford Odets's *Golden Boy,* and that it had also developed a wide range of actors like John Garfield, Lee J. Cobb, and Franchot Tone, as well as directors such as Harold Clurman and Elia Kazan.

Monty first heard about Robert "Bobby" Lewis from his friend Engel, who had composed music for one of the early Group Theater productions. He had then described "Bobby" as "bubbly and inventive" and given to violent arguments with Lee Strasberg about Stanislavski and the value of emotional memory exercises. Lewis's whole search as director-teacher was how to discover an acting style without sacrificing inner truth. Since the Group's demise in 1941 he had been conducting extremely successful acting classes at a dingy studio on Third Avenue. Monty knew he would be using exercises and improvisations in *Mural* as part of the rehearsal process. This piqued his actor's fancy.

During rehearsals of *Mural* he met four people who proved even more important to him than Lewis: the impoverished Russian exile Mira Rostova, actor Kevin McCarthy and his new wife Augusta Dabney, and Libby Holman, the former Broadway torch singer.

In 1932 Miss Holman had been charged with murdering her twenty-year-old husband, millionaire Zachary Smith Reynolds, heir to the tobacco fortune. The murder charges were dropped for lack of evidence and because she was carrying Reynolds's child; six months later a son, Christopher, was born, and after a bitter estate battle she was awarded $7 million. She returned to New York and tried without success to regain her fame as a singer.

The first day of rehearsal of *Mexican Mural,* Bobby Lewis told the cast to treat Holman, who was to be in one vignette, like any other actor. Even so, as soon as she appeared in the tiny auditorium on the fiftieth floor of the Chanin office building everybody turned and stared.

"She reminded me of a black widow spider," Augusta Dabney recalled. There was a faintly sinister quality about the way she posed at the top of the center aisle clad in a pale Mainbocher dress which showed off her perpetual tan and slender legs. Her black, rather oily hair tumbled past her shoulders and she smelled of an expensive perfume called "Jungle Gardenia."

As rehearsals progressed Holman won everybody's respect. She was a hard worker and refused special treatment, although she was backing the show as well as acting in it.

As rehearsals of *Mexican Mural* progressed, it became obvious that Holman was attracted to Monty, and he was fascinated by her lurid past. The two carried on a flirtation. Once or twice she suggested drinks during breaks. He would counter with what was then the truth: "I drink only milk."

Often she stood at the back of the house watching him during his scenes, smoking cigarettes greedily. She had always loved men younger than herself: sensitive, beautiful young men who confided their sexual inadequacies to her.

The atmosphere inside that little auditorium became, in Lewis's words, "sensual as hell. I'd organized all sorts of improvisations to free the actors physically since there was constant movement on stage. I had everybody hugging and clutching each other; during breaks there was much gliding into dark corners. As opening night got closer I could feel excitement and tension building up."

Much of the excitement revolved around Monty. "Everybody was in love with him," Lewis said. "He was absolutely mesmerizing in the show, and offstage he was like Pan, an enchanter. Everybody clustered around him and he talked and took photographs. But he refused to play favorites. One afternoon he might sit with Libby and light her cigarettes, another evening he'd go with Kevin and Augusta for dinner, but much of the time he spent with Mira Rostova and I think that ticked Libby off most of all. Libby was used to having her way with men, and yet here was this Mira Rostova, a Russian émigrée (whom Lewis had taken on as a scholarship student) with her woebegone little face out of a Kathe Kollwitz drawing—you know, *haunted*—who was monopolizing Monty."

To most people in the *Mexican Mural* cast Mira seemed proud and forlorn, given to sighs and anguished glances, moving with the air of a great tragedienne. As soon as she met Monty her face lit up, "actually shone," someone said. She began calling him "my comrade." It was obvious to everyone she was falling madly in love with him.

Monty teased and kidded her as he teased and kidded everyone else, but her dedication to the theater really impressed him. When she spoke of the great Russian actors and of her vocation—acting—her voice grew hushed, her heavy-lidded eyes blazed. They discussed Vaktangov, Boleslaski, Michael Chekov, and Stanislavski together and talked about how the truth of an actor's art is in the imagination.

Together they worked on his role in *Mexican Mural*. Mira made some suggestions, but overall Monty didn't need much help. He was doing a part that was very close to him. The neurotic, brooding qualities inherent in his own personality corresponded to those of the androgynous youth in the Naya play.

When the play opened on April 27, 1942, Brooks Atkinson wrote, *"Mexican Mural* is a strange, wild evocative sketch of an undisciplined civilization. Some of the acting is excellent, especially Montgomery Clift's superlative portrait of a brooding beaten youth who cannot endure the coarseness of his environment."

Other reviews were mixed. Some were bad, but Tennessee Williams says it remains one of the most memorable evenings in the theater, and Irwin Shaw, then a young playwright, remembered Monty.

"I was impressed as everyone in the audience that I was witnessing the performance of an actor of tragic stature who combined great power with great delicacy."

The show played three nights to packed houses. There was talk of moving it elsewhere but nothing came of it. But Monty continued toying with Mira's and Libby Holman's affections. "Once I saw them walking down the street—Mira and Monty," Augusta Dabney said. "Their arms were linked and they were talking softly with total concentration. When I got close to them they seemed to be speaking in a special language I couldn't understand. But a couple of days later I saw Monty and Libby Holman. They were moving towards her car, bodies close and swaying, arms linked. They were talking softly to each other with total concentration, and when I got near them they ignored me—and they seemed to be speaking in a language I couldn't understand."

In May 1942, Monty fell ill again with dysentery. Sick as he was, he nevertheless reported to his draft board. He said he was anxious to serve his country, he told Bill Le Massena. He wanted to be involved in a "world seized in conflict," joining the ski troops as Erik had done in *There Shall Be No Night*.

When he was classified as 4F because of the dysentery it was a terrible blow to his pride. But later he confided to his brother he'd been "scared shitless of going to war and getting his face blown off."

Meanwhile he could not seem to throw off the dysentery—it hung on, plaguing him with bouts of nausea, bleeding, and terrible cramps. More specialists were called in to confer in the Clift apartment, but still no cure resulted. He would recover only spasmodically, then fall ill again in spite of all the drugs. Desolate, he lay in his narrow room listening to the radio broadcasts of "Amos 'n' Andy" and "The Lone Ranger."

Finally the Lunts told Sunny about a Dr. Norman Brown, the foremost authority on tropical diseases at the Ochsnee Clinic at Tulane Medical Center. Monty was flown immediately to New Orleans. For two months he remained at the clinic where he had every conceivable test.

Around this time he wrote a postcard to Bobby Lewis:

I'm grossly sentimental. The most enjoyment I get in this stinking hospital are the joys of *Mexican Mural*. I've told you they were something. Imagine me at my age reminiscing. . . . Hope to be back by the end of the week. My last test here heaven help me is Tuesday. There are parts of me all over the hospital. They can't find my colon. I know they must have been looking for it for days but they haven't mentioned it to me because they think I'll get upset. I don't care. To hell with it. Love, Monty.

And to actor Kevin McCarthy a letter on Roosevelt Hotel stationery dated May 7, 1942:

Dear Kevin:
   Voila! Had lunch with Mira yesterday we talked to Mr. Lunt. He is going to do the Behrman play.
   He has lumbago.
   Saw Alfred DeLiagre in the afternoon about an English mystery play he does not want me for.
   Got the pictures of the play. I'll show them to you when I get back.
   Saw Bobby. For God's sake get the Billboard review of 'Mex M' and Candide if you think the play was panned before.
   Give my love to your wife no matter what.
   HELLO.   Monty.

The following day he scribbled another letter to Kevin and Augusta:

                                        May 13, 1942
Dear K & A
   I hope you, Kevin the unbeliever, were duly shocked by my last letter. I was not by the way bragging about the people I've seen I was trying to show I'd been in town all day long—the truth? I flew!
   Well, after putting me through Mme. Tussaud's testing machine they find I have a "strip gut"—to cure it I shall have to be here another week.
   The nurses are NOT pretty on my floor (to be read two ways). I'm not surprised only hurt. I thought that was the least you could expect—one of them shaves twice a day at least. God. Here she comes . . . please write . . . love Monty.

11

When he left the hospital in June, Monty joined Augusta at the Cape. Kevin had been drafted into the army but in July he started getting furloughs to see Augusta perform at the Monomoy Playhouse in Chatham. Bobby Lewis drove up for long weekends and spent a lot of time with the McCarthys and Monty.

Monty genuinely loved the McCarthys. They were a gregarious, exuberant, carefree young couple; they seemed a perfect foil for Monty's moodiness and precision. "We found ourselves on the same wavelength. We were never at a loss for anything to say," Kevin recalled, "and we felt completely comfortable with each other."

"What I remember most about our friendship in the early stages was the intense happiness I felt when we were all together," Augusta said. "I look back on that time, the summer of 1942, when I really got to know Monty in Wellfleet, as the most joyous time in my life. The most exciting. We had our lives ahead of us, and we laughed constantly. We were twenty-one and we thought we were terribly funny. For a couple of performances at the Playhouse, Monty played a walk-on in blackface and he made up a name for himself: T. Roosevelt Brown.

"I've never seen anyone who relished the sensual the way Monty did." Augusta went on, "God. We used to eat fresh cooked lobster out of the pot at Wellfleet, and my heart would actually pound at Monty's responses—the way he'd suck meat from a lobster's claw. . . . And Monty loved to roughhouse. We used to run on the beach together, and we would run and run alongside of each other until we were out of breath—practically sobbing for breath, and then he'd try and throw me down on the sand, and I'd run faster to get away from him, and finally we'd collapse and watch the waves rolling in.

"He was very physical too. You know, hugging and kissing everybody—men, women, and little kids. We were all very sexual with each other that summer—but it was an innocent kind of sexuality if you know what I mean."

By the time they got back to New York in September, the McCarthys and Monty were inseparable. "Our apartment became his second home," Kevin said. "We all clicked mentally. We had rapport. We agreed on everything everybody else disagreed about."

Through Monty the McCarthys went on "cultural binges." They were exposed to more ballet, art exhibits, and plays than they had been previously. "Monty wanted to see everything."

Kevin was stationed at an army base in New Jersey, so he came home every weekend and joined Monty and Augusta at plays like *Uncle Harry* with Joseph Schildkraut and Eva Le Gallienne and *The Doughgirls* with Arlene Francis. After a show they strolled up Broadway arm in arm, stopping sometimes to have a fruit drink or to watch the live turtles wriggling in their glass bowls.

Occasionally during those fall evenings Monty would gaze so ardently at the blonde, giggly Augusta, she would blush. Monty told his sister, "Gussie is never too busy to listen to me. And she has the best sense of humor. If she were free, I'd marry her tomorrow."

Monty talked to Brooks about his love for Augusta, but he said he could never betray the friendship he and Kevin had. "Stealing another man's wife is a despicable act, particularly if the man is serving in the United States Army."

Kevin recalled, "Monty never told me how he felt about Gussie. But once or twice when I saw the way he kissed her in greeting I'd think, 'Hey! that's my wife he's kissing!' "

Monty frequently embraced both McCarthys passionately in public and they reciprocated. "Monty always hugged the people he cared about," someone said, "but he hugged the McCarthys so tight you didn't think he would ever let go."

Eventually, as Monty and the McCarthys established themselves as a regular threesome around New York and were seen everywhere together, stories began circulating that they were a *ménage à trois*. Monty laughed off the stories but he insisted privately to his brother that Augusta was the only woman he could ever think of marrying.

However, Tennessee Williams felt that "a lot of people in the theater suspected Monty had actually fallen in love with Kevin and that Kevin was the love of his life."

"Monty was very oblique when it came to declaring his intentions," another actress said. "He was the kind of guy who if he wanted to make love to Kevin would make love to Augusta in the hopes the message got through to Kevin."

Whatever the private complexities of their relationship, the trio never discussed them. Only once Augusta did admit that "Monty's presence in our apartment was often disrupting," but she did not elaborate.

Both the McCarthys said that Monty was self-absorbed. "He was the star; we circled around him." They went to every performance he ever gave and afterwards discussed them with him, often for hours. However, Monty did not see either Kevin or Augusta in many of the plays and movies they did, nor did he discuss their performances. He didn't ignore their accomplishments; he was simply more interested in his own.

12

Success was making Monty more critical. He ridiculed most of the plays he was offered, he called certain actors "vomitable." He seemed more arrogant, more abrasive with people he knew; when he lambasted a young actress, a friend chided, "But Monty, she's nice," to which Monty snapped, "Most bad actors are nice."

Bobby Lewis recalled overhearing Monty in the lobby of the Shubert Theater in New Haven arguing with his agent Leland Hayward. "Monty had literally buttonholed Leland, saying ferociously, 'I don't give a shit what you think, Leland, I want to do that play, do you understand?'" Lewis had never seen the demanding and forceful side of Monty before. "I was surprised and then I thought—why the hell not?"

The play in question was Thornton Wilder's *The Skin of Our Teeth*—a cartoon comedy about mankind's blundering struggle for survival. The play was to star Tallulah Bankhead and Fredric March and to be directed by a young director named Elia Kazan.

Playwright Robert Ardrey had suggested Monty for the role of Henry, the son who used to be called Cain and has a scar on his forehead. Kazan acted on the suggestion, and the two met. Shortly afterwards, Monty agreed to play the part. Although it was not a large part, it ran through all three acts and was very important within the play.

Once again Monty played a child. Henry was fourteen, but that didn't concern Monty. What mattered was the play's theme—how man survives the Ice Age, floods, and war—and Wilder's suggestions for staging. Wilder had the actors stepping in and out of character to discuss the progress of the play and comment on its meaning and lack of meaning.

Rehearsals, beginning in September of 1942, were tempestuous. Tallulah Bankhead punctuated every day with temper tantrums. Bankhead loathed Florence Eldridge (Mrs. March), deemed Kazan incompetent, and thought the show's producer, Michael Meyerberg, was penny-pinching and vulgar. Eventually Bankhead divided the company into two factions pro and con Kazan. She maintained that Kazan's direction did not succeed in carrying the sense of improvisation Thornton Wilder intended. Wilder, in the army in California, was bombarded with letters and phone calls pleading with him to take sides. By the time the production reached New Haven, everybody was exhausted from tension.

Of all the actors (among them E. G. Marshall, Morton Da Costa and Fran Heflin) only Monty remained aloof from the squabbles. He told everyone he had to conserve his energy for performances, so he would not even voice an opinion when the cast rebelled at wearing dirty costumes.

In spite of the chaos among the cast when *Skin of Our Teeth* opened on Broadway at the Plymouth Theater on November 18, 1942, it became the most talked-about play of the season, and there were standees every night. The *Times*'s Lewis Nichols called it "the best pure theater of the forties" and Alexander Woollcott described Thornton Wilder as "a theatrical craftsman as bold, as impatient, as ingenious a sovereign in his field as Frank Lloyd Wright is in his. . . ." As for Bankhead, she won the Critics Circle Award for her outrageous and spirited performance as Sabina. Before the end of its run, *Skin of Our Teeth* had won the Pulitzer Prize as the best original Broadway play of 1942.

Monty, of course, made a personal impact once again with his vivid portrait of Henry, the faintly neurotic yet innocent son. Douglas Hubbard in *Theatre Arts* called him "a young man of quiet gallantry and great seriousness of purpose." Monty projected a blend of innocence and guile. It was these qualities combined with his good looks that made Hollywood increasingly interested in him.

It did bother some theatergoers that on occasion he fell back into Lunt mannerisms. "Opening night he sounded *exactly* Alfred Lunt," said Stephen Cole. "You know—the Midwestern drawl, combined with an English accent. Whenever he felt nervous he'd hide behind a Lunt imitation."

It was a crutch Monty admitted to Cole, "but isn't it better that I imitate the best actor in the world rather than the worst? Supposing I sounded like Johnny Weissmuller?"

Ned Smith continued to visit Monty as often as he could. "Usually we'd go and have supper after his show." Sometimes Phyllis Thaxter would join them, or Frances Heflin, but often they would go by themselves. "We'd drink a little wine and have deep philosophical conversations."

Friends who listened to them talk together referred to Smith as "the guy with the single vision. He was the scientist stating the facts; he had a blunt, rational way of viewing reality, whereas Monty had a crazy double vision. He saw things symbolically, internally. Smith served as a sounding board. It was always weird to hear them argue because they seemed such poles apart."

Midway through the run of *Skin of Our Teeth,* Monty fell ill with dysentery again, and left the production to return to the clinic in New Orleans. When he left the hospital sometime in the spring of 1943 he thought he had fully recovered, and his father gave him the family's 1937 Buick in celebration. He christened the automobile "Beulah." "God, he loved that car," Kevin said. "He treated it almost like a person—you know—patting the doors and talking to it. He was very excited about having his own car—it made him feel grown-up."

He took to driving out of New York City on short trips past West Point and the Palisades, and he visited people he knew in Westport and Sharon, Connecticut. On weekends he dropped in at Janet Cohn's place in Bedford Village. Miss Cohn was a rotund and lively spinster who worked for Harold Freedman, the well-known play agent, who handled S. N. Behrman, Robert Sherwood, Noël Coward, and Thornton Wilder.

She had known Monty since *Dame Nature,* and they had developed an affectionate, if casual, relationship. "I think he looked on me as an aunt," she said.

In 1943 Monty spent almost every Sunday afternoon at Miss Cohn's. There were always theater people there like Tallulah Bankhead or Bobby Lewis, sitting on the lawn gossiping, "and I'd have a barbecue in the garden around four," Miss Cohn said.

Thornton Wilder, then serving in Army Intelligence, was an occasional guest. An ebullient, driven man of insatiable curiosity and erudition, he was intrigued with Monty. After they met he dropped him several notes, but the two men did not become close friends until 1945.

Across from Janet Cohn's property in Bedford Village was a small lake and a compact red barn which had been renovated into a studio with a tiny bath and kitchenette. Monty took one look and signed a three-year lease.

From mid-1943 through 1947, he spent many weekends at the barn. Sometimes, Kevin and Augusta accompanied him, sometimes Mira Rostova.

Sunny kept after Monty to invite her to the barn, and finally, about a year after he had signed the lease, she came for a day, bearing tulip bulbs that she insisted on planting right outside the barn door.

Monty watched her plant, and he seemed pleased, Miss Cohn said. "He called his mother 'darling' and kept exclaiming 'how beautiful!'" But as soon as she'd gone he knelt down and yanked every one of the tulips out of the earth and threw them into the garbage can.

He wanted no reminders of Sunny around; the barn was *his,* its spare rooms in direct contrast to the gloomy overfurnished apartment on Park Avenue.

When in Manhattan, Monty frequently stayed at Mira's little place on East Fifty-fifth Street while she was away. He longed for his own place away from Sunny's intrusions and razor-sharp criticism. "Why does she keep trying to *control* me?" he cried out. "She will not leave me alone!" She opposed all his new friendships violently. Libby Holman was "perverted," Mira Rostova was "an opportunist," and Kevin and Augusta McCarthy were not of his "class." She particularly disliked McCarthy because "he's Shanty Irish and proud of it." He was an orphan, she'd heard—so where does he really come from; what is his ancestry—his genealogical tree? She repeatedly told Monty not to associate with Kevin; he was a nothing, a nobody!

13

After Kevin McCarthy joined the road company of *Winged Victory* in 1943, he was away from New York for fifteen months, and Augusta and Monty spent more time together, exploring New York and going to the theater and movies. Augusta knew she was serving as a maternal figure for Monty. Ultimately her closest friend Jeanne Green served a similar function, but neither woman minded nor did either feel any jealousy. In the beginning everything seemed blissful and adventurous. "We were both terribly naive and romantic about Monty and half in love with him in a romantic and sentimental way."

At the time Jeanne Green met Monty she was twenty-one, blonde, and vivaciously attractive. A native of Chicago, she had roomed with Augusta in New York while both attended the American Academy of Dramatic Arts; later they worked at the Barter Theater. In 1942 Jeanne married Fred Green, a sportswriter for *P.M.* who joined the air force shortly after Kevin joined the army.

While her husband was in basic training Jeanne suffered a miscarriage. "I had moved in with my mother in Larchmont, and I absolutely hated it. I felt low and very blue and I phoned Gussie and told her I was miserable and at loose ends. She invited me to stay with her in New York. I took the next train to the city.

"I remember seeing Montgomery Clift for the first time in Grand Central Station. He was standing next to Gussie in a white shirt and rumpled jeans. He was wiry and handsome and grinning broadly. When I told them both that I didn't have the strength to walk, Monty carried me out of the station past commuters and soldiers and ticket booths. He was incredibly strong."

As soon as she was feeling better Jeanne began accompanying Monty and Augusta to the theater and to restaurants in Greenwich Village for supper.

"Monty was the most wonderful person in the world to be with. He was great fun and hilariously funny. His humor was slightly cockeyed and he sparked my secret sense of the ridiculous. I told my husband naively, 'Monty knows more about living than anybody in the world.' I was hungry for what Monty had to offer intellectually. We talked books and theater and he introduced me to New York life which I had missed terribly.

"I guess I fell romantically in love with him. I don't see how any woman could help but love him he was so endearing and lovable in those days. He was also very affectionate and often kissed the back of my neck or my ear. But Monty and I were never lovers. I deeply loved my husband Fred. Monty's friendship brought no threat to my marriage."

To both Jeanne and Augusta Monty was a woman's man. As women they related to the extreme mobility of his face. "He would react to people and situations emotionally," Augusta said. "He would also tell us things about ourselves, and if we'd get mad, he'd laugh and run his finger along our cheeks. He was devastating."

They fully enjoyed their times together. But he frustrated them when they felt they were really getting close to him; he'd disappear for a couple of days at a time, and once or twice they ran into him with some shallow young man.

He never explained his disappearances or his mysterious companions, but Jeanne and Augusta refused to discuss the possibility that Monty might be homosexual. "In those days—1943-44—one simply did not discuss those things." Anyhow, as far as they were concerned, Monty hadn't made any choice. He didn't seem to have *one* sexual center. He was too mercurial, too diffuse a personality.

In January 1944, Monty acted in a revival of Wilder's *Our Town*. Ned Smith recalled, "It was the first time I realized Monty was such a special actor. He had a moment at the end of the play where he jumps over a series of imaginary rain puddles—it was quite extraordinary the way he did it."

Late in February, Monty went into rehearsals for Lillian Hellman's play *The Searching Wind*. The director, Herman Shumlin, met with Monty privately several times to discuss his part, that of a soldier wounded in the war who returns home to Washington, D.C., and finds his family has become fascist. Once Shumlin said to him, "Are you aware you've modeled your speech after Alfred Lunt?" Monty turned white as a sheet and said no, he hadn't. Shumlin told him he'd chosen an excellent model, but he didn't think Monty wanted to be an imitator.

Monty took what Shumlin said very seriously. Midway into rehearsals he no longer sounded like Alfred Lunt. He spoke in his own voice which was "extremely clear and distinctive," recalls Shumlin. "I'd call it a *pungent* voice. Monty belonged on the stage. There are certain actors who walk out in front of an audience and they *belong* there. You believed him the instant he spoke a line."

Monty opened the play with that fine old character actor Dudley Digges. The curtain rose on the two of them reading a newspaper together. One afternoon George Kaufman dropped by a rehearsal and watched the first scene. At one point he turned to playwright Hellman and rasped, "You're not going to get a laugh on those first four lines." However, Monty and Digges did get a huge laugh at every performance of the play. "We never could figure out how they got it," Shumlin said.

Lillian Hellman recalls in her memoir *Pentimento* that Monty and Digges arrived at the theater every night at seven-thirty and read scenes from Chekov and Ibsen together—until the second call for half hour. "I took to going to the theater several times a week just to stand in the wings and watch the delicate relationship between the dedicated old and the dedicated young. . . ."

Because Samuel Hazen, the character Monty portrayed, had been wounded in the leg, he spent hours perfecting a limp. He told Pat Collinge, "There is nothing harder than making a limp *believable.*" He hopped about his dressing room, experimenting first with a cane. Then without. He finally decided to use a cane, and he settled on what he called "a subtle limp."

He was just as concerned with the nuances of his delivery of the long monologue that climaxed the third act. In it, Monty as Hazen accused his intellectual parents of taking no action against the rise of fascism in the United States.

"Monty delivered the monologue instinctively with an amazing amount of intensity," Shumlin remembered. "I insisted that he perform that speech from beginning to end at every rehearsal even when we were just running through lines in the Green Room. I refused to let him walk through the scene. I wanted him to capture the essence of it technically as well as emotionally. At times he seemed infuriated that he was being forced to play in such high gear. 'I can do it, Herman, I can do it,' he'd mutter, and then I'd shout, 'Then do it, Goddamn it!' The end result was dazzling."

When Monty went out of town with *The Searching Wind,* Kevin and Augusta McCarthy were also on the road with shows. In Washington, D.C., Monty wrote Augusta the following note:

> "Admiration That's Easy to Fathom Dept."
> "Hey—love of my life.
> This is a f—— mash note. I gotta say it. I look forward
> to seeing you more than anything that will happen to me
> this spring.
> Now I've said it.
>   Yours, with a limp,
>   Clift."

When *The Searching Wind* opened at the Fulton Theater on April 13, 1944, it was enthusiastically received and lost the Critics Circle Award as best play of the season by one vote. As for Monty, the *Times* called him "superlative." The *Tribune* said, "Clift offers the year's best acting job. He is intense and can play humor and pathos with equal facility."

Brooks, who saw the play several times on leave from the army, was shattered by his brother's performance. "He was magnificent. I realized he was on his way to being a really great actor. He floored me."

Shortly after the opening, Monty was photographed by Rawlings for *Vogue*. Underneath the picture, the caption read, "Montgomery Clift gives the best performance of the season in *The Searching Wind,* Lillian Hellman's controversial play. As the wounded corporal bitter at the appeasing fumblings that have caused him to fight, Clift plays with throbbing self-control and tension of nerves that carries the third act." Brooks tore out the photograph from *Vogue* and carried it with him throughout the war.

Hollywood offers came from MGM, Warner Brothers, and 20th Century-Fox, but he turned down every one. He still felt he had a great deal to learn about acting, and he said as much in his first major interview, with Irving Drutman in the Sunday *Herald Tribune,* July 16, 1944.

> After playing with people like Dudley Digges and the
> Lunts, you feel so incompetent. Those are magnificent actors. Doing a scene with Mr. Digges you get the wonderful
> feeling of playing with an artist—not someone who's just a
> good craftsman but an actor who instinctively gets to the
> root of a role. With him on the stage you have such a glow

of self-confidence. You know that even when you come on feeling you're going to give a dead performance, his sureness, the sense of security you get from him will give a lift to your scenes together.

I've played with actors who, once they had their backs to the audience, could be so deadpan that it had a bad effect on your performance. But once he is on the stage Mr. Digges never steps out of the character he is playing. The Lunts are the same way. I played with them for two and a half years in *There Shall Be No Night,* and I've learned more from them and from Mr. Digges than I ever expect to learn from anyone.

Acting with people like that is a remarkable experience. The Lunts, for example, will go to no end of trouble to help you and point out things. It is very inhibiting at first to be on stage with them and hear them speak lines because everything they say seems so right and everything you say after them seems so phony by contrast. During the run of a play if there is ever any question on your mind about your performance you can always go to them and talk it over.

Watching them attack a scene you feel you understand the art of acting. Say there are six ways of doing a scene and you watch them instinctively choose the right way and immediately you realize why all the other ways were so wrong.

Two weeks later he wrote to Kevin McCarthy, who was still in the service and playing in *This Is the Army* in Hollywood:

Shmuck (backstage at the Fulton)
    "Why is he so damn cheerful?"
    "I don't know. I hear he opened his mailbox and found a letter."
    "He's usually kind of quiet."
    "Yeah. I guess pretty much everything is going to his head these days."
    I was happy to hear [from you]. I sat and read and read. Eventually I even got so I could figure out which page followed which and then it was even more interesting for everything meant something else than I had supposed.

From a distance that whole picture thing [movies] sounds as though it must raise such a disgust in one. I am not able to imagine even the gradual pain of being involved in your own profession [acting] and not being in it at all.
Bub.
I keep hoping Augusta will get a picture when you are away on tour (that'll be damn hard on both of us). . . . Kindly send me all bulletins good and bad.
To me—nothing happens—Nothing Nothing Nothing. Leading a Morganatic existence. Other than that . . . it's been too hot for anything but mental energy.
Couple of weekends ago I've been up to New Rochelle sailing—which is good (Sh! Don't tell Joe or he'll tell Bill [Le Massena] and then he'll tell Ned [Smith] and he'll tell Janet [Cohn]. But on those days of emptiness and sun I dislike myself so I swear I'll never go away again. Then it gets to be Sunday and it's hot and like it or not I go.
Somehow since it's practically August, October doesn't seem so far away. (Why is it nothing I ever write in a letter makes sense?) I think I shall have to call you.
Love,
Monty

Monty loved to mimic. Backstage during *The Searching Wind* he did a series of devastating imitations of Cornelia Otis Skinner, imperious and slightly deaf, trying to understand Herman Shumlin when he talked to her sotto voce in her dressing room.

Several times Monty mimed Chaplin's goofy, expectant smile in the last frame of *City Lights*. An actor who saw Monty perform the Chaplin imitation at several parties described it: "Monty's eyes would get bigger and bigger, as if he was holding his breath—the shock of simultaneous recognition hurt too much. It was fascinating to watch him become a different person without uttering a sound. He could capture the essence of a personality, a character, instantly and not only that, make you experience a rush of emotion—and you had no idea how he did it."

Long afterwards, a film director said, "Montgomery Clift knows how to use silence and fill it up."

Another illustration of his talent for mime took place at the Plaza Hotel, where Marty and Lee Swenson, close college friends of

Kevin McCarthy's, had taken Monty for drinks and sandwiches after the show.

"The setting was significant for me because what happened had a sense of unreality to it," Swenson recalled. "The room we sat in at the Plaza was very large, high-ceilinged and whitish—as though someone had antiqued the walls by brushing them with delicate strokes—just enough whitewash to permit darker hues to emerge. Dozens of empty tables surrounded us—there were only a few couples eating in the entire place. That feeling of emptiness and the shadowy color gave an almost surreal aspect to the room—as if we were in a 1920 ice-cream parlor of grand proportions."

While they were there Margaret Sullavan, then starring in the hit *Voice of the Turtle,* came in with her husband Leland Hayward and sat down directly across from the Swensons. Monty murmured that Hayward was his agent—that he had met Miss Sullavan briefly and considered her "the most talented actress in Hollywood and on Broadway and lovely beyond description."

"With that he rose to his feet and bowed to her—this gesture was acknowledged by her and her husband. Then, suddenly Monty brought off a discreet mime sketch that made it clear to Miss Sullavan how much he admired her. . . ."

He clasped his hands to his heart and swayed gently. His entire being seemed to be caught up in the spirit of letting her know how he felt about her. "It was carefully and artfully accomplished," Swenson finished. "It could have become ludicrous, but Monty didn't let it go on too long. Leland Hayward ignored the entire performance, but Margaret Sullavan understood and seemed vastly amused."

After his defeat for the presidency in 1940, Wendell Willkie had grown in social stature and political significance, and by 1944 he was one of the most popular and listened-to men in the United States.

Monty had remained fascinated by him and his career, clipping stories about him, quoting one of his favorite mottos: "Informed people make wise decisions." During *Skin of Our Teeth* Monty read *One World* in which Willkie gave a highly personalized account of meetings with Stalin, Chiang Kai-shek, and Field Marshal Montgomery. Monty recommended the book to friends "because it is so full of hope and challenge. Willkie can make anybody—kings, teachers, and factory workers—talk honestly to one another," he told Pat Collinge when he lent her the book.

Willkie died unexpectedly on October 8, 1944, and after listening to tributes from Roosevelt, Churchill, Dewey, and Harry Bridges on the radio, Monty decided to go to the funeral. Arriving at the Fifth Avenue Presbyterian Church, he found a crowd of 3,500 people milling on the sidewalk. Many were blacks or in uniform. He managed to fight his way into the church, where he stood throughout the ceremony shaken and much moved.

Late in 1944, Ned Smith helped Monty move out of his family's apartment on Park Avenue and into his own place, Mira Rostova's old walk-up on East Fifty-fifth Street and Lexington Avenue. Monty felt a sense of release and freedom alone in his new quarters. He could do exactly as he pleased, entertain his many friends, recite *Hamlet* out loud and indulge in his favorite pastime: talking on the phone.

"Monty used to call me every day, sometimes twice when I was on the road in a show," Augusta Dabney said. "We usually didn't talk about anything serious—we laughed a lot about nothing in particular."

Sunny continued to be the only obvious difficulty in Monty's life. She violently disapproved of the new apartment, and she telephoned him repeatedly to tell him he was making a "grave mistake" living apart from his family. When he explained that at twenty-four he deserved his independence, that he was enjoying the freedom to finally discover himself, Sunny snapped, "You just want to see more of your *friends.*" She scorned his new relationships with the McCarthys and Mira as "unhealthy and unwise," and she bemoaned his transformation from "thoroughbred" to "rank bum." Whenever she saw him in T-shirt and rumpled chinos she would throw up her hands and cry, "You are such a disappointment to your father and me!"

In spite of the tensions between them the bond between mother and son was extremely strong. Monty continued to drop by 277 Park at least once a week, sometimes accompanied by friends like Bill Le Massena and Phyllis Thaxter. Sunny would join them in the living room and Monty would regale everybody with stories; finally when he and his mother were alone, he'd demand, "How was I, Ma? How did I perform?" and she would answer, "I just want you to be yourself, dear."

Often their discussions would turn into arguments—mainly over Monty's language. "Monty punctuated each sentence with either 'fuck' or 'shit,' " Brooks said. "It drove Ma wild."

Invariably the conversation would get around to Mira Rostova. Sunny considered Mira "an evil influence" because she had convinced Monty he couldn't play a part without her help. He admitted himself that he had never met anyone who could dissect a role as shrewdly as Mira and reminded his mother that he was not the only one who believed this.

Mira was then teaching at the New School for Social Research in Greenwich Village, where she had gained a coterie of devoted students who praised her clear-headed approach to acting. The students also referred to her unsung talents as a great actress, Duse and Bernhardt rolled into one.

Her reputation had come about from a single scene she had performed in Bobby Lewis's acting class. It was the last scene of Chekov's *Seagull* in which Kevin McCarthy played Treplef and Mira played the sixteen-year-old Nina. Everyone who saw the scene remembers Mira's impact as Nina. Although she was too old to play an ingenue—she was then close to thirty—on the stage that afternoon she appeared miraculously youthful, passionately expressive. Her gestures were extravagant, her emotions very full.

After that little success, Mira seemed content to be in Monty's shadow. She seemed to have no ambitions for herself and devoted her energies to furthering his career. But Sunny thought Mira manipulative and opportunistic. Although she appeared docile, there was a steely side to her nature; Mira could take charge. For example, when she saw how important it was for Monty to have his own apartment, she promptly gave him hers and moved elsewhere. It was a gesture Sunny never forgave her for.

Nor could Sunny ever forgive her frequent interruptions. Whenever Monty was home visiting, Mira would phone, breaking into their dinners, their talk. "Monty was always too kind and polite," Sunny said. "He never wanted to hurt her feelings, so he never cut her off." And yet often when Sunny ran into Monty and Mira on the street, Monty would studiously ignore his mother. Later, when Sunny demanded to know why, he replied, "Oh, Ma, when I'm with Mira I have to make *Mira* feel important."

Already Monty was more loved than loving. He felt guilty about his extravagant charm and beauty and his inability on many occasions to fulfill both the men and women who loved him—to give back, in other words, some of what he was taking. He could not accept their love without ultimately paying a price. But he was so used to being alternately loved and punished by his mother that he felt uncontrollable urges to be very, very good—or very, very horrible.

14

At least once a week during 1945, Monty had lunch with the playwright John Patrick (best known for his comedy *Teahouse of the August Moon*). "We'd go to the Barberry Room at the Waldorf," Patrick said, "and Monty ate raw steak." Patrick remembers that Monty talked almost compulsively about the theater and its future. "He often generalized about the differences between audiences on Broadway and on the road. He would contradict people simply to start an argument, and although it wasn't particularly relaxing to be with him, it was never dull."

At the time Monty was starring in *Foxhole in the Parlor,* a mediocre play by Elsa Shelley. Once again he played a soldier, a musician who joins the army only to crack up under the strain and be sent home.

Bobby Lewis and Mira Rostova coached Monty in *Foxhole in the Parlor*. "It was one of the most beautifully worked-out performances of his career," Lewis said, "because Monty was starting to understand that the creative process begins with a sense of direction. He was marvelously alive and spontaneous on stage, but he knew what he was after so the spontaneity had a direction moving from it."

Lewis said they often discussed Stanislavski. "Monty loved the idea of the actor's three motors: the mind, the will, and the heart." Lewis told him that if the actor used his mind to understand the play and situation and characters, then executed exciting, truthful intentions, the proper emotion would be present.

Although all three elements were very much in evidence in Monty's performance in *Foxhole* and the critics deemed his acting "superb," "authoritative," and "brilliant," his unique performance could not save the show. It played only six weeks at the Booth Theatre.

During the run of *Foxhole in the Parlor,* Monty's leading lady, Ann Lincoln, a tiny beautiful brunette with a sweet, vulnerable quality, fell madly in love with him. Kevin recalls, "I think Monty really cared about her." Before going off on a trip to Mexico with him, Ann told her friend Nancy Lea that she and Monty were engaged.

"Gussie and I expected they'd elope," Kevin said. "But they didn't elope, and when they came back to New York, Ann and Monty began quarreling because he'd refused to marry her." For a while they stopped seeing each other, and Ann grew desperate and had a brief affair with Brando and then with Brooks hoping to make Monty jealous. Monty became enraged.

Later the two brothers had a confrontation. "It was pretty ugly," Brooks said, until he explained that he had saved Ann from suicide, whereupon Monty, burying his face in his hands, sobbed that he was reluctant to break with her because he loved her. He didn't want to marry her—but he didn't want to lose her either.

Brooks assured him Ann still loved him and wanted to come back to him on any terms. "Then Monty thanked me and said he was grateful for what I'd done."

Monty and Ann began to see each other again. They went away together for long weekends, sometimes to the barn in Bedford Village. They remained close friends until Ann was cast in *The Voice of the Turtle* and toured Australia for a year. When she came back to New York, she fell on hard times; no longer able to get work in the theater, she became an alcoholic.

Monty continued seeing Ann after he became a movie star and Ann never stopped referring to Monty as "the only man I ever loved." He sent her cash whenever she needed it; when he died he left her money in his will.

Just after *Foxhole in the Parlor* closed, Monty wrote to Kevin McCarthy:

July 16, 1945

Dear McCarthy—
   Wonderful to get your letter and luxuriate through its length. Dear boy—you do write so much like yourself that I feel very warm toward these letters. Being able to hear your thoughts keeps me in touch with you and then I am able to imagine with some sense of reality.

Arnold [Sundgaard] did get to see 'Foxhole' the night
before it closed. I have not yet read his play—he comes in
town tomorrow and may have the copy with him.

I had a personal drink of scotch—look what it does—

I have a new friend—one T. N. Wilder—novelist—
playwright. He saw Foxhole once came backstage—saw it
again (with Billy Le M who was here on furlough
before going to the Pacific) such adjectives as he had
for me—well—right then and there I was convinced he was
the greatest playwright on the continent! One night
Augusta, Billy and myself went out after the theater and
what a time we had listening to Thornton. This is a real
intellectual—I who never went to college can listen to this
extraordinary man speak with infinite knowledge and
above all Truth about that which most concerns me—the
Theater and all its allied arts. When you come back he will
be a real enjoyment for you. He has heard how we love
you and wants to meet you. A really friendly man.

I wish I could give you some idea of all of this. I was
looking at a book of Stark Young's and asked [Thornton]
if he cared for his reviews (I hope no.) All he said was
"Sensitivity without vitality is no good whatever" and
there you have the way he goes on about philosophy—
Kierkegaard, painting—Gertrude Stein, Kit and Helen
and what those two can or can't do and on and on
into any hour of the night you choose.

I presume I'll be doing Tennessee's play although
Guthrie has been such a prick about the whole business
that I shall not look forward to working with him at
all. . . . He said I would sign until June—now he's
insisting I go out of town before then if we're not a hit
here.

Oh Christ. It's terrible when you really want to play
something.

I'll write soon again. If you feel like calling me collect
—call—any time.

It's a rainy lonely day.

Monty

Monty and Thornton Wilder began to see each other frequently;
they developed an unusual rapport when they discovered they were

both twins. Monty confided how often he felt conflict and stress when separated from his sister. There was an almost mystical closeness between them, he said, of sharing and competition even though he and his twin were completely different personalities.

On afternoons at Janet Cohn's or at Wilder's home in Hamden, Connecticut, Monty probed the mysteries of being a twin. The discussions proved immensely cathartic since he was continuing to experience moments of uncertainty as to which twin he was.

Wilder assured him that all twins suffer from identity crisis, and he advised Monty to stay in close contact with Ethel. Monty saw his sister as often as he could while she was at Bryn Mawr; after her marriage to a Texas lawyer he visited the couple frequently in Austin. He felt a little less lonely as a result.

Bit by bit Wilder became Monty's intellectual mentor, but ultimately their bond went beyond books and ideas and even twinship. The two men were similar in temperament; both were remote, restless, and very secretive; loners, inveterate travelers and highly romantic.

To outsiders, Wilder was the great scholar, the playwright, the friend of such diverse personalities as Gertrude Stein, Gene Tunney, and Sigmund Freud. To Monty, he was always the affectionate teacher and surrogate father who made up reading lists for him (the first included Kafka and Kierkegaard) and who helped him choose his plays.

Together they wrestled with Monty's ambitions. He was eager and impatient to extend his talent, anxious for greater success if only as a means of establishing his identity. Wilder begged him to remain in the theater believing that "the theater is the greatest of all art forms—the most immediate way in which a human being can share with another the sense of what it is like to be a human being."

Whenever Wilder and Monty dined together they usually discussed Monty's career and the probability that he would end up in Hollywood, but they also "gossiped maliciously about everyone they knew," said a friend who sometimes joined them.

At times Wilder seemed almost enamored of Monty. "When you saw them together you got the feeling that Thornton had an actual crush on Monty," said the same friend. "It was never expressed, of course, but he would literally feast his eyes on him." And Monty, in turn, worshipped Wilder. He never missed an opportunity to hear him lecture, taking an almost childish pride in boasting, "Thornton just phoned me" or "I'm going up to Hamden to visit Thornton."

Over the years he met Wilder when he was vacationing in Key West and joined Wilder briefly in Rome while the playwright was researching Caesar for his novel *Ides of March.*

After *Skin of Our Teeth* Wilder never again produced a full-length play, although he did complete a couple of one-act plays. Moreover, he did labor over a melodrama which he called *The Emporium* and which he wrote specifically for Monty. The play focuses on a young man whose entire life is spent trying to secure a job in a vast, mysterious department store. Thousands of people seek employment in this store, but its directors invariably choose the unqualified and reject the ones with the most talent and ability.

Wilder worked for over ten years on *The Emporium,* and it was announced several times as ready for production with Monty as the lead. But Wilder was never satisfied with the play and finally abandoned it, much to Monty's dismay.

In spite of Thornton Wilder's entreaties, Monty went to Hollywood in the late summer of 1945 for his first screen test, a Warners western called *Pursued.* The screen test was not a success.

"He was stunned by Hollywood's attitude towards talent," Kevin recalled. "Actors are treated like inanimate objects to be bought and sold at a profit like sticks of wood." He marveled at the luxury of "all those lighted swimming pools with gardenias floating in them." But he perceived that "the richer and more famous you are, the more you're treated as a naughty kid and completely dominated by business managers, agents, and publicity flacks." Monty believed that most of the stars he met resented the way they were treated because "they are flattered and hated at the same time. Why don't they fight back?" he asked. Then he suddenly shifted the conversation and started talking about his future plans to become a Renaissance man in New York—an actor, writer, director, producer. It was obvious to him then that he couldn't become a Renaissance man in Hollywood.

In August 1945, Monty went into rehearsals for *You Touched Me!,* a play Tennessee Williams had written with Donald Windham.

It was based on a D. H. Lawrence short story that dealt with the impact of reality on illusions. The plot revolved around a drunken old retired sea captain and his foster son Hadrian, a pilot (played by Monty) who comes home from the wars and persuades the captain's sweet young niece to marry him and seek adventure.

(In 1943 *You Touched Me!* had been given a production at the Pasadena Playhouse but there was no interest from Broadway until

The Glass Menagerie opened in April 1945, and Tennessee Williams became the most acclaimed young playwright in America.)

Guthrie McClintic produced and directed *You Touched Me!* at the Booth Theatre. Tennessee Williams remembers the atmosphere of the first reading as "up—jittery—all the actors (particularly Monty, who was overenthusiastic) were very optimistic."

Williams recalled that Monty talked to him about Laurette Taylor's performance as Amanda in *The Glass Menagerie* and how she was an exceptional performer like Alfred Lunt. "Monty loved being in awe of people. He seemed to look on all the arts—dance, music, and theater—as if they were great mysteries. I never knew him well because I wasn't sexually attracted to him but I know one thing—his major impulse was to be an artist." Williams continued, "Monty disliked me because I was so open about being gay and he wasn't."

During rehearsals of *You Touched Me!* Williams fell into a deep melancholy that no one could relieve. *The Glass Menagerie*'s stupendous success had not brought him the expected satisfaction and he became increasingly depressed, so depressed he finally had to leave rehearsals.

He did see the opening in Boston and thought "Monty was marvelously poetic as Hadrian . . . the play as a whole didn't come off, but nobody seemed to notice—the show got great reviews and afterwards Guthrie froze the production and that was that."

Mira Rostova came to Boston too, and Monty secreted her away in his dressing room where they spent hours discussing his performance.

Monty wanted to create a gorgeously romantic Hadrian—incandescent, languid, mysterious. He kept changing his blocking on stage, much to the annoyance of the rest of the cast, but he felt Hadrian was always surprising—impulsive. He told Pat Collinge he spoke certain lines so softly he could hardly be heard—"so the audience listens more intently."

According to the actor Sandy Campbell, Monty's makeup on stage created a very special effect. "At that time most juveniles wore heavy sunburn pancake—this was when every play used footlights—and the impression on stage was very unreal. But Monty always looked *natural*. So natural I thought maybe he didn't use any makeup. One night before a performance he let me watch him make up. It was extraordinary. It took a good half hour. He used an almost yellow-colored base—greasepaint, not pancake, and he blended it into his skin until it seemed to disappear. Then he used a lighter shade on the bridge of his nose and on his cheekbones and darker shades below the cheekbones. I don't remember that he used rouge at all. He worked like a painter. He explained as he went along why he was highlighting and shadowing. He had learned it all from Alfred Lunt. I tried it later but it didn't look the same on me."

You Touched Me! opened in New York on September 26, and again Monty got excellent reviews for his performance from all the New York critics.

There was a brief lull in Monty's career after *You Touched Me!* closed; he was offered dozens of parts but he disliked most of the plays and movie scripts he was sent—he and Mira went over stacks of them in his apartment, rejecting everything. The only scripts that intrigued him offered characters who were either outcasts or exiles, and who in the course of the story survived by their wits.

Survival must have a quality to it, or it isn't worth exploring, he told Bill Le Massena. "Monty was a pathological idealist," Le Massena recalled. "He would wonder why do people do the right things for the wrong reasons or the wrong things for the right reasons? He would ramble on into the night questioning why some of the bums or dishwashers or soldiers he consorted with had more quality in their suffering than his Park Avenue pals."

On weekends throughout 1945, he escaped to Bedford Village accompanied by Mira or the McCarthys and newer friends—the Karl Maldens. He talked constantly about becoming a movie star. He was excited by the possibility, but kept saying that it had to be on his terms.

Shortly before his lease ran out on the barn, he began driving in a peculiar fashion. He seemed to momentarily lose control of the wheel, Janet Cohn said. She sometimes watched him from her house as he zoomed up the driveway revving the motor very loud. Several times he ran the car across the lawn and parked it clumsily, leaving deep tracks on the grass. When Miss Cohn pointed this out to him, he apologized profusely and promised not to do it again. But he did. "Oh, I'm sorry, dear," he'd say. "I keep forgetting."

Against her better judgment, Miss Cohn would allow Monty to drive her back to New York. "He'd go like a bat out of hell—lickety-split at least a hundred miles an hour down the Henry Hudson Parkway. It was hair raising. The tires would screech—once the car actually tilted far over to one side as we went too fast around a curve. I begged Monty to slow down but he just hooted with laughter. And we sped on, my heart in my throat. I think we made New York City in forty-five minutes instead of the usual hour and a half."

Over the New Year's holiday he took one long weekend off and went to a ski lodge in Utah. "The skiing is great," he wrote Sandy Campbell and Donald Windham, "but the only full enjoyment for myself is my after-dinner cigar. . . ." In the same letter he noted, "Hollywood is waving its fairly ugly finger at me," but he refused to stay in California even overnight. Instead he flew fourteen hours to the coast in order to discuss a project in depth with his agent Leland Hayward and then after dinner he'd fly directly back to New York. Hayward kept at him to relax in Los Angeles, and he'd laugh and say, "No, Leland, I'm too snobbish."

Finally Hayward insisted Monty remain in Hollywood for a couple of months to meet and talk with Jack Warner, L. B. Mayer, Darryl Zanuck, and Harry Cohn. And to pay for his time he even got him a six-month contract with Metro. Intrigued, Monty flew west and sent back daily bulletins to his friends in New York date-lined "Vomit, California."

When he wasn't studying scripts he visited Phyllis Thaxter or Sydney Greenstreet, who lived in an antique-filled home off Sunset Boulevard. Greenstreet often took Phyllis Thaxter dancing at the Cocoanut Grove, and Monty tagged along. Miss Thaxter was also signed to a seven-year contract at Metro, where she was playing a succession of sweet wife types. She was forced by contract to do every movie script offered her or be put on suspension; at this point almost no star—big or small—had the right to select a role or reject a role.

After seeing Greenstreet and Thaxter, Monty wrote doleful letters to Campbell. "[Hollywood] is a terrible place and I shall want an explanation when I get back as to why the hell I'm here. . . ." He had met L. B. Mayer and Benny Thau, and found Mayer to have "dashes of Jed Harris lies and Georgie Jessel schmaltz. He told me Leo the Lion is the father of one big happy unsuspended family. And I too will be happy . . . but don't you think you should stay two years and give us four months notice when you want to do a play? Nobody from here really wants to go back to Broadway now, look at . . . They keep throwing Greer Garson in my face—nostrils and all . . . as a perfect example of what . . . a career can be. Ye Gods!"

Later a story got around that Mayer broke down in tears in an effort to get Monty to sign a seven-year contract with MGM. Still he refused and gave as his reason: "Your scripts are bad, Mr. Mayer, and I don't want to be typecast—that'd ruin me."

In recalling his decision to record producer Ben Bagley, Monty said that, in effect, the studios had told him to sign away seven years of his life and be grateful. "I told them I wanted to choose my scripts and my directors myself. 'But sweetheart,' they said, 'you're gonna make a lotta mistakes.' And I told them, 'You don't understand; I want to be free to do so.'"

In May of 1946, the MGM option expired, and Monty left California with Jeanne and Fred Green. Instead of taking a plane East they drove cross-country in "Beulah."

By this time Fred and Jeanne Green had become Monty's surrogate family on the Coast. Fred Green said, "We were really a threesome, and I thought here is a guy who really has it together. We'd sit around on the floor talking till four A.M. about everything under the sun. Monty kept asking me questions about building and designing houses, which was my obsession. He looked at me with those big eyes of his and you'd think you were the only person in the world he was interested in, and, for the moment, I suppose, you were." Jeanne describes their three-way relationship as "intense—highly charged—but being close friends with Monty could never be casual, even though he could only give of himself for short bursts of time. I think our ten-day trip across country was a kind of record for him. We had ten days straight together on the road and it was marvelous."

In New Orleans, Monty and the Greens listened to jazz and drank copious quantities of French brandy at Antoine's and Galetoire's. They swam in the Mississippi River, which Monty said, "had the consistency of baked beans."

In the mornings, even with hangovers, the trio attempted to play tennis. Sometimes, after a set, he would go off by himself to the French Quarter to explore the seamier side of New Orleans. Once Jeanne asked to go, but he shook his head. "Why are you going there?" she asked, and he told her quietly, "I need to."

When they reached New York, the Greens stayed in Monty's walk-up, which was shabby and practically unfurnished. While Fred went back to work at *P.M.* newspaper as a sports reporter, Jeanne helped paint the place. "Monty wanted it terra cotta. The walls looked like dried blood when we finished, but Monty said he liked it that way."

Odd people came to the apartment at all hours as a result of

Monty's generous invitations issued to strangers in his favorite nocturnal haunts: Union Square, Harlem, the Bowery, and Chinatown.

"Monty led many lives," Jeanne Green said. "We were only part of one of them."

15

Film director Howard Hawks had not forgotten Monty's performance in *You Touched Me!* In February 1946, he offered him the role
of John Wayne's foster son in a western he was preparing called *Red
River*.

Monty was interested. He realized that pitting him as a kind of
elegant collegiate cowboy against John Wayne's bluff earthiness was
outrageous and totally against conventional Hollywood casting. He
liked the idea, but at first he said no.

Hawks persisted, and after several phone calls and an offer of a
plane ticket to Hollywood to talk over script and character, Monty
agreed to fly out. He was $1,300 in debt, and he felt he had nothing
to lose.

Hawks told Monty *Red River* had been developed from a seri-
alized novel called *The Chisholm Trail* by Bordon Deal that had appeared in the *Saturday Evening Post*. The story dramatized not only
how a group of cowboys organized the first cattle drive from Laredo,
Texas, to Kansas but also the love-hate relationship between two
strong men—Tom Dunson, an implacable rancher, and his tough foster son, Matthew Garth.

John Wayne was set to star as Dunson. Hawks wanted Monty to
play Matt. Throughout the picture father and son clash continuously
as Dunson believes in violent justice, whereas the more civilized Matt
prefers mercy.

The story and its ramifications appealed to Monty, although he
confessed to Hawks he was not sure he could cope with the brutal
fight between himself and John Wayne that occurred at the end of the
film. Hawks was unconcerned— "You're an actor aren't you?" he de-

manded. Monty, buoyed by the director's confidence and the $60,000 he was offered, agreed to do the film. He refused, however, to sign more than a one-picture deal.

When he returned to New York and told everybody of his decision, several of his friends (among them Bobby Lewis and John Patrick) questioned that he would be going against type. "What makes you think you can play a cowboy?" they demanded. Briefly, Monty was overwhelmed with doubt. He phoned Leland Hayward and said maybe he'd made a mistake; Hayward snapped that he hadn't made any mistake at all. But Monty, still acting uncertain, went to his parents. They both urged him to go to Hollywood.

Finally, at two in the morning, Monty phoned Kay Brown, David O. Selznick's New York representative and an old friend; together they went over and over his reasons for accepting the role.

He needed work, he needed money, and of course, he'd always wanted to be in pictures. And he was getting *Red River* on his terms. But he didn't want *his* movies to be trivial; he wanted each and every movie *he* was in to be conceptually interesting.

After the lengthy discussion with Kay Brown, Monty convinced himself he'd made the right decision. A few days later he flew out to Hollywood and moved into a single room at the Montecito Hotel. "My room has a wall bed and a wall kitchen," he told Pat Collinge when describing the place over the phone. "I have a great view of eucalyptus trees from my window. They stink to high heaven."

Red River was shot in Rain Valley, sixty miles east of Tucson, Arizona, from June through November 1946. Budgeted at $1,750,000—high in those days even for a first-rate western—the movie ultimately cost $3 million. A prime expenditure were the 6,000 cattle, rented at $10 a head whether they worked or not.

The first days of filming Monty burned himself on the thigh with a blank cartridge, practicing quick draws from his holster, but with practice he mastered the rodeo rider's trick mounting and the cowhand's rolling gait. His greatest triumph in the role was creating a character so forceful he more than matches Wayne's impressive presence.

Richard Schickel, in his TV series, "The Men Who Made the Movies," quotes Hawks as saying, "When [Wayne] saw Clift the first time he said, 'Howard, think we can get anything going between that kid and myself?' I said, 'I think you can.' After two scenes he said, 'You're right. He can hold his own, anyway, but I don't think we can make a fight.' I said, 'Duke, if you fall down and I kick you in the jaw, that could be quite a fight. Don't you think so?' He said, 'Okay.' And that was all there was to it. We did it that way. It took us three days to make Montgomery Clift look good enough to be pitted against Wayne because he didn't know how to punch or move when we rehearsed."

According to legend, Wayne actually burst into guffaws when Hawks staged the fight between them. Wayne simply could not take the scene seriously—something that privately infuriated Monty and probably inspired the superhuman intensity he brought to his battle with the Duke.

The fight with Wayne was the beginning of a series of bloody film fights in which he always played the idealist and loner. In *From Here to Eternity, The Young Lions, Wild River,* and *The Misfits* he was subjected to incredible beatings of one kind or another. "Monty was the man who, if physically broken, could never be spiritually beaten," writes Douglas Brode in a tribute to Clift. "His screen speciality became a brand of idealism that appeared insane in the beautiful extremity of its radical innocence."

During the filming of *Red River* in the Arizona desert, it rained steadily for almost six weeks. Most of the cast caught colds and the script had to be rewritten to include several glowering storms. The script was also being rewritten, "so John Wayne doesn't die in the end," Monty complained.

He and Wayne did not get along. Wayne told a *Life* magazine editor, "Clift is an arrogant little bastard." On the set Monty was pleasant and scrupulously polite, but between takes he stayed pretty much by himself. However, he occasionally joined the nightly poker games that were organized by Hawks and Wayne. He told Ben Bagley later, "They laughed and drank and told dirty jokes and slapped each other on the back. They tried to draw me into their circle but I couldn't go along with them. The machismo thing repelled me because it seemed so forced and unnecessary."

Whenever shooting was canceled by rain, Monty drove to Palm Springs to stay with Fred and Jeanne Green and he helped them complete construction of their house. "He hammered and plastered and painted right along with us," Jeanne said.

In Palm Springs Monty took flying lessons with Jeanne. "He flew one of those single-engine jobs, and we zoomed over the desert together," Jeanne said. "Monty was a lousy pilot but I was even worse. And neither one of us could ever land properly."

In late September, Monty started driving up to Beverly Hills to see his agents at MCA. Sometimes the Greens went along and "Monty'd rent adjoining suites at the Bel Air Hotel," Fred said. "We'd order from room service and lie around the pool. Monty was edgy." Before long a phone would be brought to him by the pool and he'd protest and make faces. His agents scheduled meetings with producers and directors who had seen some rushes from *Red River* in Hollywood and were very excited about Monty's performance.

When the phone calls and the meetings got too much for him, he disappeared into West Hollywood. "He was having an affair with a dentist's wife," Fred Green recalls, "but all I remember about her was that she was lovely looking and drove a snazzy convertible."

Bad weather continued to delay the progress of *Red River*. Filming continued in the desert until mid-November when cast and crew returned to United Artists sound stages to complete interiors. In December the picture was finally finished, and Monty wrote Ned Smith December 12, 1946:

> Well, here I am making a lousy fortune in a gold mine. Around March [of 1947] you're going to have quite a decision to make. The film "Red River" will be released. Now "do I know Clift or don't I?" "Yeah—we met—I forget where." Or do you take a more straight forward course: "No, I never met him. Ridiculous!"
>
> Lad, I have just finished up a western starring John Wayne and it's been a fine business particularly 10 weeks on location in Arizona herding cattle all day. I am totally unused to civilization.
>
> We worked very near Tombstone . . . home of Wyatt Earp . . . but the [tourists] are fast ruining this town before long nothing will stand to show what a hell of a place it once was.
>
> We went bear hunting . . . up something steeper than Katabin [a mountain Monty and Ned climbed as boys]. We led our horses up and led 'em down an THAT is something—leading a four-legged animal up and down precipices [when you're] wearing high-heeled cowboy boots like a dame. . . . . A horse should be considerably more sure-footed than me but [my horse] managed to slide considerable distances all four legs held stiffly together.

One animal blinded himself, broke a leg and had to be
killed.
    You see what happens when you turn a bunch of
fascists loose in the hills?

Although Monty told everybody he wanted to relax when he
finished *Red River,* Peter Viertel introduced him to a young Aus-
trian-born director named Fred Zinnemann who was then working
with Viertel on *The Search.* Zinnemann described the movie to
Monty in a Beverly Hills coffee shop. *The Search* was about the
fate of concentration camp survivors; the plan was to film it like a
documentary on location in Europe at the actual cities of the U.N. rehabilitation centers. Monty read Viertel's treatment and was intrigued
with both the theme and the character Zinnemann wanted him to
play—that of a carefree American G.I. who inadvertently gets involved with refugees. Monty made some suggestions to Zinnemann
but no real commitment. He wanted time to think.

    Meanwhile, he attended a rough cut of *Red River* with gossip
columnist Elsa Maxwell, who happened to be a friend of Howard
Hawks. Afterwards Miss Maxwell had nothing but praise for the
movie; she said she thought the cattle stampede was thrilling and that
Monty had "persona." But Monty disliked *Red River* intensely. He
thought the script had been watered down and that the fight scene
was ludicrous "because Joanne Dru settles it and it makes the show-
down between me and John Wayne a farce."

    As for his own performance as Matt Garth, Monty called it
"mediocre"; nevertheless, he sensed he was going to be a star. The
idea of losing his privacy terrified him. He told James Jones later, "I
watched myself in *Red River* and I knew I was going to be famous,
so I decided I would get drunk anonymously one last time."

    After visiting his twin sister in Texas, he proceeded to go to
New Orleans for his regular checkup and to get "pissed out of my
mind." He landed in jail. He wrote the Greens from his cell:

    "God—if you only had a telephone.
    "Well—I leave here tomorrow night—tests and more
tests and no fucking amoeba . . .
    "Went to the place where we'd had brandy from the
big bottle . . . sat and drank. During the evening (lost)
spent 30 dollars in one sordid way or another—wound up
having spent the night in jail—accused and booked—

'vagrancy—refusal to move on.' I was so angry at them (the anger of the innocent you understand) and every police-man within earshot of the 3rd precinct was so angry at me they wouldn't put me in one of their better suites with a running toilet. No—into the most crowded cell you can imagine. Never knew silicosis vomiting death by coughing could be so prevalent.

"Cold concrete—dead bugs—alive bugs. I had a ciga-rette. Rapturous conversation with a guard while sucking up to him to make a phone call.

"What do you do?"

"I'm an actor."

"Yeah? Know Bing Crosby?"

"No—"

"Ken Carpenter?"

"No—I—uh"

"Yeah—I used to work on the Kraft Music Hall. I went on the skids too."

Freshman asking advice of a senior cellmate: "Think they'll let me use the phone?"

"Not a chance."

IN MY OLD KENTUCKY HOME loud and off key—¾ of an hour at a time. A negro who can't sing!

"SHUT UP."

"Hey you gimme a cigarette."

"WHERE THE COTTON AND THE . . ."

"What time is it bud? Shit—I got three more hours."

Narcissus takes off his shirt and hangs it on the bars over his head—strokes his smooth belly—he wishes he had a mirror to comb his hair. God he must have a mirror . . .

"He's been here before."

"Hey—it's lights out—what time is it?"

"Everybody's been here before—UN DEUX TROIS QUATRE. Carry me back to . . ."

Heaving snores.

Fat sow. "Why the fuck doesn't somebody throw me a cigarette hey you with no shirt—she wants me to throw her a cigarette but she won't stand still . . . what time they bring you in? . . . How the hell do I know what . . . Jesus why doesn't somebody HEY WATER son of a bitch—WATER somebody.

"George Neal." Door clanks—his six hours are up
. . . colored fellow now we'll have no more chanting . . .
silence . . . COME TO ME MY MELANCHOLY BABY . . . oh
how wrong you were . . . Next night Judge Lambert—case
dismissed—mistaken charge. Well. I got that out of my system—now question is—should I send this letter?

16

As his career accelerated Monty turned to Mira Rostova and the McCarthys for their opinions and support. "We were constantly exchanging scripts from all over the world—London—Paris—Hollywood —New York," Kevin said. "Sometimes I'd write my reaction to Monty or he'd phone me his—we loved bouncing ideas off each other."

The four friends spent hours, sometimes days arguing the merits of a particular script. They sorted out the script's mistakes, rearranged situational possibilities, and pondered the reasons why certain scenes "played" and others remained dead and lifeless.

"The theater is full of illusions," Monty said, "but films are *real*." And then he would ask rhetorically, "If a role doesn't interest me, why should it interest an audience?"

All four agreed that Monty should do *The Search;* Fred Zinnemann had already signed Wendell Corey and Aline McMahon for leading roles, but there were several script revisions causing an angry Peter Viertel to bow out; he refused, unsuccessfully, to eliminate any reference to "Hitler's final solution."

This omission upset Monty as much as Viertel; he believed the movie-going public should be reminded of the Nazi mass killings. Bothered by the "goody-goody" dialogue, he told Kevin, "It's like *The Yearling* with sugar added."

But in spite of the script's weaknesses, he decided to play Ralph, an American G.I. The part appealed to him primarily because Ralph was an idealist; the part offered him a chance to explore and define the tenuous relationship between the brash soldier and a terrified little Czech boy, whom Ralph is called upon to rehabilitate.

Monty signed with Zinnemann for the part in March 1947. When he arrived in Zurich that April, Zinnemann's wife Renée welcomed Monty at the Hotel Storchen. They had lunch together and she recalled, "Monty was funny, energetic, and extremely enthusiastic about the potential of *The Search*."

Monty made no mention of Mira Rostova, whom he had put on salary as his coach. She appeared at the hotel later that day; subsequently Monty included her in most of his dinners with the Zinnemanns. He always treated her with great affection, calling her "dearest," but he never gave any explanation as to why precisely she was with him.

Years later Monty told producer Mike Weinberg, "Look, I'm a star. I can't afford to give anyone else credit for what I'm doing. It's not a question of fairness. My main concern is to give a great performance. How I do it is nobody's business."

To prepare himself for the role in *The Search* Monty lived in an army engineer's unit outside Zurich, and he dressed in army fatigues. He was particularly interested in developing a soldier's gait; he believed that character could be defined by how a person moved.

At one point army authorities invited him to a special screening of German motion pictures filmed in Nazi concentration camps during the war. There were scenes showing masses of Jews being led to the gas chambers. Some of them were smiling and waving, thinking they were about to be released. Then came ghastly shots of the piles and piles of dead bodies in the trenches, the mass shootings, and close-ups of the crematoriums and the ovens.

Monty was unable to sit through more than an hour of the films; he bolted from the screening room and vomited.

Before shooting began, Monty and Zinnemann toured the U.N. Relief and Rehabilitation camps in Germany, meeting some of the homeless Jewish children who milled about in the yards during recreation periods. "Most of their parents died in the gas ovens at Dachau or Kovno," Monty told Pat Collinge later. "Their dry-eyed little faces were grey with grief."

Shattered by the experience, he kept questioning Zinnemann over and over—what will their futures be like? They need families, they need love—a purpose in their lives. In the camps there seemed nothing to build on, no future, no incentive. Both men agreed that one of the elements in *The Search* was to dramatize the spiritual devastation of these people.

They continued their intense talks about the effects of war and anti-Semitism as they wandered through the bombed-out city of Munich where some of the first scenes in *The Search* would be shot.

Monty told Zinnemann bluntly that he still was not satisfied with his part as written. It was entirely too sentimental, and later he told the *Saturday Evening Post,* "As the script originally was written, I was a boy scout type spreading nobility and virtue all over the lot. There were no kinks." He told Pat Collinge, "I was supposed to be so damn saintly that a special prop man would have been needed to polish my halo. I felt the soldier had to be real. Exasperated with the kid sometimes—sometimes guilt-ridden over the concentration camp situation—mostly I wanted to show the relationship with the kid developing. I wanted it to be multilevel—complex—the way relationships are in real life."

As soon as filming began Mira Rostova stood behind the cameras and watched Monty going through the paces with Wendell Corey. As soon as Zinnemann called "Cut!" Monty turned to her for approval, and she either shook her head or nodded. Often the two of them went off to confer in whispers, and sometimes, after a conference with Mira, Monty insisted on a retake even though everybody else involved thought the scene was fine.

After a few days of shooting, Zinnemann told Monty that Mira could no longer appear on the set because it was disconcerting to the rest of the cast. He was the director, the only director; that was that. Monty agreed but was still not satisfied with the script's dialogue; he began writing his own. Each night in his hotel room Monty and Mira discussed the scenes involving Ralph and Karel, the eight-year-old D.P. who's like a little wild animal because he's been wandering the streets for so long. Monty wanted to show how the American G.I. tames the little boy with affection and games.

So he improvised and then rewrote the scenes in which Ralph throws the boy a sandwich, in which Ralph teaches the boy his first words of English by acting out the word "mother," in which Ralph tells Karel his mother is dead. After writing the scenes, Monty and Mira choreographed every movement right down to kicking a door shut in exasperation or lighting a cigarette to fill a beat.

The following mornings, Monty would bound onto the set bursting with all the new speeches he'd written and he'd rehearse them with Ivan Jandl, the little Czech boy who played Karel. Ivan spoke no English and learned his lines by rote, but somehow Monty could communicate beyond words. Monty always had a special affinity for children, and he worked with Ivan slowly, patiently cueing on his lines until the cameras began to roll.

The producer, Lazar Wechsler, was infuriated when he heard the new dialogue. His son David had already rewritten Viertel's script, and he wanted their words kept intact. He thought Monty's improvised speeches were sloppy and might ruin the movie's "message." He even hated the chewing gum Monty kept chomping on as part of his characterization.

For a while the two argued between setups. Monty was adamant about holding onto the new dialogue. Wechsler called him a "stupid actor" and questioned where he got the idea that he could write. Monty ignored his insults and continued to improvise dialogue for *The Search*. Wechsler in turn barraged him daily with special delivery letters demanding that Monty stop tampering with the script and reminding him that he was just an actor, and could easily be replaced. Monty threw the letters away and went on bringing Zinnemann new scenes and new dialogue, much of which was incorporated into the movie.

When Wechsler realized that Monty was still reworking the script he stormed onto the set with his lawyers. Monty brought his own lawyers, and tense discussions between the opposing attorneys turned into shouting matches.

"I am having battles with this spastic . . . of a producer," Monty wrote the McCarthys dolefully. "Then I go trembling with rage and try to act."

Shooting dragged on in bad weather, causing delays on location in Munich as the battles with Wechsler continued. The entire cast was demoralized by the producer's interference and carping. One afternoon everyone threatened to quit. "Such a depressing bunch of people you have never seen," Monty wrote to Kevin from Munich.

Then a new crisis emerged. Monty's three-month contract ran out, and he refused to sign another until Wechsler agreed he could rework the last big scene in which Ralph tells the little boy his mother is dead.

To the McCarthys, Monty wrote on September 14, 1947:

Dear Children of Light—I am involved right now in the grim results of a legal error. All [this] anguish is the result of not having put in writing my changes or thoughts on the script when I read it so the day I went before cameras I

lost all right of approval. My heart is really breaking. The
dialogue that stares up at me is not hard to fix . . .
OHGOD. . . ."

"This Wechsler is incredible. He forces everyone he
hires to spend their time writing or talking to their lawyers.
From a distance this is funny. Close to you've never seen
so many tense tight-lipped faces. I wish I were dead.
Augusta—Kevin—my love. And if James Kevin [the
McCarthys' six-month-old son] should ever meet one L.
Wechsler spit on him & hurl at him the McCarthy curse.
These are my sorrows. I have no good news. Old
Montgomery.

Throughout the dispute between Wechsler and Monty, Fred
Zinnemann tried to remain neutral. The gentle, pipe-smoking director
hated bullying or shouting; he simply wanted to complete the movie
without antagonizing either side.

It was obvious to everyone attending the rushes, including
Wechsler, that Monty was responsible for a startlingly original contribution to *The Search*. "His scenes bristled with life," Zinnemann
recalled. "And he filled the screen with reverberations above and beyond the movie itself." After studying the rushes, Wechsler grudgingly agreed to let Monty rewrite the last scenes of the picture in exchange for an extension of his contract, but the two men were never
on speaking terms again.

In fact when the movie was completed October 2, 1947, Monty
wrote Kevin: "The last day an orgy of hate. After dubbing, I picked
the stilettoes off my back and went to the hotel. There awaited two
letters from Wechsler. One instructing me to get out of Switzerland,
the other saying his board of directors was going to take action
against me as 'they see fit.' I better get to the border quick . . ."

Two years later Lazar Wechsler and Richard Schweizer (who
had written an earlier version of the script) won an Academy Award
for the screenplay of *The Search*.

17

Monty returned to New York in the fall of 1947. He couldn't stop talking about Fred Zinnemann and *The Search*. Making the movie had been what Monty had always imagined film making should be: a collaborative effort between actor and director. He did not talk about his fights with Wechsler, but he bragged to Brooks that he had rewritten the entire script with Zinnemann's encouragement. He showed Brooks his version covered with copious notes and the new dialogue in the margin of the dog-eared manuscript scrawled in his tiny, almost indecipherable hand. When Brooks commented on the brevity of the speeches Monty snapped, "In movies you *see* first and *hear* second. Words aren't as important as visual images."

He seemed tired and edgy, but actually Monty was happy—extremely happy. He always referred to *The Search* as the most fulfilling artistic experience of his life.

For a while that fall he camped at the McCarthys and helped them paint their apartment, having conversations while he stood on his head.

In late October, Howard Hawks wired Monty after the first public preview of *Red River* and said the enthusiastic audience reaction on written preview cards exceeded even his expectations. "Were the cards from cretins?" Monty joked delightedly to Kevin. "What do you suppose *was* the audience's expectation?"

He could not quite believe what was happening to him. His agents called daily with new movie offers. Broadway producers begged him to return to the stage. He knew he had the potential of enormous success, and working with Zinnemann had made him believe he could control his career. But he had to keep moving. That fall he drove up to Bedford to see the Greens and their newborn twins, taking them along on one of his several visits to Thornton Wilder's. "Lots of talk about Kierkegaard and Camus," Jeanne recalled. "We'd also go on book-buying binges at Brentano's in New York where Monty bought stacks of books that he didn't read but just lay piled in his apartment."

He went back to Stillman's gym where he exercised vigorously, determined to develop himself as a "Renaissance man." He would direct, write, and act, he said. He would not do another movie unless it was the perfect movie.

He took singing lessons, and he worked with Mira Rostova on a variety of roles. For a while he took a course with Josh Logan in musical comedy. Invited to join the newly formed Actors Studio, he began attending its first classes with Julie Harris, Marlon Brando, Maureen Stapleton, David Wayne, and Kevin McCarthy.

Elia Kazan, Bobby Lewis, and Cheryl Crawford, all Group Theater alumni, had evolved the concept of the Studio and rented space in the ramshackle Malin Studio building on Broadway and Forty-sixth Street in the heart of the theater district. The aim of the Actors Studio was to provide a permanent place for talented actors to work on their craft, with an emphasis on the inner psychological approach to acting—the Stanislavski system—which may simply be defined as a codified formalization of the technique of acting.

Stanislavski stressed as vital the knowledge of one's action or objective in a role. "What do you mean to *accomplish* in this scene?" was a common question at the Studio. Stanislavski also stressed "work on oneself" (on one's body movements, speech, imagination).

When Lee Strasberg, an authoritarian actor-teacher, took over the Studio classes from Lewis and Kazan he went a step further and developed "The Method." "The Method" *personalized* Stanislavski. Strasberg said, "The more an actor knows about *himself,* the more he will be able to make use of himself. Good acting exists when an actor thinks and reacts as much to imaginary situations as those in real life. Gary Cooper, John Wayne, and Spencer Tracy . . . try *not* to act but to be themselves, to respond or react. They refuse to do or say anything they feel not to be consonant with their own characters."

At the Studio, Strasberg devised a series of exercises to trigger that special something inside the actor to impel him to "come alive" on stage. Basic preparation for "The Method" included sense memory exercises and "Private Moments"—perhaps the most controversial element of Strasberg's teaching. In "Private Moments" actors sang, stripped, played with themselves, or thought about their dead mothers in order to release their emotions. Some Studio members (including Monty) found "Private Moments" exhibitionistic, not artistic, but the majority believed "Private Moments" broke down inhibitions.

Throughout the late forties and well into the fifties, the Actors Studio was *the* place to study and be discovered. The atmosphere was often vulgar and highly competitive—but it was never boring. The most talented actors, directors, and playwrights in America vied for attention in classes that often included celebrities like Noël Coward, Laurence Olivier, Joan Crawford, and the members of the Kabuki and Moscow Art theatre companies. Eventually an entire generation of "Method" actors streamed out of the Studio: Jane Fonda, Joanne Woodward, Paul Newman, Geraldine Page, Kim Stanley, Rip Torn, to name a few. Monty is generally included on the Studio's roster of famous names, but although he attended classes and was one of the original members of the Studio, he was never truly a "Method" actor. Many "Method" actors never created characters, Monty felt, but instead merely played variations of themselves. Although he knew he could never get away from himself, Monty felt he must use his imagination to explore a part. His approach was to create the character in his mind and decide how he moved and behaved. Monty's scripts were covered with tiny jottings which pinpointed the way to the character's objective. Character motivation fed his imagination.

The essential Clift character tended to be a loner, outside the mainstream, isolated—intense but always struggling against conformity, and within that framework Monty's range was extraordinary; his characters were by turn extroverted, withdrawn, articulate, or monosyllabic, assertive, passive.

He was a great believer in the psychological gesture: the physical manifestation of an emotion. It could be expressed in a look—how he stares into Shelley Winters' face before he kills her in *A Place in the Sun,* the sidelong glance of astonishment and desire when he sees Elizabeth Taylor for the first time in *Place,* the way he phones his mother in *The Misfits,* as if he's just been slugged; in his greatest performances Monty personified, rather than impersonated, character.

In 1947, Monty had not made any final judgments about the Actors Studio, and he enthusiastically attended classes with Kevin, David Wayne, Tom Ewell, and Jerry Robbins among others.

For a while he labored over a scene from Dostoevsky's *Crime and Punishment* with Maureen Stapleton, a plump, intense young actress from Syracuse, New York. "Monty played the murderer so sympathetically I felt sorry for him," Miss Stapleton said.

The two rehearsed in her cluttered apartment, one she shared with the singer Janice Mars, in a dilapidated brownstone next to Leon and Eddie's on West Fifty-second Street. "Everybody crashed there, from Marlon Brando to Wally Cox," Maureen Stapleton said.

"Wally used to say, 'I'm not shy—I'm antisocial.' He was making silver jewelry to support himself. He wore a watch with an alarm on it, and whenever it went off he'd bolt out the door even if he was in the midst of a conversation."

Monty had first met Marlon Brando in 1944 when Brando was doing *I Remember Mama*. On another occasion Monty went up to New Haven to replace Brando in *The Eagle Has Two Heads* after Brando was fired. After Monty saw the play, he decided against taking the part, and on the train back to New York he ran into Brando. The two had a very long, tense conversation, carefully avoiding mention of *The Eagle Has Two Heads*.

At the Actors Studio they ran into each other constantly, and it was obvious to those who observed them that there was an unspoken rivalry between them. Before Brando came along, Monty was the hottest young actor in New York; Brando, at twenty-three, was competition. He had already gained a reputation around Broadway as an exceptionally talented, unpredictable actor. He dressed in leather jacket and blue jeans, kept a raccoon in his apartment, and zoomed around town on a motorcycle. He described himself in a theatrical bio as having been born in Calcutta.

In fact, Monty and Brando were both born in Omaha—the similarity ended there. Brando was bluff, relaxed, and openly sensual. He drank, ate, and made love so indiscriminately he often complained loudly of "crabs."

Monty, on the other hand, was more reserved and shy with people he didn't know. He found Brando "too clownish and a slob." Brando thought Monty was overly serious and intense. "What's the matter with your friend?" he asked Kevin McCarthy. "He acts like he's got a Mixmaster up his ass and doesn't want anyone to know it."

"Whenever the two of them appeared at parties it was really something," says a girl who was part of the Actors Studio set. "You didn't know whom to look at first. Marlon had such basic animal magnetism that he stopped conversation when he entered a group. Monty, meanwhile, was elegance personified."

Ellen Adler, Stella Adler's daughter, recalls, "I was dating Marlon at that time. I was around sixteen. I think we went to somebody's apartment after the theater for drinks. Anyhow, Monty was there with some other people. We got to talking. He was so polite and charming, always with the match for the cigarette. Marlon stood it for as long as he could, and then he came barging over and pulled Ellen Adler away. 'She's my Jew, Monty!' he roared. Monty just grinned and shrugged."

After *Streetcar Named Desire* opened, Brando mesmerized the entire theatrical world with his performance as the brute Stanley. Mira Rostova confided in Monty that she wanted to meet him but she was too shy to go backstage. She talked about Brando so much Monty finally arranged to have Jerry Robbins give a dinner at his apartment to which Brando and Mira were both invited.

"It was the damndest thing," says a costume designer who was present. "Everybody knew that the party had been given so Mira could meet Brando, but it never happened. The two never spoke. Mira just circled him all evening but they never exchanged a word or even were introduced."

At the time, Monty was working at the Actors Studio with Jerry Robbins, improvising a scene from *Romeo and Juliet.* The young, innovative choreographer, fresh from his triumphs in *Fancy Free* and *High Button Shoes,* was curious about "The Method." When Monty had difficulty understanding the feud between the Montagues and Capulets, Robbins put it in modern terms and suggested that it was "as if" there were a feud between two ghetto street gangs in New York, the blacks and Puerto Ricans. Monty understood immediately.

While he was at Actors Studio, Bobby Lewis asked Monty to play Treplef in his workshop production of *The Seagull.* Monty procrastinated. "For some reason even though he was ideal for the part of the young poet, Monty kept telling me, 'I don't want to limit myself,'" Lewis said.

"I told Monty all great artists are limited," the director went on. "Charlie Chaplin was limited, but remarkably versatile at the same time. The artist who knows his limitations and is not frustrated or embittered but works within the framework, perfecting, shaping out of his own specialness, can be enormously fulfilled."

Monty wasn't sure. His Hollywood agents were urging him to make more movies where his specialness would be promoted. Advance word on *Red River* and *The Search* was extremely enthusiastic —Montgomery Clift was considered a "hot property." This unnerved him; he was jittery about the public's reception of his work. His own critical sensibility had been thrown out of focus by the piecemeal method of movie production. He knew he'd done all he could to make his characterizations come alive, but he had no idea how either one of his film performances would stand up.

Once out of work, Monty, like many actors, lost his confidence, and his sense of identity. He was existing in a savagely competitive culture and a profession in which 80 percent of actors were permanently unemployed. Almost nine months had passed since the completion of *The Search,* and he was feeling pressured to do something else.

18

On March 26, 1948, *The Search* opened all over the United States to unanimous acclaim. Suddenly Montgomery Clift was famous. "He became," wrote Joe Morella and Edward Epstein in their book, *The Rebel Hero in Films,* "a new hero to postwar audiences—a man with a conscience whose vulnerability and disillusionment with the world he wasn't the least bit embarrassed at revealing."

The *New York Times* said, *"The Search* is absorbing, gratifying, an emotional drama of the highest order"; "Montgomery Clift is superb," said the *Tribune.* "As the young soldier who brings back the little European waif into the fold of humanity Clift gets precisely the right combination of intensity and casualness. . . ." Photographer Richard Avedon, who saw the movie shortly after it opened, told Brooks, "The minute Monty came on the screen I cried because he was so realistic and honest and I was deeply touched. He seems to be creating a new kind of acting—almost documentary in approach. It has the style of reportage."

His young soldier in the film is never an impersonation—the composition of the performance is multileveled and filled with details. Monty knew how to play to an audience, and because of his stage training, he also knew how to get an audience to share in his characterization. He had the ability to create a world for himself. "Who's that soldier you got to act?" people would ask Fred Zinnemann, who said, "Monty was so damn real on the screen people didn't believe he was a professional actor."

In close-up, Monty was absolutely riveting. One was practically absorbed into his eyes, which were clearly formidable and perhaps his best asset as an actor. Large, grey, infinitely expressive in his beautiful but rather deadpan face, they could register yearning, intelligence, and despair in quick succession.

"Monty could have been in *Snow White and the Seven Dwarfs*," said the actor Bill Gunn. "His impact as a new kind of hero went beyond the material in *The Search*. Monty was the first actor with whom audiences could identify instead of look up to, and yet at the same time he became a fantasy figure and a romantic visual icon for moviegoers. And he had an individual attitude about himself. He wasn't bland, or all grins. He wasn't even that nice. He just *was*."

Within weeks after *The Search* opened and while it played to capacity crowds at the Victoria Theater on Broadway, Monty's phone rang incessantly. He had to have his number changed. He went to buy an umbrella at Bloomingdale's, and a small crowd surrounded him. When he tried to have a quiet dinner with David O. Selznick at Maria's, one of his favorite Italian restaurants on East Fifty-second Street, customers watched him eat and two waiters came out of the kitchen and asked for his autograph.

He accepted both the praise and recognition graciously. By this time he'd seen *The Search* (he'd arranged a special screening at MGM for his parents and the McCarthys), and he was proud of his performance. He knew he'd been good. So that even Sunny's whispered comment in the darkened theater, "You *act* like Kevin on the screen," didn't bother him too much.

In June, Monty went out to Hollywood to star opposite Olivia deHavilland in *The Heiress*. He was paid $100,000, and Paramount, who was producing the picture, decided to take advantage of his sudden fame and popularity by promoting him as their next big sex symbol. Max Youngstein, then head of publicity, tried to convince him to have lunch with Louella Parsons, to appear at premieres and nightclubs with ambitious starlets of the moment like Terry Moore.

But Monty refused to do any publicity. Instead, he holed up at a tacky little hotel and studied his script with Mira until late into the night.

He had agreed to play the cold-blooded fortune hunter Morris Townsend in *The Heiress* (based on Henry James's *Washington Square*) because he didn't want to be typecast. Augustus Goetz, who wrote the screenplay for *The Heiress* with his wife Ruth, first met Monty on the Paramount set. He was then clad in tattered jacket, jeans and a T-shirt. "He looked like a bum, and I thought, how can he ever play the suave, elegant Townsend?" But the next time Goetz saw Monty in makeup and costume he was flabbergasted. "The transformation was startling. He was the most fashionable youth I ever saw."

Monty told Goetz he was looking forward to working with William Wyler, whose earlier films, *The Letter* and *Wuthering Heights,* he had greatly admired. He was a bit fearful as well. Wyler, a former prop man, was precise and tyrannical, known to shoot fifty takes of a scene—goading and criticizing an actor before he got the results he wanted.

The first day of shooting, Wyler recalled, "Monty came to me on the set and said quietly, 'If you ever bawl me out, don't do it in front of the crew.'" The director assured him he wouldn't, and the movie was subsequently made without much open disagreement, although none of the actors got along. Filmed entirely on the Paramount sound stage amidst sumptuous and tasteful sets representing New York's Washington Square of the 1850s, the entire cast (which included Ralph Richardson and Miriam Hopkins in addition to Monty and deHavilland) behaved with the utmost politeness to each other—"like we were made of glass," Monty confided to Pat Collinge.

On camera, Monty acted the eager boyish lover as enthusiastically as he could, and deHavilland seemed properly smitten with him. Off-camera, however, the two barely spoke, as Monty was sure Wyler was favoring her. He made his feeling known: "She memorizes her lines at night and comes to work waiting for the director to tell her what to do," he wrote Sandy Campbell. "You can't get by with that in the theater and you don't have to in the movies. Her performance is being totally shaped by Wyler." (That performance won Miss deHavilland her second Academy Award.)

Later he accused Wyler of letting Miriam Hopkins upstage him and hog scenes. As for Ralph Richardson, the great actor's consummate technique intimidated him. "Can't that man make any mistakes?" he groaned after Richardson repeated a take with him for the thirtieth time in the same polished manner. "I cannot—will not—do a scene the same way each time," he told Pat Collinge over the phone.

Monty watched himself closely in the rushes. It didn't take him long to realize he wasn't doing his best work in *The Heiress,* although he and Mira labored over intentions and subtexts every evening after shooting. In the mornings, he would try to discuss the nuances of his characterization with Wyler, but there was never any feeling of camaraderie between himself and the tiny, dictatorial director as there had been with Fred Zinnemann, who had often gone along with Monty's suggestions as to which were his best takes. He found Wyler cold and unemotional—a master technician without a heart.

As the weeks rolled by he stopped listening to deHavilland and made up his own dialogue for her "because she isn't giving me what I need to respond." When he told Kevin McCarthy that over the phone, Kevin was shocked. "He was too meticulous, he had to have everything worked out, but he was going too far, and I told him so. Monty has this strange thing, his own kind of truth.

"As far as he was concerned, most of the actors he played opposite weren't doing their parts as well as they should, so in essence he did the parts for them!"

When Mira went back to New York, Monty moved in with the Greens, who had just bought a beautiful, Robert Neutra-designed house in the Hollywood hills. "Monty insisted on lending us part of the money so we could swing it," Jeanne said. "Of course, we paid him back."

Sometimes, late at night, when the Greens were asleep, Monty would leap onto their bed and curl up beside them. Jeanne would wake up, then fall back asleep holding Monty in her arms. "I don't remember how many times this happened," she said, "but Monty suffered from acute insomnia—he also hated sleeping alone." There was never anything sexual about the three of them sleeping in bed together. He would just cuddle against them like a baby and doze off, "then in the morning there would be pillow fights and laughing. . . ."

Monty often played with Jeanne's twin girls, and he would talk to Jeanne about being a twin, telling her how lucky her twins were to be fraternal instead of identical. "It's hard enough to *find* an identity," he would say, "but if you're an identical twin it's almost impossible."

On weekends, he would drive his dilapidated Buick out to Santa Monica beach where he would swim or lie in the sun and try to forget *The Heiress*. Occasionally, he would have a game of tennis with Charlie Chaplin on William Wyler's court, which was part of the director's manorial estate above the Beverly Hills Hotel.

Brooks said Monty was absolutely floored when Chaplin asked him to play. "Afterward, Monty said Chaplin told him, 'If you weren't a great actor you'd have been a great tennis player.' Naturally, Monty told him the same thing." In truth they were downright mediocre, according to director Robert Parrish, who often kept score for them at Wyler's, "but they both had such flash and energy they *looked* like champs."

To his friends Windham and Campbell, Monty wrote, "I have taken up tennis. Out here it's called 'social tennis.' It's a vitriolic game full of bile, craftiness, and hypocrisy, if played well. I'm playing much better."

Often after a game Monty would go with Chaplin to Salka Viertel's for Sunday supper. The Viertels' unpretentious but comfortable little house on Mayberry Road in Santa Monica was not only a gathering place for European intellectuals such as Thomas Mann, Bertolt Brecht, and Aldous Huxley, but for Norman Mailer, James Agee, and other young American artists.

Salka Viertel was a Polish actress-writer who'd been Max Reinhardt's mistress in Vienna before marrying director Berthod Viertel and moving with him to Hollywood in 1929. She joined the MGM story department and worked closely on all of Garbo's major films, including *Anna Karenina, The Painted Veil,* and *Camille.* When Monty first knew her she had just been blacklisted and was giving drama lessons to earn money. Her left-wing activities ultimately ended her screen career during the days of Joseph McCarthy and the House Un-American Activities Committee.

Monty admired her for her courage and her zest for life. She once told him she never worried about growing old because she had neither the time nor the patience to think about it.

After they met, she invariably included him in her glittering Sunday gatherings and introduced him to writers like Franz Werfel and Christopher Isherwood, who was then renting her garage apartment, and Garbo, her closest woman friend.

"Eventually Salka became another mother figure to Monty," her son, writer Peter Viertel, said. "He sought her out for advice. She listened to him pour out his troubles, his plans. They were never out of touch with each other even after she moved to Switzerland."

As Monty's career bloomed, he phoned Salka or Pat Collinge almost daily, often to harangue about Hollywood, which perplexed and frightened him. He was terrified of having his private life supervised by press agents—he thought Hollywood agents' aesthetic values were all "caflooey. Either something is good or it isn't," he told Pat Collinge.

Urged by his agents to knock off a few fast pictures to capitalize on his sudden popularity, he refused. Instead, when offers came, he demanded final script approval, which at that time no actor had. MGM showed him a few final drafts, among them *The Atom Bomb*

Story, and *The Stratton Story,* about a baseball player who loses his leg.

Later he would quote an F. Scott Fitzgerald letter describing the magic land of the movies as a "soft, slack place where withdrawal is practically a condition of safety, where everywhere is corruption or indifference."

In 1948, Hollywood was at a major transition point. Screenwriters and directors still chattered bravely around their fireplaces, but the fact remained that the star systems and the great studios were starting to crack. After prospering mightily during World War II grinding out hundreds of dreamy escape films and developing new stars like Van Johnson, movie profits slid from $90 million in 1941 to $55 million in 1948. Low-budget European movies such as *Shoe Shine* and *Open City* gained a wide following. Postwar audiences were demanding reality with their entertainment. Worse still, the Supreme Court's decision that the studios rid themselves of their theater chains in five years meant that the highly lucrative union of production and distribution which had stabilized the industry for two decades was to be completely dissolved by the Sherman Antitrust Act.

Over everything hung the postwar cloud of "The Red Menace," and the atmosphere in the film community palpitated with hysteria and guilt, as the careers—and sometimes lives—of actors, writers, and directors were systematically destroyed by Senator Joseph McCarthy, the House Un-American Activities Committee, and the blacklists. Fear triggered the McCarthy era, and the public mendacity and moral evasion it generated repelled Monty. "There seems to be a prevailing attitude of acquiescence," he told Pat Collinge. "Everybody is so good and meek, and yet everybody suspects everybody else of being a secret member of the Communist conspiracy."

He ran into Dalton Trumbo and Lester Cole, both of the Hollywood Ten, now writing scripts under pseudonyms. When he visited the once-ebullient Clifford Odets, he found the playwright broke and despairing. He had become a friendly witness to HUAC and named names to save his career. Now his career was ruined, and nobody would talk to him.

Monty was not well informed politically, but he did believe actors should refrain from being political patriots unless they really knew the facts. He found many of his show business cronies who were still involved in left-wing causes "silly and hypersincere—as if they're playing a role."

One actor, however, had to be exempted from this—Robert Ryan, a striking, complex man whose recent performance in the movie *Crossfire* as the sadistic bigot who murders a Jew almost won him an Academy Award. Ryan fought to abolish the House Un-American Activities Committee, and helped found the Committee to Ban the Bomb. Once Monty asked him, "Why weren't you ever blacklisted?" to which Ryan replied, "I'm a Catholic and an ex-marine. Hoover wouldn't touch that combination."

Just before *The Heiress* finished shooting, *Red River* opened around the country. The picture received great notices, and Monty superlative ones: "Montgomery Clift plays the thorny young cowboy in *Red River* with a fresh blend of toughness and charm," said *Time*. "He is that rare bird—with both screen personality and acting talent."

Years later Caryl Rivers wrote in the *New York Times:* "All the girls in the eighth grade fell in love with Montgomery Clift in *Red River*. His face had the perfection of a fragile porcelain vase. His beauty was so sensual and at the same time so vulnerable it was almost blinding . . . his dark eyes like the deep water of a cavern pool holding the promise of worlds of tenderness; the straight perfect blade of a nose that could have been the work of a sculptor the equal of Michelangelo."

With the tremendous personal success from *Red River* ("Clift is the hottest actor since Valentino," wrote *Look*), Monty found himself in even more demand, and Paramount now insisted he cooperate with the press. For once he didn't fight them, although he told Max Youngstein that he "hated behaving like a trained seal." It was a terrible ordeal being a movie star, he said; there was so much to the experience that had nothing to do with acting. All he really wanted to do was to be left alone to act.

Yet he endured a dinner with Louella Parsons at Romanoff's: "Monty is boyish and charming," she gushed. He spoke at length with Kyle Crichton of *Collier's*. Crichton later ridiculed his lofty determination to share time between Broadway and Hollywood. He also posed for *Life* magazine, but he insisted the Greens come along while he clowned for the photographer on the site of a house Fred was building.

All this time Lew Wasserman, Monty's principal agent, then the thirty-two-year-old president of MCA, was fighting to come up with an unorthodox movie contract which would please his difficult client and please a studio as well.

Wasserman was a slender, soft-spoken man who'd started out in show business hawking candy in a Cleveland burlesque house.

When Monty knew him he arose at five in the morning to read scripts and then, as now (he is chairman of MCA today), he shunned publicity, one of the reasons Monty originally liked him. The two often played tennis together in Palm Springs, along with Wasserman's wife Edie.

Both of them were pleased when Monty finally signed with Paramount for three pictures with the then unheard-of stipulation that he would have script approval and the movies could only be directed by Billy Wilder, George Stevens, or Norman Krasna. He also had the freedom to work at any other studio of his choice.

He should have been jubilant about this arrangement. He had obtained what he wanted, and his fierce independence from producers would be a future model for other actors to emulate. But instead he felt sobered by this rush of fame and fortune, and he was still concerned about the outcome of *The Heiress* because he felt his performance was mediocre. He was playing against the bounder image (with Wyler's blessing), but he felt the result—he had studied the rushes—was too glib, too modern, and in too much contrast to Richardson's and deHavilland's theatrics.

Now that he was more in the public eye, he felt unusually vulnerable. In the space of a few weeks he'd been misrepresented by Crichton and misunderstood by the producers who called him spoiled and snobbish because he openly disagreed with their taste and ideas.

He started thinking about success and failure; he told Pat Collinge over the phone late one night that he disliked both words. "To survive . . . you have to be completely self-centered and believe in yourself so totally or people think you're nuts. Success out here has nothing to do with accomplishment," he told her. "Some of the biggest successes here are the grandest slobs."

He elaborated on the same theme with old friend Ned Smith, who had written congratulating him on his great success in *Red River* and *The Search*.

October 20, 1948

Dear Smythe
    . . . a fine letter. You speak of things close to me.
Your letter has remained in the back of my thoughts all
through my work here. . . . I want to agree heartily—only
disagree with a certain conception of actual movie making

and add some thoughts which may or may not be applicable in large part only to the artist.

You say, "You planned a route for your conquests, have followed it exactly, each point of stepping being just as preconceived" and "You have finally mounted your peak happy and contented with your recent success."

"Happy and contented . . ." obviously if this state existed I could find no affinity within myself in the rest of the letter and could answer you only from a sense of guilt.

Not so.

The first part of the sentence is misleading for it is so oversimplified. It leaves out all together the gamble involved in each venture. "Each point of stepping being just as preconceived . . ." I was only sure what I would *not* do—most important—not to give away my freedom and not to do what did not genuinely interest me. The fact that these two pictures (*Red River* and *The Search*) have turned out so well was a big shock to me. I have worked 10 months in the last three years and it might well have gone on like that.

I must tell you where the satisfaction lies in me that things have gone so well. From now on I shall not have to be idle for such long stretches as before. Interesting things do not actually abound but they are here, they are for me, and I can take them. So another person goes to college—so all this now enables me to work and not lose valuable years. The gate is open to grow.

Outward success. I do agree with you about man as a judge of himself, etc. Specifically—I am embarrassed by myself in *Red River* and proud of *The Search*. That's important. I could wish it were not so but there it is. There is one thing I feel more and more as I sweat my heart out at work. Failure and its accompanying misery is for the artist his most vital source of creative energy. I mean inner failure—failure to achieve what one strives for—Outward success has little or nothing to do with this. Perhaps [success] deludes people long enough so you yourself can try again. It's silly—with each new failure one can become more and more popular.

If you have a goal—and you're busy growing—you're safe.

It's only when you believe of yourself what the general public believes that you start losing the courage to risk outward failure. That is the biggest pitfall.

LOOK OUT!

I'm hoping you'll concede that I have much the same high regard for money as a means not an end as you. The accumulation of gold as an objective would so eat into one's other goals—that I long ago resigned myself to having it only if it is earned in the accomplishing of other things. Shallowness and deadness beckon anyway—so why reach for them in seeking outward satisfactions?

Well—after reading all this you can see what a model creature I am!

I believe Nov. 4 I shall be going to Paris. . . . It is a fine feeling to have a friend such as you.

Monty.

PART TWO

PART TWO

19

Monty's trip to Europe and the Near East in 1948, shortly after he wrote his letter to Ned Smith, was one of his most intensive.

Traveling alone, clad in windbreaker and crumpled chinos, often unshaven, he flew first to London to catch the Old Vic and dine with his idol Laurence Olivier. He next went by boat train to Paris where he spent days wandering through the Louvre and the Left Bank. At night he attended the Comédie Française and the ballet.

Thornton Wilder and his sister Isabel were in Paris too. The three of them had tea with Alice B. Toklas at Rue Flores; afterwards Monty was taken on a tour of Gertrude Stein's collection of Picassos, Matisses, and Cézannes, with Wilder describing the history of each painting in his vigorous, delighted manner.

Monty's favorite stopover was Rome—"Everywhere you go you hear churchbells ringing," he wrote. He loved walking all over the city because it had "views like San Francisco." Rome is a city of hills and walls and hills, he said.

He loved the gushing fountains of Rome, the shadowy cobbled streets, the unique color of the sky "pink over pink." He loved in particular the Campidoglio and its endless beautiful stairs.

Someone pointed out that at the top of the stairs were the crumbling statues of the heavenly twins Castor and Pollux. After seeing them, Monty began making a list of historical twins—Jupiter's twins, Apollo and Diana, Helen and Polus. Hercules was a twin; and there were the "other" twins as Monty called them—Romulus and Remus, who suckled at the teats of a wolf.

Monty spent Thanksgiving in Rome gorging on the past and drinking cup after cup of espresso (and he brought an espresso machine back to New York).

After Rome, Monty stayed briefly in Athens. Then he met Fred Zinnemann in Israel, and the two of them traveled to the Dead Sea, Haifa, and Jerusalem. For a few days Monty lived in a desert kibbutz which was under Arab attack.

A letter to Sunny dated December 16, 1948 sums up his travels:

Dear Mom—

Hello . . . I feel as if I'd been around the world 6 times—London, Paris, Rome, Athens, Tel Aviv, Jerusalem, Tel Aviv, Negev, Haifa, Cyprus, Athens, Geneva, Rome, St. Moritz, Paris, London. . . .

Health—a cold—slight flu—bronchitis. With no rest since Hollywood I am going to try and take two weeks in Switzerland and then head home (in case the cable was unclear Hotel Stefani St. Moritz). . . . In Jerusalem drove in an amored car as near as possible to Mt. Zion—climbed up on to the top of Mt. Zion then very carefully looked from this vantage point over the walls of the Old City. There was still sniping periodically at Mt. Zion and Zion Gate—listening to the tales of the siege of Jerusalem is amazing . . . more of that when I'm home. . . . Well I'm off to St. Peters. . . . my best love to you all for my sake I wish I could be [home] at Xmas time. Me spending Xmas with no silver ornaments radiating through the holidays? Incredible. Much love Monty.

He was so immersed in his travels he didn't realize he was on the cover of *Life* magazine (December 7, 1948) until he reached St. Moritz—several people there recognized him on the ski slopes and told him about it. He promptly wrote Kevin and asked him to "send me a copy, bub."

Then his agent cabled him he'd been nominated for the Academy Award for his performance in *The Search*. And on New Year's Eve he was notified that he'd been chosen as America's most eligible bachelor by the Barbizon Models of New York.

By the time he returned home, *Variety* had stated, "One of the most unusual rises to stardom in all of Hollywood history is that of Montgomery Clift. With only two films released, *Red River* and *The Search,* and with no studio backing, he has suddenly become one of the two or three most in demand male players in Hollywood and can pretty much have his choice of parts at any studio. He's also demanding—and getting—$150,000 a picture."

His "unusual rise to stardom" actually seemed inevitable; excitement had been building for some time. After the Oscar nomination, *Time, Collier's, Look* and the *Saturday Evening Post* followed with major profiles, all attempting to analyze his appeal. Obviously he was not another Gable or Tracy, a traditional leading man; he was instead quirky, remote, taciturn, a loner—and almost androgynous.

In both *The Search* and *Red River* he played gifted, driven outsiders, dealing with reality in a very personal, hard-edged way. What made these performances so fascinating was not that they revealed new facets of either cowboy or G.I., but that he managed to find new contexts for them to exist in. He was both surprising and familiar at the same time.

And the triumph of these performances was the hidden motor that propelled him, which helped create the web of complexity and ambiguity that was part of him as an actor.

Without being aware of it, audiences were witnessing a new kind of eroticism on film—an eroticism and vulnerability which sprang from the contradictions in Montgomery Clift's personality: Monty was open—he was hidden—he was gay—he was straight; in essence he seemed to represent a new kind of man—a man who refuses to make judgments on sexual preference. "He was so ambiguous sexually it was a relief," said press agent Mike Mazlansky.

For Monty, however, his sexual ambiguity was a private torture. He lived in New York between pictures so he could conduct his complicated private life without too much publicity.

He always made it clear to reporters that he disliked discussing romance: "I have no time—no time!"

For the record, he was dating Terry Moore; for the record, he escorted Mira Rostova to parties and dinners. Off the record, he had been until recently emotionally committed to a Broadway choreographer—a "theatrical genius," Monty called him early in their affair.

"Monty broke up with the choreographer when the guy named names for HUAC," Brooks said. "Monty told me he'd lost all respect for him."

In spite of his precautions, gossip often surfaced about Monty's "double life." Once a reporter thought he spotted Monty Clift coming out of a gay bar in San Francisco. In New York it was rumored Monty went occasionally to the public baths on the Lower East Side.

Herman Citron recalls Hedda Hopper phoning MCA shortly after Monty had been nominated for the Academy Award for *The Search*. "Is it true Montgomery Clift has been arrested for pederasty in New Orleans?" she demanded. Citron told the gossip columnist: "No, that is preposterous, and besides, Monty is visiting his sister in Texas."

As soon as he hung up the phone, Citron phoned the police in New Orleans and discovered Monty had been detained briefly in jail for drunkenness and then released. However, not long after that he was arrested on Forty-second Street for trying to pick up a young boy. His lawyer hushed the incident up.

Meanwhile, Paramount was busy promoting him as their next great sex symbol—the most eligible bachelor on the screen. Monty hated the publicity campaign; he began drinking more than brandy, and he complained to Bobby Lewis, "Look, I don't feel particularly sexual and besides, what does sexuality have to do with my work?" To which Lewis replied, "Remember, please, the most potent thing an artist has is his imagination."

"Becoming a public figure—a celebrity—tore Monty up," said Bill Le Massena. "Monty hated, loathed, and despised deception, and here he was having to hide. In the theater he could have swung both ways and it wouldn't have mattered. But as a Hollywood star he had to be the all-American male one hundred percent or else."

Because of this, Monty occasionally went to extreme lengths to promote a heterosexual image. Herman Citron recalls getting an angry phone call from Monty saying, "I'm taking a plane to L.A. tonight; I have to ask you something very important face to face." When Citron murmured, "Couldn't you ask me over the phone?" Monty snapped no and hung up. Fourteen hours later he appeared at MCA, and he hustled Citron into a conference room and shut the door. "Did you tell so-and-so I was a fag?" he almost whispered. His eyes were huge.

"No, Monty, I didn't, honestly," Citron answered. With that Monty began shaking the agent's hand, "Thanks, Herm. I didn't think you would, but I had to make sure." Turning on his heel he walked out the door, and took the next plane back to New York.

The more successful Monty became, the more he attempted to remain nonchalant, uncaring. He was almost studiously messy in old chinos and frayed shirts. He told Elsa Maxwell when he had brunch with her that he would not give up his $40-a-month flat because "I like living in New York. New York is where I can still be around so-called ordinary people. The inbred hothouse atmosphere of Hollywood makes you lose contact with the real world. Suddenly real people don't exist for you."

Whenever he was in New York, Monty haunted night court, studying the faces of prostitutes and petty thieves. "The miracles that happen to their expressions by accident!" he told Kevin McCarthy. He also attended the trial of Judith Coplon, a government worker accused of stealing secret U.S. documents and giving them to her Russian boyfriend at a meeting at the Museum of Modern Art. Photographed leaving the courtroom, surrounded by fans, Monty refused to comment on the guilty verdict.

Now he spent time with Karl and Mona Malden, who lived in the brownstone next to his on Fifty-fifth Street. If he felt like seeing them he would climb over the roof and down the fire escape and then tap on the window, hissing, "This is Monty! Whatcha doin'?"

Malden was then appearing in *A Streetcar Named Desire,* and he was competitive, intent, stolid, puritanical, and a bit put off by Monty's manic energy. He also disapproved of his critical arrogance when it came to judging other actors' craft. "Monty and Kevin were too artsy-fartsy for Karl, although he tried not to show it," said actor Don Keefer. Still there were frequent get-togethers in the Malden apartment with Marlon Brando, Barry Nelson, Mary Welsh, Don Keefer, and Maureen Stapleton all arguing about acting.

Monty spent most evenings with the McCarthys in their new apartment in Peter Cooper Village. "He practically lived with us," Augusta said. "Stanley Kubrick photographed him for *Look* at our place playing with our baby son Flip. He'd have other reporters come down to interview him but always when we were there. He seemed more relaxed when we were around."

Augusta would make him Dagwood sandwiches, his favorite snack. He might bathe Flip before he and Kevin would go off to a foreign movie at the Beverly. "And we never stopped talking," Kevin said. "We'd stay up 'till four A.M. discussing everything from Alger Hiss (who we both thought was guilty) to what we could do to keep the double-decker buses from disappearing on Fifth Avenue. And we talked about acting endlessly. Monty was an absolute genius when it came to perceiving a character."

"He was in no way an intellectual," said actor Don Keefer who sometimes joined in these discussions. "Monty's gift was emotional and intuitive. He had extraordinary imagination as well as extraordinary empathy for the characters he worked on. So much so that he could give each one of them a shape and you could almost imagine what they were feeling and seeing."

Beneath the surface, the relationship between Monty and the McCarthys, though good-natured, was highly volatile. Monty phoned the couple constantly, and he thought nothing of barging into their apartment at all hours of the day and night.

"He did the same thing with us in California; banging on our door at two A.M., waking us out of a sound sleep," Fred Green said. "I yelled at him a couple of times and eventually he stopped. Kevin never said anything. He took a lot from him."

Others say there was tension in the marriage because Augusta was getting more acting jobs while Kevin, encouraged by Monty, kept turning down scripts because they weren't good enough. And Monty seemed closer to Augusta than to anybody, including Mira Rostova. He told others he was deeply in love with her.

When Kevin was rehearsing Romeo for CBS's "Omnibus" and he was having trouble with the death scene, "I asked Monty to help me and we worked one entire night in our living room with Gussie playing the dead Juliet, Monty playing Romeo. He was agonizingly brilliant," Kevin says. "He seemed totally assured in his conception of the character. His Romeo was impetuous, romantic, fumbling with words as he expressed his love for Juliet. He also brought a physicality, an athleticism to the role. His entire body seemed part of the work. And then there was this power—this originality behind the concept. He played young love so *intensely,* so *truthfully*."

They rehearsed till five in the morning; after Gussie staggered off to bed Monty went over the scene for the last time using a pillow as Juliet. "I remember he covered it with passionate kisses, then rocked it back and forth in his arms like a baby."

20

In the early spring of 1949, Monty made one of his quick trips to Hollywood. He saw his agents and discussed Dreiser's *American Tragedy* which he was going to make later that year, getting first billing opposite Elizabeth Taylor. ("Who's Elizabeth Taylor?" he reportedly asked his agent when the deal was being negotiated.) He also conferred with Billy Wilder on a script called *Sunset Boulevard,* which Wilder was writing specifically for him. According to Herman Citron, Monty was very excited by the material, calling it "the definitive Hollywood ghost story."

On this trip he dropped by Salka Viertel's for supper. Publisher Frank Taylor, then a story editor at MGM, hurried forward to introduce himself. "I didn't know the guy, but I'd just seen both *Red River* and *The Search,* and I thought he was sensational. I told him so and we talked a little, but he put me off. He seemed to have a sixth sense about me—he stared at me with those strange unblinking eyes of his. It was as if he was stripping me bare psychologically. It was very disconcerting."

After their chat, Taylor watched as Monty darted about the living room, conferring with Chaplin, getting Garbo a drink. Then he wandered over to the buffet and fixed himself a plate of food. And then he carried his plate through the glittering throng of celebrities—Thomas Mann, Artur Rubinstein, Aldous Huxley, Lotte Lenya—he climbed over the white sofa and perched on top of it, eating from his plate with his hands like a monkey.

"It was repulsive," Taylor recalled. "I found out later he did this periodically, stuffing his mouth with food like an animal. But, somehow, he still managed to appear elegant."

As he often did when he was in California, Monty stayed with the Greens in their Hollywood Hills house. He found Jeanne in a deep depression, sometimes crying. She was pregnant again, and they didn't have much money. She wasn't sure she wanted another baby right away—the twins were a big responsibility. Monty talked to her for hours and finally said, "If you don't want this baby I'll get you an abortionist." Together they weighed the pros and cons.

"I remember it was eleven o'clock at night," Jeanne said. "I was exhausted from crying and talking—I agreed to let him find a doctor for me. Monty then took my face in his hands and kissed me very gently and said, 'Don't worry. I'll arrange everything.' And he did. He left and then came back around three A.M., tapped on our bedroom window and made the high sign—'it's OK'—and then he pantomimed going to sleep and disappeared into the dark."

The following morning, Monty gave Jeanne the name of a Beverly Hills doctor, and she went to him "very hush-hush"; he in turn gave her the phone and address of an abortionist who had an office in the industrial section of Los Angeles. She made the appointment, but then she panicked. "I couldn't eat, I couldn't sleep—I fell apart." She and Fred discussed the situation at length—she then told Monty she couldn't go through with it. He suggested that perhaps she needed some therapy. "I found an analyst and after a couple of sessions I realized I wanted my baby terribly. I decided not to have the abortion. Monty gave me a thousand dollars as a present to use for more therapy which, he said, was essential for everyone."

He did not tell her why. He did not tell her he was so worried about his drinking he thought he would have to seek psychiatric help. He couldn't stop drinking. He and Ned Smith got "roaring drunk" and finished an entire bottle of brandy the night Ned helped him move to his new apartment. Bill Le Massena recalls Monty getting terribly drunk on martinis. "I remember thinking, 'My God, Monty likes his booze' and then I realized before 1949 all he ever drank was milk."

Arthur Miller once said, "An era ends when its basic illusions are exhausted." For Monty, 1949 still held some illusions; but it was a frenetic, exacting year. On the surface he seemed to be moving constantly, rarely sleeping, talking obsessively. He was constantly talking to his agent Lew Wasserman (whom he was depending on more and more). He met people like Nicolas Nabokov and John Huston. He became friends with Roddy McDowall.

He had already begun preparations on *An American Tragedy* (now entitled *A Place in the Sun*). He wanted to play George, the fortune hunter, realistically—not romantically. "He is not a nice person," he told Elsa Maxwell when he had breakfast with her again at the Waldorf. "George would kill for five bucks if he had to. Everything he does is calculated."

In 1949, Monty flew to Europe and back at least a half dozen times—to London and Rome to see producers and directors, to appear at the opening of his movies. Once he flew to Paris on a chartered plane with Gene Kelly and Betsy Blair as the only other passengers. He asked Ned Smith to join them, but Smith refused. "I could tell Monty was extremely impressed at having practically an entire plane at his disposal."

On weekends he would drive up to Stamford and sleep over at Libby Holman's lavish estate, Treetops. He had a special little room —"Monty's room"—which was treated like a shrine and always kept in readiness. He would bring with him some of the scripts he was considering: Mailer's *Naked and the Dead* (screenplay by Lillian Hellman); Thomas Wolfe's *Look Homeward Angel,* which Wyler wanted to direct; a western called *High Noon,* two untitled comedies by Norman Krasna.

He frequently spent Sundays at Thornton and Isabel Wilder's house in Hamden. Wilder was in a despondent state, demoralized by the critical indifference to his book *The Ides of March.* At one lunch, a guest remembered, Monty tried to entertain him with anecdotes about Hollywood. He described Louella Parsons sitting drunk and cross-eyed in a corner at a party trying to make conversation with all the movie stars who came sucking up to her. He did an imitation of L. B. Mayer in his office at MGM, seated at his desk, which was on a rise. "He's like a gangster on a throne," Monty said.

But these stories seemed to depress Wilder, who murmured that his own life was a failure. This astonished Monty, and he said as much, arguing rapidly that success has nothing to do with achievement—original achievement; he simply could not comprehend how someone as remarkably talented and productive as Wilder, someone with such a capacity to appreciate and understand life in all its glories and terrors and complexities, should denigrate himself in this way.

Wilder had recently abandoned work on a play called *Alcestis* for Garbo, and he was currently trying to write *The Emporium,* inspired by Kafka's *The Castle*. He was writing the play expressly for Monty, and Monty, much moved, urged him to finish it. He would play it anywhere, any place, he said. As if to spur Wilder on, he began to read the entire works of Kafka, and he tried to discuss them all: *The Castle, Metamorphosis, The Trial*. Monty found the writing "baffling, exquisite, tortured."

During his reading he came upon a photograph of Kafka taken in Prague the year of his death. His face is sharp, chiseled, skull-like, his ears stick out like a bat; his eyes are startled, full of fear and yet oddly contained. Monty kept the picture and ultimately tore it out of the book so he could study it more closely. He gazed at that picture almost every day. Years later he used it as the basis for his characterization of Noah in *The Young Lions*.

Monty saw a great many shows in 1949—*South Pacific, Gentlemen Prefer Blondes*, Richard Whorf in *Richard III, Caesar and Cleopatra*, the Lunts in *I Know My Love*. He went to the Philadelphia opening of *Death of a Salesman* with the McCarthys, and he left the theater sweaty and shaken, muttering, "It is fantastic! Arthur Miller is saying the American Dream is full of shit!"

Don Keefer, who was in the cast, joined him and others at a local bar for drinks; everybody waited for Monty to elaborate on the play, and on Lee J. Cobb's and Mildred Dunnock's performances. Usually Monty was very critical, but that night he just slumped on a bar stool and drank the way Baudelaire describes Poe drinking: "Barbarously—with a speed and dispatch altogether American, as if he was performing a homicidal function, as if he wanted to kill something within himself, a worm that would not die."

After *Salesman* opened at the Morosco in New York, where it swept every award, Monty saw the play numerous times, often standing at the back of the house so he could see the audience as well as the entire stage, so he could "absorb the total goddamn picture."

Privately, he had begun to scribble in a notebook: "From Julien Green's diary—what I have against a life of pleasure is that it kills in a man all aptitude for love. The theater is no place for a man who bleeds easily—Sean O'Casey. Self-esteem must be held high—vanity and pride working in inverse proportions. The sadness of our existence should not leave us blunted, on the contrary—how to remain thin-skinned, vulnerable and stay alive?"

He was receiving so much fan mail and so many scripts he finally hired a full-time secretary named Arline Cunningham—an effervescent brunette of nineteen who came from an impoverished family somewhere in the hills of Pennsylvania. After seeing *Red River* she took the Greyhound bus to New York with the express purpose of meeting Montgomery Clift.

She arrived at the Clift apartment on Park Avenue and rang the bell. Brooks happened to answer the door. He recalled, "There was this ravishing girl asking, 'Does Montgomery Clift live here?' Monty was away but I asked her in and we talked about *Red River* and then I helped her find a hotel."

Within weeks Arline got a job as a typist at MCA and soon worked her way up to being Jay Kantor's secretary. Kantor was one of Monty's principal agents in New York. Sometime in 1949 Kantor asked her to go out in a limousine to Idlewild and "pick up Monty Clift. He's coming in from Hollywood—meet him—give him these scripts—take him back to his home," he ordered.

Arline did as she was told, but she also kept Monty quietly entertained on the ride back to Manhattan. Monty was entranced by her serenity—her seeming inner calm. He subsequently hired her part time to read and comment on his scripts, answer his mail and his phone, and in general organize his crowded schedule. Very quickly he began depending on her judgment, her opinions—and she became absorbed into his life. She began accompanying him to screenings and to the theater. She went up with Monty and Roddy McDowell to Libby Holman's estate on weekends. She fantasized vaguely about being an actress, but she never went beyond the talking phase.

"Arline fell in love with Monty, but then everybody I knew was in love with Montgomery Clift," said Rosemary Santini, who knew Arline when they both lived in Greenwich Village. "Monty represented a new kind of man in the bleak 1950s, a guy who was poetic and vulnerable and disturbed and not afraid to show it. I think Arline even lived with Monty for a while, but nobody seems to know whether they ever consummated the relationship.

"She was absolutely gorgeous—breathtaking," Miss Santini continued. "I'd say she was as lushly beautiful as Elizabeth Taylor, whom she sort of resembled—big breasts, velvety skin, huge sparkling eyes, very, very sexy. She could be lots of fun and laughs and then suddenly she'd close herself off and get unreachable, and you'd think, 'Oh-oh, there's a weird one.' "

Miss Santini remembered seeing them together at one party, "Arline was crying and I heard somebody say to her, 'You're knocking your head against a stone wall trying to make Monty love you the way you love him.' "

Whatever the outcome of the relationship, Arline stayed close to Monty's life for almost five years—and during that time, until 1954, he depended on her for advice and comfort. She was the only one who accompanied him when he went to Germantown, Pennsylvania, to see the Foggs and try to comprehend his mother's beginnings.

Arline also went with him and Ned Smith (who found her "absolutely bewitching") to a bar in the Camden Airport where a handwriting expert analyzed Monty's scrawl and told him bluntly: "You're the most disturbed man I've ever seen—you'll die young."

21

Throughout 1949 people drifted in and out of Monty's apartment on East Fifty-fifth Street—women like photographer Inge Morath and actress Betsy Blair—casual friends like Artie Shaw and Norman Mailer. The one constant at 131 East Fifty-fifth Street aside from the McCarthys was Mira Rostova who lived in the apartment next door. "She was always around," actor Don Keefer said. Monty would say, "Mira and I are the Europeans in this crowd. We don't like Coca-Cola. Kevin is American and he does."

Over the past six years, Mira and Monty had developed an almost symbiotic relationship in which their identities were constantly shifting and blending. They responded to each other as mother and son, as antagonists, and as intimate friends. When someone asked Monty, "What does Mira mean to you?" he replied grandly, "Mira is my artistic conscience."

Although Mira claimed often to know what Monty was thinking, there was a part of Monty he kept hidden from her. "His underground existence," she called it. "But he introduced me to all his homosexual friends. I knew them all.

"Monty was totally split sexually," she continued. "That was the core of his tragedy, because he never stopped being conflicted and he never stopped feeling guilty about being conflicted."

It was this conflict—this warring between his yielding receptive feminine side and his self-asserting questing male side—that prevented him from ever realizing complete fulfillment.

This split also kept him from loving anyone completely. "He wanted to have a lasting relationship with someone. He tried to have lasting relationships, but he was unable to."

Sometimes when he felt relaxed and affectionate he would cry,

"Oh Mira dearest, if I were a different person we would have been married long ago."

And he would laugh. "I knew he didn't mean it," Mira said. "Would I have married him? Oh, I cannot say. Monty was one of the most important people in my life, but marriage? He was too troubled to be married."

The trouble stemmed in part from his drinking. His drinking was still increasing. "I love to drink!" he said. It made his problems disappear, his tensions reduce; he no longer felt lonely or fearful. He was drinking much more than he should, and yet he always concealed it.

By May of 1949, Monty knew he would soon be filming two movies back to back: *The Big Lift* to be shot in Berlin, and *A Place in the Sun* to be filmed partly on location at Lake Tahoe. He was looking forward to doing the pictures, but he also dreaded the experiences because (he imagined) he would be fighting with the director, disagreeing with the actors, and wanting the scripts rewritten.

"Monty was a perfectionist," said Kevin McCarthy. "After making only three movies he already felt thwarted, frustrated, isolated in his needs to express himself on film."

Monty constantly had to submit himself to inferior tastes (like L. B. Mayer's, who thought mainly in clichés and formulas) or to superior powers like Darryl Zanuck and Lew Wasserman, who saw in his client the potential of a superstar like Tyrone Power or Valentino and wanted to build him as such.

Monty would often come back from California muttering, "I'm not called an actor out there, I'm called a hot property. And a property is only good if it makes money—a property is lousy if it loses money at the box office."

The film community was aware of Monty's contempt for Hollywood values, and they disliked him heartily for it. "Right off he was labeled an outsider," said a press agent who used to drink with Monty at the Bel Air Hotel. "The minute you refuse to play the game in Hollywood exactly as they want it, and that means totally giving up your body and your soul and your guts to becoming a STAR, you become an outsider. The minute you have integrity, which is what Monty had—you are an outsider. The minute you refuse to sell yourself as a commodity, a product, the agent and producers and directors who literally feed off talent call you an outsider, and it is much harder to survive. Hollywood couldn't have cared less that Monty preferred to live in New York and disapproved of the pap about himself in fan magazines. To survive being a star in Hollywood like Humphrey Bogart or Gary Cooper, you have to be sensitive and ruthless, humble and arrogant. Monty was sensitive. Period."

That May, almost as a protection against Hollywood, Monty optioned *You Touched Me!*, surprising its authors Tennessee Williams and Donald Windham, both of whom thought the play had been totally forgotten. And after optioning the play, Monty then announced to the *New York Times* he was forming a production unit, Kemont. He and Kevin McCarthy would adapt *You Touched Me!* for the screen, after which sometime in 1950 he would produce and possibly direct the movie version. He would also star.

He was elated at obtaining the property—it meant he had committed himself to being involved with an artistic adventure in the most complete sense. And it had always been one of his favorite plays. He saw it as an allegory, representing the closed versus the open attitudes towards life. "This play is not only about the glory of relationships," he told Kevin, "it's about the greatness and glory of being alive."

Right after he optioned the play he and Kevin and Karl Malden went up to visit Martin Swenson in Brookville, Maine, where Swenson and his wife were trying to farm. They shoveled chicken shit out of the henhouse, took walks through the dense woods, strolled down to the Bagaduce River. Monty loved Maine; the hardy climate invigorated him, the Maine characters amused him. He listened to the lobstermen who smelled of salt philosophize about the weather and pinching pennies. That weekend he and Kevin decided to set *You Touched Me!* in Maine rather than England, its original location.

As soon as he returned to New York Monty started conferring with Kevin on *You Touched Me!* "We'd meet at Monty's place," Kevin said. "We'd make notes, then we'd go around the corner, pick up some fresh red meat at the butcher, come back and eat it raw, and continue our discussions."

The discussions didn't last long. "We met only a couple of times," because, in June, Elia Kazan cast Kevin as Biff in the London company of *Death of a Salesman* which was to star Paul Muni and open in the West End on July 23.

Naturally Kevin was overjoyed. He began working immediately with Mira on the role. And he couldn't wait for rehearsals to begin. There was only one catch. "Although Monty seemed happy enough for me, he kept repeating, 'You know, you're going to have to leave the show during the run to continue working on *You Touched Me!* ' "

Augusta remembers how startled she was at Monty's attitude. "He planned to go back to work on *You Touched Me!* as soon as he finished *A Place in the Sun* in December and he saw no reason why Kevin shouldn't do the same. He gave little or no consideration to the fact that *Death of a Salesman* was the biggest break of Kevin's career —he barely seemed to acknowledge it. As far as Monty was concerned, Kevin would leave the show at the appointed time. Kevin didn't know what to do."

Almost as soon as the McCarthys arrived in London with their baby, Flip, and moved into a little rented mews house in Chelsea, Monty began bombarding them with letters—funny, affectionate letters from New York—but most of them were filled with references to *You Touched Me!*

He was concerned about the dialogue and the characterizations; he was concerned about opening up the play for the film—hence the relocation to a sea town rather than a house away and above the water. He talked of casting Walter Huston as the drunken sea captain, and he said he would try and meet with him the next time he was in California.

He also directed some thoughts to Kevin regarding Kazan's rehearsal tactics for *Death of a Salesman,* having heard that he was trying to recreate the most effective moments of the New York production.

> I wonder and wonder about each day of rehearsal of yours. I wish to God you were going out of town so the Powers that Be would disappear for a few days. Work in progress means nothing to them. And the prospect of becoming a shit in front of all those people in order to experiment oneself about something which is tentative anyway is nothing to look forward to. I beg of you if you have the *slightest* qualm about something you are wanting to do don't even try to do it fully their way. The novelty of any approach will make you do it well at first, and since it is neither the way your instinct wishes nor if it were had you arrived at it yourself—the truth of it will vanish and you will be continually chastised with 'you did it fine that day.' Inside one wants to please and this way the hurdles to your truth will mount.

In another letter, dated July 9, 1949, he enclosed articles by
Fred Allen and some snapshots of himself taken in Maine, where he
had gone briefly to escape the heat of New York "because otherwise
I would have turned into an oversize Empirin tablet."

His agent, Lew Wasserman, was still dickering with Paramount,
trying to postpone shooting *Place in the Sun* for a couple of weeks so
Monty could also do George Seaton's *The Big Lift* in Germany first.
Monty thought the movie was particularly important because it not
only described the drama of the Berlin airlift, it reflected the contrasting attitudes of Americans during the Cold War.

He wrote in a letter of July 9:

> Yesterday I read in the paper that Montgomery Clift
> is going to star opposite June Allyson (June Allyson??) in
> *The Big Hangover*. My worst fears are that Lew is perhaps
> giving assurance to Metro that I will do *The Big Hangover*
> and thus they will be able to get Elizabeth Taylor. I think
> secretly the powers that be are afraid (if I go to Germany)
> I might get deathly sick or break a leg and they'd much
> rather have me . . . on the home lot of Metro where they
> can watch the bone heal. . . . I sit stewing in this pissmire
> having no idea what the next blab of the telephone will
> bring. . . . Yesterday Mira and I saw that specially flown
> screening of *Alice Adams* (with Katharine Hepburn). A
> horrendous disappointment. Not only Mr. S. [director
> George Stevens] as a potential for us [for *You Touched
> Me!*] but even more immediately definitely the wrong
> man to tackle "Tragedy."
>
> Other movies for you not to miss. *The Barkleys of
> Broadway,* Oy. *The Great Sinner*. Oy. Oy. *The Stratton
> Story*. A Metro film. But now a great piece of news. If
> anybody thinks our movie is broader than an Abbott and
> Costello farce wait till you see *The Bank Dick*. I never
> laughed so hard. It's a great picture—and I gotta go again
> and take notes and send you some of the gags in the
> picture to relieve the monotony of London. . . .
> Man to W.C. Fields—I heard you buried your wife.
> Fields (hardly overheard) I had to—she died.
> Man (excitedly) You're not wanted here.

Fields (murmuring) That's silly, I'm wanted in every state in the union.

In *My Little Chickadee* Mae West puts a goat in her bed and leaves the room. Fields enters. The room is dark. He thinks she is in bed. He climbs in and drawls out very slowly, "Dear why don't you take off your coat? It would feel so much better. . . ."

Well, dear hearts, good night. I hope things are going well for you. All America wants to know—were you sick Augusta [meaning seasick on the ocean crossing]. I say no. I love you. Monty.

By August everything was decided, and Monty left New York to make *The Big Lift*. On his way to Germany he and Mira stopped off in London to see the McCarthys. There were jaunts through Regents Park and lots of theater, and there was much talk and laughter punctuated by Monty's reminder that Kevin tell Binky Beaumont, *Salesman*'s English producer, that he would be leaving the show before the end of its six-month run.

Kevin hedged. He had just opened—it wasn't the proper moment, he said, but he was determined to tell Beaumont; he gave Monty his word.

Afterwards he panicked. "I realized I could never go back on what I'd said. And I did want very much to collaborate on the screenplay. But I also wanted to stay in *Death of a Salesman*."

Since he had a run-of-the-play contract he decided the only possible way to break it was to obtain a medical release. He must persuade a doctor to write a letter saying there was something physically the matter with him.

Over Augusta's objections he phoned critic Cyril Connolly, a friend of Mary McCarthy's. Connolly in turn put him in touch with Sonia Orwell, who put him in touch with an analyst who'd worked with Anna Freud.

"I told him my problem—that I must leave *Death of a Salesman* —and I went over and over my feeling of commitment to Monty and *You Touched Me!* When I finished my story, he told me he'd give me the necessary papers, but then he added, 'Why are you so influenced by this Montgomery Clift? What does he mean to you? How do you really feel about him?' "

Kevin had never given his friendship with Monty close scrutiny. "I knew I looked up to him. Admired him. Enjoyed his company enormously. I felt as close to him as a member of my family. As far as I was concerned he was a member of my family." Still, Kevin put off going to Beaumont although there was now added pressure from Monty, who called frequently from Germany asking whether he'd got his release.

Finally, in desperation, Kevin spoke to Paul Muni and implied he'd have to quit *Death of a Salesman* for personal reasons. With that Muni retorted he would refuse to act with his understudy, so he'd better stay.

Late that summer in Berlin, Monty prepared for his role in *The Big Lift* by walking through the city he would be filming in, soaking up its atmosphere.

Afterwards he told Pat Collinge: "Berlin has a blasted quality—it reminds me of an overexposed black and white photograph—it is grainy—two-toned—slightly eerie. Berlin is a city with no trees and few buildings still standing. Streets piled with rubble—it is a filthy city —with thin whiny dogs, a city with little sunshine. Families survive in unbelievable conditions. . . . They huddle in the cellars of gutted apartments. They are sullen and unfriendly. Everybody queues up for hours for food. They will hassle for an hour over a single piece of cheese."

Monty took a few walks with director George Seaton, whom he initially felt complete rapport with. Seaton, born in South Bend, Indiana, had been both an actor and director in stock before going out to California and turning his hand to scripts, among them *The Song of Bernadette* and *The Eve of St. Mark*. His *Miracle on 34th Street* screenplay won the Academy Award in 1947.

Monty was enthusiastic about *The Big Lift* script, which Seaton had written and would direct. "The dialogue is fantastic," he said, as it combined so many playable elements—comedy, romance, and suspense—told in character terms.

He agreed with Seaton that one of the movie's principal intentions was to dramatize the contrasting American states of mind during the Cold War. These were reflected right in Monty's role of Danny, the wise-cracking, moody, liberal flight engineer who is part of the Berlin airlift, who underestimates the terrible moral corruption in Germany as a result of Hitler. He falls in love and is completely betrayed by a German girl who "uses" him.

Seaton had gone to a lot of trouble to get Monty a nice little house in a suburb of West Berlin. He'd had it specially furnished with couches and beds from Paris. There was one floor for Monty and one floor for Mira Rostova who was written into his contract as Mr. Clift's "secretary." Seaton thought it was perfect for both of them.

However, when Monty saw the house he said coolly, "I visualized something with a garden." Seaton laughed and said, "Oh, come on, Monty, this will be fine." And Monty repeated with an edge to his voice, "I visualized something with a garden."

This was the hottest, most demanded star in Hollywood talking, Seaton said. He realized if he didn't get him something with a garden he might fly back to California in a huff. So he phoned Gen. Lucius Clay, Commander of the American Occupation, and explained the situation; eventually, a colonel and his family gave up their house (and garden) in Berlin for the duration of the filming to Monty.

The Big Lift was shot entirely on location in Frankfurt and West Berlin, with the bulk of the cast, aside from Monty, Paul Douglas, and the young actress Cornell Borchers, made up of General Clay's honor guard platoon, as well as hundreds of airmen who had actually flown the lift. A great many scenes were filmed at Tempelhof Airbase in West Berlin where only months before American Air Force planes had landed every three minutes, twenty-four hours a day, bringing in food and coal to thousands of West Germans.

No trouble was expected with the cast, but almost immediately friction developed between Paul Douglas and Monty. Douglas, who was playing a crude, cynical sergeant, was a tough-talking former sports announcer—turned Broadway actor. Before starring in *A Letter to Three Wives,* he'd gained fame playing the gangster Brock opposite Judy Holliday in Garson Kanin's comedy, *Born Yesterday*.

During the filming of their first scene, Douglas noticed that Monty would lean into the two-shot so much that he practically pushed Douglas out of the frame. At a break, he marched over to Seaton and informed him of what was going on. "Look," he said, "Duke Wayne warned me that this kid's a little shit. If he causes any more trouble during our mutual close-ups . . ."

The next time Monty leaned into a two-shot, Douglas slammed down on his big toe and Monty cried out in pain. Then Douglas hissed, "You do that again and I'll break your fuckin' foot." Monty never leaned into any more of their two-shots, but for the rest of the shooting they weren't on speaking terms.

An even more serious problem arose: Mira Rostova. She appeared on location every day, standing behind the camera, either shaking her head or nodding as soon as Monty completed a take.

William Perlberg, *Lift*'s producer, brought this to Seaton's attention after Monty insisted on redoing a scene seven times when everybody else thought the first two takes had been brilliant. Calling a break, Seaton walked Monty arm in arm out of earshot. He asked bluntly whether Mira was a secretary or his drama coach? Monty didn't answer. He just smiled.

Controlling his temper, Seaton assured him the movie was going exceedingly well—he was terrific in the rushes and there was absolutely nothing to worry about in his performance, so why did he need this woman?

Monty reportedly replied, "She is helping me find truth." Exasperated, Seaton told him he had hired Montgomery Clift to star in *The Big Lift,* not Mira Rostova. "But George," Monty answered, "you don't understand. When I'm on the set Mira Rostova *is* Montgomery Clift."

Finally, during one big scene shot at the airport, Seaton's wife wheedled Mira away from the location for a cup of coffee. "Things were so tense I decided I'd better go with her," Mira said. "The crew was taking a long time to set up."

As soon as they disappeared into the airport bar, Seaton shot the scene and Mira was not there to oversee it. "Monty was furious. He said I'd let him down." Seaton, however, was jubilant.

After that Mira never left Monty's side. The two conferred after every shot, and in the evenings they would attend the rushes, whispering as the takes rolled onto the screen. Then Monty would argue with Seaton as to which take was more effective, finally causing the cameraman to crack, "That woman is directing the picture."

The remark so enraged Seaton he ordered Mira off the picture completely. "If Mira goes, I go, George," Monty said. Mira stayed.

"No director likes to be second-guessed," said a reporter who covered *The Big Lift.* "Seaton was constantly being contradicted by this little Russian lady, and he didn't like it, and I don't blame him."

Nor did Mira Rostova. "I understand how George Seaton felt," she said recently. "It was an impossible situation, one I always felt uncomfortable in. Who wants to be disliked? I was always the heavy. But I don't regret it since the end result—Monty's performance— benefited from my suggestions. It was worth the trouble, but it was never a pleasant experience for me."

Seaton has few happy memories of Monty. "Near the end of the filming he was jittery—jumping around. I guess he was under a lot of pressure. But he could be very unpleasant. I remember he used to buy cigarettes at the PX and then sell them on the black market."

In the middle of filming *The Big Lift,* Monty was airmailed the final version of *Sunset Boulevard,* which was scheduled to go into production in the middle of 1950. Agent Herman Citron phoned Berlin a few days later to get a reaction.

"At first I thought the connection was bad," he recalled. "Transatlantic phone calls were pretty difficult to hear then, but I heard correct all right. I heard Monty shouting over the static, 'I don't like it, Herm. I'm not gonna do it!' "

Citron remembers being flabbergasted because the script was "absolutely sensational, and Monty had liked it so much originally. We yelled at each other back and forth—Monty gave me no specific reason other than he didn't think the part was right for him and could I tell Billy Wilder?" Citron replied he could not. Monty would have to do that himself which he ultimately did—over transatlantic phone, and Wilder was momentarily infuriated.

Sunset Boulevard went on to become an acclaimed movie, of course; it made William Holden a star and regenerated Gloria Swanson's career. But Monty always maintained he did not regret his decision, and whenever asked, he praised the movie.

(Years later Citron surmised Monty might have been reluctant to do the picture because the relationship in the script between the handsome young writer and the middle-aged, fading screen star resembled ever so slightly his own closely guarded [at the time] affair with the forty-eight-year-old Libby Holman.)

Seaton grudgingly admitted that Monty gives a "terrific performance in *The Big Lift.*" Whether or not Mira Rostova is partially responsible is beside the point. The fact remains Monty's performance is one of the most significant and underrated of his career. Once again one sees that indefinable quality of his which is neither a matter of looks nor acting ability. It's a rather weird chemical relationship with the camera so that what appears on film is not just a marvelous face but a complex, compelling *presence.* In this role his style is exuberant and less restrained, even comical (for instance, the nightclub scene, where he sings on stage with a trio of Germans). He has picked up assurance and flair on camera—he smiles more, a flashing, eager smile. It's almost as if he is now aware he has a magnificent career ahead of him and he is looking forward to it along with everybody else.

Watching Monty on the screen in *The Big Lift,* particularly in

Monty's mother, Ethel "Sunny" Clift, just before she entered Cornell in 1910.

◀
Monty and Sunny, St. Moritz, winter 1930.

Monty and his twin sister, Ft. Lauderdale, Florida, 1933.
▼

(Top) Monty at the age of one in Omaha, spring 1922.

(Bottom) Monty, Brooks, Sister and nurse Wilke in Hendaye, France, 1929.

a. Monty photographed when he was a John Robert Powers model, New York, 1933. (Theatre Collection, The New York Public Library at Lincoln Center. Astor, Lenox and Tilden Foundations)

b. With Thomas Mitchell and Georgette McPhee in *Fly Away Home.* (Theatre Collection, The New York Public Library at Lincoln Center. Astor, Lenox and Tilden Foundations)

c. Jackie Kelk and Monty (right) in the Cole Porter musical *Jubilee,* 1935. (Theatre Collection, The New York Public Library at Lincoln Center. Astor, Lenox and Tilden Foundations)

d. With Lois Hall and Morgan James in *Dame Nature.* (Stephen V. Russell collection)

a

d   e

e. With Tallulah Bankhead, Florence Eldridge, Frederic March, and Francis Heflin in Thornton Wilder's *The Skin of Our Teeth,* 1942. (Playbill, © American Theater Press, Inc., All rights reserved. Used by permission)

f. With Lynn Fontanne and Alfred Lunt in Robert Sherwood's *There Shall be no Night,* 1940. (Theatre Collection, The New York Public Library at Lincoln Center. Astor, Lenox and Tilden Foundations)

Monty and his father, Bill Clift, at Sister's wedding in Milwaukee 1945. (Brooks Clift collecti

Mira Rostova, Monty's coach and confidante.
(Kevin McCarthy)

The actress Ann Lincoln, after she appear
with Monty in *Foxhole In the Parlor.*

y as he looked when he played the lame soldier in Lillian Hellman's *The Searching Wind*.

a

b

c

d

a. Between takes in Munich for *The Search* with director Fred Zinnemann and Ivan Jandl. (Stephen V. Russell collection)

b. As the cowboy Matthew Garth in Howard Hawks's classic western *Red River*. (Ethel McGinnis collection)

c. The famous fight scene in *Red River* between Monty and John Wayne. (Ethel McGinnis collection)

d. With John Wayne, on location in Tuscon, Arizona. (Ethel McGinnis collection)

e. With Olivia de Havilland in *The Heiress*. (Culver Pictures)

e

d

e

a

b

c

a. Monty's cover photo (reproduced by permission of *Life*, Dec. 6, 1948, © Time Inc.).

b. Kevin and Monty in London.

c. On vacation in Italy, 1950. (Kevin McCarthy)

d. At Visconti's Costume Ball in Rome with Augusta Dabney and Kevin McCarthy.

e. After the Command Performance of *The Heiress* for King George VI in 1949. (Ethel McGinnis collection)

At Paestum, an old Greek colony south of Naples. (Kevin McCarthy)

the love scenes, one sees in him the potential of a grand romantic hero—full of erotic promise and seductiveness and charm. But his sex appeal is subtle and indirect—his sexuality has a poignance and a vulnerability, a "please don't hurt me" quality. He seems to be projecting his own value judgment on the act of love. Behind his beauty is a striving, a determination that keeps him from succumbing completely to narcissism. This inner tension makes Monty fascinating to watch. Sex isn't everything, he seems to say with his eyes, it's just a beginning.

22

Monty did not want to take Elizabeth Taylor to the premiere of *The Heiress* at Grauman's Chinese Theater in Hollywood. He hated crowds, the anxious perspiring autograph hounds who tore the buttons off his jacket if they got close enough. He hated having to kiss producers' wives. "Last time I went to a premiere in New York Mrs. So-and-so stuck her tongue in my mouth," he informed Max Youngstein.

Who was this Elizabeth Taylor anyway? He'd just come from spending the night in San Quentin's death house in preparation for *A Place in the Sun,* and he was preoccupied with the emotions of playing a condemned man, not a celebrity. All he knew about Elizabeth Taylor was that she was a gorgeous seventeen-year-old movie star who had recently made the statement, "I have the emotions of a child in a woman's body," and she had written a book about her pet chipmunk called *Nibbles and Me.*

He pleaded with Max Youngstein and Lew Wasserman to let him stay at his hotel and study the *Place* script with Mira Rostova in peace. But both men were adamant—he must go to the premiere. It was a command from Paramount, they said. He was the hottest property in Hollywood (he winced at the term), and since he and Taylor were about to play lovers in the Dreiser tragedy and the sex angle of the picture was going to be very much exploited, it was a natural publicity gimmick that they appear in public together.

A natural, Monty scoffed. Well, he didn't have a tuxedo. One was already rented, he was told. Angrily he made a last stipulation. His coach Mira Rostova must accompany them to the premiere. Youngstein agreed and quickly arranged to have one of his assistants go with Rostova as her escort.

The press agent Harvey Zim who went along on that evening recalls, "It started off a little like *Day of the Locust*—there was a kind of funny red color in the sky as if a fire had started in the hills or something. There was Mira Rostova sitting like a stone in the limousine's back seat. Her silence was ominous. There was Monty hung over—jittery—saying he had terrible stomach cramps."

As they drove along Sunset Boulevard, he insisted on stopping at a drive-in where he chomped on raw hamburger. Throughout the ride he fingered his lucky red dice as if they were worry beads.

The atmosphere brightened considerably as soon as Elizabeth Taylor joined them. "She looked ravishing, and she was so foul-mouthed and unconcerned about going to this premiere that everybody else relaxed in the limousine too."

Having been in the movies since the age of ten, Taylor was used to incessant promoting—she had lived virtually all of her life on public display. After she and Monty became close friends, she used to chide him for refusing to cooperate with media. "If you did, you'd not only be the biggest superstar in the world, you'd win an Oscar too," she said.

A block away from Grauman's Chinese Theater the press agent and Mira hopped out of the limousine and proceeded on foot so that "Liz and Monty could make a romantic entrance together." The crowd gawked and cheered as they marched up the red carpet and into the theater.

Once in his seat Monty confided he felt like crawling into a hole and covering his head with sand. He'd already seen his performance in *The Heiress,* he told Taylor, and he hated, loathed, and despised it; he proceeded then to explain why in detail.

Taylor shushed him—the movie unfolded on screen. Within minutes after his first scene with Olivia deHavilland she was whispering how wonderful he was, but he only muttered something inaudible, then began to shake beside her. At one point he took her hand and gripped it so hard she almost cried out in pain. He kept muttering, "I'm so awful, Bessie Mae. I'm so awful." But when the movie was over there were bravos and applause; as the lights went up people from all over the theater crowded around him, congratulating him, telling him how marvelous he was. He listened, writhing in his seat, and then jumped up, giving a hooting laugh. "Let's get out of here, Bessie Mae," he said, and he yanked her up the aisle.

"Why do you keep calling me Bessie Mae?" Taylor demanded after they had got into the limousine and were speeding off. "The whole world knows you as Elizabeth Taylor," he said, "only I can call you Bessie Mae." Monty gave nicknames, often silly ones, to people he felt a special affection for. Ned Smith was Smythe—"You're too much of an original to be called Smith," he said. Brooks was "Boof." Mira was "Mupa," the Russian for Mira.

On the way to William Wyler's party after the premiere, Monty continued his tirade against the movie and his performance. Later, Taylor told her mother she had never met anyone as complicated or "wound-up" as Montgomery Clift. He talked terribly fast—jumped from subject to subject—and smoked one Pall Mall after the other.

When they arrived at the Wylers', the mansion was ablaze with candles and fresh flowers. It was one of those splendid old-fashioned Hollywood parties. Music drifted through the rooms; the guests included David Niven, Gary Cooper, and David Selznick.

Once again Monty was surrounded by admirers—agents, producers, directors swarmed around congratulating him on his performance, wishing him well on *A Place in the Sun*. He moved from room to room with Taylor on his arm. One of the guests, Diana Lynn, recalled, "The combination of their beauty was staggering. Elizabeth was hypnotically beautiful—almost embarrassingly so. She was a perfect voluptuous little doll. And those great violet eyes fringed by double lashes. But there was an enigmatic power and magnetism behind her looks which gave her beauty—and his—a sultry depth. One could see her as goddess, mother, seductress, wife. One could see him as prince, saint, and madman."

That night Monty seemed properly inscrutable in his rented tux —except when he let loose with his wild hooting laugh. "What I remember—aside from his very disturbing cackle," Robert Ryan, who attended that party, said, "what I remember were his eyebrows. They seemed to dominate his face, and they would have been too fierce if it had not been for the hypnotic quality in his large dark eyes."

Although *The Heiress* failed at the box office, it was a success critically, and deHavilland won her second Academy Award for her performance. Bosley Crowther called Monty "vital and charming," but "a wee bit too glib, modern in his verbal inflections and attitudes." Other reviewers found him hard to understand; "he strangles his words," said one critic. But Howard Barnes in the *Herald Tribune* called Monty and deHavilland "superb." "Clift plays the suitor with immense conviction."

George Stevens, who had directed such movies as *Gunga Din*,

Woman of the Year, and *The More the Merrier,* had been working on *A Place in the Sun* since 1947. Stevens's doubts about the clumsy, sprawling structure of Dreiser's book had nothing to do with his belief that it was a fierce, profound indictment of America's false standards.

Dreiser, however, had objected violently to an earlier film version (made in 1931) because it protrayed his youthful and ambitious killer as a sex-starved drugstore cowboy, and he was not at all sure he would allow another movie to be made on *An American Tragedy* until Stevens convinced him he could do his novel justice.

He had to convince Paramount as well. Ever since the blacklist, all the major studios were terrified of doing anything that could be construed as un-American. Stevens's original script was rejected as being "too strong."

"I read that first version—so did Monty—it was superb," said Anne Revere, who played Monty's evangelist mother in the film. "They kept to the plot, which was based on an actual killing and subsequent trial in upstate New York. But the characters in this version made perfect sense. They were almost archetypal. The murderer (Monty) was more frankly ambitious—conniving. Liz Taylor's part was originally a rich, spoiled, mean bitch. Shelley Winters was actually lovable, and, as for the mother, there were some very powerful scenes which dramatized the influence she'd had on her son."

Miss Revere had not yet been blacklisted when she was cast in *A Place in the Sun.* (She wasn't blacklisted until 1951.) "But I was lucky to be in the picture at all. As it turned out, most of my big scenes were cut." Stevens kept toning the characters down, making them and the story more romantic. The title *An American Tragedy* was scratched, and before *A Place in the Sun* was chosen, the picture was called *The Lovers,* since Elizabeth Taylor and Montgomery Clift had been signed for the leads and Paramount was determined to build them up into a romantic, saleable legend.

Even with the sentimental overlay, critics would eventually call *A Place in the Sun* a vivid reflection of middle America's attitude towards money and social status. Stevens himself observed: "The greatness of *An American Tragedy* lies in the fact that it is all things to all people. . . . In the main this might have been the love story of any Johnny or Mary in America. . . . Dreiser was factual; a man of great compassion, a tremendous realist. . . . he made his central character, Clyde Griffiths [the name was changed to George Eastman for the film], one of the most fascinating and controversial figures in literature. You can spend weeks debating Clyde's guilt or innocence, his legal immorality over his spiritual immorality."

Having started in films as a cameraman at the age of seventeen (he directed over thirty Laurel and Hardy shorts before he was thirty, and he also worked as a gag writer), Stevens had a shrewd understanding of cinematic values. The *Place in the Sun* screenplay (written and rewritten by Harry Brown and Michael Wilson—later revised and rewritten by Stevens's close assistant, Ivan Moffat) was carefully designed to indicate exactly what the film would look like. The composition of scenes *flowed*. Stevens would visualize a shot of Taylor, seductive and infinitely beautiful, which would dissolve to Shelley Winters, hair in curlers, staring dejectedly at a row of mailboxes.

He said, "I'm one of those directors who believes every element that goes into a picture affects the viewer, although the viewer may not realize the impact of tiny minor things" (such as the soft playing of the radio on the windowsill during the Clift/Winters seduction scene, the repetition of fire and water images, the owl's eerie hooting on Loon Lake which punctuates several scenes before and after the murder).

The filming of *A Place in the Sun* proceeded in October 1949 almost without incident. The set was kept as quiet as a cathedral so that the actors could concentrate without being diverted in any way. The crew tiptoed about, moving props and scenery as if they were precious crystal. Most of the time between takes Stevens played music, "to keep the actors in the mood." He played, for the most part, Franz Waxman's score for *Sun,* mainly the "party theme."

A favorite ploy of Stevens's was to have Monty and Taylor or Monty and Winters run lines for him and then rehearse the scene without speaking—just looking at each other. "In such a way it becomes more powerful because you have to communicate your thoughts," Shelley Winters said. Stevens was always very conscious of creating a specific kind of energy from scene to scene.

Monty worked with such highly charged concentration and intensity as George that he would often finish a take drenched with sweat. "That's the worst part about acting," he told Elizabeth Taylor. "Your body doesn't know you're acting. It sweats and makes adrenalin just as though your emotions were real."

Throughout much of the filming he was tense and preoccupied. Believing Dreiser's tragic killer was essentially unsympathetic, he played him with his head cocked to one side and drawn back like a turtle. "He's the kind of a guy who has some charm, but basically he conceals and dissembles about everything," he said. "He's tacky and not that bright," Monty told Robert Ryan, "but he's overwhelmingly ambitious." Motivated by the passion to make money and make it big in society, George, Monty felt, was also a quintessential mama's boy. "He has no style, no sophistication." In the film, Monty demonstrates that when he makes his entrance into the big party where he meets Angela (Elizabeth Taylor), his ideal woman—the rich, spoiled, pampered woman he's dreamed about. Somebody asks him, "Are you having a good time?" and he answers with a perfect blend of shyness and hostility—"How should I know? I just got here."

With Mira Rostova at his side, Monty worked out every beat in every scene in restrained and poignant detail.

In almost all his movies, "Monty, like Garbo and Brando, had the extraordinary faculty for giving you a sense of danger," recalled Richard Burton. "You were never quite sure whether he would blow his lines or explode."

Before completing the interior scenes at Paramount Studios in Hollywood, *A Place in the Sun* shot for two weeks on location at Cascade Lake, Nevada, as well as Lake Tahoe. It was near the end of October; the Sierras were so cold that snow had to be hosed off the trees and melted from the ground before Monty and Elizabeth Taylor could shoot their scenes lakeside.

Most of Monty's free time was spent conferring with Mira Rostova or arguing over interpretation with George Stevens. Shepherd Strudwick, who played Taylor's father in the film, recalled, "Monty came over to me after a disagreement with Stevens, shaking his head wearily and saying, 'I'm right, I know I'm right, but it doesn't make any difference to them. I'm right and I'll keep saying I'm right.'"

He was referring to Shelley Winters' approach to her role. "She played it all wrong," he told Judy Balaban later. "She played her tragedy from the minute you see her on screen. She is downbeat, blubbery, irritating." (Earlier, Monty had fought to get Betsy Blair the part, believing her wistful, sweet quality was better than Winters' rattled pathos.)

He pleaded with Stevens to at least redirect Winters in the remaining scenes so that she would appear more sympathetic. If she was made more appealing it might also make the romance between himself and Taylor more bittersweet. Now, he said, the picture was very much off kilter.

Stevens told Monty he was being too sentimental. Alice Tripp, Winters' character, was *supposed* to be drab and pitiful, and Shelley Winters was being just that, and giving a marvelous performance (some say the best in her career).

Later, Stevens told the American Film Institute, "The thing that interested me most about *Place* was the relationship of opposing images. . . . Shelley Winters busting at the seams with sloppy melted ice cream . . . as against Elizabeth Taylor in a white gown with blue ribbons floating down from the sky. . . . Automatically there's an imbalance of images which creates drama."

Because he wanted such imbalance visually as well as emotionally, Stevens was hardest of all on Elizabeth Taylor, who'd never really acted before. He demanded constant retakes of her scenes with Monty, and when he couldn't get the results he wanted he would argue or bait her until Taylor, unused to criticism, flared up angrily.

She had just completed *The Big Hangover* with Van Johnson and was being costumed for *Father of the Bride* on weekends, so she felt under particular strain. Also, her mother, Sara Taylor, was chaperoning her so relentlessly, she could rarely be alone with Monty for whom she felt a growing attraction. Occasionally she would sneak into his dressing room, presumably to run lines with him while Mira Rostova held the script. But often she would lounge in a chair chewing gum loudly and complaining about her mother whom she called "a large pain in the ass."

Monty sympathized but he invariably changed the subject to *A Place in the Sun*. What did she think of George Stevens as a director? Why had she decided to play Angela Vickers and, more important, how did she see her as a character? Was she sweet, quiet, voluptuous, innocent?

"It was my first real chance to probe myself," Elizabeth Taylor wrote later, "and Monty helped me. . . . It was tricky because the girl is so rich and so spoiled it would have been easy to play her as absolutely vacuous, but I think she is a girl who cares a great deal."

Together they went over their roles, with Monty guiding her into the nuances, the objectives of the part. Angela wants George Eastman more than anything, he would say, but she is perfectly confident she will possess him—she is always confident. Just let the character unfold within you—keep thinking of this girl, and then she will suddenly grow and bloom in front of the camera.

Sometimes Monty would demonstrate by acting the part of Angela Vickers himself. He always had authority when he performed,

and when he mimed a woman, he could almost conjure up a smolder-
ing female essence. (Michael Billings, in his book, *The Modern
Actor,* says, "There is an androgynous bisexuality that underpins
great acting." During most of his career Monty made the most positive and creative use possible of his femininity.)

His commitment to his work "affected Elizabeth almost physically—like electric shocks," wrote her biographer Richard Shepherd.
"[Monty] gave of himself in a scene to such a degree that soon
she began to respond in kind and the chemistry they produced eventually illuminated the screen like heat lightning."

Their memorable first love scene (shot entirely in close-up with
a six-inch lens) is a record of how they responded to each other on
film. Taylor is achingly tender and maternal; Monty presents a tantalizing paradox of a cool facade hiding great inner passions.

Stevens rewrote the dialogue for that particular scene at two in
the morning. "I wanted the words to be rushed—staccato," he said.
"Monty had to let loose—he was so enormously moved by her. Elizabeth must be compelled to tell him how wonderful and exciting and
interesting he is all in the space of a few seconds. . . . Anyway, it
had to be like nothing they had ever said to anyone before."

When Stevens handed her the new dialogue, Elizabeth looked at
it and said, "Forgive me but what the hell is this?" Stevens told both
of them to memorize it, then they'd rehearse and shoot, but when
filming he wanted them to hurl the words at each other as fast and as
compulsively as possible.

"Elizabeth dissolved when she had to say 'tell Mama,'" Stevens
recalled. "She thought it was outrageous she had to say that—she was
jumping into a sophistication beyond her time." But Stevens insisted
on that phrase. He wanted to create a mood that was at once primitive and basic, "a kind of preordained meeting."

When he edited the scene he did not use a movieola. Instead he
set up two projectors and viewed the reels of Monty's close-ups and
Taylor's close-ups simultaneously on a projector screen which covered an entire wall, then spliced the film in such a way that the cameras seemed to roll from Monty's face to Taylor's face "thus creating a
tempo—with the thing in which as fast as it could be said it was said.
Monty had that kind of emotion—he got all steamed up," Stevens
said. Taylor dissolved when she looked at him and spoke. "I wanted
to get the feeling of them both being totally lost in each other."

What one finally sees on film is the almost jittery sensuality of the young lovers as they circle each other verbally, then swoon into a passionate embrace.

During the filming, Monty and Taylor became attached to one another. "The tenderness they expressed in *A Place in the Sun* is the kind of tenderness they felt for each other in real life," says Judy Balaban, a friend of both actors.

At Lake Tahoe, Monty played games, pretending to reject her sexually—telling her, "I'm too old for you—I'm an old man" (he was twenty-nine, she eighteen). But by the time they returned to Hollywood to complete the film there was no question that she aroused him more than any other woman ever had. He loved everything about her, he told photographer Blaine Waller. "And her tits! They are the most fantastic . . ."

Occasionally, when they were together, Monty would exclaim, "I've found my other half!" Elizabeth Taylor was very much like him —mercurial, secretive, enigmatic, warm, shy—and resembled him physically in ways his real twin, Ethel, did not. She had the same thick brows and perfect features, the same rather oddly hirsute body. (When Ted Davis met Elizabeth Taylor with Monty at the Plaza, he joked, "Give her a razor and shaving cream for her arms.") Monty, for his part, went monthly to an electrologist on West Fifty-seventh Street to have the thick pelt of hair removed from his shoulders and chest. ("In a bathing suit he looked like a monkey," Frank Taylor said.)

A Place in the Sun took over four months to finish. (Stevens shot over 400,000 feet of film.) They were still shooting over Christmas, and by then Monty's and Elizabeth's flirtation had ripened— some say into an actual affair. Once they were seen necking in the limousine going to and from Paramount Studios. "It was the one time Mrs. Taylor and that Russian lady didn't go along," said the chauffeur who drove them.

The gossip columnists had a field day, calling them "the magnificent lovebirds." Hedda Hopper predicted marriage. One columnist actually announced their upcoming wedding, forcing Monty to phone and demand a retraction. "We are just good friends," he said. (Later he howled at Elizabeth, "I never thought that phrase was actually used.")

One night they attended a big party Norman Mailer gave for himself after selling *The Naked and the Dead* to the movies. Shelley Winters and Marlon Brando accompanied them. "It was a fiasco of a party," Miss Winters recalled, "because Norman had invited *every-*

body in Hollywood both left and right, and you didn't do that in 1949. Adolph Menjou was there snubbing Charlie Chaplin. Bogart was giving Ginger Rogers the fish eye. Monty and Elizabeth and Marlon were very uncomfortable. So we left early." But they got caught in a driving rainstorm. Brando had lent somebody his raincoat and his car keys were in the coat, "so we all stood around in the parking lot getting soaked to the skin."

Monty could detach himself from everyone when he wanted to, and on the last days of *A Place in the Sun* he did just that, shutting himself off with Mira Rostova—speaking to no one, not even Elizabeth Taylor (who was hurt by his behavior). He was trying to prepare himself emotionally for the rigors of the death cell scenes, the first of which he played with his mother (Anne Revere) and the chaplain; the second, the good-bye scene with Elizabeth Taylor; and finally, walking "the last mile."

He and George Stevens argued incessantly over how to play the last seconds of the film. The director wanted him to conjure up some awesome, terrifying emotion in the final close-up. Monty argued that a man on his way to the electric chair has no expression—he is numbed, paralyzed, in a state of shock.

On January 20, 1950, in the midst of his arguments he wrote Brooks, who, after several careers, was now an actor.

> A half a day. Tomorrow I walk to the electric chair. No
> more dialogue. At last I can afford to collapse. Oy. Never
> thought this day would come. . . . I'm glad you're
> concentrated on what you're doing. Somehow if one is not
> being productive life becomes quite a travesty. But your
> talk of television is just a drop of the dissatisfaction you'll
> feel the farther on you go. In this country the arts are
> mixed up with a crock of people most of whom are just
> stretching the silver . . . a lot of craftsmen but no artists.

He labeled George Stevens a craftsman. He was bitterly disappointed in what he felt was his lack of flexibility, his lack of imagination in working with actors. "George preconceives everything through a viewfinder," he said.

So on the last day of shooting *Place* he refused to give Stevens the "big look" he wanted in the death cell. When the cameras rolled he gave him instead a look which reflects a special kind of agony. His mind and body appear to be floating elsewhere—as if he has punished himself physically and mentally until purged of superficiality. It is a peculiarly austere gaze, heightened by the harsh light of the prison cell.

23

As soon as shooting was finished on *A Place in the Sun,* Monty went to stay with Libby Holman at Treetops for a few days, then he flew to Acapulco with Mira, where he lay in the sun and baked away some of his exhaustion.

There were stacks of scripts waiting for him in New York, but he was refusing to do any more films for the time being. Before leaving Hollywood he had turned down in quick succession *The Girl on the Via Flaminia,* an untitled Howard Hawks film, *Shane,* and a Broadway production of *Hamlet,* in which Gertrude would have been played by Katharine Hepburn.

He wanted to finish *You Touched Me!* and he wrote to Kevin accordingly. (They were planning to meet in Paris in ten days; Kevin had just closed in *Death of a Salesman.*)

> Plans and provisions. Etc. We have Feb. and March
> to write and granted we turn out something we both like
> we have left a month in which to hire people have locations
> picked—I saw John Huston. . . . His father is going to
> Italy to play in *Quo Vadis.* . . . These carefully chosen art
> director, cameraman, cutter can save our lives AND
> deciding whether the film should have any director at all!
> I've come to a decision in my life—no more great men—so
> except for the two flesh payments [his other two pictures at
> Paramount] I expect to be doing just that. . . . it seems
> to me that you and I should have only one project is
> disgusting . . . the point is now we're FREE. During the
> shooting of A.T. I became much more aware of what goes

into the making of a film—before I never cared so I never asked—so I now feel with what I see that what I thought before was folly. True, people spend a year on a picture and arrive at next to nothing on our terms. . . . Stanley Kramer shoots a pic in 16 days works on it 2 months and it closes up but the results would embarrass us I think . . .

The McCarthys had never traveled extensively with Monty before, but in Paris that February 1950, they found him an ebullient and easy-going companion. It was their first trip to Europe so they trudged all over the city together.

Monty was recognized wherever he went. Once a small crowd followed him along the Champs Élysées. *Red River* and *The Search* had been big hits in Paris. Monty would let the crowd surround him and then he would say a few words in French before darting off to catch up with the McCarthys.

The traffic seemed exceedingly heavy in Paris that winter, especially at night, and to cope with it the police wore white capes and carried lighted night sticks to direct the lines of honking traffic. When he came back to New York, Monty told Pat Collinge he'd tried to steal one of those lighted night sticks for his nephew in Austin, Texas, but he'd found it impossible.

Together he and the McCarthys saw *Hamlet* with Gerard Philipe; they cheered a former factory worker, Yves Montand, a protégé of Piaf who was singing a series of ballads at L'Etoile, a popular vaudeville house. They also managed to get tickets through MCA for *Un Tramway Nommé Désir* at the Theatre Edward VIII. The Tennessee Williams play was a huge success in spite of critical pans. Cocteau had done a very free translation (adding Negro dancers who wafted in and out of the action). And the part of Blanche was played by the great comedienne Arletty. Her interpretation, Monty felt, was "crazier than either Jessica Tandy or Vivien Leigh."

Just before they left for Italy, Thornton Wilder took them to lunch. He had just read Simone de Beauvoir's *Second Sex,* which he had reservations about: "too literary—not enough genuine documentation about modern women." But he was much more interested in Jean Genet's *Journal du Voleur.* "It is unique in literature!" he exclaimed. "Genet writes about crime as easily, as effortlessly, as Conrad writes about the sea!"

Every so often Monty would disappear, saying he had parts of the city he wanted to discover on his own. Once he came back full of excitement because he'd found the Rue du Faubourg St. Honoré's open markets. "There are fantastic foods there—charcuterie, turkey pâté—barrels of fresh oysters. . . ."

"The only thing that bothered me about Monty then," Augusta remembers, was "that he was taking all sorts of pills. Red pills, green pills, blue pills, yellow pills." She did not know whether these pills were tranquilizers, diuretics, antidepressants, vitamins, or barbiturates. When she asked him he replied grandly they were all those things. Drugs made him feel better. They helped him sleep, lessened his allergies, increased his energy, and stopped his pain. He would still turn white and sweaty with an attack of colitis, and when this happened he would pop a few pills in his mouth and swallow them down with wine. "But he never looked to see what the pills were," she said.

In Rome they stayed at what Kevin considered a "dreary hotel," the Albergo Savoia, on the Via Ludovici, but Monty was amused by it because Mussolini had lived there for a while.

It was cold and damp in Rome but they would walk over to the nearby Via Veneto in the evenings, and would sit in the outdoor cafes sipping tiny cups of strong espresso, watching the crowds of late strollers.

Some of them recognized Monty as the cowboy in *Red River*. He was asked for his autograph. Occasionally too many paparazzi flashed cameras at him and then Monty would shout "Basta!" But he enjoyed the attention.

During the days they toured museums. "We have been wandering around Rome," Monty wrote Brooks on February 22, 1950. "Ours is the osmosis type of sightseeing which, of course, is aided by liquor consumption, spaghetti consumption, etc. Squeeze Augusta and you get fettucine with butter sauce. Squeeze Flip [the McCarthys' son] and you get the same thing with meat sauce. O! what an indulged existence. . . ."

During their stay, they ran into Tennessee Williams who invited them all on a carriage ride through the Borghese Gardens.

They also lunched with the Italian novelist Alberto Moravia and through Paramount's European head, Pilar Levi, they met director Luchino Visconti who, along with Fellini, De Sica and Rossellini, was a force in founding the influential neorealist school of postwar filmmakers. Visconti had just made a very controversial film called *La Terra Trema,* a three-hour fictional saga of an impoverished

Sicilian family. It was said to have been financed entirely by the Italian Communist Party.

Visconti had seen both *The Search* and *Red River;* he was anxious to talk at length with Monty and arranged a luncheon at his villa. "We had a marvelous meal," Kevin recalled, "but we seemed surrounded on all sides by gardens, dogs, and *objets d'art.*"

Later Visconti asked them to a big party. "It was a masked ball," Kevin remembered. "There were dozens of Roman noblemen wandering around in business suits with Halloween masks over their faces. Franco Zeffirelli, Visconti's young protégé, painted a beard on Monty's chin and gave him a turban. Monty resembled a high school magician."

By the middle of February, they were speeding down the Amalfi Drive. On the way they took dozens of pictures of the spectacular southern coast. They stopped off in Capri and Porto d'Ischia. They spent an entire day at Paestum; a strong wind whistled through the ruins the afternoon they were there, so Monty tied a scarf about his head like a gypsy. And Kevin snapped him doing an exultant little dance against one of the great battered pillars.

A few days later in Milan they sought out Vittorio De Sica, who was filming *Umberto D.* Monty admired De Sica's film *Shoeshine.* When he told him how overwhelmed he'd been by that artless study of two poor boys involved in postwar Rome's black market, the director replied he wished his fellow Italians had been as moved. The picture was not a success in Europe.

At the lunch break everybody moved to a trattoria for minestrone and thick bread, while De Sica held forth on gambling—his passion. He hoped someday to make a movie about gamblers, about one of those rich old lonely ladies who smoke and gamble all night in the casino. Gamblers feel their fortunes, their destinies are told in money, he said.

By the end of the meal, Monty and De Sica were embracing with promises they would work together someday. They did work together less than two years later, but it was not as comradely and pleasant as it had been at the trattoria; it was total disaster.

On their last stop—Florence—Kevin photographed Monty hanging out of his hotel window. He came dangerously close to falling into the Arno.

When he wasn't clowning around or buying presents for his family in the expensive leather shops along the Via Tornabuoni, he sat in the Piazza della Signoria writing postcards to Elizabeth Taylor. He'd received a number of letters from her during the trip, which he carefully kept in the pocket of his tweed jacket. Every so often he would take them out and reread them, one by one.

In early March, on the way back to New York on the liner *Queen Mary,* they sailed right into a hurricane. "Augusta got very seasick," Kevin recalled, "but Monty and I were out on the streaming deck and took pictures of the storm. The crew and even some of the passengers kept shouting at us to come inside before we were swept overboard. We did go inside but then Monty decided to open a porthole—which you're not supposed to do when there's a gale force wind. Of course, the porthole was locked, but Monty got somebody to open it. He could get anybody to do anything for him. Then he told me he was bored and he was going to hang out of the porthole over the waves. I told him, 'Don't be a fool!' and he said, 'Why not? And take a picture of me so you'll have a record of it, McCarthy,' so I took the picture and it was sort of a record, I suppose. I don't think anybody had ever dared hang out a porthole in mid-Atlantic in a hurricane before. But then Monty liked to dare. . . ."

In Europe, *You Touched Me!* was rarely mentioned; however, the minute they settled back in New York, Monty and Kevin plunged into a day-to-day routine of writing, attempting to turn the Windham-Williams play into a precise, colloquial scenario. "But we didn't want to lose the lyricism."

Most mornings, and often into the late afternoons, they worked in a borrowed apartment on East Fifty-fourth Street. Sometimes Arlene would type up what they'd written.

For the first time in their friendship they began fighting. "We had really fierce arguments," Kevin recalled, "arguments that would leave us shaken afterwards. Never have two such different sensibilities tried to collaborate. I was a bumpkin, a clod in comparison to Monty. He had so much taste and class, and he was funny in an offbeat kooky way. I'm into corny humor. Well, we'd get into blazing arguments about jokes: 'You think *that's* funny?' Monty would shout, and then I would put him down for his lack of understanding as to what I was getting at. We had one particularly violent argument over punctuation. Monty didn't like any kind of punctuation— periods, question marks, exclamation points—he thought they inhibited the actor. We really fought over that."

Sometimes, for no apparent reason, he would cry out to Kevin that he wanted to see the "inner circle of hell." He wanted to see and experience debauchery, depravity. He had been such a puritan, so disciplined, so intent on leading a pure life. But now he wanted to come to terms with ugliness. He wanted to "march through the Inferno and come out unscathed. He was confident he could do that," Kevin said.

Monty and Kevin were frequently interrupted by long-distance phone calls from Elizabeth Taylor in Hollywood, reporting on her romance with hotel heir Nicky Hilton. They were about to be engaged, she would inform him. Fine, Monty would say. During the next call she would announce, we are engaged and what do you have to say to that? And Monty would answer, "Nothing, Bessie Mae, except are you sure Nicky Hilton is the right man for you?"

As soon as he hung up he would dash off a letter to her, presumably elaborating on the subject.

The two of them kept up a frantic correspondence until her wedding day in May of 1950. Until that time, one friend insisted, she kept pleading with Monty to marry her so she wouldn't have to marry Nicky Hilton. "Elizabeth's prime objective in life was to find a husband. It is still her prime objective." More often than not after a phone call from Taylor, Monty would pour himself a big beaker of Jack Daniels with lots of ice and gulp it down.

In late April, *The Big Lift* opened at the Rivoli to disappointing reviews. The movie was criticized for being a "hodgepodge of impressions about the Berlin airlift." Otis Guernsey, Jr., in the *Tribune* said, "Douglas and Clift have color . . . but the script tends to stay too close to the slangy G.I. Joe. . . ."

That June a disappointed Monty and Kevin went up to Brooksville, Maine, and stayed at the Swensons' to finish the script of *You Touched Me!* They also scouted for location sites. Then, after completing a final draft in July, they flew to Hollywood and tried to find a producer.

They rented a suite at the Hotel Élysée, sending out dozens of copies of the script, hanging on the phone making appointments to discuss the project with all the major studios. But nobody was interested. "We had no luck," Kevin said. "The only positive reaction—it reminded some people of Marcel Pagnol. Everybody thought the script was humane and loving but fanciful—meaning it wouldn't make any money. I remember Lew Wasserman telling us you gotta throw out the first forty pages of dialogue, which we thought were beautiful, and get right to the story."

Their main problem was they had no idea how to operate. "In those days an actor—even as big a star as Montgomery Clift—didn't go around hat in hand with an original far-out script. Orson Welles was the one guy who'd had savvy enough to pull it off with *Citizen Kane*. We were babes in the woods. Now stars like Robert Redford and Warren Beatty produce their own movies brilliantly sometimes, but even they take a long time to do it."

While they were in California, Kevin began hearing unflattering stories about himself and Monty—"about how I hadn't written any of the script—about how Monty was carrying me careerwise."

Then he returned to New York and went up for a movie at 20th Century-Fox. Henry Hathaway, who was to direct the picture, interviewed him, then had him read a couple of scenes from the script.

"In the middle of the audition Hathaway stopped me with 'You act exactly like Monty Clift.' I said, 'That's funny, because Monty's mother always accuses Monty of copying my style for his role in *The Search*,' and Hathaway retorted, 'Tough shit, kid, he got there first. You better stop shackin' with him. It isn't doing you any good.' I'm sitting there at the 20th Century-Fox offices on Fifty-sixth Street and Tenth Avenue, and I looked at him stunned and said, 'What the hell are you talking about?' and he said, 'Everybody in Hollywood thinks that!' and I said, 'You're not serious?' and he said, 'I am. Do yourself a favor. Lose that guy.' Here I was with a life to think about and a career to think about, and I couldn't believe what I was hearing. It was totally untrue. Monty and I had never had a homosexual relationship—we had a man-to-man relationship—I never had a clue he was gay all those years. If he was gay. Later I was reproached for not having my eyes open, for not being aware. Monty had a great many young men friends, and I remember Mira saying around this time, 'Don't you see all those young men?' and I said, 'So what? Monty is a famous actor, a movie star, he has a lot of admirers.' And Mira said, 'They are the wrong kind of admirers.'"

In August, Monty flew to London for the command performance of *The Heiress*. He was deluged by fans wherever he went; some even hid in the hall near his suite at the Connaught. The phone never stopped ringing. Tennessee Williams begged him to star in *Summer and Smoke* in the movies. The producer Binky Beaumont asked him to tea. Leland Hayward called from Paris and set up a cocktail date so Monty could meet his new wife Slim. The high point, of course, was a scheduled dinner with the Laurence Oliviers.

And then, before *The Heiress* was screened for a very select Mayfair audience, Monty was presented to the Queen. He wrote to Ned Smith, "There I was standing in line next to Ty Power and Jimmy Stewart. We were all in white tie and tails, top hats, canes—you never saw anything like us!" And to Kevin he wrote, "I feel like a pasha!" It was part of Sunny's dream come true—he had become an important world figure—acclaimed, famous, rich—clearly being a movie star wasn't all bad—he enjoyed the limousines, the bowing and scraping. Marlene Dietrich and Noël Coward called him "Monty darling," and they didn't even know him. Being famous is like belonging to an exclusive club, he told Pat Collinge.

After the command performance he flew to Italy to do more publicity. At a press conference in some drafty old palace ballroom near the Forum, he was introduced to a chubby Roman journalist named Giuseppe Perrone. "Reporters from all over Europe were talking very fast, asking questions in French, Italian, and German about *Red River* and what is Elizabeth Taylor like?" Perrone recalled. "Monty had a translator but some of the questions got garbled. He was very good natured about it, but finally after about an hour he begged off, and that's when we got into a conversation."

Perrone, then twenty-seven, wrote a gossip column called "Roman Hollywood" for *Il Progresso*. "Monty and I hit it right off. We talked movies—mainly European movies like *Shoeshine* and *Open City* which he'd been very impressed with—then he asked me to have dinner with him at his hotel."

He was staying at the Hassler. After they ate, they went up to his suite for brandy, and Monty impulsively brought out some letters from Elizabeth Taylor. They were still corresponding. "He let me read some of her letters," Perrone recalled. "And one he was composing to her. They both sounded childlike and innocent. Monty called Taylor his 'ideal woman.' He spoke of her as his 'twin.' 'We are so much alike it's *fan*tastic!' he said. They'd both been child actors; they'd never really been kids, he said—no fantasy life—no games or fun. . . . He seemed upset about Taylor's marriage to Nicky Hilton but he didn't think it would last. "Suddenly, there's a knock on the door," Perrone continued, "and a bunch of roses is delivered to him. He laughs a strained, choking laugh. Right after that a blonde appears at the door clad only in a robe—she is naked underneath—and offers herself to him. He gets very embarrassed—pushes her out of there bodily—slams the door shut, then runs into the bedroom. I can hear him yelling angrily on the phone something about 'my private life is my private life if I wanna fuck a goat I ought to be able to—this is fascist-Nazi tactics—who the hell do they think they are?' Then he comes back into the living room trying to be calm and polite. But after another drink he starts pouring out his anguish to me about how all this was a publicity gimmick. The girl had been a setup—Paramount was doing this to make him seem like a virile he-man of an actor. Jesus Christ! He was livid with rage. I assured him I would never write about what had happened, and he was all over me with thanks. Then we got very drunk together."

Monty and Perrone dined together again during his stay in Rome. "We went to some little restaurants on the Via Condotti or to my parents' apartment. My mother and father loved Monty. He was so kind and interested in them as people."

Whenever he was with the Perrones he would play with his little red dice, shake them in his clenched fist—worry them in his hand. Before he made any kind of decision he would throw them out on the table.

The last time he saw him, Monty gave Perrone one of the dice. "It'll bring you luck," he said. Perrone says he believes it did—he is now a successful lawyer and producer. "But I don't think that remaining one of the dice brought Monty good fortune. He seemed so unhappy when I knew him."

Monty was supposed to do more publicity in Milan and Paris, but Libby Holman's son Topper was killed in a mountain climbing accident on Mt. Whitney. Without consulting Paramount, he immediately left Italy and flew back to New York to be with her.

24

Since they lived less than a block away from each other on East Sixty-first Street, it was easy for Monty and Libby Holman to see each other almost every day. If they didn't, they stayed on the phone for hours, Monty doing most of the talking. He tried very hard to cheer her up while she stayed in seclusion mourning the death of her son.

He would tell her about the ballets and plays he'd seen. He'd loved *Member of the Wedding* and Arthur Miller's controversial version of Ibsen's *Enemy of the People*. The night he'd gone liberals and conservatives argued loudly at one another during the performance; the play was frightening audiences since it seemed to reflect the ugly repressiveness of Senator Joseph McCarthy.

On his own, however—by himself and not working—Monty was restless. He wandered around the city during the day—over to Forty-second Street to see a second-run movie or to the latest exhibit at the Modern Museum.

He was very careful about "cruising"; he tended to avoid the obvious homosexual hangouts. The risks of exposure, blackmail, and entrapment were too great. The search for sexual partners was discreet and usually done through friends and at parties.

Usually he could be seen sauntering down Lexington Avenue past Bloomingdale's to the fruit and vegetable stand on Fifty-eighth Street. He haunted the Dover Delicatessen, often charging huge orders of imported canned goods to be sent back to his apartment where Arline waited, typing up his correspondence, answering his ever-ringing phone. "She was still hopelessly in love with him," said a friend.

A couple of times a week he would drop by MCA at 575 Madison Avenue. Whenever he appeared on the sixth floor the secretaries would blush and giggle, but he would ignore them and shoot into Jay Kantor's office to begin arguing over the latest batch of scripts.

He was being offered everything—more than Brando because "Monty seemed less *extreme* than Brando," agent Edie Van Cleve said. He was offered movies in CinemaScope and 3-D; he was offered westerns, melodramas, mysteries, war pictures, spy thrillers. "But everything is crap!" he would explode.

He had to experiment, he would say—he had to meet and create new challenges for himself, but when he tried explaining further "how the audience is my barometer . . . how I always ask myself when I read something, 'Will the audience like what I'm doing; will the audience respond to this character, believe in this story, be interested, care?'" the producers and the agents would often look at him blankly.

"They act threatened when I say I must *care* about what I do," he confided to Brooks. "Sometimes when I'm up at MCA I think all those little men in their identical black suits care about is *profits*—and you know some of them seem to hate my fuckin' guts?"

He talked about losing his optimism, and he was in a despairing mood the night Norman Mailer called and asked him to come to a party at Vance Bourjaily's. "It's for Jimmy Jones," he said.

Monty rarely went to parties—he disliked parties full of strangers—and he didn't enjoy being fussed over as a celebrity. Mailer assured him he could just get "bombed very privately," so he hopped a cab and went to the Village.

Bourjaily's apartment was crowded when he arrived. Bill Styron was there and Marshall Allen, his very rich friend and benefactor; so was Betty Ford, the lady bull fighter, and her husband, actor David Ford; so were novelist Chandler Brossard and Philip Harrington, one of *Look*'s biggest photographers.

Almost everybody was trying to talk to guest of honor James Jones. The burly crew-cut novelist sported Italian silver jewelry on his wrists; he wore blue jeans and puffed on a big cigar. "It wasn't a very good party," he recalled, "even though it was for me. A lot of New York literary types standin' around talkin' self-consciously about their advances and the books they were gonna write—Norman began arguing away, as always, arguin' to win—suddenly I see this haunted face kinda floatin' through the cigarette smoke and noise and I think, Jesus H! It's Monty Clift!"

Jones introduced himself; the two of them went into a corner "and we got pretty loaded." Around midnight, "we decided the party was so boring we had to leave." Which they did, accompanied by Mailer and Styron. "For a while we walked around in a kinda circle— I think we ended up at some Irish bar where Monty knew the bartender."

They continued to drink until the place closed. "We got into a big discussion about *From Here to Eternity*." Jones had just sold his best-selling novel about corruption in the U.S. Army before Pearl Harbor to Columbia for $82,000. "I'd like you to play Prewitt," he recalls telling Monty.

"Monty got all excited—he *loved* the idea. I told him Harry Cohn wanted John Derek for the part, but that *I* didn't want him. 'But can I play a fighter?' Monty wanted to know. I told him he sure as hell could!"

After that night, the two men kept in touch by phone and postcard, and Monty eventually visited Jones in Tucson and in Ohio. Shortly after he was signed for the part, he began studying Jones, questioning and free-associating with the novelist.

"All my girlfriends said Monty Clift acted just like me in *From Here to Eternity*," James Jones said.

Monty never stopped studying people. He had a favorite bar, Gregory's, no longer in existence, on Lexington Avenue and Fifty-fourth Street, where he would go and watch people drift in and out— the winos and the pimps and the middle-aged divorcées who coughed into their drinks and the college kids getting high on Scotch and ginger ale and the serious alcoholics . . . .

Gregory's was a dark, dingy place with wooden booths to the right of the bar—there was a jukebox near the wall telephone; it smelled perpetually of beer and fried steak grease. But nobody ever bothered Monty when he came in, so he took to dropping by almost every afternoon in 1950 and 1951. He would invariably start drinking Scotch at the bar with old Max, the owner of the Dover Delicatessen, and they would discuss baseball or what was happening in Korea.

By evening Monty would have moved to a booth to be joined by Kevin McCarthy, nineteen-year-old photographer Blaine Waller, and, on occasion, Elizabeth Taylor, who had left Nicky Hilton and wanted a divorce.

Taking a break with Elizabeth Taylor during the filming of *A Place in the Sun*.
(Peter Stackpole, © Time Inc.)

As Private Robert E. Lee Prewitt in *From Here to Eternity*. (Culver Pictures)

a. With Donna Reed.

b. With Frank Sinatra, who played Angelo Maggio.

c. Prewitt goaded into fighting.

a   b

On location in Kentucky for *Raintree County*.

With Elizabeth Taylor in *Raintree County* ▶ before the accident.

Monty's car directly after the accident.
At right Kevin McCarthy tries to tell police what happened.

"She wanted to marry Monty—she was very much in love with him," Blaine Waller recalled. "He would bring her into Gregory's and introduce her as Bessie Mae. She wore an awful lot of makeup, she smoked like a fiend, and used more four-letter words than any of us put together, and boy was she gorgeous! I have never seen anybody as beautiful. She was supposed to be staying at the Waldorf, but she was actually staying at Monty's place. He didn't bring her into Gregory's too much, mostly they were by themselves—they were very private."

Monty did bring Elizabeth to dinner at his parents' apartment. "For someone so beautiful, Elizabeth Taylor seemed to have a huge inferiority complex." Waller went on, "Monty seemed to be one of the few people who could actually break through her facade and relate to her."

Sunny Clift recalled, "Elizabeth was very sweet. And very much in love with Monty. She was basically a decent young woman. When she got a raise at Metro—or a new contract—she'd give her father a new car even if she'd given him a new car six months before. She'd never been given the chance to be good. To be a good actress or to be good at anything else. She'd been pushed into being a movie star from the time she was six years old. She never had a chance to find out what *she* wanted to do—or how to assert herself. Everything was done for her. She was very generous—thoughtful. She sent me the most beautiful flowers. Still does. But I think at that point in her life she was starting to realize what her parents and what MGM had done to her. She once said, 'I've never had a chance to even breathe for myself.' Monty tried to get her to act more natural. She'd been raised in such an artificial atmosphere—such a hothouse environment. She'd never carried money—never taken a walk by herself."

Once when she was with Mrs. Clift she blurted, "I never want to see my parents again!"

Monty also would take Elizabeth to Camillo's Restaurant, one of his favorite Italian restaurants. They would sit in the back very quietly and talk till the place closed. One night they remained until long after the last customer had left. The owner, Lawton Carver, suddenly got an urge to paint the dining room, so he came over to their table and said, "You kids just sit there if you want; I'm going to paint."

To his surprise Monty and Elizabeth took off their shoes, picked up brushes and proceeded to paint the walls. They stayed till three in the morning, Carver said. "We had an awful good time talking and painting up a storm."

Before Elizabeth went back to California, she and Monty discussed marriage again. "He seriously considered it," Blaine Waller said. "He alluded to it often enough and he wanted kids. But anyhow, he finally decided against it."

"Monty wasn't the kind of man who should be married," his mother said. "He was too involved with his career."

And with his drinking. It had become such a problem by November of 1950 that Monty finally went to see Dr. Ruth Fox, a New York psychiatrist who specialized in treating alcoholics. Dr. Fox recalls, "When Monty came to see me he said he didn't want to stop drinking—no alcoholic ever does—all he wanted me to do was to help him control it because he was getting into so much trouble."

Dr. Fox treated him on and off for several months and she got him into group therapy. "Everybody was so excited at having Montgomery Clift in group—he talked about his problem with liquor and the others in the group urged him to join A.A." For a while Monty attended A.A. meetings but then he stopped. He kept on with his weekly sessions with Dr. Fox and she said, "Monty told me he thought he was a homosexual and he wanted to know how to deal with it."

Dr. Fox went on: "While he was with me he stayed sober for an entire month. He was so grateful. He had a terrible lack of self-esteem for someone who was such an achiever. He would go off on terrible secret benders. Much of the time he seemed in acute distress almost close to a mental collapse. One morning around 6 A.M. my bell rang, and when I opened the door Monty literally fell at my feet dead drunk."

Dr. Fox got him into Neurological Center at Columbia-Presbyterian Hospital and had him detoxified. But by that time she decided he was so complicated and had so many emotional problems her therapy wasn't helping. She decided he should go into analysis so he could find out why he drank.

After he left the hospital she sent him to her former analyst, Dr. William Silverberg. "I considered Silverberg a very liberal, enlightened guy as far as drinking was concerned." Most of the medical profession believed that drinking was caused by a "weakness of will." But Silverberg had first-hand knowledge of alcoholism—his secretary, Ed Shipley, was an alcoholic who had just joined A.A.

William V. Silverberg, at age forty-nine a unique figure in New York psychoanalytic circles, became one of the most controversial people in Monty's life. Known as a brilliant teacher of analysts, a neo-Freudian and an innovator of psychiatric techniques (in his paper "On the Origins of Neurosis" he introduced the concept of effective aggression—the ability to achieve what one wishes to achieve regardless of the obstacles), Silverberg helped found, along with Karen Horney, the Association for the Advancement of Psychiatry. His greatest contribution, according to his colleagues, was his insistence on the development of a three-year graduate course at New York Medical College, said to be the first psychoanalytic training program attached to a medical school.

Friends called him Billy; Monty called him Billy, too. To friends and patients alike, his rosy cheeks and cherubic smile belied an almost frosty remoteness. He had a biting sense of humor and a boundless curiosity about people, as well as a vast fund of knowledge which ranged from horse races to Beethoven to the best recipe for cheese soup.

His spacious apartment overlooking Central Park West served as both office and home. Divorced, with two teenage sons, he shared these quarters with Ed Shipley, his secretary-companion for over twenty-five years.

In psychiatric circles Silverberg was known to be a homosexual. "It was taken for granted," Dr. Fox said, "but it was rarely discussed. I sent a great many artists-writers to Billy for consultation. They would always phone me afterwards and say, 'Why he's one of us.'"

Silverberg was a close colleague of Harry Stack Sullivan, whose theory focused on interpersonal relations as the main determinant of the psyche. Sullivan called his own homosexuality the tragedy of his life. He believed one cannot evolve fully if one remains homosexual. However, he also believed it was better to accept and confront one's homosexuality than suppress it. One assumes that Silverberg believed this, too.

Monty began seeing Silverberg every day. Dr. Richard Robertiello, who was first a patient, then a student of Silverberg's, had the session after Monty in 1950 and 1951. "I remember Montgomery Clift walking slowly out into the waiting room. He had the most intensely tormented expression of anyone I'd ever seen."

Nevertheless, at first Monty seemed enthusiastic about his analysis and he was soon hero-worshipping Silverberg as he hero-worshipped Thornton Wilder. "Billy is so learned, so erudite!" he would say. "He knows all about music, art and science, and he thinks having relationships with different people shapes your life."

Possibly Monty felt emotionally drawn to the remote and courtly doctor because he bore a physical resemblance to his father, Bill Clift. In any event Monty would come back from a session and describe what happened to Mira. He told her how he would lounge in a chair facing Silverberg, or lie on the floor (still his favorite posture), and he would talk about whatever came to mind. He soon began to see how much he was suppressing in his subconscious.

"Silverberg told him his adolescence had been too passive, that he had never had a real childhood," Mira said. This may have been the reason Monty began hanging out in bars, getting into fights, trying to act aggressive.

He also free-associated about his mother to Silverberg. He admired her valiant struggle to survive and better herself—he was in awe of her strength of will. What bothered him was her obsessive need to control other people's lives, including his own. Currently she was attempting to oversee the life of her grandchild Suzanne, Brooks's oldest daughter, who lived in Boston. "If she has her way she'll present her at Versailles!" he cried. And then he would flash back to his own past, recalling the countless instances where she'd interfered with *his* relationships, shattered *his* privacy, attempted to dominate *his* thoughts, *his* very impulses. All in the guise of "doing what's best for you."

As his analysis progressed Monty's drinking increased. His moods became more manic—he was hostile to his friends; he actively pursued women.

He kept having his phone number changed to prevent the increasing number of strange calls. Lately there had been threats of blackmail too—from people who imagined he was a homosexual and said they had seen him at the old Bickford's all-night gay cafeteria on Fifty-first Street and Lexington Avenue, gazing into the mirror waiting to be picked up.

He was suffering more than ever from insomnia, but he wanted to get off barbiturates and away from their deadening effect. However, he always carried a collection of vitamins, phenobarbitals, Tuinals, Nembutals, and Seconals in his jacket pocket.

"I just want some sleep," he would tell Max Youngstein. Then he blurted out: "How can you tell whether you're a homosexual?" He'd had relationships with both men and women. He enjoyed both, he didn't know *what* he was. Youngstein urged him to seek therapy. "He didn't tell me he was already seeing someone."

To some people Monty referred to Silverberg as "Victor"; and he usually denied that he was in analysis. He felt self-conscious about admitting it; in 1950 being psychoanalyzed was considered daring, unorthodox; it implied guilt, personal failure, and emotional disturbance. Sunny Clift was horrified when she found out: "What a total waste of money."

Monty paid Silverberg for his sessions whether he went to him or not. If he was on location for a movie he might not see the doctor for three or four months, but he insisted his lawyer pay his weekly fee of $150 "to keep my hour mine," he would say. Monty continued seeing Silverberg for over fourteen years; the money added up.

Only once during 1950 and 1951 did he confide to Max Youngstein that he was afraid his analyst might be a queer—wasn't that a bad thing? Should he stay with this doctor? He liked him, he didn't like him, Youngstein recalled. He kept repeating that he didn't want to turn totally queer—he felt he could go either way. Should he remain with this doctor? "I told him, 'Make up your own mind, Monty.' He was in obvious torment about it. A couple of times he showed up at my apartment in despair—my wife would let him in. We never asked him what was bothering him—he would just pass out on our living room couch and go to sleep."

When Elizabeth Taylor flew back to Los Angeles to start divorce proceedings, Monty went to Nassau and joined Barney Balaban and his family at their hotel.

Monty revered Balaban, the tough-talking energetic sixty-five-year-old president of Paramount Pictures. "Daddy was *heimish*—warm—outgoing, he had gusto," his daughter Judy said.

Before going to Hollywood, Balaban had built up a highly lucrative movie theater chain throughout the Midwest in the 1930s. Since then he had, along with Cohn, Zanuck, Skouras, and the Schenck brothers, virtually run the motion picture business. He worked out of New York, where he lived with his family at the St. Mortiz hotel, walking distance from the Paramount Building on Times Square. On weekends, he stayed at his estate in Westchester.

Until Monty, he had never socialized with "the talent," as he called actors. "But Montgomery Clift became an exception to the rule," Judy said. "We started hearing about Monty after he and Daddy spoke at a United Jewish Appeal fund raiser. Daddy was profoundly impressed with Monty's feelings about Israel. After that fund-raiser they started meeting to talk about Israel and God knows what else. All of a sudden we started hearing about this Montgomery Clift—this phenomenal human being who had so much charm and erudition. Frankly, I didn't think such a perfect person could exist."

Judy Balaban was then sixteen, a beautiful wisecracking redhead. "I was very rebellious. I had gone to Nassau to be with my boyfriend whom my parents disapproved of, so they went along as chaperons. They invited Monty along."

She and Monty met in the hotel bar around three in the afternoon, "right after we got off the plane. My parents went off to rest—we stayed in the bar for a while, then went back to my room where we started talking about everything under the sun. I remember we got into this long discussion about astrological signs. We were both Libras, which was an immediate bond between us. We talked about Libra characteristics. You know, how Libras hate to be rude? Libras seem good-natured and pleasant, but they won't let anyone tell them what to do. Libras are supposed to be bright, but they're also very gullible. Well, Monty confided as to how the inconsistencies in his nature maddened and baffled him. I said I felt the same way. We started roaring with laughter. Then I looked at my watch. It was eight-thirty at night. We were supposed to be meeting my parents in the dining room and we hadn't even unpacked."

After that evening Judy and Monty spent most of their time together swimming, playing tennis, walking on the beach, while Judy's boyfriend sulked. Then came a night "like out of a B movie. Monty and I were on the hotel terrace staring up at the moon, and my boyfriend—my ex-boyfriend, really—comes up, very jealous and bombed out of his mind. He and Monty have words—they almost got into a fight. After that fight I was with Monty permanently."

The Balabans left Nassau after a week and went on to Palm Beach secure in the knowledge that Judy was being chaperoned by Montgomery Clift. "They considered me a silly kid and Monty was an older man—a family friend."

In late January, Elizabeth Taylor obtained her divorce. She saw Monty again in New York before flying to London to begin filming *Ivanhoe*. They continued to correspond and to talk regularly on transatlantic phone.

Even so—as far as Judy was concerned, "Monty and I were going together. We hung out at Gregory's—with Blaine. We went to movies, to jazz joints like Condon's. I was in love. I was deliriously happy.

"One night my father took us to dinner at Larue. Suddenly it dawned on him that Monty was not just a family friend, my chaperon. He was emotionally involved with me, and I was emotionally involved with him. Daddy got furious. After that dinner he never spoke with Monty again. Oh, they had little conversations, but cool, abrupt ones. Monty was traumatized by this—he had looked up to my father, admired him enormously. But Daddy simply could not approve of our relationship. Number one, Monty was an actor, number two, he wasn't Jewish, and number three, he was 'older.' Monty tried talking to Daddy about it, but he got nowhere with him and this was very upsetting to both of us. We used to spend hours figuring out how we should talk to my father—how we could persuade him that it was okay—that we were happy with each other—that we were good for each other. . . ."

The tension didn't prevent Monty and Judy from having a marvelous time together, however. "*Fan*tastic! as Monty would say. We would walk through Central Park—have picnics there, read Salinger to each other—we'd drive out to Jones Beach . . . and we'd take cabs. We'd get into a taxi and Monty would say expansively, 'Drive all over the city,' and the driver would glare at him, 'What d'ya mean, drive all over the city, bud?' and Monty would glare back. 'Look, if you don't know what drive all over the city means, who does?' Then we'd collapse with laughter."

They drove up to Palisades Park—they drove down to Wall Street and explored Chinatown and the Battery. "Monty had the gift of making life larger and more vivid," Judy said. "I saw more with Monty."

They spent part of each day at Gregory's, usually with Blaine Waller. "First there would be a round robin of phone calls in the morning," Blaine said. "Monty to Judy, Judy to me, me to Monty—we'd plan all sorts of things to do and end up at Gregory's. Monty invariably paid for all the drinks and food. He was very generous—he seemed to really want to do it."

Brooks would drop by with Kim Stanley, and Roddy McDowall, too, frequently joined them, with his roommate, Merv Griffin, who was singing with Freddie Martin's orchestra.

"Monty didn't approve of Merv—he spoke of him contemptuously as 'that band singer.' And Merv sensed this. Once they got into a wild pie-throwing fight," Blaine said. "It's funny, Monty could really be shitty—not at all nice to someone he didn't dig. This was the first time I realized I had to separate his artistic life from his private life—he was a great actor, but it didn't mean he was always a great person—not by a long shot."

Usually when hostility arose among the group, Roddy McDowall would save the day by telling some hilarious anecdote. "He was one of the funniest people I've ever met," Blaine Waller said. "We would actually fall on the floor laughing at him."

But there were serious discussions too, with Monty as the catalyst. They all knew he was a presence—somebody a little freaky and difficult, but very special. His concentration was intense, almost palpable when he talked to them. "He had a tremendous effect on all of us, Roddy—Blaine, me, even Elizabeth," Judy said. "We used to talk about it later. He was like a father confessor, a teacher. We looked up to him. We were still kids—barely twenty; he was thirty—he called himself an old man. He had enormous perceptions about all of us. He'd seem to talk almost nonsensically—mystically—about our drives, our instincts, our urges, and then zap! he'd make a point as clear as glass. He talked a lot about how we should learn to live in the present, how we should gamble with energies, our talents—and most of all how we should accept ourselves as we were. 'Don't conform,' he'd say. . . ."

He could not follow his own advice. He was as guilty as ever over his hidden homosexual involvements. Most of them were short-lived and tempestuous, but he did have one regular lover, a young movie actor who had moved to New York to be closer to him.

Monty occasionally appeared in public with Judy Balaban and this young actor. "I never thought anything of it," Judy said. "Of course I was eighteen and it was 1950. I assumed they were just friends."

Judy said she was so naive and so in love with Monty she rarely thought about Monty's "separateness. I knew he was different. I knew he was deeply unhappy about something. He drank too much. I tried to get him to talk about what was bothering him when we were alone together, but he never would."

She recalled the weekend they spent at Richard Avedon's in East Hampton. "We had a chance to sleep in separate bedrooms or together. Monty said I should make the choice. We shared a bedroom that weekend."

Judy described their affair as "tender and beautiful," but many other women say he was a passive lover and often impotent. He needed constant sexual reassurance, and he was able to get that from men more easily than women. According to Ben Bagley, Monty had a small penis and was extremely embarrassed about it.

"He talked about it all the time to me," said record producer Bagley. "I think it was the secret tragedy of his life. A lot of homosexuals gossiped about Monty's problem because gays put great importance on the size of their cocks."

In the unexpurgated version of Kenneth Anger's *Hollywood Babylon,* Monty is called "Princess Tiny Meat." When he got a copy of the book he hooted, "Jesus H. Christ! is nothing sacred?" and he had his lawyer see to it that in subsequent editions of the book the reference was cut.

Back in 1951, Monty had not yet experienced much brutality or coarseness in his personal relationships, and he still had the capacity for astonishment, for joy. "He was such an organizer, such a do-gooder for his friends," Mira said, and she told how he would drive Thornton Wilder five hours to see a specialist for his back trouble, how he would plan special outings for Roddy McDowall and herself so they could all take photographs when the light was just so.

He wanted everybody to like him, but sometimes his generosity of spirit backfired. Mira recalled how he impulsively befriended the superintendent of her apartment building, "a really unpleasant, disreputable fellow." Monty began hanging out with him, buying him drinks at Gregory's, listening to his problems. The super eventually reciprocated by asking him to a beer blast in Queens. Monty turned the invitation down, and the super got furious. "Really mean," Mira said. "Monty couldn't understand it. I reminded him how he was always talking about being selective."

"He was constantly talking about choices," Judy Balaban said. "He taught me the positive use of the word discriminating. He said the word usually has a sense of ugliness about it, but it can be an important and positive addition to your vocabulary because it means being *selective,* it means making choices, which is what life is all about. It has to do with forming values, deciding whether this is a loving thing or a hateful thing."

He was trying to make choices himself. He still read almost every script that came to him—he still searched diligently for something new and fine to do.

He told Pat Collinge he sensed that most of the producers and directors he met felt insecure with him because he had so many ideas and opinions of his own. This may have made him drink more, Miss

Collinge recalled, "but when I said I was worried about his heavy drinking, he laughed and told me it wasn't a problem."

In July, Monty went up to Ogunquit in Maine, where his analyst, Dr. Silverberg, had a summer home, and he continued his sessions. Once he attended a musicale at Silverberg's, accompanied by Libby Holman, but mainly he didn't socialize with the doctor that summer. He stayed in a motel, and only saw him for his fifty minutes.

Back in New York, friends like the McCarthys were shocked that Monty would visit his analyst on vacation—"It sounded unorthodox, and it didn't seem to be helping his drinking," Kevin recalls. When he came back from Maine, "he was drinking more than ever, and he seemed more depressed." (Dr. Robertiello, Silverberg's former patient and student, said, "Silverberg was non-interfering—as most analysts were during that period. He never tried to direct a patient. Also, no alcoholic has ever been cured by an analyst; the process of analysis is to bring conflicts and anxieties to the surface. Drinking represses both.")

At the beginning of the summer, screenings of *A Place in the Sun* were held. Charlie Chaplin attended one of them in Hollywood, and afterwards told George Stevens, "This is the greatest movie ever made about America." That quote was repeated in the press, and an excellent word of mouth began on the film. In New York, Dr. Silverberg attended one screening. Monty seemed both pleased and nervous introducing him to his friends.

The movie opened officially in August. Monty took Judy to the New York premiere at the Capitol Theatre. "Fans swarmed all over our limousine—we had to fight our way through the crowds. Afterward, what seemed like thousands of people surged forward at us, and the buttons on Monty's tuxedo were yanked away and a great clump of my hair was cut off as a souvenir!"

The following morning they read the reviews. "As produced and directed by George Stevens the movie is first rate all along the line," wrote John McCarten of the *New Yorker*. Bosley Crowther drew attention to the director's use of close-up and to the sharp dissection of "the pitiful working of the minds and moods of three young people correlated by varieties of loneliness, ambition and love." Crowther went on to describe Monty's performance as "terse, hesitating, full, rich, restrained . . . and poignant. . . ."

A Place in the Sun became one of the emblematic films of the 1950s. "A new generation of soul searchers reacted to the tormented youth portrayed by Clift," wrote Joe Morella and Edward Epstein in their book, *The Rebel Hero in Films*.

Film critic Andrew Sarris, who saw the movie countless times, says, "Clift and Taylor were the most beautiful couple in the history of cinema. It was a sensuous experience to watch them respond to each other. Those gigantic close-ups of them kissing was unnerving—sybaritic—like gorging on chocolate sundaes."

Then, of course, there was Monty's cruising sexual swagger (which Brando and Dean picked up on). Few audiences in the 1950s were aware of the meaning of that androgynous swagger—it was very subtle and Monty only did it for a few seconds on film—but it was almost as if he was telling the millions of women who swooned over him—"You think you're beautiful? Well, I'm beautiful too, more beautiful than you. So who needs you?"

A Place in the Sun was named the outstanding picture of 1951 by the National Board of Review of Motion Pictures, and Monty received his second Academy Award nomination as best actor.

Judy knew Monty was seeing a great deal of Libby Holman. "We often visited her together." She knew too that he was continuing to write and phone Elizabeth Taylor. "I understood he had a life separate from me, but I still felt we were very, very close."

They never discussed breaking up. "It just happened," Judy said. "Suddenly he stopped calling three or four times a day, and instead he called me once a week. I was very hurt, very upset, but I knew there was nothing I could do about it."

Late in the fall of 1951, she began dating Merv Griffin; they became engaged briefly. The following year she married Jay Kantor of MCA. Monty did not attend the ceremony, but Marlon Brando did; he was Kantor's best man.

In November, Elizabeth Taylor came back to New York. She phoned Monty immediately, and they began seeing each other every day, all day. This time they went to restaurants like Le Pavillon and Voisin, and allowed photographers to take pictures of them. Whenever they appeared, Elizabeth showed off a huge sapphire on the fourth finger of her left hand. She called it her engagement ring from English actor Michael Wilding, although she'd bought it herself.

Elizabeth had met Wilding in London while she was filming *Ivanhoe*. He was old enough to be her father, but she maintained she'd fallen madly in love with him. Some friends felt she was still trying to persuade Monty to marry her, using Wilding as a ploy. "I remember being at Monty's apartment when Elizabeth phoned from the Plaza where she was staying and begged him to reconsider marrying her before Wilding arrived in New York," a friend recalls. "Monty was sweet but adamant. Arline stood next to the phone frozen-faced."

Not long after that, Elizabeth got word she would have to do retakes of *Ivanhoe* in Hollywood. When she informed the Plaza she was leaving they immediately sent her a bill for $2,500. She'd thought her two weeks at the hotel was complimentary. The management said no.

She became enraged. "She acted spoiled, threw a tantrum," said a press agent. Then she phoned Monty and started complaining to him. He rushed over with Roddy McDowall, and the three of them got drunk on martinis and ran around the hotel suite hanging pictures upside down, unscrewing all the bathroom fixtures, strewing toilet paper about. "They ended up dueling with a huge bunch of chrysanthemums. Yellow petals littered the carpet. Afterward, Monty waltzed away with a supply of Plaza Hotel embossed towels. He always set them out whenever Elizabeth stayed in his apartment in later years."

The Plaza Hotel incident was much publicized; Michael Wilding read about it and flew to New York immediately. He and Monty subsequently met and they saw each other frequently, "but one always got the sense they were competing for Elizabeth's attention and affection. Monty felt very loving and protective and rather superior when it came to Elizabeth Taylor."

"Nobody knows Bessie Mae the way I do," he would say.

After Elizabeth Taylor married Wilding, Monty confided to Inge Morath that he hated living by himself and he didn't see how anyone could do so successfully. "He'd take me to Le Chambord or the Colony, and we'd discuss the ways one could live alone successfully." Miss Morath was then Henri Cartier-Bresson's assistant, and traveling quite contentedly all over the world by herself. "Monty didn't see how I did it even though I tried to explain if you had some inner resources, if you even half liked yourself. . . ."

Often he would phone her in the middle of the night and recite German poetry to her. "He spoke beautiful German—and his knowledge of German poets was quite marvelous, but they were all young, tragic, beautiful poets who'd died before they were thirty. . . ."

Around this time he asked Blaine Waller to live with him. "The message was explicit. Monty often came on with me, but I finally made it clear I didn't swing, and he just smiled and shrugged—eventually he stopped. I wasn't ac/dc; Monty was. No crime in that. Except in those days you didn't talk about it. I think he dug men and women running after him. And he liked seducing both sexes. It turned him on. He was very sexual in 1950 and 1951."

For a while he kept an aspiring actor. They lived in Monty's new apartment—a spacious duplex he'd just rented at 207 East Sixty-first Street. "We thought the guy was taking him," Blaine said. "But Monty gave him money, helped him get established, even helped him get a big movie in Hollywood. He was a dislikable punk; he had a very unattractive personality."

Monty was still seeing Silverberg. But he no longer talked about his analysis. Max Youngstein recalls, "He no longer mentioned that his analyst might be a faggot."

Silverberg's student-patient Robertiello once accused Silverberg of homosexual behavior during a session. "Silverberg ignored the accusation and behaved in his usual cold clinical manner. While Silverberg was known as a homosexual in the psychiatric community, it would have been career suicide to go around talking about it. In those days homosexuality was considered a serious psychiatric illness."

Not long after Elizabeth Taylor got married Monty stopped mentioning the possibility of ever marrying himself. He did not go into Gregory's any more, not since an angry drunk had broken his nose and dislocated his shoulder in a freakish barroom brawl. Instead he began spending more and more time with Libby Holman.

He was continuing to suffer from insomnia. Often before he could sleep he would knock himself out with Nembutals and Scotch. Libby had a hard time sleeping too—she took Seconals.

They would crawl into her huge bed covered with white satin sheets and pass out. The walls around them were covered with photographs of Libby's men—all of whom had died tragically—her first and second husbands, her lover, and her son, Topper Reynolds.

"Libby Holman wanted to possess Monty. To *possess* him!" Sunny Clift recalls. "But how could she possibly possess anyone who was more important than she was? She wanted to influence him, but how could she influence someone who was going to influence an entire generation?"

25

Long before Libby Holman met Montgomery Clift, when she was twenty-four and the toast of Broadway, she told a reporter: "I want to have at least one great love. A man who has achieved something in the arts. He must be more than a match for me in physical vitality and artistic achievements. I never want to envy youth. I never want to be dependent. At fifty—sixty—seventy—eighty—I want to have enough charm and fascination inside myself to draw admiration and love of men. I want to be rich inside."

She was born Elspeth Holzman, daughter of Alfred Holzman, a noted Cincinnati attorney. She had a sister who committed suicide, and two brothers, one who was very close to her, and another estranged from her.

Throughout her childhood she was considered precocious. She played the violin and piano. She read through her father's legal briefs. "I studied Jung and Oscar Wilde before I got the curse," she once said. As soon as she was given her first car she was stopped for speeding. "I'm going to have to pinch you," the cop said. "I'd much rather be tickled," she retorted. In Europe she was arrested for sunbathing nude.

At sixteen, she entered the University of Cincinnati where she immediately got the reputation of being the most original student in her class. And ambitious. "The thing you remembered about her was how strong her ambition was," Howard Dietz said. "I want to be somebody special," she used to say.

After graduation she went to New York and enrolled at Columbia Law School—she planned to follow in her father's footsteps and become a lawyer. But her secret dream was stronger—to be a singer. She made her debut in *Garrick Gaieties* of 1926, but she didn't achieve stardom until 1929 when she sang "Moanin' Low" in a review called *The Little Show*.

When she made her entrance on stage stumbling and pawing at the scenery, she seemed overwhelmed with emotion. Actually she was terribly nearsighted and couldn't see a foot in front of her. But everybody in the audience sat up and took notice as she belted out her song in an earnest throaty voice. According to one witness, "Libby's voice was so compelling she made the entire theater sweat and forget home and mother." Brooks Atkinson called her a "dark purple menace."

Next she appeared in *Three's a Crowd,* opposite Fred Allen and Clifton Webb. Her throaty renditions of "Body and Soul" and "Something to Remember You By" were so provocative she became a celebrity overnight.

For a while she and Jeanne Eagels lived together, danced together openly at clubs, got roaring drunk in speakeasies all over the East Side. "She seemed to reserve the best part of herself for women," said a woman friend. "Libby was tender, compassionate, generous—enormously sensual with all her close women friends. With men for the most part she acted like a ball breaker."

Her best friend was a slender, blonde, Southern aristocrat, Louisa Carpenter, an heiress to the Du Pont millions. The two of them often dressed in men's suits and bowler hats and went to the Clam House to eat spareribs and cole slaw with Tallulah Bankhead and Beatrice Lillie.

Libby was pursued by many men. When she turned thirty her most ardent admirer was twenty-year-old Zachary Smith Reynolds, heir to the $700 million Camel cigarette fortune. At the height of their courtship, she made him jealous by planning a round-the-world cruise with Louisa Carpenter; Reynolds threatened suicide, saying he would crash in his own plane if she took the cruise. Libby refused to listen to his threats and went gaily off with Louisa. The two of them stayed in Paris several weeks with Josephine Baker, because Libby thought she could play Miss Baker in the movies.

In 1932 Libby abruptly gave up her career and married Smith Reynolds. She moved with him to Reynolda, the tobacco family's huge estate four miles outside Winston-Salem, North Carolina, and she tried to get used to living on a thousand acres and taking care of a big white gabled house. Sometimes she swam by herself in the lake on which swans glided.

Eight months after the wedding on July 5, 1932, Libby and

Smith gave a lavish barbecue to which dozens of people were invited from all over the South. During the party Libby and Smith quarreled violently; the following morning Smith died of a gunshot wound; after an inquest Libby was accused of his murder. Later, during an emotion-packed trial, she was defended by her lawyer father and she was cleared for lack of evidence.

The trial ended November 15, 1932. Libby moved immediately to Louisa Carpenter's secluded Delaware mansion. Two months later she gave birth to son Christopher Smith Reynolds, a sickly infant weighing only two pounds. A bitter estate battle ensued. Libby was ultimately awarded $750,000 and Christopher got $6,600,000 of the Camel cigarette fortune.

For the next four years, Libby lived in virtual seclusion in a house near Louisa's in Wilmington. For a while she commuted to Hedgerow Theater in Philadelphia three days a week and studied drama with Jasper Deeter, paying $10 a lesson. She talked of coming back to Broadway in a revue with her good friend Clifton Webb. She sang at the Derby Ball in Grosvenor House in London; she appeared in Miami; she was photographed at a roller skating party in Philadelphia.

In 1937 Libby moved back to New York, and, renting a brownstone on East Seventy-ninth Street, she tried unsuccessfully to rebuild her career; she then left the city and bought Treetops, the twenty-four-acre estate outside of Stamford, Connecticut, that Monty would so frequently visit. She spent thousands of dollars decorating the place. For a while she hired seven bodyguards and three Great Danes to protect her baby. Christopher—she nicknamed him "Topper"—had the best doctors, the best teachers, toys, clothes, and travel while he was growing up.

Off and on Libby drank so heavily she would have to go to a private nursing home to be dried out. Her most important relationships continued to be with women like Louisa, or her analyst, Else Brickner, whom she saw daily; later, one of her most intimate friends was writer Jane Bowles.

In 1939 she married Ralph Holmes, a handsome, moody actor twelve years her junior. Earlier she'd had an affair with his brother, who died in a plane crash. Ralph died from an overdose of sleeping pills in 1945. Then, she met Montgomery Clift.

The minute she saw Monty she was enormously moved by him. She always had respect and wonder for talent and achievement, and she thought he was by far the most brilliant and exceptional actor of his generation. "I bow down before you," she would say grandly.

But she was equally aroused by his mercurial nature and by his androgynous quality—that almost inhuman ability to synthesize the temporal and the timeless in his nature. "He identifies with men and women equally," she would say. She felt the same way about Garbo, who seemed as poetic and mysterious as Monty. Libby had photographs of Garbo all over her house.

But her son Topper, slender, reserved, intelligent, was the center of her life. They went on long trips together to Morocco and Europe. They worked together in the summer theaters. Libby would sing, Topper stage-managed. She visited him at Putney School in Vermont and stood by proudly when he graduated near the head of his class.

After his frozen, broken body was found lodged in a crevice on Mt. Whitney, Libby lay in a state of near collapse for weeks. Then she drank herself into a stupor, blaming herself for his death because she had not seen to it he was properly chaperoned. She kept crying that everyone she loved was doomed—husbands, child—and for a while she refused to get too involved with Monty, warning him, "Watch out! Something terrible's gonna happen." And he just laughed and said, "You're *fan*tastic! Shut up!"

A couple of months after Topper died, there was another bitter estate fight with the Reynolds family, but Libby was ultimately awarded her son's $6,600,000. The added wealth made her more suspicious and shy of people. She told Monty she had an increasing fear that everybody was after her money. "Her mail was extraordinary," her accompanist Gerald Cook said. "Everybody asking for a handout."

Eventually she invested part of her fortune in a foundation to promote civil rights. She named the foundation after her son. One of the first Christopher Reynolds grants went to Martin Luther King, Jr., then a young Atlanta minister, enabling him to go to India and study Gandhi's techniques in nonviolence. He and his wife, Coretta, later became close friends of Libby's.

She couldn't drink much, because her ulcers were so bad that she would double up with pain after one glass of white wine. To combat her depression and her ulcers, she tried practicing Zen. She spent several hours a day meditating, and she would come out of her silence bursting with questions about Korea and Truman and the exquisite beauty of Gloria Vanderbilt. She punctuated everything with "I'm such a stupe!"

Throughout the fifties she spent most of her time at Treetops with Monty. "I remember her brown as a berry but very emaciated," Augusta said. "She would smoke cigarette after cigarette through paper filters."

On many Sunday afternoons, Monty and Libby could be observed floating on rubber mattresses in the pool, sometimes nude. Libby never stopped looking at Monty, and always with desire and love. Sometimes he would return her look. "It was a little embarrassing to watch," said a friend.

Libby loved Treetops. It was home. Every spring she gave a party to celebrate the blooming of her million daffodils. They grew in golden profusion across a hill opposite the house. "It was a spectacular sight," Kevin said. "The daffodils seemed to flood and shine and ripple across that hill."

After her son's death, Libby continued to entertain as she always had, giving lavish impeccable luncheons and dinners with Monty sitting at the head of the table, sometimes very drunk. The finest of Chateau wines flowed and the best fruit was squashed into napkins, and Brie ran gooey off the plates. And some of the guests—male models, chorus boys—"male hustlers some of them, let's face it," said an interior decorator friend of Libby's—were loud and bombed out of their minds by the end of the meal.

"Libby didn't seem to know or care who came to these parties," Augusta Dabney said.

"There was a lot of running around on the lawn nude, falling into the pool, and getting stoned on pot," said Stephen Cole. "All of that sounds pretty tame now."

Marijuana, cocaine, mescaline were available at Treetops. Libby had got into the so-called exotic states of consciousness in the twenties with Tallulah Bankhead, who took cocaine before the Crash. Paul Bowles recalled discovering a supply of "very good grass" in a humidor in Libby's brownstone the day Allen Ginsberg and Peter Orlovsky came to call.

When they weren't in Morocco, the Bowleses—Paul and Jane—actually lived at Treetops for months on end, partly because they were almost always completely broke. Libby had a special fondness for Jane, the quick-tongued fragile writer who was going slowly mad. She and Monty developed a strange rapport. They both empathized as to why the other drank. "We drink to suppress our panic," Monty would exclaim, and then he and Jane would dissolve into laughter.

Whenever Jane got drunk enough, she would confide to Monty that she was in love with Libby, and Monty would counter with, "But so am I!"

An endless stream of people visited Libby throughout 1952 and 1953—some remember Monty fondly, others do not.

One of his agents, Edie Van Cleve, said, "Monty was always so kind and considerate—he was the only person who ever seemed really interested in my horses. We'd talk for hours about them." (Miss Van Cleve owned several show horses, and her office at MCA was filled with trophies and medals they'd won.)

Designer Oliver Smith said, "Monty acted like a spoiled brat around Libby—I couldn't stand him." Alice Byrd, Libby Holman's maid, spoke of his thoughtfulness. "He brought me the prettiest scarves from Paris." Libby's nephew David Holman remembers Monty acting "silly—so babyish, hugging, kissing, biting you sometimes, and often falling down drunk."

Producer Lyn Austin recalls coming to the opening-night party Libby gave for Jane Bowles's play, *In the Summer House* (which she backed). "Montgomery Clift was in the kitchen necking with Libby. They were being very lovey-dovey right in front of Judith Anderson and Roger L. Stevens."

At the same party Augusta Dabney went upstairs to powder her nose. "I walked into their bedroom and I got the feeling Monty and Libby must have very kinky sex. Everything seemed erotic and faintly decadent—the low lights, the slippery white satin sheets on the bed, the overpowering fragrance of Jungle Gardenia perfume. And then I saw this huge bottle of Seconal on the bedroom table. It must have contained a hundred pills—the prescription on it read 'Libby Holman Reynolds.' "

When her homes got too crowded with hangers-on, Libby and Monty would escape to a motel in Amagansett, Long Island, and they would take bike rides or walk on the beach. "They were trying to get off the booze," said a painter who knew them. "I used to run into them holding hands and plunging through the dunes. They were cold sober and quite morose." Libby would always talk about her plans for a one-woman show. She never stopped thinking about her singing career. She kept someone on retainer to "light" her, and she still worked with accompanist Gerald Cook almost every day in New York.

Libby did not go out to Hollywood with Monty in March of 1952 when he attended the Academy Award ceremonies. He was up against Brando, Fredric March, Arthur Kennedy, and Humphrey Bogart, and he did not think he had a chance of winning, although he confessed he wanted to. "Why not?" he said.

As usual, Monty stayed with the Greens in their Hollywood Hills home. He insisted they accompany him to the Awards as his guests. Jeanne recalls, "We were terribly flattered; we were also stone-broke." She went out and bought a cheap little dress at Bullock's, which she hoped she'd be able to return. Fred rented a tux. "He wore a boiled shirt and the shirt kept popping out all evening." Monty howled with laughter every time it happened.

At the ceremonies in the Pantages Theater they sat on the aisle —in front of Karl Malden, who was nominated for best supporting actor for *Streetcar,* and Kevin McCarthy, very excited and proud because he'd been nominated for his role as Biff in *Death of a Salesman* (the same role he'd done in the London stage production).

The proceedings, emceed by Danny Kaye, went on interminably. *A Place in the Sun* won for best director, best screenplay, best camera work, best film editing, best scoring, best costume; but Monty did not win best actor—Bogart won, for his performance in *African Queen.*

"Afterward we all went to a very posh party at Perino's," Jeanne said. "Fred and I felt uncomfortable and out of place. We didn't know any of the movie stars or directors who came over to talk to Monty. But Monty was wonderful—he made us sit with him at the head of the table, and he directed most of his conversation to us."

He seemed preoccupied with creating a real home for himself, "a very private place." He wanted Fred to come to New York and redesign the duplex he'd just rented on East Sixty-first Street. Monty said he would pay all expenses and Jeanne would come along as decorator—"it would be an adventure."

Since Fred was now a full-fledged builder/designer, and since he and Jeanne loved Monty like a brother, they agreed immediately. As summer approached they arranged to have their three young children taken care of by a nurse. From June through September they flew back and forth from California to New York—"It was an utterly exhausting summer emotionally and physically, but one we never forgot," Jeanne said.

26

Instead of hiring an outside contractor, Fred Green did almost everything himself on Monty's duplex—tiling, plastering, breaking up rooms. "It was a God-awful task—it took over four months and it was made much worse by Monty's behavior," Fred said.

"Remember, I was working a fourteen-hour day—for free. All I wanted was a little appreciation, some gratitude. Monty used to waltz in before going out to dinner or a party and he might make some criticism—never a compliment. Once he came by with Augusta, I was down on my knees scraping the floor. It was one of those brutally hot humid nights and Monty says, 'Wish you could join us at the theater'; without waiting for my reply he left. I was furious."

They fought when Monty insisted that Fred construct a fourteen-foot long medicine cabinet in his bathroom. Fred told him it was unheard of—he wouldn't be able to fill it. Monty said he would, and as soon as it was built he did; the contents of that enormous cabinet with its mirrors and its louvered doors became legendary. There were pain relievers such as Darvon, antibiotics, such as Terramycin; there were anticonvulsants, antidepressants, tranquilizers. There were paregoric, decongestants, antispasmodics, antinauseants, muscle relaxants, and all sorts of sleeping pills: Seconal, Tuinal, Nembutal.

Even with so many barbiturates around, Monty couldn't sleep. By this time, his system had developed a tolerance for most pills, and he had to take them in greater amounts for them to have any effect. Late at night he would climb to the roof of his duplex and peer into other people's apartments to take his mind off his insomnia. Once or twice Fred found him hanging over the edge of his house drugged and thick tongued, and he would carry him, protesting, downstairs.

While the reconstruction was going on, they all stayed in Libby Holman's brownstone half a block away. Throughout that summer they played Frank Sinatra's record of "I've Got the World on a String." "We played it over and over again," Jeanne Green said. "I used to cry when I heard it."

Libby was staying up in the country at Treetops for most of July and August, so the furniture in her house remained draped with white dustcovers. "We'd sit in one tiny patch of her living room drinking brandy and listening to the Sinatra record," Jeanne said. "But the atmosphere was vaguely creepy because Libby didn't approve of us. She was jealous and suspicious of my relationship with Monty, and she thought Fred was too inexperienced to renovate a brownstone."

Sometimes she appeared to be "sneaking up" on Jeanne, eavesdropping on her conversation with Monty. "We'd be out in her garden in the evening, and suddenly this figure would emerge and hover in the background and then disappear, and Monty would stop what he was saying to me and go off with her."

The heavy sensual fragrance of Libby's Jungle Gardenia scent seemed to insinuate itself into every nook and cranny of the house, "even the broom closet." And whenever Jeanne embraced Monty, "I smelled it on his shirt, on his skin."

Fred Green flew back frequently to California on business. While he was away Monty insisted Jeanne stay with her friend Ginnie Paisley on Twenty-seventh Street. "Monty didn't want me to stay over at Libby's alone with him, even though all we did was sit up until four A.M. talking. I'd get exhausted and plead with him to just let me crawl on the sofa, since we'd be shopping early the next morning. But he refused to permit it. I kept saying, 'Oh, Monty, it would be so much easier if you just let me sleep here, please,' but he said no."

Jeanne had the feeling Libby kept Monty "on a long leash. One morning I came back from Ginnie's—Monty and I were going to Bloomingdale's. We decided to play 'I've Got the World on a String' once more. We were sitting on the couch listening to it when suddenly this figure—half hidden by a great bunch of flowers—appears in the doorway. It was Libby, unexpectedly home from the country. Monty got very clutched. He crawled over to her on his hands and knees and started telling her how gorgeous and wonderful she was. It was a frightening image."

Almost every day Monty and Jeanne went on an extensive shopping expedition for the house. Monty wanted everything to be perfect for his duplex—nothing but the finest—china, silver, crystal. They searched everywhere for extra thick carpets so he could lie on any part of the floor.

Once they were in Hammacher's pricing some very expensive brass hangings, and he pocketed one. Jeanne reprimanded him sharply, and he shrugged, "What the fuck!" Another time they were in Hammacher's European lift and he "peed on the floor. I said, 'Oh, Monty, why did you do that?' and he snapped, 'I didn't know where the men's room was.'"

Often, when they returned to Libby's laden down with packages, he suddenly asked Jeanne to leave. "Walk around the corner, get a cup of coffee—I have a gangster coming over."

Gangsters, why? To supply him with extra pills? She never knew and never questioned, but she left.*

When he wasn't in New York overseeing the renovation of his duplex, Monty was moving about—flying to Hollywood or Las Vegas or San Francisco or visiting James Jones in Tucson, Arizona.

According to writer John Bowers, Monty and Jones sat around restaurants talking about *From Here to Eternity,* posing for photographs together. "Monty talked a lot about Elizabeth Taylor. He says that she can instantly catch a mood. Nothing has to be explained. 'I'd rather work with her than any actress in the world. It's all intuition with her.'"

According to Bowers, "Monty ate his salad with his fingers—he calls salad garbage . . . in the late evening he fell out of the car and rolled all the way down a clay hill." When the others got down to him on the bottom he was giggling. "Shit," Jones is supposed to have remarked, "he'd a been dead if he hadn't a been drunk then."

When Monty got back from Tucson, he drove up to Hamden to see Thornton Wilder about the play he was writing for him. He also went to Ogunquit, Maine, for his sessions with analyst Silverberg.

Monty came to a decision that summer. After almost two years

* Years later a drug runner nicknamed "Bird," who now works for the New York police department in a Harlem drug clinic, admitted supplying Monty, Judy Garland, and Libby Holman with pills. "I supplied a great many New York celebrities with pills in the fifties," he said. "Bird" was then in his teens and working for a "Mafia guy" who lived in Harlem. "Every couple of months I'd deliver Clift a roll of pills— that's a thousand pills—Seconals, Tuinals, and Doriden, which wasn't even on the market yet. A roll of pills cost $450 in 1955—today it would cost a thousand."

of not working he signed to do three movies: *I Confess* for Alfred Hitchcock, *Terminal Station,* to be made in Rome by Vittorio De Sica, and James Jones's *From Here to Eternity.* He was excited about the roles in these pictures because "they are all characters faced with a terrible crisis."

However, when he returned from Maine, his moods became extreme; he was at once perverse and despairing. He had barred his mother from ever visiting the duplex because they invariably argued violently over his relationship with Libby Holman. Even so, Sunny couldn't resist dropping by. She wanted to see what the Greens were doing with the apartment, and she would trot through the torn-up rooms making suggestions, making criticisms.

Monty always tried to be very polite and loving, but as soon as she left he would bark out orders to Fred and Jeanne: "Do this! Do that!"

Lately Bill Clift had been pressuring Monty—gently—to let him invest the $250,000 a picture he was now making. Monty very firmly said no. "If there's one person I don't want to handle my money it's Pa," he told Brooks. But rejecting his father upset him.

As for Brooks, he was stage-managing TV shows such as *Hit Parade* and *Matinee Theater.* His second marriage to model Leslie Dixon had broken up shortly after the birth of their daughter Cathy. Their divorce became final in 1951. He was now involved in an affair with actress Kim Stanley, whom he declared was the love of his life. Stanley's husband, actor Curt Conway, refused to give her a divorce.

She ultimately became pregnant and bore Brooks a son, Jamie. When she refused to give the baby Brooks's name, or to leave her husband, Brooks became "emotionally unhinged. I considered murdering her. She was the most important person in my life. I worshipped her." He eventually began therapy with Anaïs Nin's psychiatrist, Dr. Inge Bogner.

"Monty was the only person I told about the child Kim and I had. He was very sympathetic. I talked to him a lot. He encouraged me to stay in therapy until I resolved some of my problems."

As for his own problems, Monty never discussed them. Arline was still his secretary, and still in love with him. She made no specific demands, but her presence in the duplex was a continued reminder that he had once rejected her.

They finally came to an understanding, and she left his employ and later married a musician. But she never forgot Monty. "When-

A scene from *A Place in the Sun*. (Ethel McGinnis collection)

As Father Michael Logan [in] Hitchcock's *I Confess*. (Ethel M[c]Ginnis collectio[n])

◀ Costumed in Berlin for *The [Big] Lift*. (Ethel McGinnis collectio[n])

Jeanne Green and Monty in [his] brownstone during its renovati[on] (Kevin McCarth[y])

(Far right) At "Treetops." L[eft] to right: Kevin McCarthy, Lib[by] Holman, Monty, Augusta Dabn[ey,] a cousin of Libby Holman, a[nd] Tony, one of Libby Holma[n's] adopted sons.

Kevin McCarthy and Monty in their controversial off-Broadway production of Chekhov's *The Seagull*.

With Dolly Haas in *I Confess*. (Steph[en] V. Russell collection)

The young Libby Holman. (The Bettman Archiv[e])

Dining out with Elizabeth Taylor at Camillos, their favorite New York restaurant.
(Brooks Clift collection)

ever I was around him he gave me the illusion of being more alive," Arline said. "He made me aware of a kind of truth and density in life."

He did this, she said, by "making me pay attention to the smallest details. We'd be sitting in Gregory's and suddenly he would begin examining the graffiti on the wooden table—he'd cry out, 'This is a veritable map!', or he'd start talking to Sol, the newspaper boy who came in to sell us the *Daily Mirror,* and by the time he was finished, he'd have collected all sorts of minutiae about Sol, including the dreams he'd had last night. Monty forced you to open your eyes and look and listen to the world, and by osmosis you started listening and looking at yourself."

He could show others how to be fulfilled, but his own fulfillment was another matter. After being with people all day he would often leave everybody in a high state of tension and go back to Libby Holman's irritated and depressed.

"He had extreme changes of mood," Blaine Waller said. "Sometimes you knew he had to be by himself."

Often Jeanne Green would find him late at night fully clothed but passed out on Libby's white satin bed. The buzzing telephone would still be in his hand. (He loved phoning friends all over the world, at all hours.) She and Fred would undress him like a baby, and clean him like a baby too. He often wet his pants.

As the summer progressed, the Greens and the McCarthys became more and more worried about Monty; they sensed his suffering and felt powerless to help him. They wondered why Dr. Silverberg, who was still seeing Monty every day, had not been able to ease his torment or stop his drinking.

Dr. Ruth Fox said, "Billy would phone me periodically and say 'Oh dear, Monty's off his Antabuse* again.' Billy was aware Monty was an alcoholic. We discussed it frequently. But looking back on it I don't think Billy ever really believed alcoholism was a disease."

Mira was so concerned about Monty's drinking and his manic moods that she begged Thornton Wilder to go to Silverberg. Wilder demurred; he was too busy, but he admitted that Monty had changed radically since he'd gone into analysis. He no longer seemed so respectful with Wilder—he broke lunch dates with him, he was rude.

Mira finally spoke to Monty about Silverberg. They had several arguments. "I told Monty that Silverberg hadn't helped him with his

* A drug which is used as a deterrent against alcohol.

drinking or his other problems. I said I thought he should try another doctor."

Monty retorted, "Billy is right about everything except my work."

Mira sensed Silverberg believed Monty was too dependent on her and wanted him to break that dependence. When she tried to discuss Silverberg again, Monty cut her off with great rage. "I realized he'd told Silverberg what I'd said about him. From then on, we began to separate. Monty and I were never the same, never as close, as intimate."

Kevin and Augusta tried talking to Monty about his drinking, his pill taking, but only when he was the "old Monty," sober, vigorous, nervy, still relishing life. He still had long periods of lucidity when he seemed perfectly normal. Then he would deny anything was bothering him. He always disliked talking about himself.

By September, the duplex was finally painted, and Jeanne began rearranging the hundreds of books in Monty's study, where she came upon Dr. William Silverberg's *Childhood Experience and Destiny*. Opening it to the flyleaf, she read the inscription "To Monty, my hero, Billy." She snapped the book shut and returned it to a shelf. Later she told Fred and the McCarthys about the intimate inscription, and the four friends began speculating about Silverberg.

Was it possible that the psychiatrist had been caught in Monty's web? Seduced by Monty's magnetic personality and fame, seduced by his charm, his deep, deep needs?

"Dad never discussed Montgomery Clift," said his son, J. William Silverberg, M.D., who practices psychiatry in White Plains. "There was always a rule of silence. I only found out Monty had been a patient after he died, and I was told that my father who was then very ill (he died in 1967) could not be informed of his death right away because he would have been too upset."

"Billy always went out of his way with Monty although I can't tell you why," says Dr. Lily Ottenheimer, Silverberg's most intimate colleague. "Billy advised him on his choice of roles. Billy understood the artistic temperament. But as for a countertransference, or a relationship other than doctor-patient—absolutely not. Billy was far too aware of his own complicated private life, his own psychohistory, to ever allow such a thing to happen."

Possibly, but Silverberg's former student, Dr. Richard Robertiello, feels "something might well have been going on within that very rigid structure Silverberg always set up between himself and his patient. I doubt if Billy ever acted out his feelings to Monty—he was too self-contained, too remote—but the emotions were probably there."

"It was not characteristic of my father to reach out to anyone," his son, J. William Silverberg said. "People came to him."

That may be, Robertiello says, but he found the inscription "very unusual—mysterious." In any event, given psychiatric transference, the results must have been disastrous for Monty, who kept telling everybody how much he admired Silverberg.

Several years after *Childhood Experience and Destiny* came out, Silverberg presented a paper (never published) at the New York Psychiatric Institute. It was obviously a thinly disguised case history of Montgomery Clift, Robertiello said. Everyone who listened to it recognized the personality as Clift. "It could have been called a 'breach of discretion.'" In the paper, Robertiello recalled, Silverberg described his patient as a highly successful artist—an asexual man he likened to Leonardo da Vinci; his creativity and his energy were focused on his work, but he was overwhelmed by a fierce anxiety which he suffered from night and day. The patient had periodic blackouts. He was also carrying on a relationship with an older woman—a mother figure—who allowed him to give in to all his excesses, to liquor and pills.

Monty no longer discussed his analysis or how it was progressing, but it was obvious to everyone who knew him that his secret fears and guilts constituted a puzzle he was unable to solve. What he was most concerned with, and this he expressed in a drunken moment to Bill Le Massena, was how others perceived him. "I don't want to be labeled as either a pansy or a heterosexual. Labeling is so self-limiting. We are what we do—not what we say we are." In another revealing talk, he confided to Mira Rostova, "You know? Billy Silverberg is becoming my Mephisto!"

The work on Monty's duplex was finally completed in late September. Fred was never paid for anything he did on the apartment, but he said, "I never asked for money. I did it out of friendship for Monty."

Before the Greens returned to California, Monty presented Fred with a gold watch inscribed, "to a timeless friend." Fred suspected Monty had been given the watch as a present and hadn't liked it. Fred didn't like it either, so he never wore it. Later he and Jeanne discovered that the watch had indeed been sent to Monty the previous Christmas by an agent from MCA.

Ned Smith came back from Spain in the fall of 1952, and he and Monty saw each other frequently. "We'd been corresponding as we always did, but we had a lot to catch up on."

Smith recalls being very impressed with the renovated brownstone. "You walked upstairs to a high-ceilinged living room with huge casement windows overlooking East Sixty-first Street. Hundreds of books lined the shelves, ranging from Boccaccio to G. B. Shaw to Sandburg's *Lincoln*."

There were oak coffee tables made to order in Scotland, mixed with antique English chests. Monty seemed to have chosen his charming mixture of modern and antique pieces for their satiny woodwork. Everything was highly polished; he talked appreciatively to Smith about the various kinds of wood in the apartment.

He took Smith upstairs to view his bedroom—the giant headboard of his outsize bed was made of dark mahogany. And his workroom contained a piano stripped down to four varieties of blond wood and a desk seven feet long. "The top of the desk is really an old fire door made of many layers of wood," he said.

"Monty had an answering service, which not many people had in those days," Smith recalled. "He was listed with Celebrity Service, he told me. He was one of the people to get the first issue of *Sports Illustrated,* which I couldn't understand." But he was acting differently, and Smith didn't quite know why.

"He talked about meeting Laurence Olivier, whom he was very impressed with—he thought he was absolutely wonderful. He talked about Marlene Dietrich, and he was very specific about her comeback in Las Vegas, which he'd gone to, and the dress she had on—all spangles which seemed stuck to her body—and he did an imitation; he mimed the dress. He talked about how Dietrich and Ernest Hemingway had come over to the brownstone and how Hemingway was a tremendous bore, he seemed so self-important. He talked about Vivien Leigh and how hard she was on Laurence Olivier: 'She is very neurotic and very nervous, and she holds her teacup *like this,*' and he imitated Vivien Leigh and the gesture was totally effeminate, and it distressed me greatly. He talked no more about doing many things in his life—broadening his life—he talked only about 'I have my work to do and this and that.' He took singing lessons; he went to the gym; he had to go to the dentist's. He talked about the movie *African Queen,* and he said, 'I can't stand the way Katharine Hepburn plays the part.' He said, 'When she pours gin overboard she doesn't do it right.' I said, 'What do you mean? I thought that was a terrific scene, one of the greatest scenes I've ever seen in a movie,' and he answered, 'Terrible job.' He spoke a lot about *From Here to Eternity* and Frank Sinatra, who he thought would be great for the part of Maggio. . . . I wanted to tell him about my experiences—I had been to Spain and lived there and learned the language and had been turned upside down by the experience. But, well, there were things about Monty now that I'd been sensing about him that made me uneasy. . . . Still it was so pleasant knowing him, and I felt I could help him." Smith paused in the recollection. "That's not the right way to put it. I felt I was still very much part of his life. . . ."

27

Monty's decision to play a priest in Alfred Hitchcock's film *I Confess* was influenced partially by his friendship with Brother Thomas, a young French monk who had only recently taken his final vows in a cloistered monastery in Quebec.

Monty often referred to Thomas as the only person he knew who lived in a "state of grace." "But he also has a sense of humor," he said. "When he heard I was playing a priest in a movie, he wrote me, 'I'll never forgive you if you come out looking like Bing Crosby.'"

Brother Thomas and Monty had met—by chance—in Grand Central Station in 1945. Thomas was then only seventeen and a postulant over from France and unable to speak a word of English.

Monty noticed him sitting on his suitcase by the information booth crying his eyes out. He went over to the boy. Soon they were conversing in French, and Thomas was explaining how he'd been on his way to his new monastery in Quebec to begin his novitiate, that he'd missed his train, and since he couldn't speak any English had no idea how to find out when the next train was.

Monty quickly obtained the information for him. Since the train didn't leave for several hours, he invited him back to his apartment for a warm meal and a talk.

Afterwards he and Brother Thomas corresponded regularly. Monty would write about his struggle to work well and truthfully "to solve the problem of how to become what I want to become. I am in anguish because the odds are I won't. . . ." and Thomas would try to describe his own struggle to accept joyfully a life of contemplation and solitude. "What's amazing," he wrote to Monty, who read the letter to a friend, "what's amazing is that you don't give up much of life in a cloister. Maybe you'd find some peace on a retreat. Because you are in fact *more aware of reality* in the purest most vivid sense. You begin to value natural beauty as never before—the color of the sky just as the sun comes up—the sounds of a candle flickering. . . ."

Just before Monty went to Hollywood to begin filming *I Confess,* he spent a week at Brother Thomas's monastery outside Quebec.*

He attended Mass every morning at four. He told Pat Collinge later how moved he'd been by the solemn dignity of the services "in that great chapel." He observed the monks at work and at prayer. "Some of them, like Thomas, have a fundamental sense of reverence —of tenderness—they seem to believe like Blake that 'everything that is is holy.' "

"Priests walk in a special way because they wear robes or habits," he told Jeanne Green. "When they walk they push the material forward with their hands." (François Truffaut said in his famous interview with Hitchcock that in *I Confess,* "Montgomery Clift is always seen walking; it's a forward motion that shapes the whole film. It also concretizes the concept of his integrity.")

While he was at the monastery, Brother Thomas taught Monty how to say the rosary and the Stations of the Cross. He showed him how to genuflect, and he helped him start memorizing the Mass. Near the end of his stay he was also allowed to talk briefly with some of the other monks. Monty said later to Pat Collinge, "Their passion for saints is like ours for movie stars."

In the Hitchcock movie, Monty played a priest who hears the confession of a murderer and through a bizarre series of coincidences is indicted for the murder himself. Because of his holy vows on the inviolability of confession he makes no move to clear himself.

Monty asked Thomas if it would be feasible for a priest to risk his life in order to keep the sanctity of the confession. Thomas assured him it would. "It's like being a lawyer or a doctor. It's a bond of trust."

Monty left the monastery refreshed. He had taken neither liquor nor barbiturates during his five-day stay.

He did, however, begin to drink heavily again when he went out to California to film *I Confess.* Fred Green recalls being phoned late

* Brother Thomas came to Monty's funeral in 1966 dying of cancer. At the time he told Brooks, "If a book is ever written about Monty, I don't want my name or religious order revealed." He died a few weeks later.

one night by the Los Angeles police because Monty had been stopped somewhere on Wilshire Boulevard for drunken driving. "I came down to pick him up. The cops hadn't taken him to the station or anything. They were just sitting with him in his car, talking. They told me, 'He is such a sweet guy. Take care of him.'"

Karl Malden recalled going to a dinner party at Alfred Hitchcock's with Monty around this time. Mira went along with them carrying a rose which she held throughout the meal and kept sniffing. Nobody seemed to think it was unusual. Monty got so drunk he finally passed out, and Malden picked him up in his arms and carried him out to his limousine.

But he was not always drunk, Jeanne Green contended. He was staying with the Greens as usual, and when he was there he was usually sober. "We'd run lines in the evening and discuss the script." He talked compulsively about playing a priest, Jeanne said, and about how this priest must choose between betraying the secrets of the confessional and becoming a martyr—he kept talking about how priests assume the guilt of the world if they're good priests. She had the feeling "Monty wanted to be all things to all men—saviour,—father confessor. He had a superimage of himself that he couldn't possibly live up to on the screen, of being the rebel hero and nonconformist. But at the same time he felt he was flawed and he couldn't be perfection in these roles."

"He had a strongly developed sense of guilt," said Pat Collinge. "The guilt sometimes paralyzed him, but it was also a basic part of his nature. I used to tell him when he'd cry on my shoulder, his greatest weakness was self-pity. And he would say, no, I have no will power, it's a lack of will."

His mother, Sunny Clift, said, "Monty's biggest weakness was he didn't want to hurt people. Instead he'd hurt himself. He'd go along with what others said simply in order not to hurt feelings. He had a very hard time saying no."

While he was filming *I Confess* at Warner Brothers, he never appeared at Romanoff's, preferring the tacky darkness of The Beachcomber. He saw old friends like Salka Viertel, suffering from the horrors of the House Un-American Activities Committee. He saw new friends like Jack Larson, who was playing Jimmy Olsen on the TV series *Superman,* opposite George Reeves.

Sometimes he would go down to Strip City, a burlesque joint in Hollywood off Pico where comic Lenny Bruce was playing, or visit couples like Jean Simmons and Stewart Granger, who had a lavish home and pool atop the Hollywood Hills. The English contingent was usually there, including the Richard Burtons, Michael Wilding, and Elizabeth Taylor.

Taylor was pregnant with her first child and she was enormous—150 pounds. When he wasn't on call at the studio Monty would sometimes drive her over to Oscar Levant's house in Beverly Hills, and they would sit and listen to him play Gershwin on the piano.

After her baby, Michael Jr., was born, Monty began showering the infant with gifts. He even bought him a tiny chair and table which he put in a place of honor in his New York apartment. Whenever Elizabeth and the baby came to stay, the table and chair were put out especially for him.

Friends kidded him about the attention he lavished on Michael Jr. "You act as if he were your son—is he?" And Monty would reply, "I wish he were."

Much of the filming of *I Confess* took place on location in Quebec during chilly October weather. During the shooting most of the cast, including Brian Aherne, Dolly Haas, and Anne Baxter, rarely got a chance to speak to Monty, because as soon as he completed a take he'd disappear into his dressing room with Mira Rostova.

"He wasn't drinking. He was sober—but then he never drank when he was working," Dolly Haas said. "But he seemed mighty unhappy about something."

He and Alfred Hitchcock were not getting along. Monty disliked the director's "enormous bag of tricks, his endless devices!" He despaired over the fact that Hitchcock kept telling him bluntly and firmly how to act. "Alfred is too arbitrary—too calculated," he would exclaim to co-star Karl Malden after the director ordered him to look a certain way in a scene. Hitchcock and Monty fought in civilized fashion throughout the movie. Both were stubborn. Sometimes they made compromises and resolved their differences, other times Monty would play a scene Hitchcock's way but with variations. Then it was done still another way, and Hitchcock would choose the take he preferred.

When Monty accepted the role in *I Confess,* the priest was to be hanged at the end, then proven innocent. But the Hollywood censors thought it would offend Roman Catholics; a silly happy ending was tacked on while they were shooting the picture, making Hitchcock upset. He thought that "Montgomery Clift always looked as if the angel of death was walking alongside of him," and it would have been very powerful cinematically to watch him stride to the gallows for a crime he didn't commit.

Privately, Hitchcock was extremely dissatisfied with the production. Years later he told François Truffaut that he never should have made *I Confess,* because the basic concept of the movie was wrong. Most audiences could not accept the idea of a priest remaining silent and sacrificing his life over the sanctity of the confessional.

At the time he was worried about the heavy-handedness of the screenplay—the lack of humor. "My approach has always been ironic," he told Truffaut. He was also not happy with the casting of Anne Baxter as the woman who loved Monty before he joined the priesthood. He wanted Swedish actress Anita Bjork, but Warner Brothers had insisted on Baxter; Hitchcock met her for the first time in the dining room of the Chateau Frontenac just before filming started.

Then, of course, there was the brooding presence of Mira Rostova. She was on the set at all times. "Monty doesn't need that little pigeon!" Hitchcock told Karl Malden. He steadfastly ignored her, but he didn't ban her from coming on the set as other directors had done, "because whether she believes it or not, I know bloody well more than she does."

Malden, who played the police inspector investigating the murder, was the only member of the cast who socialized with Monty. "He had asked me to do the picture. I'd been dying to work with him."

Malden recalled, "I remember we worked on all the scenes we had together three nights running in our hotel room. I'd always loved discussions with Mira since she was right there in terms of bouncing ideas back and forth—in terms of dissecting a character. I'm very competitive as an actor—it makes me energetic—guess it's my background as a basketball coach, but I am always very specific for my objective in a scene—I fight for it."

In all of Malden's scenes—which are interrogation scenes—his objective was to break Monty's character down, make him talk, make him admit his involvement in the murder since all evidence points to that. But Monty will not break his vow of silence on the matter. "We rehearsed and rehearsed and I thought Monty and I had those scenes going like gang busters. Then we filmed the first one and I thought, wow. This is good. After three takes I watched Monty's reaction and instead of letting me know whether it had been OK—I mean I had been playing the scene with him—he'd turn to Mira and they'd have this sign language going. They would ignore me completely. The second time it happened I said, well, to hell with it. And things were never the same between us after that. It was like a conspiracy behind your back."

Even so, Malden admits that "Monty was marvelous in *I Confess*. His ability to project mood and a held-back strength is quite extraordinary—it's a high point in the film." Truffaut believes "he was truly remarkable. Throughout the picture his attitude as well as his expression is consistent. He has an air of dignity at all times. It's only through his eyes that we see his bewilderment at all the things that are happening to him."

During filming in Quebec, Vittorio De Sica came to see Monty about his film *Terminal Station,* which the two planned to make together starting in December in Rome. "They carried on a long discussion in French," Mira Rostova recalls. "It turned into an argument after De Sica informed Monty that since he couldn't speak English he was going to hire an Italian actor who would stand in for Monty in front of the camera. De Sica would direct this actor to move and speak exactly the way he wanted and then Monty would copy him!"

Monty retorted angrily he would never do the movie under such circumstances. With that, De Sica laughingly changed the subject and went into a wild monologue about his plans for another movie to be filmed in Chicago, with Monty starring as a babyfaced gangster.

When Monty returned to New York, it was on the eve of the presidential election. He had been very impressed by the eloquent speeches of Adlai Stevenson, "that civilized man," he called him. He was so impressed that when he was asked along with Lauren Bacall and Henry Fonda to speak at a rally at Madison Square Garden, he instantly agreed.

As soon as he informed his father, Bill Clift argued hotly against it. "As a Taft Republican, I'll be laughed off Wall Street if any of my friends read my son is campaigning for Stevenson." He and Monty fought about it over dinner at the Clifts' Park Avenue apartment. Brooks was present and he sided with Monty; he then accompanied his brother while he made the speech.

On the following morning, the Stevenson rally at the Garden and Monty's involvement were carried in all the newspapers. "There were photographs and everything," Brooks said. "Pa became livid with rage. This was the final treachery as far as he was concerned. His anger was actually a culmination of a lot of things. Monty had never listened to him about anything—about his career or how to handle his money—he'd been crushed when Monty refused to allow him to invest his dough. He disapproved of Monty's clothes, Monty's friends, Monty's language, and now this—this was utter betrayal, to support [his words] 'a Commie liberal for President.' He and Monty had another knock-down, drag-out fight ending with Pa crying out, 'When I die, I don't want you at my funeral.' That hurt Monty a lot. But of course he never said anything."

A few nights later, Monty flew to Rome to begin work on *Terminal Station* for Vittorio De Sica. He wrote to Brooks almost immediately, thanking him for his "moral support," but other than that he did not refer to the fight with his father. He just finished with "I hope my speech didn't help Adlai lose the election."

28

Right from the start *Terminal Station* was in big trouble. The day Monty arrived in Rome he learned that Carson McCullers, the original choice, was no longer writing the screenplay. She had been fired by David O. Selznick and replaced by a series of writers including Paul Gallico, Alberto Moravia and Truman Capote (who was given total credit for the screenplay but claims to have written only two scenes). But director Vittorio De Sica and producer Wolfgang Rheinhardt had no say in the matter; Selznick was putting up all the money for the picture as a vehicle for his new wife, Jennifer Jones.

The plot of the movie was based on a story written by Cesare Zavattini (who also wrote *The Bicycle Thief*). It concerned the ending of a passionate love affair between a Philadelphia housewife (Jones) and an Italian-American professor (Monty) who spend their last hours together in a train station quarreling, losing each other, reconciling, even making love in a conveniently empty railroad car.

The picture was filmed in its entirety in Rome's new deluxe depot, and shot only from ten at night to five in the morning. De Sica, who spent his own money to rent the station at night and fill it with people and clanging trains, told critic Charles Samuels he had "terrible problems with the production." Not the least of these was Selznick, who wrote De Sica forty or fifty page letters every day. "I would agree with everything David said, and then do things my way."

De Sica could speak no English. He was used to working with amateurs he could shape on film, so he also clashed constantly with Jennifer Jones and Monty, both of whom had very definite ideas as to how they were going to portray their characters.

One of the scenes—filmed in the terminal's elegant dining room—

was shot more than twenty-three times while De Sica tried in various ways, including pantomime, to make himself understood. Finally he and Monty ended up in a shouting match, and Monty threatened to quit. Selznick had to talk him out of it.

Away from location, Monty got very little sleep. He would work all night and then return to the Hassler Hotel around six in the morning, so keyed up and anxious about the film that no amount of pills could relax him. He would write feverish letters or talk to friends by transatlantic phone, and he would take long walks through the Borghese Gardens.

He saw friends like Pilar Levi from Paramount and journalist Giuseppe Perrone. Perrone recalls, "He hated being in the movie, he was exhausted all the time, he was drinking. I remember how generous he was with his money. He seemed obsessed with helping people less fortunate than himself. He had enormous empathy for almost everybody he met due in part to his imagination—he always wanted to see how everybody ticked. But it was more than that—it was a function of his essential humanness. He listened to other people's dilemmas and instantly responded. I visited once on location at the train station, and I felt the extras were taking advantage of him. He was literally handing out money to them—giving it away. Once he asked me, do you need any money? I said of course not. He was looking for help, but he was always giving help at the same time."

But, he was not an angel—in spite of his generosity. He could be tricky and insensitive and two-faced, and he often manipulated people with tantrums.

His rages were directed at Selznick, whom he called "an interfering fuckface" behind his back. Selznick wanted the movie to look like a slick little love story, complete with a happy ending. Monty sided with De Sica, who thought the picture should depict a ruined romance.

"Love relationships are ludicrous, painful, and gigantically disappointing," Monty ranted at the producer of *Gone With the Wind*. "This couple loves each other but they become unconnected."

The only person Monty felt sympathetic to was Jennifer Jones. Miss Jones, then thirty-three, was an edgy, beautiful Kansan who had won an Oscar for her performance in *The Song of Bernadette*. While she and Monty were working on the film, she remained preoccupied with the recent suicide of her former husband, actor Robert Walker. She also missed her two young sons, who were in school in Switzerland.

Married to Selznick less than two years, she seemed unable to adjust to his energetic domination. "Jennifer is madly in love with David, but she talks openly about his emotional instability to me," Monty confided to Pat Collinge. "She says it's almost as bad as her own. They are both in deep analysis."

Every so often, Jennifer Jones would try and patch up the differences that kept arising between her husband and Monty. After one particularly fierce argument, she gave Monty a very expensive leather briefcase from Gucci. It was of the finest emerald-green Moroccan leather, but the brass clasp kept unfastening. Monty loved to show it to friends with the comment: "Jennifer Jones gave this to me. It's beautiful but it doesn't quite work—how like Jennifer!"

As soon as *Terminal Station* was complete, Selznick took the film back to Hollywood and proceeded to cut and edit it himself, eliminating most of De Sica's colorful but unnecessary vignettes with other travelers, eliminating as well a good deal of footage of the outside of the train station. "It looked like a documentary." The story itself was so fragmentary, the final version, retitled *Indiscretion of an American Wife,* lasted only sixty minutes.

When it was screened for him Monty declared he hated the picture and denounced it as a "big fat failure." But strangely enough—with all the pressures involved and without Mira Rostova—he gives a lively, provocative performance, which also was perhaps his most sexual one.

He plays the cliché situation (the breakup of two lovers) with drama and urgency and a sense of style. Passion clings to his every move, every gesture, every look. At the core of his characterization is his exasperated absorption, both in the situation and in Jennifer Jones; he seems unable to talk or think of anything else.

Their lovemaking scene, done in close-up in an empty train car, has a bold, voluptuous quality to it. Monty is caught in the throes of a grand passion—he is a man in love, rapt, intuitive. It is one of the few times Monty ever played a man in love, an intelligent sensitive man, and he plays the character with a flourish—ending his performance with an operatic leap across the train tracks to embrace his mistress for the last time, narrowly missing being crushed to death by an oncoming express.

When *Indiscretion of an American Wife* was finally released in 1954, it received universally bad reviews.

29

Monty had been waiting to play Prewitt in *From Here to Eternity* for almost two years, but in spite of entreaties by author James Jones, Harry Cohn wanted Aldo Ray. For months, director Fred Zinnemann fought with Cohn over casting.

They fought while the mammoth screenplay was being written first by Jones, on the Columbia lot. They continued to fight while screenwriter Daniel Taradash reshaped and compressed the 816-page novel into a 161-page shooting script. They were still fighting after other stars like Burt Lancaster and Joan Crawford had been set for leads.*

Zinnemann finally threatened to quit unless Cohn agreed on Monty. Columbia's president asked why. "Because," Zinnemann answered, "I want to make a good picture and Montgomery Clift is the only actor who can play Prewitt."

Cohn acquiesced—Zinnemann promptly phoned Monty to tell him the news. "Hooray," he cried, "now I'm a fuck-up!"

"Fuck-up" was his way of describing what turned out to be the most complex and subtle performance of his film career. (Later Leslie Fiedler would write an essay about the character of Prewitt, calling him a "hero-bum," "a slob philosopher," "a modern Ishmael.")

Time magazine put it another way: "Clift's Prewitt is a man who can't play it smart because he is cursed with an ultimate piece of wisdom—it's reflected in one of his lines, 'If a man don't go his own way he's nothin'.'"

* Miss Crawford later quit in a dispute over costumes and was replaced by Deborah Kerr.

Robert E. Lee Prewitt is a wanderer, a loner—a soldier who refuses to join his army division boxing team on moral grounds: he
once blinded a friend in the ring. As a result he is given "the treatment" by a vicious army officer—but in spite of the treatment he will
not give in, he will not box.

Monty saw Prewitt as a man who had no place to go but the
army—he had to end there after bumming around the country. "Pru
is a limited guy with an unlimited spirit," he said, "an inarticulate
man, never a 'word' man." During filming he worked for hours over
his scenes, cutting his own lines back in the script to a bare minimum. "Good dialogue simply isn't enough to explain all the infinite
gradations of a character," he said. "It's behavior—it's what's going
on *behind* the lines."

His Prewitt never says much; when he does it means a lot.
"How can you love the army when it treats you so badly?" his
hooker girlfriend asks, and Pru replies, "Just because you love something don't mean it has to love you back."

He decided from the first that part of Prewitt's strength comes
from revealing as little as possible about himself except when he
plays the bugle. Then, and only then, can he express himself richly
and fully—honking, smearing, trilling out the notes in a spray of jazz
and blues. The horn becomes a key to his world, and when he plays
he disturbs, and soothes, all who listen to him.

For weeks, Monty hunted through every music store in Los Angeles trying to find the same kind of crystal mouthpiece Prewitt used
"when he played the taps at Arlington." But the mouthpiece was no
longer being made.

For weeks before filming started Monty also worked with a musician religiously until he learned how to play the bugle himself. Even
though he made no sounds on film he believed it was essential that
his mouth and throat movements be just right—and they were. In the
movie, his entire body seems forged with the notes blaring out from
his horn.

Monty had Mira Rostova fly out to Hollywood before filming
started on *From Here to Eternity*. She analyzed the script with him
and she also worked with him and Frank Sinatra on their scenes. But
Dr. Silverberg was pressuring Monty to break with Mira—he didn't
want him to be so dependent on her—and so, just before shooting
started, Monty informed Mira she had to leave. Mira angrily replied,
"All right, I'll go, but you'll never be able to perform without me."

This remark offended Monty so deeply he started to drink heavily. They were supposed to meet Merv Griffin for dinner but Monty got so drunk Mira was afraid to get in the car with him. Monty drove off without her. She waited, terrified, for his return. "I was afraid he was going to have an accident."*

When he returned from dinner that night—still drunk—Mira asked him if she could phone Silverberg for him and Monty agreed at once. He kept repeating, "I feel so lousy. . . ." Mira then phoned the analyst, who told her curtly to mind her own business. When she interjected that Monty had asked her to call, Silverberg broke in with, "Stop interfering with my patient. He is perfectly all right."

Mira said she was shocked by the doctor's refusal to deal with somebody who was obviously very ill and needed professional help. "He wouldn't do anything." She called him once more and was again told to stop interfering. "So I did, but I had a premonition something terrible was going to happen."

As soon as filming started Monty did not drink at all during the day. "He was very excited about the movie," Jack Larson said. "I remember he wanted to get to the airport very early to make sure he'd be sitting next to Deborah Kerr on the plane."

The first weeks of shooting began in Hollywood, March 2, 1953; then the entire company flew to Hawaii to shoot all the exterior scenes outside Schofield Army Barracks. Cohn was demanding they keep a tight schedule—they arrived at five in the morning and were filming by ten.

"We had a lot of fun," Zinnemann recalled. "We'd have dinner together every night—Deborah Kerr, Burt Lancaster, Frank Sinatra, and Monty. Frank tried to phone Nairobi where his wife, Ava Gardner, was making a movie—we'd kid him about being jealous of Clark Gable, Ava's costar."

The fun ended for Sinatra when Zinnemann gave in to an order by Cohn, who insisted that the big drunk scene with Monty and Sinatra be played standing up rather than sitting down. Zinnemann went along with Cohn after a bitter argument with Sinatra—they never spoke after that; nobody on the picture ever forgot the incident.

Nobody ever forgot how Monty worked either. "Monty was so

* He'd already had one since his arrival in California; he'd driven through somebody's hedge in Beverly Hills after a party. The police picked him up, but instead of taking him down to the station they talked to him, telling him how dangerous it was to drive when drunk and not to do it again.

intense about being Prewitt he raised the level of the other actors. He cared so much they started caring," Zinnemann said.

He approached the script like a scientist, said Burt Lancaster. "I've never seen anyone so meticulous."

"He worked out all sorts of broken speeches for himself," Jack Larson said. "In that long scene with Donna Reed, where he explains why he can no longer box, he must have worked over a single speech for at least twenty-four hours straight. Finally he came up with the sentence, 'And then I hit him—and he couldn't see any more.' He said that he couldn't use the word blind because it didn't mean anything to him, but the word 'see' did."

Monty carried around the novel *From Here to Eternity* until it was dog-eared, referring to the book as a character guide. "If we had dinner," Deborah Kerr recalled, "we'd start discussing something other than the movie and then he'd slip back into talking about Prewitt. 'You think I should move that way—how do you suppose Prewitt feels about this?' He was deeply immersed in the part," Miss Kerr went on. "His concentration was positively violent. We had only one scene together. I walked behind him and Monty was supposed to say to Burt, 'Who's that?' He spent two days figuring out how to say, 'Who's that?'"

Every so often he would talk on the phone to Pat Collinge in New York about "Prewitt's relationship with his parents" and how that connected with his affair with the hooker, played beautifully by Donna Reed. "Prew's father beat him regularly," he informed Miss Collinge. "His father didn't give a shit about him, but he loved his old man anyhow—that's why he joined the army, that's why he played the bugle, that's why he wanted to get married, to be a respectable man, someone his dad could accept."

"He would be making superb actor's sense," Pat Collinge recalled, and then "out of the blue he would start ranting against Burt Lancaster. 'He gets top billing, he doesn't deserve to!' he'd yell. 'He is a terrible actor. He thinks he's a dynamo; he's nothing but a big bag of wind, the most unctuous man I've ever met!' and then he'd drop the subject and go back to talking about Prewitt."

When Monty returned with the company to California to shoot all the interiors at Columbia Studios he moved to a suite in the Roosevelt Hotel in downtown Hollywood.

Every morning at dawn he could be seen jogging around a high school track directly across the street from the hotel. He also continued boxing with a trainer, and he also boxed with James Jones, who had once been a Golden Gloves contender. He was going to have two fights in the picture, and he wanted to be in superb condition, "which he was," said Jack Larson. "He was lean, sinewy, stronger than I'd ever seen him."

He could not bear to be alone, and if he was, he would often hang out of his Roosevelt Hotel window tootling on his bugle. He had friends with him constantly, particularly the Greens and actor Jack Larson; above all, he spent endless hours with Jones and Frank Sinatra.

The three of them became inseparable during the filming of *From Here to Eternity*. "They were a motley trio," a press agent said. "Jones looked like a nightclub bouncer with his thick neck and broken face. And there's this edgy cocky little wop Sinatra always spoilin' for a fight, and then Monty who managed to radiate class and high standards even when pissing in the gutter."

The three of them went almost every night to the same Italian restaurant. "I can't remember the name of it—it was somewhere in West Hollywood," Jones said; "Frank knew the owner. We'd sit in the back and talk."

Still, Jones was miffed because his version of the screenplay had not been used—and he was even madder because the story had been toned down. The stockade brutality so explicitly expressed in the book was out, and the commanding officer who gave Monty the treatment was forced to resign, rather than being given a commission as in the book. The result was a not too unflattering portrait of the U.S. Army, which had not been Jones's intention.

"Columbia Pictures ass-kissed the army so they could shoot the exteriors of film at Schofield Barracks in Hawaii without being bothered." Jones remained furious about this and complained about it to Monty and Sinatra.

"We talked about the injustice of life and love," he said, "and then Monty and I would listen to Frank talk about Ava Gardner." He seemed obsessed with her—she had left him, unable to cope with his rages and his entourage, which followed him everywhere.

Once during the course of the filming he became so depressed by her rejection he threatened suicide. Monty talked him out of it.

"We would get very, very loaded," Jones said. "After dinner and a lot more drinks we would weave outside into the night and all sit down on the curb next to a lamppost. It became our lamppost and we'd mumble more nonsense to each other. We felt very close."

Often, when Monty and Jones and Sinatra returned to the Roosevelt where they were all staying they would become loud and obstreperous. They would shout obscenities in the lobby—they would throw beer cans from the windows onto startled passersby. Twice the hotel management threatened to throw them out. Twice Columbia Pictures intervened.

If they weren't too drunk, and sometimes when they were, Monty and Sinatra worked on their scenes together. "Monty really coached Sinatra in the part of Maggio," said Jack Larson. "He spelled out every beat, every moment, and Sinatra was grateful." At that moment the singer was considered a has-been. He had fought and begged to get the part of Maggio—accepting, almost humbly, a salary of $8,000 instead of his usual $150,000.

Occasionally, after working with Sinatra, Monty would visit Jones alone. "He'd come crawling down the fire escape, agile as a monkey, and then swing into my room. He'd be brandishing a bottle of Scotch and a pot of espresso. First time I ever tasted that kinda coffee. I hated it, but I drank it 'cause Monty did. We'd sit around and booze it up. I don't remember much of what we talked about. Monty talked more than me. He was an odd man, but I felt a strange rapport with him while we were making the movie."

Monty tried to draw him out about his childhood in Robinson, Illinois, and about his years in the peacetime army. Jones had been serving at Schofield Barracks in Hawaii the morning the Japanese attacked Pearl Harbor.

"I told him I felt cut off from a lot of experience being a writer, working by myself so much, and he said actors were cut off too! 'Except you writers don't need to hear the sound of applause,' he said. I said, 'What in hell are you talkin' about?' and he stares at me with those funny blazing eyes of his and then he starts laughing that crazy-sounding laugh.

"Monty had a special kind of pain," Jones went on, "a pain he could not release. He had a tragedy hanging over his head like a big black comic-strip cloud. It was so distinct you could almost see it. I never heard him talk about himself personally."

Sinatra and Jones spent so much time with Monty the Greens got to know them both. But Jeanne, for one, did not like the novelist. "Jimmy Jones was on a real macho kick, which I found phony as hell. This was 1953, but he was wearing a silver Navaho belt, silver bracelets, and tight jeans, and he came on very strong sexually."

Once Monty asked the Greens to drive them all to "somewhere.

To an airport, I think. They were going to Las Vegas or Palm Springs. I don't know how we got into this slave-master situation, but we did. Fred and I were furious about it in retrospect. I remember we were in our station wagon. Fred was all by himself in the front seat like a chauffeur. Frank and Monty were in the second seat and Jimmy Jones and I were in the back."

Driving out of Los Angeles Jones talked sotto voce to Jeanne about Monty, saying he found him strange and asking if he was a homosexual. Jeanne said, "I got very prim and said I have *no* idea. With that Jones suddenly confided, 'I would have had an affair with him but he never asked me.'"

From Here to Eternity was being made very fast—it would take only forty-one days to shoot—and Monty was exhausted from the pressure of long days on the set. Midway through filming he decided to go to Baja California for the weekend. Columbia said it was all right, as long as he didn't fly.

Monty asked the Greens to accompany him, and when they agreed he immediately chartered a plane. "We got caught in a dense fog; the plane landed in Tijuana, and we could have been killed," Jeanne said. "It was madness. We finally reached La Paz and stopped there. We did some pearl fishing and lying in the sun. Monty was in terrible shape. He must have started drinking at nine A.M.

"A couple of times I went to his hotel room to cut his hair for him. He had the shakes so badly I had to hold his head against my chest. I knew he had to be on more than liquor."

By this time Monty had become addicted to a whole spectrum of sedative drugs, including barbiturates, tranquilizers, and his almost daily bottle of Scotch. Monty, of course, believed he was drinking and taking sedatives in order to survive—to survive his success, his fame, his dreams of greater power and achievement. He would sometimes say the pressures in his life made him drink more, but he would never admit that drinking was causing pressure—nor would he admit to the conflict he was continuing to have about his sexual identity.

"He wanted to love women but he was attracted to men, and he crucified himself for it," Deborah Kerr said.

How he managed to function creatively remained a mystery to people who saw him stumble and fall at parties, who listened to him ramble and free-associate almost nonsensically when he was on a combination of alcohol and drugs. "His drinking was more deadly than Spencer Tracy's," said a cast member. "Drunk or sober,

Spencer knew who he was, but when Monty drank he seemed to lose his identity and almost melt before your eyes." "But Monty wasn't always on something," Jack Larson insists. "While he was working he was cold sober. Withdrawn maybe, but sober, intense, involved. He felt tremendously responsible to his work."

He couldn't have been on pills or liquor when he shot the fight scene with Ernest Borgnine, who played the sadistic sergeant, "Fatso" Judson, in *Eternity,* who tortures Maggio until he dies in the stockade. Prewitt decides to avenge Maggio's death. He stalks Fatso in an alley, they have a knife fight, and he murders him. This brutal sequence, which runs only three-and-one-half minutes in the film, took twelve hours to produce. The stars performed the scene themselves after Zinnemann found the stunt men's version too slick and professional.

"It was a Saturday afternoon at five o'clock when we started shooting," Borgnine told newspaperman Hal Jacques. "We finished the scene at 4:40 A.M. Sunday. They were the most grueling hours I've ever been through—I felt as though I'd been through a meat grinder."

Monty and he were bruised from head to toe. They took literally hundreds of falls. They threw each other against walls, kicked, punched, slapped and gouged each other.

"Once Monty caught me with a good wallop in the stomach that really hurt," Borgnine said. "For a moment I was tempted to pay him back in kind. I forgot I was acting. I really felt ready to murder him."

That feeling passed, but it was a fight to end all fights. "We went all out and gave it everything—both of us. We tried to wrestle our knives away from each other—we used plastic knives so there was never any real danger, but the falls were real. There weren't any mattresses, or pads, to land on. When we fell we really fell. We hit the pavement hard."

After each sequence they would stop the camera and rehearse the movements for the next one in slow motion. "After we got it down, we'd do it again for the cameras."

Fatso, of course, doesn't know why he's being killed. When Prewitt sees that in the dying man's eyes, he realizes what a senseless thing he's done.

Monty managed to carry that thread, that piece of knowledge right up to the end of the picture to his last scene, where he passively allows the soldiers to fire on him without identifying himself.

The day Monty played that death scene a lot of people on the set cried. He played it as if he knew the murder of Fatso had been to no avail—that he had to die. It was inevitable. "How he evoked that feeling I don't know," said James Jones who watched the scene being shot, "but he ran into his death like someone running into a gigantic tidal wave. His face was gaunt—tense, chalk white—he looked as if he'd had the guts pulled out of him, then he rolls over on the grass and Zinnemann calls cut! And someone says, 'Prew's dead,' in a hushed voice."

As soon as shooting concluded for Monty, May 2, 1953, he made plans to go to the McCarthys on the Cape. But before he left Hollywood he allowed himself to be interviewed by Hedda Hopper at the Brown Derby.

"In one sentence, what is the story of your life?" the columnist asked.

"I've been knifed."

"What are you going to do on Cape Cod?"

"Lie on the beach and grovel in the sand."

The interview continued in rambling fashion; finally, Miss Hopper's last question: "What other professions would you like to go into?" "Bartendering," Monty replied.

Throughout their talk he played with a pencil—now he stuck it into a piece of bread. When anyone paged him at the restaurant he would yell, "Montgomery Clift is dead!"

Miss Hopper watched him leave the Brown Derby—he was dressed in his usual grey flannel slacks, an open shirt and dark glasses. When he got outside he chinned himself on a building that was being constructed while workmen cheered him on—then he ran like a sprinter across the parking lot to hunt for his rented convertible.

While he was on the Cape, Monty stayed in Mary McCarthy's small house in Wellfleet. It was a compact place which Miss McCarthy kept immaculate. When she returned in September she found the rooms full of cigarette burns—on the windowsills, under the bathroom cabinet. "Mary thought Monty wasn't paying attention," Kevin said.

There were other signs that summer that all was not well. Monty swam, lay in the sun, and read a great deal, but he complained to the McCarthys of having blackouts.

During his blackouts that summer on the Cape, Monty drove his car into a ditch on the way to the dump with the garbage. He had no

After the accident Monty's jaw was wired and the left side of his face was virtually immobile.
(Culver Pictures)

Occasionally Monty's left profile was photographed with the following results. (Stephen V. Russell collection)

His right profile was the least damaged, so cameraman Robert Surtees photographed him mainly from the right. (Culver Pictures)

a. In Tennessee Williams's *Suddenly Last Summer* with Katherine Hepburn.

b. With Elia Kazan in Tennessee for *Wild River*.

c. With Hope Lange in *The Young Lions*. (Culver Pictures)

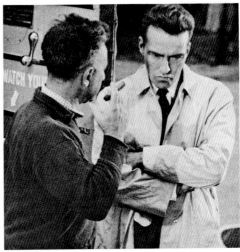

As the lovelorn columnist in *Lonelyhearts*. (Stephen V. Russell collection)

Monty's seven minute scene in *Judgment in Nuremberg* won him his fourth Academy Award nomination.

With Marilyn Monroe. (Eli Wallach)

As Perce, the punchdrunk cowboy in Arthur Miller's *The Misfits*. (Stephen V. Russell collection)

With Marilyn Monroe, Eli Wallach, Arthur Miller, John Huston, and Clark Gable in Reno, Nevada. (Stephen V. Russell collection)

Playing Freud while suffering from cataracts. (Stephen V. Russell collection)

Freud's wedding. (Culver Pictures)

Comedienne Nancy Walker in 1958.
(Joseph Abeles)

Myrna Loy. (The Bettman Archive)

Lorenzo James,
Monty's secretary from 1964 to 1966.

The final movie, *The Defector*.

memory of the incident, nor did he remember running over Mary McCarthy's herb garden. At a restaurant in Provincetown he addressed a waiter, "Hey, fuckface!" but he expressed disbelief when chastised about it later. "I didn't say that!"

One evening he broiled a steak in the fireplace, and as he attempted to place it on a platter it sailed onto the white shag rug. Laughing wildly, Monty proceeded to carve the meat on the rug before serving it to his astonished guests.

Mary McCarthy diagnosed Monty's behavior as, "hebephrenic-schizophrenic reaction that is characterized by silliness, delusions, hallucinations, and regressions."

According to Dr. Lily Ottenheimer, a psychiatrist who knew Monty, "such a diagnosis is nonsense. Montgomery Clift was in no way a hebephrenic—if he had been he could not have functioned so successfully as an artist." It didn't seem to occur to anyone that Monty's hallucinations and blackouts were caused by the vast amounts of liquor and pills he was consuming.

On August 6 he went down to New York for the opening of *From Here to Eternity*. He and Sinatra sneaked into the Capitol Theater and watched a matinee from the balcony. Afterwards, Monty called Jack Larson from a Times Square pay phone and told him he didn't like his performance. Later he reversed his opinion.

The film, of course, went on to get superlative reviews. "It tells the truth about life and about the intolerability of the human spirit," said *Time* magazine. And Bosley Crowther in the *New York Times* wrote: [This is] a film almost as towering and persuasive as its source. . . . It captures the essential spirit of the James Jones study. . . . It stands as a shining example of truly professional moviemaking."

As for Monty, Crowther wrote: "Montgomery Clift adds another sensitive portrayal to an already imposing gallery with his portrayal of Prewitt. . . ." In the *New York Herald Tribune,* his performance is singled out as "taut and sensitive as he takes what is dished out to him, suppresses his love for the bugle except for one ringing 'Taps' and transfers his emotions to a pretty prostitute. He makes himself indigestible to the army, almost willfully, but he always has sympathy on his side, even in an occasion of murder."

From Here to Eternity went on to win the New York Film Critics Award for best director, best movie, and best actor (Burt Lancaster). It won seven Academy Awards (Sinatra and Donna Reed both won best supporting Oscars). Monty was nominated for best actor, but he lost to William Holden, who won for *Stalag 17*.*

For the first time in his career Monty was very upset about not winning. "What do I have to do to prove I can act?" he demanded of *New York Times* movie critic Howard Thompson over drinks at P. J. Clarke's.

Kevin joined them later and said, "Monty appeared in despair." In the past he had joked about award giving, calling it the most meaningless American pastime. Now, suddenly, he wanted to win the Academy Award very much.

Karl Malden has his own theory as to why Monty's performances were often undervalued. "Because he always became part of the warp and woof of a script. So much so that his artistry wasn't always appreciated. If you watch him in *From Here to Eternity,* he completely immerses himself in the character and situation of Prewitt, so much so that he actually sinks into the flesh of the story." Burt Lancaster and Sinatra bulge out of the picture, but Monty is one with it.

Monty and Sinatra remained close. For a while they phoned each other constantly; and they drank together in Hollywood and New York.

Monty idolized the singer. He played his records until they wore out, he kept his photograph in a place of honor in his duplex, and he showed off the gold lighter Sinatra had given him on Christmas that was engraved "Merry merry buddy boy. I'm with you all the way. Maggio."

The two kept in close contact until one night Monty got very drunk and came on sexually with a man at a party in Bel Air. Sinatra witnessed the incident and he had his bodyguards throw Monty out of the party.

---

* The night of the Awards he phoned Renee Zinnemann in despair over not winning. She subsequently sent him a miniature gold trumpet mounted like an Oscar which he treasured for the rest of his life.

30

By late 1953 Monty was beginning to hear a lot about a twenty-one-year-old actor named James Dean. "He's a punk and a helluva talent," Elia Kazan said. "He likes racing cars, waitresses—and waiters. He says you're his idol."

"Jimmy was affected by Brando, but he was more moved by Monty," Dean's good friend, actor Bill Gunn, said. "Jimmy dug Monty's fractured personality—his dislocated quality. Brando was too obvious. Monty had more class."

According to Gunn, people put Dean down for mimicking Monty and Brando, but imitation was absolutely necessary in the desolate fifties. "Monty and Brando fathered a whole generation of actors—Al Pacino, Jack Nicholson, Dustin Hoffman, Bob DeNiro. Monty was the first movie star to seem *obsessed*—slightly nuts. There was a tremendous resistance to craziness in the 1950s and Monty was disturbing—he had an edge."

Dean, a former high school basketball star from Indiana, had hitchhiked to New York to become an actor in 1952. After months of near starvation he began working regularly on live TV. His biggest competitors were Paul Newman and Steve McQueen; they all went up for the same parts, but everybody remembered Jimmy Dean. During auditions he used to lie on the floor to relax.

Ultimately during his stay in New York, Dean obtained Monty's unlisted phone number and called him repeatedly. "Mainly to listen to the sound of my voice," Monty said. He tried to discourage these calls. "He'd just say 'Uh—hello, man—uh—this is Jimmy Dean—uh—how are you?' What the fuck was I supposed to say? 'Hello, man—uh—how are you' back?"

Later he found out Dean phoned Brando regularly too, and he also signed a couple of his letters "James (Brando-Clift) Dean."

After watching Dean on a TV show where he played a psyched-out teenager reminiscent of himself in *Dame Nature,* Monty became even warier. (His only comment was, "Dean is *weird.*") He would not see him on Broadway in Gide's *The Immoralist,* where his sensuous portrayal of a homosexual Arab houseboy won him both a Tony and a Daniel Blum Award, and he refused to meet him whenever he had the opportunity. Nevertheless, he followed his career avidly and questioned all their mutual friends about him.

In the spring of 1954 Kazan cast Dean as the rebellious twin Cal Trask in John Steinbeck's *East of Eden.* Paradoxically, the screenplay had originally been offered to Brando (to play Cal) and Monty (to play the good brother, Adam).

While it was being filmed, Monty heard a great deal about the production. Apparently Dean was rude and generally disruptive with other members of the cast. He carried a gun; he refused to speak to anyone unless it had to do with the movie, and spent a great deal of time in the dressing room meditating. "But his behavior doesn't matter," said a friend. "He is giving an incredibly intense performance as Cal. He is giving *everything.*"

Even more intriguing to Monty was the gossip about the screen test made by Dean and Dick Davalos (who played the good brother). The scene, set in Cal's bedroom, had homosexual overtones, so much so that in the final version of the film the scene was cut.

Although no actor, with the possible exception of Brando, was so sought after as Monty in 1953 and 1954, no actor turned down as many roles.

"Monty could have been the biggest movie star in the world," his agent, Herman Citron, said. "He was always considered before Brando, but he was too choosy. We'd scream at each other over the phone. 'I will not do it Herman,' he'd say. 'It's crap!'; and I'd yell, 'Can't you lower your standards for once?' "*

---

* In the next year Monty said no to the following, among others:

PLAYS
Reclining Figure by Harry Kurnitz
All Summer Long by Robert Anderson
King of Hearts by Jean Kerr
Desire under the Elms by Eugene O'Neill
Traveller Without Luggage by Jean Anouilh

Original screenplays were rare in Hollywood during the fifties. There had always been a tendency to "play safe" and adapt hit plays or best-selling novels into movies. Now, amidst financial anxiety, CinemaScope, and political unrest, this tendency became even more prevalent. "As a result, most of the scripts Monty looked at were absolute crap," said Bill Gunn.

Monty seemed to realize that he needed the kind of role that would give his career mythic weight. John Wayne and Gary Cooper had made picture after picture and the cumulative effect became legend. Monty had played a priest, a killer, a cowboy, and two soldiers, and everything seemed scattered somehow. His mastery of craft worked against him. Unlike Wayne and Cooper, he did not lend himself to type-casting. "You could place Yul Brynner but you couldn't place Clift," critic Andrew Sarris said. "On screen Montgomery Clift was a chameleon—furtive. In every movie he seemed to be looking for himself."

Since *From Here to Eternity,* Monty's standards for perfection had continued to rise. He was pitting himself not only against Laurence Olivier's technical prowess but against Brando's brooding sexual intuitive style also.

He had seen all of Brando's films, the most recent being *The Wild One.* He'd hated the picture but thought, "Marlon is continually creative even with shitty material. He shows you what is going on inside himself."

Monty believed he could achieve anything Brando could in terms of character, and he knew he was as skillful, if not more so, in transcending mediocre scripts, but it was a battle. In the beginning

---

MOVIES
Desiree
Friendly Persuasion
Babylon Revisited
Speak to Me of Love
Marco Polo
Joseph and His Brethren
Prince of Players
Miracle in the Rain
Ethan Frome
End of an Affair
The Wanderer
Fahrenheit 451
Moby Dick
The Trouble with Harry

with *The Search,* it had been an exhilarating challenge, but with each movie the struggle—emotionally and physically—had become more unbearable to him, and it also seemed to do no good.

He believed, somehow, that Brando would eclipse him in both popularity and critical acclaim. "It's a chemical thing," he said, "Marlon connects more immediately with an audience than I do." And yet Monty felt wronged because he believed he'd worked harder. "Working harder doesn't seem to matter."

There was no question about it, Brando was a huge, brute force. Whether in *Viva Zapata, The Men,* or *Streetcar,* his personality over-powered, and to the public at large he was already a cult figure in torn T-shirt, scowling, alienated. As a character on screen he never rationalized or accepted, he simply rebelled. Monty rebelled too, but his impact was more intellectual, reasoned, oblique.

Their relationship was never a close one. "Prickly would be a good way to describe it," said a friend. Monty became very touchy whenever comparisons were made between the two of them as actors. He maintained he felt neither superior nor inferior to Brando, and said, of course there could be no competition between them—they were too different. "We're both originals," he said. But after he started hearing about Brando's shattering performance in *On the Waterfront,* he told several people, including some press, that he'd turned down the role of Terry Malloy, the punch-drunk fighter. He said he kept turning movies down because he was more interested in developing his special Chekov project.

He and Mira Rostova and Kevin had decided it was about time they worked on something together, and that something was *The Seagull.* They would work on it for the sheer pleasure of it, they said, rehearsing it in workshop until it became perfection. After reading through seven published English translations of *The Seagull* (including Stark Young's and Constance Garnett's), they decided to draft their own translation of the Chekov masterpiece.

The trio sat in Monty's duplex, and Mira began by translating each line from the Russian literally. Then she and Kevin and Monty would fight and argue over what Chekov really meant. "It took months—it was a labor of love," Mira said. "Kevin and I ended up doing most of it because Monty kept flying back and forth for picture conferences."

One weekend they went up to Treetops, and while Libby Holman kept them supplied with excellent food and wine, they continued working on the project. "It was all very pleasant," Mira said, "but I had no idea why we were *there*."

When they finished the final draft Thornton Wilder polished it and made line-by-line changes. (Masha's "It's mourning for my life; I'm unhappy" became, in Wilder's words, "I'm mourning for my life; I'm unhappy.")

Arthur Miller also dropped by the duplex to read the manuscript. Both playwrights were enthusiastic about the new version and urged them to do it professionally. *The Seagull* had not been produced in New York since 1938, when the Lunts did it on Broadway.

Eventually word got around that Mira, Kevin, and Monty had done an idiomatic and admirably playable treatment of *The Seagull*. There were many conversations about it in Bobby Lewis's special acting class held at eleven-thirty at night weekly at the 48th St. Playhouse. (In attendance: Kim Stanley, Gaby Rogers, John Fiedler, Maureen Stapleton, Roddy McDowall, Mira, Monty, and the McCarthys.)

The class had been formed with the express purpose of working the actors through every step of a production from auditions right through opening night. "I did it," Lewis said, "because a lot of actors do brilliant work in scenes, but when they get into a production they tend to fall apart."

Lewis thought that working on *The Seagull* in front of the class would be a marvelous opportunity to test his theories, and he suggested it to Monty who nicely but firmly turned him down. (Lewis was shocked and hurt. He was then at the peak of his career, having just directed *Teahouse of the August Moon*.)

"We didn't want a good director," Kevin said, "a strong director like Bobby. We thought we could direct ourselves. Which was probably our biggest mistake."

They still had no plans to do the show professionally. They talked simply of working on scenes in a leisurely manner—possibly in class or in workshop but where they could take plenty of time, without pressure, and luxuriate in Chekov's characters and situations.

Months went by—they continued to procrastinate until producers began to call and tried to pin them down. Everybody wanted to see Montgomery Clift back on Broadway—it had been ten years.

After much deliberation ("because he didn't really want to act on stage again—he was in no shape and he knew it," Mira said), Monty agreed to let T. Edward Hambleton and Norris Houghton present *The Seagull* for a limited run off Broadway at the Phoenix

Theatre. Kevin would play Trigorin, Monty would be Treplev, and Mira would do Nina.

When Mira timidly said she thought perhaps she shouldn't play the seventeen-year-old ingenue, that she would be miscast and considered too old (she was then forty), Monty scoffed, "That's ridiculous! You must play Nina—you're the only one who can." He added, "Norris Houghton will direct so you can do exactly as you want— Norry's going to direct as if he was hosting a cocktail party!"

Privately Monty told Kevin he was doing *The Seagull* for Mira. "She has given me so much—dedicated so many years of her life to me—with so much love and commitment, I want her to have the opportunity to show the world what a rare and gifted actress she is."

Shortly before rehearsal of *The Seagull* began in April, Monty flew out to Hollywood for more movie conferences. While he was there he stayed at Elizabeth Taylor's house. Her husband, Michael Wilding, was away making a picture.

The Greens said his drinking was becoming worse, but they were still trying to ignore the problem. One night Monty was supposed to take everybody out to dinner, but at the last minute a very distraught Elizabeth phoned and said, "Monty's in bad shape. I don't know what to do."

The Greens drove immediately to her house in Benedict Canyon. The place was a mess. Taylor had a veritable menagerie: four cats, two poodles, a golden retriever, even a duck. Some of the expensive furniture was scratched or shredded by the cats' claws. On the big coffee table were six months' worth of movie magazines, all with Monty and Liz covers.

Monty was falling-down drunk when he greeted them. "He made no sense at all," Jeanne Green said. She canceled the restaurant reservation, and she and Fred proceeded to try to cook a meal.

"I was appalled by the state of the kitchen—hardly any food in the refrigerator—a few eggs, butter not too fresh, a couple of pieces of ham. Monty kept interfering. 'I know how to make an omelet better than you.' He broke some of the eggs into a bowl, ended up getting yolk and shells on the floor."

Elizabeth didn't appear for at least an hour, and when she did, Jeanne said she could tell she'd been crying. "The heavy makeup she'd put on couldn't cover her swollen eyes." She was also pregnant with her second child.

It turned out to be a very unpleasant evening, and there were other evenings like that with Monty, since by now he was drinking constantly—before meals, before any public appearance—whenever a crisis arose. There were more and more occasions when his behavior and his judgment were being affected by his alcoholism.

Elizabeth Taylor kept phoning the Greens, begging them to help her with him. Finally Jeanne Green got fed up and said, " 'Look Elizabeth, if you can't handle Monty why don't you let him move in with us? We love him and we know how to handle him. Obviously you don't.' Elizabeth got bitchy right back, and said, 'I love him too,' and hung up on me."

Not long after that the Greens decided to stop seeing Monty. "We just couldn't take his behavior," Jeanne Green said. "We had treasured his friendship and he had thrown it away. I don't love easily. Neither does Fred, but it was an accumulation of a lot of things, a couple of years of things—we felt we could no longer cope with such self-destruction."

The first reading of *The Seagull* was held in Monty's duplex in late March of 1954. The entire company was there: George Voskovec, John Fiedler, Maureen Stapleton, Sam Jaffe, Will Geer, Mira, Kevin, and Judith Evelyn, who'd just been cast as Madame Arcadina. "She knew she was a last-minute replacement for Stella Adler, who'd suddenly backed out of the play," John Fiedler said. Miss Evelyn, a distinguished Viennese actress who'd created a sensation on Broadway in *The Shrike,* felt uncomfortable and insecure.

Even so, the atmosphere was almost courtly—everybody was very well-mannered and in awe of Monty, John Fiedler remembers. "But nothing was ever discussed then, or later, about characterizations, interpretations—a point of view."

The first two weeks of rehearsal passed pleasantly enough. Thornton Wilder sat and watched the proceedings but never said a word, although he conferred periodically with Monty and Norris Houghton. And then suddenly everybody realized nothing was coming together. There were all sorts of acting styles floundering around on stage—Actors Studio, Max Reinhardt, Hollywood, summer stock, Berliner Ensemble. Then there was Mira Rostova's performance as Nina, which everyone tried to ignore.

"It was very unfortunate," said a cast member. "There she was, a mature sophisticated Russian lady playing a seventeen-year-old virgin. It didn't work. She had low energy—didn't project anything but a kind of gloomy Dostoevsky quality."

While they were rehearsing at the Malin Studios, a terrible argument ensued between Judith Evelyn and Kevin which disintegrated into personal criticism. Everyone in the company, Monty included, just walked away from it.

Later, after another argument erupted (nobody remembers about what), Monty threatened to quit the show and his old friend, musical conductor Lehman Engel, was called; Engel came down to rehearsals and talked him out of it.

"We walked around and around the block," he recalls. "Monty was deeply disappointed. In Kevin, in Mira. He loved them both but he thought they were both terrible in the play—in particular Mira—and he would never be able to tell them to their faces. He knew he wasn't as good as he could be either—the entire production wasn't as good as it should be. He was devastated by the entire experience."

After a long conversation, Engel convinced him to remain with the production, and Monty went back to rehearsal.

Finally came the first preview at the Phoenix Theatre, which was a disaster. The audience complained of no energy on stage—and inaudibility. Dorothy Parker was overheard in the lobby saying, "Judith Evelyn looks like a female impersonator in the cheap wig she's been given to wear." Herbert Berghof thought Mira Rostova had been "betrayed" by her so-called friends—Kevin and Monty, "All she needs is some *specific* direction."

After the curtain came down Bobby Lewis came darting backstage to complain about the language in some of the scenes: "What about such and such a speech in the first act?" he demanded of Mira. "It sounds much too modern." To which Mira replied, "Thornton Wilder wrote that line." Lewis murmured, "Oh, I thought Chekov wrote *The Seagull*."

That night Kevin phoned Arthur Miller and asked him to come in and help. "Everybody was waiting for somebody to take over, and Arthur did," Maureen Stapleton said. "In three days he redirected the entire show. His first note was I can't hear you, his second note was I can't hear you, his third note was I can't hear you."

"Arthur really pulled it together," John Fiedler said. "He talked to us about Chekov and about the interior eloquence of the play which he really understood. He told us what was working and what wasn't. He told Monty to stand up, you're an aristocrat, don't slouch. He talked about energy and pace and how, although the play is deceptively episodic and seems to drift, every line is pertinent."

A specific example of Arthur's direction: "Maureen as Masha

had to waltz around the stage at one point, so Maureen asked, 'Why am I waltzing?' and Arthur said, 'If Masha doesn't waltz she'll scream her head off.' Right away Maureen knew what she was doing and she was off and running and she gave one of the best performances in the show."

Judith Evelyn was never able to adjust to the role of Arcadina, the shallow, possessive actress-mother, nor was she able to adjust to the many diverse acting styles in the company; she kept complaining to Stapleton about not being able to respond to the other actors on stage. Finally Stapleton told her a story: "Once there was a march of the animals in the jungle and all the animals were supposed to come out to march—the giraffes and the monkeys and the lions and the tigers and the orangutans and the rhinos—only the elephant refused to join, and finally the monkey asked, 'Aren't you ever going to join the march?' and the elephant replied rather haughtily, 'In the cool of the evening when you all start fucking each other, I can assure you I'll be there.'"

Opening night of *The Seagull,* Maureen Stapleton and John Fiedler were waiting in the wings for their cue when Judith Evelyn sailed past them. She had played her first scene and made an exit to a burst of applause. For a brief instant she paused and hissed, "It's the cool of the evening, darlings," and then she floated off to the other side of the stage to await her next cue.

As soon as the curtain came down on the last act, Judy Balaban and her new husband, Jay Kantor, fought their way backstage to see Monty, "because I thought he'd been wonderful." His dressing room was already crowded when they arrived, and he greeted them "maniacally. He kissed me passionately, and he started crying, 'I love you! I love you!'" Judy said. "Of course, he didn't mean it—he acted quite strange." They left as soon as they could and they didn't go on to the opening night party promotions tycoon Ben Sonnenberg was giving in his elegant, art-filled Gramercy Park brownstone.

Brando, Marlene Dietrich, Harry Belafonte, Lee Strasberg, Thornton Wilder and Arthur Miller were just a few of the guests. Everybody milled about, but most of the people avoided talking about what they'd just seen, except those who couldn't resist tearing apart Mira Rostova's "dreadful performance."

Only a few friends waited for the reviews, which weren't so bad. The *Daily News* called *The Seagull* "a splendid piece of work." Brooks Atkinson of the *New York Times* wrote, "There are some remarkably good individual performances in the Phoenix production of *The Seagull,* notably by Judith Evelyn, Montgomery Clift and Maureen Stapleton. Unfortunately there is also a bad one by Mira Rostova in the vital role of Nina and a colorless one by Kevin McCarthy as Trigorin who is also a pivotal character . . . but the performance is illuminating enough to make the venture worthwhile . . . it is intelligently though imperfectly staged. . . ."

The *Herald Tribune*'s Walter Kerr singled out Monty: "Mr. Clift does not really work any more openly, any more showily than the others but there is a secret, a very clear line of emotion behind the terse facade. The actor's edgy anxiety before the performance of his adventurous play; the elusive contempt with which he tells a novelist his works are charming; the management of a difficult soliloquy in which he edits his own work—all are casual bits of playing and completely telling ones, and Mr. Clift's groundwork is firm. When the play rises to its few passages of explosive emotion—the boy's rage at his mother, his abandoned gratitude for a compliment—the performance enlarges without effort and expands into furious fire. . . ."

Later, in the *New Republic,* Harold Clurman chided, "The real pathos of Clift's performance . . . is not only that he makes Treplev more downcast than he need be and thus more American than Russian, but that as an earnest actor he believes he can pay his debt to his ideals by attempting a challenging role for four weeks out of ten years. He needs ten years' of work on stage to act as well as he potentially can in the kind of parts he aspires to. It is not idealistic and it is certainly not healthy to reserve oneself for certain rare occasions to do what one wants to."

Clurman's scolding reminded Monty that only a decade ago he had told Bill Le Massena and Ned Smith he intended to be the greatest actor in the world, he was going to play Hamlet and Chekov, he didn't care about money or celebrity.

"Monty still talked about being the greatest actor in the world, but he no longer seemed to mean it," Bill Le Massena said. "I'd drop by the duplex and Roddy would be there and Kevin and maybe Maureen Stapleton, and they were all discussing what should Monty do next? *Hamlet* was mentioned frequently, but it was just talk, and Monty would be sitting there drinking . . . ."

In spite of the mixed notices, *The Seagull* sold out for its entire run—there were always lines at the box office and crowds backstage after the show. "Monty was a huge draw," Norris Houghton said. "We could have run indefinitely."

As time went on (the run was extended into July), underground admirers of the production surfaced and theater buffs such as Mike Nichols came back to see the play again and again. Brooks Clift recalled, "It was an unforgettable collection of talents on stage and it made the ensemble playing almost touchingly painful."

But there was a different kind of pain being experienced backstage during the run of the play—the private agony of Mira Rostova. She never said a word about her terrible reviews. Naturally, no one in the cast mentioned them, yet they hung over her head like an evil cloud. "She'd always be polite and dignified," said John Fiedler. "She'd come in before half hour, go into her dressing room to make up. She behaved as if everything was just fine—just dandy. But sometimes when she smiled, her big tragic eyes would be swimming with tears. Underneath she was probably dying. Appearing in a play is a very public thing, and Mira had got the most savage notices of any actor in recent years, and yet night after night she went gamely on— she had guts. Because at almost every performance there were snickers, sometimes laughter, when she spoke, and catcalls and yells of 'Nina, speak louder, we can't hear you, Nina.'" (For some reason Mira was never able to project beyond the first couple of rows.)

And then Monty turned against her. "They had been as thick as thieves during rehearsals," John Fiedler said. Now, although they appeared friendly enough, there was an element missing in their relationship. "They stopped being intimates. She no longer confided in Monty—he no longer confided in her. When they were together in a room there was visible strain."

Although Monty rarely talked about his disappointment with *The Seagull,* he confided to his friend Bill Le Massena that as far he was concerned, Mira had let him down.

When Le Massena argued that she had been grossly miscast, Monty argued back that no matter, he had expected great, luminous things from her as an actress, and even miscast she should have delivered *something.* He had spent years defending her talent to his family and friends, and now he'd been proven wrong.

Le Massena repeated that she'd been miscast in *The Seagull,* and he reminded Monty how much she'd helped him with *The Search* and *Red River, A Place in the Sun* and *From Here to Eternity.* Then he added, If you feel bad, how do you think Mira must feel after those horrendous reviews—going out on stage in front of hostile audiences?

Monty groaned in sympathy, but he never went to comfort Mira. From then on they were estranged.

For Mira, "It was the most excruciating time in my life. I bitterly regretted doing Nina—my first impulse had been to say no. I'd just wanted to work on it in class, never do it commercially. Of course, I was too old for the part. I wasn't right—but Monty kept insisting, insisting, insisting. He always persuaded me to do things, often against my better judgment."

After the show, Monty went somewhere every night. "He was in great demand," playwright Bill Marchant remembers. "Once after a performance of *The Seagull* I ran into him at a party. Monty seemed bored and started to leave. We walked out together. It was a lovely spring evening. We strolled over in the direction of Central Park. You could smell the grass—the moisture in the air—I think there was a full moon. When we reached the Plaza Hotel, Monty said, 'Let's take a carriage and I'll drive you home.' A carriage was approaching and he tried to hail it but it wouldn't stop so he ran after it calling; it still wouldn't stop. Suddenly Monty sprinted in front of it and threw himself in front of the horse! The horse reared, then froze, hooves dangling in midair. I managed to drag him from under the animal's heaving, sweaty belly—and then I gasped, 'What in hell do you think you're doing?' Monty grinned, 'I stopped the horse, didn't I? John Huston said if you throw yourself in front of a cab or a limo or a carriage they *stop* every time.' Then we got in and he drove me home in the carriage, but I was quite shaken up for some time afterwards."

Ned Smith came back from Ireland in the summer of 1954 and went to see Monty immediately. "It was a Sunday afternoon. He was in the duplex and there was an actor with him, a well-known actor whom I disliked immediately. Monty filled me in on everything he'd been doing: *From Here to Eternity, I Confess*—his movie with Jennifer Jones was about to open."

The atmosphere between the three men was rather strained, and Ned said, "Eventually this well-known actor left. I'd made no notice of him as an actor. Pretended I had no idea who he was, although I'd seen him in the movies dozens of times. He even spelled his name for me, and I said, 'I've never heard of *you*.' I said it viciously. As soon as he left I turned to Monty and said, 'Well that's the closest thing to a homosexual you're ever gonna find. I don't like 'im.' And Monty suddenly looked whipped. He didn't like me at all for saying that.

"I said, 'What's goin' on with you?' He didn't answer, just slipped away for a minute, and then I said, 'Oh, for Christ's sake! Why don't you spend the night with a girl and screw the hell out of her?'

"'I already did that and I didn't like it,' he said despairingly."

After *The Seagull* closed in July, Monty drove directly up to Ogunquit, Maine. He'd rented a rambling, grey, shingled house down a wooded road near Perkins Cove. It was a large house with a cathedral living room, stone fireplace and plenty of summer wicker furniture on the porch. Secluded, comfortable, he intended to rest, read scripts, and see Dr. Silverberg.

Bruce Robertson-Dick, a young fisherman and sometime sea captain, recalled: "Everybody in Perkins Cove knew that Montgomery Clift had rented the Wyer place, and my wife at the time was so excited about it, the day he arrived she decided she was going over to welcome him and ask him to come to our town dances. I couldn't persuade her he might want to be left to himself. Against my better judgment we drove over to the house. Sure enough, there's a car with a New York license plate parked under the trees. We go and thump on the door. It's midafternoon. No answer, so we thump some more. Then the door opens and it's Montgomery Clift—hairy as a bear—dripping wet with only a towel wrapped around him. He blinks at us, stammers something. My wife pipes up how much she admires him in the movies, and would he like to come to our town dance Saturday night? Monty says he's come here for a vacation, but he'll try, and then he shuts the door."

Dick's wife was thrilled to have actually seen Montgomery Clift in the flesh, and she hurried back to the village to tell all her friends—and one of them declared she was going to seduce him. After much discussion, it was decided everybody would go back to Monty's that night to catch another glimpse of him. "Looking back on it, we acted like a bunch of prize idiots, but you've got to remember Perkins Cove is a very small place—only seventy-five residents—this was the biggest thing that had ever happened there."

After dark they returned. "All you could hear was the crickets and the mosquitoes. There were no lights in the house, we figured he was having dinner somewhere. Suddenly, we hear a car coming up the road and we scatter into the bushes. Sure enough, the car stops,

Monty gets out. One of the girls giggles. Monty cocks his head; he senses he's surrounded. Rather sheepishly we come out of the bushes —oh, I guess, there were about seven of us. He asks, a little exasperated, 'What do you want now?' My wife steps forward and says, 'I brought some of my friends over to say hello.' Everybody choruses 'Hi' sort of weakly. Monty grins and shrugs. 'Would you like to come in for a drink? All I have is Scotch.' We pile into the house laughing. We were pretty broke that summer. Nobody had enough money to buy beer, let alone Scotch. Anyhow, after that we dropped by Monty's place a couple of times a week. The liquor really flowed. He was very generous with it. He liked his booze. He was a heavy drinker, but I personally didn't think he was an alcoholic. He went out a couple of times on my boat to fish. He took walks along the cove by himself. I don't recall he ever swam—I had the feeling he was embarrassed at being so hirsute."

Eventually the more conservative older neighbors on Perkins Cove complained about Monty's parties. "Drunken revels," they called them; there was talk of drugs and "fairies." Captain Dick remembers, "Our parties were fun—sure we got drunk, but they weren't orgies. Monty did have other parties for his New York friends, but we weren't invited." He went on to say that long-time residents of the cove disapproved of Monty's behavior because he was so different. "He was erratic, difficult, convivial, funny—weird and bitingly perceptive about the townspeople who cricitized him."

He did not talk about his work while he was there, but he had a stack of scripts "two feet high," Dick remembers. "The only one he seemed interested in was the one about a Private Slovik.* He had me read it and we talked about it. I told him it wasn't too cheery, and he laughed his crazy-sounding laugh."

Monty's exit from Perkins Cove was a rather ugly one. He was supposed to leave July 31 to make room for new tenants coming August 1.

The Wyers, who owned the house, drove up the morning of the 31st to say good-bye to Monty and to make sure the place was in good shape. When they opened the door they found the rooms a shambles—chairs overturned, rugs rumpled, glasses broken, liquor and soda bottles strewn all over the floor. And in the center of the room lay Monty stark naked, passed out.

* The brutal account of the only American soldier who was executed for desertion during the Second World War.

When they tried to rouse him they found it almost impossible. "He seemed under the influence of both booze and drugs," Evan Smith, the real estate man, said.

Eventually they managed to dress him, and they propped him up on the front porch while they scoured the house from top to bottom—they cleaned until midnight, and they never forgave Monty, who did nothing but slump on the porch for hours as if half alive. Finally he staggered down to his car and drove off.

31

By the fall of 1954 Monty was being compared to Jekyll and Hyde by many of the people who saw him regularly. When he was sober and alone with a friend he was relaxed, articulate, the "old Monty." But after a couple of drinks he often acted almost deranged, sometimes getting down on all fours and barking like a dog. Beyond a certain point he was growing possessed; his tolerance for liquor diminished as alcoholism increased its hold.

"Monty started going downhill after *The Seagull* with frightening rapidity," Mira Rostova said. "He was not nearly as focused—on his life or on his work." One of his doctors bluntly told him he was reaching the breaking point, and although he still refused to acknowledge his dependence on liquor, the ravages of drink were beginning to systematically destroy his dignity, his possessions, his friendships, and his health.

Intimates like the McCarthys no longer permitted him in their house at Dobbs Ferry—this after Monty had tipsily dropped their son Flip on the floor. The Greens refused to see him, and the Lunts, who had never tolerated drinking, had long since stopped proffering invitations to their East End Avenue home.

Kevin still came by the duplex regularly, but "we were afraid to have him [Monty] around our kids." Still, Libby Holman accepted him as he was; she seemed immune to his behavior. At a dinner at Treetops, Monty got very drunk and kept resting his face in the soup, and Libby would jerk him up like a doll, wipe his cheeks, and go right on talking to her guests.

Friends like Nancy Walker, Jack Larson, and Bill Gunn also tried to ignore Monty's drinking problem "because he wasn't always drunk." And his new secretary, Marge Stengel, who replaced Arline in late 1953, fended off the press and organized his life as much as she could.

"Marge was always there when Monty needed her," Bill Gunn said. "She would stay upstairs in the study all day going over scripts, over correspondence. She was tough, she was efficient, and she became very important to him. He depended on her. She took care of shopping, made sure the maids really cleaned the duplex properly. Monty had to have everything perfect—even his Perrier water had to be in a certain place in the living room."

It was Marge who screened the dozens of phone calls that came in from New York and Hollywood, who made appointments for Monty's friends to come and go. A few friends like Elizabeth Taylor, Roddy McDowall, and Bill Le Massena were always put through immediately on the phone, and they had special entree; they dropped by the duplex frequently. They often left very depressed.

Another friend, Jack Larson, started telephoning Dr. Silverberg, suggesting he put Monty in Silver Hill Sanatorium so he could be cured of drinking, but the analyst always cut him off, telling him not to interfere.

"Here was this doctor taking Monty's money, his time, fucking him over and letting him kill himself by inches—it was criminal," Larson said. At one point Larson brought Monty dead drunk to the psychiatrist's office at ten in the morning and deposited him on the doorstep, but it did no good. Silverberg still would not acknowledge that Monty had any problem with alcoholism.

Sometimes when it became almost uncontrollable, Monty would go up to Treetops to dry out with Libby's help. Libby had dried herself out on many occasions; she knew just what to do. She also believed that addiction was not only an illness but a central human fact, a drama; that one can't use will power to get off booze, one has to reach a state of mind where one doesn't want or need it.

She was no longer drinking herself because her ulcers were too bad, and she'd cut down to four mentholated cigarettes a day to protect her throat. She was involved in rehearsing her one-woman show, *Blues, Ballads and Sin Songs,* which was to open October 5, 1954, at the Bijou Theater for one week only.

It was something she had started working on ten years before when she performed with Josh White at the Vie Parisienne. Later she sought Carl Sandburg's advice, and she researched at the Library of Congress. "Oh, gosh!" she would exclaim to Monty, extending her arms and flapping them, "I want to do more than torch songs! I want to do songs that are really Americana, not just blues."

She went all over the United States collecting songs: songs sung in chain gangs, in cotton fields, jails, and bordellos. In the fall of 1954, after trying out the highly stylized program in London, Paris, Milan, Amsterdam, and The Hague, she and her accompanist, Gerald Cook, rehearsed for hours at Treetops, rehearsed numbers like "On Top of Ol' Smokey," "Proud Mary," and "Love for Sale," which they performed for Monty. "Gerald's oriental accompaniment sounds like a drug pusher's cry," he told them gleefully.

He also liked Libby's unorthodox use of a kitchen chair in her show. "It's more than a prop," he said. Rocking it back and forth, she would twist her body around it, kneel and pray before it, huddle on the floor next to it, sob over it before stretching herself full length on top of the piano to finish her recital.

Just before the show opened she gave a rare interview (her first in ten years) to the *New York Times,* in which she explained, *"Blues and Ballads* is not a concert per se. I don't know what it is. It is, however, what I want to do." She paused, smiled, then shouted, "I sing anger or passion!" Then, lowering her voice, she said, "Out it comes. I don't spare the vocal cords. A lot of the tones are hideous, but they're hideous for a reason. They're anguish and when you're anguished you don't have a pure tone. It's not like singing torch songs, all that precious special junk."

The interviewer, J. P. Shanley, asked her if she thought her career had been altered by the tragedies that had marked her life, the sudden death of her husband and her son.

"My professional life has been going a certain way, and no matter what happened to me, I think it would have taken the same turn. I may have acquired another dimension, but my course would have been the same. I'm really of the Maude Adams school. Private life is one thing, and professional another."

Blues, Ballads and Sin Songs opened to much fanfare on Broadway and got respectful reviews; "artful and often interesting" was the general consensus of opinion. But Walter Kerr in the *Herald Tribune* thought "there was a private studied quality to the program. . . . Holman seems to be listening to something the audience can't quite hear. . . ." John McClain in the *Journal American* joked, "I expected her to wind up balancing that chair on the tip of her nose. . . ." Atkinson said he missed the old 1920s vulgarity in her voice: "Her best songs are still torch songs. . . . Then the deep, sultry voice has a chance to express broken-hearted passion and there is a marvelously self-assured cynical humor, insolent, wheedling in her rendition of 'Body and Soul.'"

Libby was exhausted after the show closed. She and Monty immediately went to Havana together, staying at the Hotel Nacional near the Du Pont property on which Louisa Carpenter had an estate, and they lay in the sun all day and sometimes attended porn shows, strip joints, and brothels at night. They had a chance to be completely depraved in Cuba. Money was no object, so they could buy all the sex and drugs they wanted.

Magda Vasquez Bellow recalls seeing them almost every day either on the beach or in the gift shop of the hotel. "Libby Holman was a middle-aged woman informally dressed, not too well groomed, and always giving the impression of being slightly high—perhaps on dope. Montgomery Clift was always somewhat loud, not too well mannered, and like Libby seemed to be more or less high or on dope. Their relationship seemed a happy one but . . . there was something wrong and not healthy somewhere.

"They laughed a lot in a stupid, rather childish way. They argued from time to time. Monty's table manners were obnoxious. He was anything but the timid, sensitive person he gave the impression of being in his films. She looked very much the part of a tough cookie, and must have had him—quote—'under her spell.'"

Most of the time Monty seemed unembarrassed by his excesses —his displays of cruelty or his bursts of extreme tenderness and generosity (huge wet kisses, tears, gifts of money, of advice).

"He couldn't say no," said Bill Le Massena. "When he was sober he still had enormous energy and curiosity. Jesus—he seemed inexhaustible and he reacted excessively to everything and everybody. He allowed people to come into his life who had no business in his life—the lowlifes, the degenerates, eccentric losers from New York and California. He allowed them in and he gave to them as deeply and fully as he did his friends."

And yet he treated the man who was living with him then "like shit," Bill Le Massena said, "and this guy took it because he loved Monty and thought he was an inspired human being. Monty would get him to do all his parties—you know, order the food, the liquor, even do the inviting, and then just before the guests arrived Monty would say, thanks a lot and good-bye, and the poor guy would leave. He knew better than to come back before the party was over."

Monty was giving a great many dinner parties throughout 1955. He gave one dinner for Greta Garbo, and he invited Libby, Thornton Wilder, Arthur Miller, the McCarthys, and businessman George Schlee, who was supposedly Garbo's lover. Throughout the dinner Schlee kept baiting Libby Holman about the mysterious death of her husband, Reynolds, and her own trial until finally Garbo, sensing everybody's embarrassment at the table, grunted, "Shut up," and Schlee did.

Garbo said nothing more until much later in the evening, when she suddenly began talking animatedly about the glories of the Hammacher-Schlemmer store. Apparently she went there to browse almost every afternoon of the week.

Monty took her out several times alone. "He had a violent crush on her," Blaine Waller said. " 'She is a veritable Sphinx—*fan*tastic!' " he would say. At the end of one date he managed to kiss her goodnight. "Her lips are chapped," he said.

32

Throughout 1955 and into 1956 Monty didn't work, although he had plenty of opportunity—he was offered every screenplay of note from *The Devil's Disciple* to *Trapeze* to *Bus Stop,* but nothing pleased him.

"If he had only concentrated on something then," Bill Gunn said, "to hell with being picky—his life might not have turned in on itself. He was a terribly bright, concerned human being, but like all of us he needed something to focus on, something to believe in."

The winter of '55 Monty skied in Canada; he went to Cuba again and to Italy, but in New York, except for occasional forays into Bloomingdale's or the Isle of Capri restaurant, he remained holed up in the East Sixty-first Street duplex.

There were scripts all over the apartment—dozens of scripts from Hollywood, New York, Europe—he read them all and made notes but he found nothing he liked. He had a terrifying time sense. At thirty-four he called himself "an old man." Part of him believed in the eighteenth-century romantic's view of life—that exquisite artists like Keats and Shelley died young—that for the artist *life* tends to corrupt—that the intensity and true life of creation and feeling simply cannot survive middle age.

He was beginning to wonder if he would ever have a lasting relationship with anyone. He still dreamed of getting married. He was sick of the pickups, the one-night stands. He was even tired of his most recent lover, a young actor who borrowed money from him and seemed to be using him to further his career.

So Monty would drink. And then he would end up in bed with someone. "It didn't matter what sex you were," Jack Larson said. "If Monty really liked you—man or woman you ultimately went to bed with him. If he liked you, he couldn't keep his hands off you—touching—caressing—hugging—he was very physical and very, very affectionate. And of course he was always passing out with you and then you were undressing him and putting him to bed and finally you were ending up in bed with him too."

Still Monty was lonely. Director Herb Machiz said, "The real tragedy in most homosexual lives and for a person as sensitive as Monty was having to accept the tremendous disappointment of never finding a mate worthy of him."

He clung to old friends like Bill Le Massena, Libby Holman, Ann Lincoln, and Roddy McDowall.

He was restless—edgy, he'd move around the duplex with a kind of jerky rapidity—or he'd sprawl shoeless on the floor. He'd make fun of President Eisenhower's atrocious grammar. He'd become a fan of Mickey Spillane: "D'you think I could ever play a sadistic private eye?" he once demanded. He was a great observer of all things American, and he kept a list in his head of fads. "Boy, they die fast," he'd say, "remember the bomb shelters and Davy Crockett T-shirts? I bet they're moldering somewhere. And how about chlorophyll toothpaste, mon vieux?"

When he went out it was usually to a screening or to a show: "But it was always a big deal to appear anywhere in public with him," Bill Gunn said. "You'd have to sneak into your seat after the lights went down—dash up the aisle before curtain calls. Monty said he hated being recognized or fussed over."

Even so, he could occasionally be persuaded by Gunn and a few other close friends to go to some "cheapie" restaurant in the Village or on the West Side. But such outings often turned into disasters.

"One night," Gunn recalled, "we were in this Italian place on Eighth Avenue. We're just eating pasta and rapping. Out of the corner of my eye I see a girl at another table staring at Monty. She gets up to make a phone call. I think nothing more about it till we've paid our bill and are on the street. Suddenly Monty's yelling, 'Let's get out of here!' because a gang of people including the girl from the restaurant have appeared out of nowhere and are rushing hysterically at Monty, flinging themselves at him, yelling, touching. They just had to feel close to someone they believed was special."

In a moment they managed to hail a cab, but not before Monty was mauled and tugged and pinched. Once in the cab that wasn't the end of it. The kids remained glued to the windows pressing their faces against the glass. "As we take off there's a big smack as if somebody hit the car hard. Monty is leaning back on the seat his face red and sweaty with disbelief."

When they arrived at the duplex and got out to pay the fare they noticed the door of the cab was dented as if some huge force had jammed into it.

"It was weird being with him sometimes," Gunn said. "Here I was, a twenty-one-year-old black kid from Philadelphia with a genuine culture hero of the 1950s. I sometimes couldn't believe I was with Montgomery Clift. I had hero-worshipped him too when I was growing up. He was a symbol—he'd had a definite effect on me and thousands of other kids. He used to pooh-pooh the fact that he'd had an influence on anybody. 'I'm an actor not a magician.' And he used to quote from Emerson, 'Heroes usually become bores.'"

Monty did take a great interest in Bill Gunn's career. (Gunn was then giving a highly acclaimed performance in Lou Peterson's play *Take a Giant Step*.) "Monty encouraged me in everything I did. He kept telling me, don't copy anybody. Be proud of yourself." He frequently worked with Gunn, breaking down roles he played on TV. "He wasn't a very patient teacher, but God he knew what he was doing as an actor. He made me aware of how essential it is to be specific."

When Gunn appeared off Broadway in other shows, Monty would watch his performance from the wings, and as he exited, he would give him whispered directions or comments between scenes.

Later, when Gunn wrote his first Broadway play, *Marcus in the High Grass,* Monty came up to see it at its Westport tryout. "He sat on the aisle and sobbed—loudly—throughout the performance. I thought his expression of emotion was wonderful!"

At one time, Monty told Gunn he'd like to take some cocaine with him. He talked about it being a speedy high and with no bad aftereffects like the amphetamines he often swallowed. There's a golden glow of self-confidence, he said, and it kills the pain of being yourself. Gunn said he didn't want to; Monty never brought up the subject of drugs after that. "He wasn't a junkie, contrary to rumor. Sure, I know he took uppers and tranquilizers. But he wanted to feel up, and heroin is not a high—you nod off and contemplate yourself. Monty was never like that."

Every so often Monty would bring up—inexplicably—the subject of his family. "He told me he hated his mother and how she bullied his father, and he told me how he'd recently called her a cunt at the dinner table because she had been rude to the maid. He talked about

Brooks and how he wasn't living up to his potential. He was wasting his time screwing too many women."

Once Gunn came over to the duplex and found Monty cold sober but in a rage. "He had these beautiful Daumier lithographs—originals—on the floor and he was smashing his bare feet into the glass. Miraculously he hadn't drawn blood. I grabbed him away and said, 'What in the fuck are you doing? Those are valuable.' And he said, 'My *mother* gave them to me,' and I said, 'Well, they're too valuable to ruin like that, stop it.' And he said, 'I don't want them—you want them?' I guess I nodded—next thing I know he'd packed them up for me in a tote bag. They're now hanging in my house in Nyack."

After a while Gunn said he ducked the subject of Monty's parents. "It was too heavy, too painful for me to deal with." Gunn knew in spite of their disagreements that Monty still saw his mother regularly.

"He may have said he hated her," Bill Le Massena said, "but Sunny remained the most important person in his life, and he was maddened by this. They still had a very close, almost conspiratorial relationship. Early on she had confided in him all of her secrets—now they were two-faced with each other. Sunny was always tender and affectionate when they were together; when speaking about him to other people she was often unduly harsh."

She was particularly critical of his continuing relationship with Libby Holman. They were virtually inseparable and Monty called her "my best girl." Holman was then actively supporting Martin Luther King's bus boycott in Montgomery, Alabama. The civil rights leader dined frequently at her home, often with Monty in attendance.

As long as Monty and Libby remained together* there were constant references to them in the columns and their antics were duly reported—how they sat in "21" picking their teeth, how they entered a Museum of Modern Art opening and were so boisterous they had to be quieted by one of the Rockefellers. Monty often kissed Libby in public and occasionally perched on her lap. He also had an X-ray of her skull in a shadow box in the duplex and when anybody asked him what it was he'd chuckle and say, "That's my steady girl."

When Libby traveled to Europe alone Monty would lend her his watch, "then he'd telephone me in Paris or London and ask the time.

---

* Eventually a play about their affair entitled *Single Man at a Party* played briefly at the Theatre Manqué off Broadway. Ruth Merrick starred in it, and Joan Crawford optioned it for the movies.

He'd figured out the difference and knew what hour it was back in New York."

They both shared expensive tastes—one in particular, fresh caviar. "Whoever loses a bet pays with a pound of caviar," Libby told Eleanor Harris. "Last time we bet we went to the Madison Avenue Fruit Market, so the loser would have to buy the caviar, but neither of us could bear waiting till we got home so we ate the entire pound with our fingers during the walk home." Libby called such indulgences "royal madness."

Mostly they stayed for weeks on end in Connecticut at Treetops. Actor Roddy McDowall was often there, too, as was Thornton Wilder; he dropped by to discuss *Alcestis,* which Monty said he would star in at the Edinburgh Festival that summer. He was even growing a beard for it.

Late that same spring McDowall took dozens of photographs of Monty—shadowy, romantic portraits in which his features are taut and intense and his expression is pure and steadfast. In many of these photographs, Monty's hair is chopped off unattractively close to his head. Whenever he wasn't working he'd always go to the barber and get a G.I. It looked terrible, but he seemed to want to look that way. "It was a way of forgetting his narcissism," Bill Gunn said. "And I've never known anyone who liked being in front of a camera as much as Monty. He was the same way in front of a mirror—never ashamed; he enjoyed looking at his reflection. He was like a woman in this regard. He could stare for minutes on end at his image unself-conscious—totally relaxed."

While he was up at Libby's he had a nasty accident in her car—a brand new Simca which he smashed into a tree, and he landed in the hospital. The newspapers were going to run a story about it, but Libby's lawyers managed to hush it up. After that Monty was so leery of driving he gave away his own car—a green MG—to a friend. Later the friend sent him a bill for a thousand dollars for having the car overhauled. Monty couldn't believe it. "Everybody tries to take advantage of me because I'm a movie star"; he refused to pay that bill.

That summer he went up to Maine again to see Dr. Silverberg and to confer with Thornton Wilder on *Alcestis.* After much thought, he had decided that he could not do the play unless there were major changes. He found much of the dialogue forced and pedantic and told Wilder that as they sat on the beach together. "Thornton became so enraged at my criticism he almost jumped into the Atlantic Ocean,"

Monty informed Mira afterwards. "He said not one word of his dialogue would be changed, and he stormed off."

Soon afterwards Monty and Libby Holman flew to Europe and traveled all over Italy for almost three months. When they returned to New York it was October. Monty stayed over in Libby's brownstone. She would often wake him up with coffee and the newspapers; one morning not long after they got back she did just that and also said, "Isn't it terrible what happened to Jimmy Dean? He was killed in an automobile race on Highway 66. He was driving his silver Porsche. His neck was broken; his chest crushed when it smashed into the steering wheel."

Monty sat up and threw up across the white satin sheets. "James Dean's death had a profound effect on me," he told Bill Gunn later. "The instant I heard about it, I vomited. I don't know why."

Ned Smith had been reading in the papers about Monty and Libby Holman. He was concerned for his friend, concerned and irritated too because the last times they'd spent together had not been pleasant. Smith felt he was going ahead with his own life—progressing "in my own small way," but it seemed to him that Monty was standing still. "This bothered me tremendously—because until recently Monty had the world by the tail—he'd had absolutely everything, and now he was blowing it."

One evening Smith dropped by the duplex. "We sat around talking. Monty was by himself—and I just asked him point blank, 'What is all this talk about you and Libby Holman?'

"He was very arrogant, as well he should have been—it was none of my business what he did with his life. 'I'm having an affair with Libby Holman,' he told me definitely. 'Is it any business of yours?'

" 'No, it isn't,' I said, 'except I think you'd want a younger girl.' "

Monty didn't answer. Instead he changed the subject and began asking Smith rather sarcastically if he enjoyed being out of work (he'd just quit his job). "He seemed to take pleasure that I was out of work—'Now you're like us, Smith,' he said, 'like actors—I've been out of work for months and months. Now you know what it feels like.' "

Something prompted Smith to demand, "Why don't you play Hamlet then?" and Monty said, "I'm not ready to play Hamlet. People say I am, but I'm not." "Now that should have been enough but I kept at him and at him as to why he wasn't working more or wanting to achieve or progress. I wasn't smart enough or perceptive enough to realize the psychological mess he was in, and a damn mess it was too."

Smith continued needling him as to what was the matter, and why he seemed different—had he lost enthusiasm and interest in everything? When Monty wouldn't respond, Smith blurted, "Get rid of my letters—throw 'em away!" With that Monty cried, "Smythe! Don't say that. Your letters mean a great deal to me. I reread them all the time. I care about those letters. . . ."

Until that evening Smith thought Monty did care. For nineteen years they'd shared a rich correspondence which seemed to reflect their growth as men, as adults. Since the very beginning of their friendship Monty had written compulsively of his world, his dreams. And Smith had done the same. "In all my letters I tried to show Monty *my* world, my experiences—sailing, my love and fascination with the sea, my adventures as a chemical engineer in Iceland or Spain. I thought as an artist he should be aware of different, opposing things in life, but now I felt he no longer cared, which is why I told him to destroy my letters. And I think he ultimately did."

They didn't talk much after that. Eventually Monty left the room. Smith thinks he must have taken something—pills—because "when I turned a few minutes later, he was leaning against the wall, and he'd lost all outward zip and seemed peaceful and quiet, and his eyes were glassy. 'You're sick aren't you?' I said, and he said, 'Yes, I am.' "

There seemed nothing else to say. Smith got up and left the duplex, and after that evening he did not see Monty for ten years. He moved to Stamford subsequently, married, and had two sons. He said he kept telling himself he was glad to be free of "Monty and that mess. I didn't want to be associated with a guy like that. But every so often his name would come up and I'd say, 'Montgomery Clift, he's an old friend of mine.' I dropped his name so often it was disgusting. You'd think the only worthwhile thing in my life was to have known Montgomery Clift."

One afternoon in November 1955, Blaine Waller phoned Monty and suggested they get together. "Monty said great, and he invited me to come along with him to a screening of *Guys and Dolls*. 'I'm dying to hear Marlon and Sinatra try and sing together,' he said. 'It oughta be a gas.'" Waller agreed, and that evening went over to the duplex to pick him up.

He found Monty "smashed but not too smashed—he was in a very good mood." The two had a lot to talk about in the cab on the way to the movie because Monty had helped Waller get a job as a photographer at MCA, and he wanted to hear how it was working out.

When they reached Loews 86th Street they found the theater teeming with people; the lobby was jammed. "Some studio bigwig was guarding the box office waiting to pass Monty in." They were given the VIP treatment, "roped off seats, the whole bit." They sat down just as the picture started and settled back expecting to be entertained.

But the picture turned out to be terrible. Not long after it started Monty began making very loud derogatory remarks: "Marlon is vomitable—oh, look at poor Frank!" He got so noisy people in the audience were shushing him. Finally, in the middle of it, he said, "This picture sucks, let's get out of here." So they hustled down the stairs.

When they reached the lobby, he was still fulminating against Hollywood corruption and lousy values. "He was really steamed up. Suddenly, for no reason at all, he smashed his fist through the display case, you know, where all the glossy photographs of Marlon Brando, Sinatra and Jean Simmons were pasted up. Glass shattered everywhere. Ushers came running. At first they were furious—then when they recognized Montgomery Clift as the culprit they were tongue-tied. Monty was immediately contrite. He keeps saying, 'I'm sorry, I'm so sorry, I don't know what possessed me.' By this time the manager of the theater is there and some guys from Sam Goldwyn and MCA. This was the big preview, the last before the movie opened. . . . Monty keeps apologizing and apologizing—then he says, look, he'll pay for everything, and with that he darts into the street. I follow.

"He starts running up Third Avenue—running like a jackrabbit chased by dogs. He's laughing, his hooting crazy laugh—" He ran for blocks before Waller told him to stop or he'd bust a gut.

33

Monty had never lost touch with Elizabeth Taylor. They were in fact closer than ever, scribbling notes to one another, talking for hours over long-distance phone. Whenever he flew out to California for a picture conference he stayed with Taylor and her husband, Michael Wilding, and when she came to New York she usually moved into Monty's duplex, sometimes with her two baby sons.

Monty would sleep a half a block away at Libby's, but he would return to his place for all meals and, as he described it, "Elizabethan discussion." "He'd get all excited and fuss over diapers and bottles if the kids were there," Bill Le Massena said. "Mrs. Wilding is visiting me, he'd say, and everybody knew better than to bother them."

By late 1955 the Wilding marriage was in the process of breaking up and Elizabeth, emotionally traumatized by the thought of another divorce, was using Monty as her prime confidant.

She talked endlessly to him about Michael Wilding; they had nothing in common any more—he was twenty years older; he treated her like a child, not a wife. She anguished over the future of her children and over the possibility of being alone again without a man.

Often she would sob hysterically in Monty's arms, and he would hold her until she calmed down. Sometimes he massaged her back for hours and fed her hot milk to soothe her jangled nerves. "He was the kindest, gentlest, most understanding man I have ever known," she told journalist Eleanor Harris. "He was like my brother; he was my dearest, most devoted friend."

Monty loved her deeply. "You know how it is when you love somebody terribly but you can't describe why? That's how I love Bessie Mae." Although he had grown fond of the debonair and charming Wilding, he thought he was weak. He knew Elizabeth resented supporting him and her entire household and always had. Since their marriage, she had made eight films. Once she told Monty how she yearned for a "big, strong guy to take care of her completely, to buy her lots of jewels and pay every bill." She had been supporting her family since she was ten years old.

Occasionally when they were together, Monty recalled his own adolescence when he supplemented the family income by his earnings in the theater. "If you start making money at a tender age the way Bessie Mae and I did," he said, "you become suspicious of everybody's motives, no matter how much they say they love you."

It was Elizabeth who urged Monty to star in *Raintree County* with her. Neither of them thought it would be a particularly good movie, certainly not another *Gone With the Wind* as it was touted by studio flacks. But it would be a chance to work together, which they'd wanted to do since *A Place in the Sun.*

Metro was sinking $5 million into the project—big money in 1956. For the previous year, set decorators, architects, costume designers, scenic artists, and makeup personnel had been at work all over the studio in Culver City. One of the biggest sets, which would take up an entire sound stage, was to be a recreation of Sherman's march into Atlanta. It was a scene that would require a thousand extras.

After being offered $300,000 plus top billing, Monty agreed to star in the movie "so I can work with Bessie Mae." But it was also to pay his debts. He had absolutely no money to speak of, and he'd had to borrow from his agents at MCA to live. However, when he actually signed to do the movie he asked for $250,000. "Use the $50,000 you don't pay me to make the movie better!" he said. MCA tried to argue him out of it, but to no avail.

He thought the screenplay, based on Ross Lockridge's 1948 best seller about the Civil War, resembled a "soap opera with elephantitis." *Raintree*'s plot concerns the tempestuous love affair between an idealistic Yankee schoolteacher, Johnny Shawnesee (Monty), and a neurotic, predatory Southern belle, Susanna Drake (Taylor). It also involves slavery, secession, suspected miscegenation, suicide, and attempted murder. As soon as Monty got the script he began crossing out and rewriting speeches, "so the picture could move a little!"

Before he flew out to Hollywood to begin filming *Raintree County,* Monty made a firm decision—he would no longer drive.

MCA found him a chauffeur named Florian, a Filipino who would drive him everywhere and cook and clean for him as well. MCA also found him a house on Dawn Ridge Road in the Hollywood Hills.

Almost immediately his entire life began revolving around *Raintree County*. He arose at six in the morning. After breakfast, Florian drove him to Culver City. Monty usually drowsed in the back seat, the script on his lap. As soon as he got to Metro he primed himself with more coffee and went immediately to makeup. He thought it was "a riot" that makeup artist William Tuttle had insisted on casting a "Montgomery Clift life mask" ("Like a death mask" he told his ex-lover Josh over the phone. "Bill supposedly needs it to design 1860 whiskers for my chin.")

Some of the scenes requiring the most extras were shot first. The long hours under the glaring banks of lights bothered him. "He was constantly putting drops into his eyes," *Raintree* director Edward Dmytryk recalled. "And cool pads between takes—because he was drinking, his eyes were often bloodshot. He knew they were his best feature—it bugged him when they got puffy or weren't clear."

After his usual lunch of raw steak, Monty would pose for publicity stills or be fitted for more costumes. He had daily sessions with newspaper people and with his agent, Lew Wasserman. Wasserman was pressuring him to sign up for more films. Already the trade papers were filled with items listing Monty's future plans. "Clift will probably star in *Sons and Lovers* after he completes *Raintree County,* and he is considering playing the lead in Fitzgerald's *Tender Is the Night.*" Monty maintained neither was true.

Kevin McCarthy visited him on the set and found him concerned about the movie, concerned about the script. McCarthy tried to kid him about the various turns in their careers. "You're doing a costume picture of epic proportions," he said, "I'm doing a thriller." His latest movie, *Invasion of the Body Snatchers,* directed by Don Siegel, was a science fiction movie which neither of them realized would go on to be a classic of its kind.

Monty was so concerned with the weaknesses in the *Raintree* script he harried Dmytryk with suggestions and changes he'd stayed up half the night thinking up. A burly man with cold eyes and an abrupt manner, Dmytryk had his own problems. He had made forty-seven movies, among them *Crossfire* and *Caine Mutiny,* but he was a former member of the Hollywood Ten who had gone to jail, then recanted to save his career.

"Monty and I met as often as possible for drinks or lunch. I agreed to listen to his suggestions. He was obviously a great actor—very inventive. But I sometimes felt he worried things to death, little things."

He recalled his preparation for a "flash" scene—a scene lasting no more than a second or two on the screen—the scene called for Monty to enter the room and see his baby for the first time. Monty practiced opening and closing the door countless times; he tried it abruptly, tentatively, fearfully, joyfully, excitedly, all to find the one entrance which would convey exactly the emotion he wanted.

One afternoon Dmytryk said Monty planned to have coffee with him. But before doing so he apparently wandered across almost the entire MGM lot, which spanned some 187 acres. On the way he phoned a poetess friend back in New York to tell her what he was seeing.

"He said he'd walked past film laboratories, business offices, police force, fire department, and that he'd gone into warehouses filled with costumes and props. He said MGM was like a complete little city unto itself. He said they were already burning Atlanta on one lot. On another he saw a white Colonial mansion, on rolling lawns, and beyond that a murky swamp where *Raintree County* reaches its dramatic climax."

When he met Dmytryk he was briefly elated by what he'd seen. "It's going to be an epic production," he said. The director was rehearsing one of the big ballroom sequences in the picture. There were dozens of couples waltzing around the set. "Many of the male dancers happened to be homosexual," Dmytryk said. They watched for a while and then strolled over to the coffee urn. "Oh, Christ, Eddie," he whispered, "don't let any of them behave like fags!"

By the beginning of May, there had been so many whispered comments about Monty's drinking that Metro's production chief, Dore Schary, visited him in his dressing room for several private talks. "He'd been causing trouble. Elizabeth was very upset but not saying anything because they were so close. I explained to him how important it was for him to be sober at all times on the set—that it was essential during the actual shooting. He would always promise me with complete sincerity that he would and not to worry."

But Schary worried enough to insist that the studio take out a $500,000 insurance policy against a possible production breakdown. "It had never been done before," Schary said, "but I had a funny premonition that we should."

The morning of May 12, 1956 dawned foggy; fog hung over the ocean at Malibu and curled around the green hills of Bel Air. The entire University of California campus in Westwood seemed festooned with pearl-grey mist.

Jack Larson dropped by Monty's house on Dawn Ridge Road and spent part of the afternoon there. Monty was exhausted—exhausted from his intensive filming schedule (he was in almost every scene in the movie) and exhausted from listening to Michael Wilding talk. Apparently Wilding had been driving over to the house after Elizabeth went to bed, and he'd been telling Monty his side of the story of his marriage. How much he still loved her and didn't want to lose her—the twenty-year age difference didn't matter, he kept saying.

Monty had listened with growing exasperation. There had always been an undercurrent of tension whenever the two men discussed Elizabeth Taylor. Each believed he understood and loved her more.

For the previous three years, Monty had spent so much time with the Wildings that many people in Hollywood imagined their arrangement was a *ménage à trois*. There was even talk that Wilding had grown jealous enough to beat Monty up. "It's true Liz did pit Monty against Michael for a while," said the late Diana Lynn, who used to watch the trio at parties. "But I never heard about violence. It's just that Liz had this almost *iridescent* sensuality. Her lips, her breasts, *gleamed*. She was so damn sexy and flirtatious she made every man want to unzip his fly and stick it into her.

"At first Monty was driven up the walls by her behavior," Miss Lynn continued. She'd known them both when they were filming *Place in the Sun*. "He wanted her badly—he got very cut up after she married Nick Hilton—and they tried to start up their affair again after she got divorced. They kept trying until she married Michael Wilding."

Eventually Liz and Monty worked out a special relationship between them that was at once intimate but not the least sexual.

Monty's deep emotional involvements were always with women —with Elizabeth Taylor, Libby Holman, Augusta Dabney, and, later, Myrna Loy. "He'd pick up guys and bring them to the duplex," said Bill Le Massena. "He'd sleep with them and that would be that. He'd get bored. Once he said to me, 'I don't understand it. I love men in bed but I really love women.'"

Until recently some of Monty's friends had suspected he'd set up the same kind of familial situation with the Wildings as he had with the McCarthys and Greens—where he was in a sense the child figure, the focus of attention.

In the first two relationships, Monty would retreat whenever problems arose between husband and wife, but in the Wildings' case both Elizabeth and Michael forced him to listen—separately—to their joint problems and to help them come to a decision as to whether they should get a divorce.

He'd grown sick of it, he told Larson that foggy afternoon. He wanted to hear no more. "He was drained from the situation. He'd heard about it from every angle—he told me under no circumstances was he going out that night. He wanted to stay home, maybe study his script, nap a little, then go to bed."

Every so often while they talked the phone rang. It was always Elizabeth Taylor. She kept trying to persuade Monty to come to a little dinner party she was giving that night. He kept saying no, he was too tired. But she wouldn't take no for an answer and neither would Wilding. At one point he got on the extension phone and told Monty he must come.

After one conversation Monty told Larson, laughing, that Elizabeth was giving a dinner for some young priest who had admired his performance in *I Confess*. "This young priest is so modern he says 'fuck,' but I don't care what he says, I want to stay home."

Monty continued to refuse the invitation while Larson was there. "I heard him say no to Elizabeth again and again—I think she called him three times." He was so determined not to go anywhere that night that he gave his chauffeur the evening off. Before he left in his own car, Florian fixed a little cold supper which Monty planned to eat. He'd watch some TV and then go to bed.

When Larson said good-bye around six, Monty was again on the phone telling Elizabeth Taylor no, he wasn't coming to dinner. She apparently kept phoning him until finally, although he didn't want to go, he said yes, because he never liked disappointing her and it was so hard for him to say no.

Around seven—before it got dark—he got into his car, a car he hadn't driven for months, and he started off to the dinner party.

"The dinner was subdued," Kevin McCarthy said. "Rock Hudson was there with Phyllis Gates, his secretary whom he later married." The priest never showed. Michael Wilding lay half awake on the couch; he was heavily sedated for back trouble. Elizabeth kept putting records on the hi-fi—Sinatra and Nat King Cole. She served lukewarm rosé. Monty didn't drink more than one glass. He slouched by the door, moody and unshaven."

He told Kevin he wanted to leave early, he was very tired and afraid to drive down the steep hill. Kevin said he'd guide him to Sunset Boulevard; Monty seemed relieved.

After they said their goodnights, they stood outside in the foggy darkness and "we leaned against our respective cars and talked. Monty was depressed. He talked about *Raintree* and how disappointed he was in it—and with Hollywood in general. God, how he hated that place! He felt he had no control over the situation."

Kevin said he finally got into his own car and drove off. Monty followed right behind him. "Suddenly," Kevin said, "I looked in my rearview mirror and I saw that Monty's car was coming much too close to my car. I got the idea he was going to play one of his practical jokes—he was going to give my car a little nudge. He never did bump my car, but I had the feeling he might, so I put my foot on the gas and went a little faster. Monty's car seemed to be almost on top of me. I wondered if he was having a blackout. I got frightened and spurted ahead so he wouldn't bump me. We both made the first turn but the next one was treacherous. We were careening now, swerving and screeching through the darkness. Behind me I saw Monty's carlights weave from one side of the road to the other and then I heard a terrible crash.

"A cloud of dust appeared in my rearview mirror. I stopped and ran back. Monty's car was crumpled like an accordion against a telephone pole. The motor was running like hell. I could smell gas. I managed to reach in the window and turn off the ignition, but it was so dark I couldn't see inside the car. I didn't know where Monty was. He seemed to have disappeared.

"I ran and drove my car back and shone the headlights into Monty's car. Then I saw him curled under the dashboard. He'd been pushed there by the force of the crash. His face was torn away—a bloody pulp. I thought he was dead.

"I drove back to Elizabeth's shaking like a leaf and I pounded on the door. 'There's been a terrible accident,' I yelled, 'I don't know whether Monty's dead or alive—get an ambulance quick!' Mike Wilding and I both tried to keep Elizabeth from coming down to the car with us but she fought us off like a tiger. 'No! no! I'm going to Monty!' she screamed, and she raced down the hill.

"She was like Mother Courage. Monty's car was so crushed you couldn't open the front door, so Liz got through the back door and crawled over the seat. Then she crouched down and cradled Monty's head in her lap. He gave a little moan. Then he started to choke. He pantomimed weakly to his neck. Some of his teeth had been knocked out and his two front teeth were lodged in his throat. I'll never forget what Liz did. She stuck her fingers down his throat and she pulled those teeth. Otherwise he would have choked to death." (Later Monty gave her the two front teeth as a souvenir.)

When Dr. Rex Kennamer arrived, Monty was half-conscious, and in that dazed state he managed to mumble through swollen lips, "Dr. Kennamer, meet Elizabeth Taylor."

It took Rock Hudson and Kennamer at least half an hour to extricate Monty from the car. Elizabeth rode with him in the ambulance to Cedars of Lebanon Hospital, maintaining enormous control until he was wheeled into the operating room; then she became hysterical.

Dr. Kennamer recalled, "It was a miracle he lived. He was bleeding like a stuck pig. He had heavy lacerations on the left side of his face. His nose was broken as was his sinus cavity—it was crushed. His jaw on both sides was crushed as well. He also had a severe cerebral concussion. He went into the operating room immediately. No, he had no plastic surgery. The biggest reconstruction job was his teeth."

Kevin saw him later that night. "He looked like a David Levine cartoon. His face had ballooned to six times its normal size. He was propped up in bed unable to speak because his jaw was wired. His eyes glared out at me helplessly."

In the next week Hank Moomjian, the assistant director of *Raintree County,* collected money from the entire crew for flowers and sent them to the hospital. "Monty called me as soon as he got them," Moomjian told Eleanor Harris. "His broken jaw was all wired up but he talked through clenched teeth to tell me the flowers were the nicest thing that could have happened to him. He said he'd leave the flowers on his dresser till they rotted. He did, too."

During the next nine weeks Monty recuperated, first in the hospital, then in his rented house on Dawn Ridge Road. For a while he lay in traction—the car crash had caused him to suffer from severe whiplash. The swelling gradually went down on his face—it seemed to be healing nicely—and miraculously there were few scars. His broken jaw gave him the most pain; it was excruciating. After it was wired for three weeks, the doctors discovered it had been set incorrectly—the jaw had to be broken again and then reset.

An unending stream of visitors came and went from the house on Dawn Ridge. Elizabeth Taylor appeared almost every day; so did Kevin McCarthy, who recalls, "He seemed in relatively good spirits and I don't know how he managed it, but he got friends to get him liquor—he was drinking martinis through a straw."

His secretary, Marge Stengel, flew out from New York; so did Libby Holman and Bill Clift.

Both women stayed at the house; Bill spent hours with him. Monty made him promise not to let his mother see him. Bill Clift promised; he was privately appalled by his son's condition, by his shattered, almost unrecognizable face. Monty told him through clenched teeth he intended to finish *Raintree County*.

Everybody was against it. Libby Holman was the most vehement. After ministering to him for several weeks, during which time she tried to persuade him to take a year off, she packed her bags and went back to Treetops. Jack Larson said he tried to stop her. "I told her, 'Don't go, Monty needs you.' And she answered, 'No, he doesn't, if he's going to be so foolish as to go back to work now there is nothing more I can do. I can only help him if he'd be sensible.'"

MCA and Metro-Goldwyn-Mayer were pressuring Monty. Lew Wasserman and Dore Schary had been among the first visitors at Cedars of Lebanon Hospital right after the car crash, and they came regularly to the house on Dawn Ridge Road. "At first they seemed genuinely concerned for Monty's recovery," said Larson, "but pretty soon you realized they were really concerned about that $5 million movie *Raintree County*. It was the highest budgeted domestic film in MGM's history—they didn't want to lose any money."

Schary recalled, "About half of *Raintree* was shot when the accident occurred. Yes, Monty was in terrible shape, yes, he was in pain, yes, he'd lost his looks and was going to have to adjust to a new face. Yes, we considered replacing him. But it would have meant reshooting two million dollars worth of footage. We'd already shot a lot of stuff with him in Kentucky and Tennessee. We figured we could do makeups shots from his right profile—since that profile wasn't so damaged. After conferring with Elizabeth and with Monty's doctors as well as with Monty himself, we all decided it would kill him to take him off the picture. Elizabeth was afraid he might kill himself if he wasn't allowed to go back to work. It was Monty who made the final decision. He really wanted to go back."

"Monty convinced himself he could do it," Jack Larson said, "but it was too soon." And one of his agents, Herman Citron, said, "he wasn't ready to go back to work. He was in too much pain."

"When I first saw him I almost went into shock," said Larson, "but I think I hid it because he said, 'I don't look *too* different, do I, mon vieux?' I think he was testing me. He wanted the truth and I assured him no, no, you don't. Of course, he looked completely different. His mouth was twisted. A nerve had been severed in his left cheek so that the left side of his face was practically immobile—frozen. His nose, that perfect nose! was bent—crooked—out of shape. He looked stuffed, that's the only way I can put it—the only feature that remained the same were his eyes—they were still brilliant and glittering and they stared right through you, but they were now brim full of pain."

Just before Monty went back to work at MGM, he wrote his brother a letter:

Dear Brooks,

Thank you for your well wishes and particularly the way you expressed them. Do you want to hear the gory details? Well, skip the next part if you don't. Had four teeth knocked out (fortunately bottom teeth) my nose was broken had a fracture of my upper jaw just below my nose a cut clear through my upper lip (please don't ever have stitches taken in your lip) a fracture of the upper jaw near my ear. I was lovely. I didn't get a mirror until two days after I was in the hospital and I can safely say there was not one characteristic of my face remaining. My eyes were a pool of blood. I was swollen out to here.

After leaving the hospital I was lucky enough to meet up with these two dentists, see, and they agreed to wire my jaws together so that not everybody would have to understand the things I said. This lasted three and a half weeks. During that time I could only have soup (courtesy of the missing teeth) aspirin and soup or soup and aspirin. Then the wires came off.

Now they've started trying to save a loose tooth which in becoming loose cracked part of the jawbone. I must say I admire the dentists for that. So the three of us wired that tooth to the remaining tooth next to it. Then an abscess formed that had to be lanced. Then they decided to dig for

oil through the canal of that tooth. The nerve was dead.
They dug but they didn't find any oil. They cleaned out the
canal and slapped cement in there. . . . NOW . . .
everything starts to swell. Anyway I'll cut this short by
saying it's been a long painful process. I used to think of a
dentist as someone who cleaned your teeth. Not any more.

We go to work Monday and I can't say I'm looking
forward to working the first couple of weeks. . . . I hope
everything goes well with you . . . thank you for your
thoughts

love Monty

p.s. just got your latest letter I'm very glad you got the
job particularly such a picture you describe Intriguing . . .
from a time point of view I won't be free til like November
. . . I've . . . told MCA not to send me any scripts
because if I like something I'll kill myself because I won't
be able to do it . . . I *certainly* thank you sir. Good luck,
love Monty

PART THREE

34

Once filming of *Raintree County* was underway again on location in Danville, Kentucky, Monty became almost manic with tension. "I've never seen anyone under such pressure, except in combat during the war," said screenwriter Millard Kaufman. "He gave the impression of being charged up all the time without ever exploding."

During the day, while waiting for filming to begin, he would sit by himself with the script; often when spoken to by other members of the cast (Eva Marie Saint, Rod Taylor, Lee Marvin), he didn't seem to hear. Perspiration poured from his body. He had to change shirts eight times a day. He was not eating. Instead he drank skim milk with three eggs broken into a glass. "It keeps me starving but concentrated," he said, "and at the peak of tension." Finally his agent, Herman Citron, came on the set and persuaded him to have steak for lunch. Monty said he would try but it was almost impossible for him to chew solid food. His jaw was still wired—and made terrible snapping sounds when he spoke. "I sound like the Frankenstein monster," he'd joke. He was in excruciating pain, but he tried to make light of the ordeal. "It's costing me thirty thousand bucks to have one bridge put in my mouth, and I'll never have enough money to have my teeth cleaned."

Every so often, as if maddened by his physical suffering, he'd inflict more pain on himself. One night he dined with director Eddie Dmytryk and his wife Jean. The Dmytryks served beef fondue. Monty dipped a piece of steak into the bubbling hot oil and offered it to the director. "I told him no thanks, I'd like mine better done. With that he stuck his hand deep into the boiling oil—but he never reacted to the pain."

Another time, Dmytryk dropped by the house Monty was renting in Danville early one morning to talk over some script changes. He found the place empty but the shower doors shattered in the bathroom and blood all over the floor. He raced around trying to find Monty and discovered him in the makeup trailer calm and collected. "Are you all right?" he screamed. "Of course I'm all right, Eddie," he answered. "Why shouldn't I be?"

But he wasn't all right, and when Bill Le Massena came to visit him Monty confided he was sorry he'd gone back to work; he hadn't realized how supremely difficult it would be.

They talked about his near-brush with death. He had kept a photograph of his smashed-up car as a reminder. "It's a miracle I'm still alive," he kept saying.

When he tried to sleep he suffered from insomnia and nightmares. Twice he ran naked into the streets, to the consternation of Danville residents. Twice he had to be escorted back by police who guarded his house night and day from autograph hunters.

"I'm so worried about the next day's scenes I can't sleep," he explained to reporters who questioned him about his sleepwalking. "Finally I doze off; I wake up terrified, think I'm in my own apartment—then I get up and crash into a wall."

He didn't say he was frantic about the way he now appeared on film. In close-up his still-swollen face seemed immobile so, when he could, Dmytryk shot him in long shot or from his right profile which hadn't been so badly damaged.

He remained in such acute back pain from the car accident that he would periodically give himself shots of codeine in his dressing room. Whether or not he became addicted was never established because he took so many different kinds of pills. By now, he was conditioned to a future of amphetamines, barbiturates, and tranquilizers, and he was accustomed to having a large supply close by at all times. "Bird," his regular dealer in New York, sent him rolls of pills. Fortified, he could cope with the pressures of *Raintree County,* the incessant demands to speak to journalists, to perform in front of the camera with a new face he could neither control nor move.

Occasionally he would experiment with a new drug with dire results. During *Raintree*'s exhausting five-month schedule, Elizabeth Taylor's own health broke down several times. In Natchez she suffered a hyperventilation syndrome and heat exhaustion (the contributing cause was a very tight corset). Monty insisted being in on the consultation along with Dmytryk, and while she was being checked he went through the physician's bag and named the entire contents. "There wasn't a drug in there he couldn't define," Dmytryk said.

The doctor left a bottle of forty chloral hydrates for Elizabeth to take in case she had trouble sleeping. "Chloral hydrates are a fantastically strong mickey finn," Monty said. The following evening Dmytryk and Millard Kaufman were in Elizabeth's suite waiting for Monty to join them at supper when Elizabeth noticed that twenty of her chloral hydrates had disappeared. "Millard and I looked at each other," Dmytryk said, "and we raced down to Monty's room. Sure enough, he was passed out on his bed with a cigarette stub between his fingers. The cigarette had burned the flesh right down to the bone." Dmytryk managed to pry the stub out with a pencil and then he and Kaufman ran back upstairs to Elizabeth to confer as to what to do.

They were phoning a doctor when Monty appeared ten minutes later, awake and sober, his hand bandaged. He made no comment, and everybody sat down at the table and tried to act as if nothing had happened. But before dessert Kaufman and Dmytryk excused themselves on some pretext and went back to Monty's room to see if they could find the rest of the capsules. "It took us a while, but eventually we found this leather satchel filled with about 200 different kinds of pills—barbiturates, tranquilizers, pain killers. We found the chloral hydrates, too. He'd taken two. There were eighteen left—so we got a druggist in Natchez to open his store and replace the chloral hydrates with vitamins that resembled them. Monty never said anything, but with his knowledge of drugs he probably knew exactly what we'd done."

He was also drinking—mainly off the set, but sometimes on. "When that happened and he was too drunk to work, I told him to go home and sober up," Dmytryk said. "He'd get mad and throw tantrums. Once he kicked a tree so hard in his anger that he broke a toe."

Libby Holman visited him to see how he was. "They'd get drunk together," a press agent said. "She seemed to want to control him."

Periodically he seemed all right—sober, lucid, even helpful. Horrified when he discovered Millard Kaufman was walking around on location with pleurisy and had been ordered to take Empirin with codeine, Monty argued he should take plain codeine and he promptly gave him some from his own supply. "He had an enormous knowledge of medicine," his doctor, Rex Kennamer, said. "He stayed with me until I felt better," Kaufman said. "I used to tell him, you're a humanitarian without a cause—that's why you play doctor."

Throughout the shooting Monty remained furious with MGM for allowing the press on location. After his accident he'd been promised a closed set. "Jesus Christ!" he yelled, "I am at my absolute worst. Everybody thinks I've gone round the bend."

When Eddie Mannix, a Metro vice-president, came on the set to see how the picture was progressing, Monty had just finished filming a swamp scene and was covered with mud. As soon as he saw Mannix he ran over and gave the astonished man a bear hug. "How are ya, Manny?" he cried, hugging him close and dirtying his shirt front. "I'm fine, Monty," Mannix replied, struggling to free himself. "How are you?" "Fine, Manny, fine—I particularly like Hedda Hopper telling the world I'm a drug addict. She saw me shooting vitamins in my dressing room."

Eventually Mannix managed to free himself and hurried off the set dripping with mud. Monty's howling laugh followed him all the way to his limousine.

The only person he relaxed with was Elizabeth Taylor. During *Raintree* he became totally involved in her new love affair with Mike Todd. "I serve as father confessor and go-between," he said.

It was Monty who met Elizabeth at the Louisville airport after she'd made a quick weekend trip to New York where Todd had proposed marriage. Monty arrived at the airport in a chauffeur-driven but battered sedan so the press wouldn't recognize them when she returned to location. As soon as she got into the car he presented her with a prearranged gift from Todd, a huge pearl ring. "You'll get your real engagement ring soon." Much later, when Todd wanted to meet secretly in the East, Monty arranged to have them rendezvous at Libby Holman's estate in Connecticut.

Miss Holman and Taylor did not get along, but Holman agreed to the meeting at which Monty and she were present. During it Todd presented Taylor with her "real" engagement ring—a huge diamond said to be worth $92,000. As they left around midnight, Taylor could not fit her glove over the enormous jewel; impatiently she flung both gloves on the sofa, and Holman saved them. At her death a pair of tiny white kid gloves was discovered at Treetops, stuffed into an envelope marked "L. Taylor gloves, 1956."

As soon as *Raintree County* finished shooting in October,

Monty returned to California to another house he'd rented in Brent-
wood, on Kenter Avenue. He hung heavy black curtains on every
window and on the glass doors facing the pool. No light got in. The
bedroom smelled like a hospital. He spent a great deal of time lying
in the dark during the day.

He was still going to the dentist and also to a physiotherapist as
he was suffering from "delayed action whiplash" from the accident.
Jack Larson drove him to and from the various doctors in Beverly
Hills, and he kept him company "when he wanted company. He was
very despondent that fall—nobody seemed to cheer him up."

Friends phoned him regularly—Libby Holman, Bill Gunn, Elizabeth Taylor, to tell him excitedly about the premiere of Mike Todd's
Around the World in 80 Days. He did not want to talk to his mother,
so he tried to keep Sunny's calls short. He was dreading having her
see him. "She'll say something which will sound perfectly harmless
but it will be designed to lay me low."

He tried to relax. He enjoyed sitting by the pool, staring into the
water. His face was finally healing; his jaw no longer snapped and the
swelling had gone down in his cheeks. Some deep facial scars remained, but he had begun to lose the look of a man who had been
terribly beaten up.

He knew the worst part of his disfigurement was his upper lip. It
had been ripped in half during the car crash. Sewn together, the flesh
seemed pulled, almost curled back and blotted like a repaired harelip.
He'd never had plastic surgery; instead the doctors had tried to preserve his appearance, so his features were not changed so much as
thickened. The once-perfect nose and mouth seemed slightly off-
kilter.

While he recuperated scripts came daily to the house, and his
agents from MCA dropped by to visit. But his health and energy had
not returned so he would just sit and listen. He was becoming a shy,
evasive person; every so often he would cover his entire face with his
hands—like someone who'd been terrified by a flesh-crawling horror
movie.

One Saturday afternoon, Larson came by with books and newspapers to read. They sat together by the pool saying nothing. Suddenly Monty got up and excused himself and went into the house.
Larson thought he was going to the john. When he didn't come out
after about a half hour he went inside to find him.

As he reached the kitchen he heard a peculiar moaning sound
and he called out, but there was no answer. When he reached the

bedroom he saw that the curtains had been torn from the windows leaving the room flooded with light. Monty was sitting in a corner sobbing. Larson waited a moment before tiptoeing back to the pool.

It was late afternoon when Monty came outside again. He sat down next to Larson and after a moment he reached out and touched his arm. "Jack," he said, "when I went into the bedroom I looked at myself in the mirror. Really looked at myself for the first time," and he began to choke up. "You know what?" His eyes filled with tears. "I think I can still act. I think I still have a career."

Larson says he realized then that he'd gone back to *Raintree* believing it was his last picture; he felt he'd never be able to work again.

Monty's spirits rose after the crying jag, although any questions about possible changes in his face got him agitated. He began considering screenplays; John Huston wanted him to star in *Moby Dick*. He even started thinking about returning to Broadway. Larson would drive him out to Santa Monica beach, and they'd lie on the sand, and he'd recite chunks of Shakespeare and Chekov. "He wanted to play Hamlet someday—he wanted to direct. He'd start casting in his head for a production of *The Cherry Orchard*."

Just before he left Hollywood to go back to New York in late November, a man drove up to the house and informed Monty that "Marlon Brando wants to talk to you seriously and in private about something. Are you agreeable?" Monty said, sure, tell him to come on over, and the man drove off.

No more than ten minutes later another car drove up, and out stepped Marlon Brando. Dressed in work clothes, he was scowling as he approached the house. He'd had his eyebrows shaved off for the role he was then filming: Sakini in *Teahouse of the August Moon*.

Monty came out to meet him; then the two men went into the house and conferred in the living room for about an hour.

Larson, since he was going to drive Monty in to the doctor's later that afternoon, waited by the pool. From his vantage point he could see the actors pacing about the living room, then sitting down opposite each other at a table in the foyer. An hour later Brando strode out, got into his car, and disappeared down the hill.

Larson didn't ask questions, but later, on the way to the doctor's, Monty told him what had been said. Apparently Brando had been hearing all sorts of stories about Monty destroying himself with pills and booze. Brando wanted to communicate something: Monty must stop this shit. He must take care of himself not only for himself but for Marlon Brando.

"Then he got into this rap about competition—the healthy competition that should exist between actors—that existed, say, between a Laurence Olivier and a John Gielgud, between a Richard Burton, then, and a Paul Scofield. These men challenge each other, he said. Now, didn't Monty know the only actor in America who interested Brando was Monty? Didn't he realize they had always challenged each other, maddened each other, intrigued each other, ever since they started their careers? Brando said the year he'd been nominated for *Streetcar* Monty had been nominated for *Place in the Sun*. 'I went to *Place in the Sun* hoping you wouldn't be as good as you were supposed to be, *but you were even better,* and I thought, hell, Monty should get that award.' And Monty answered 'I thought the same thing! I saw you in *Streetcar* praying you'd be lousy—and at the end I thought Marlon deserves the Oscar.' Brando said, 'In a way I hate you. I've always hated you because I want to be better than you, but you're better than me—you're my touchstone, my challenge, and I want you and I to go on challenging each other . . . and I thought you would until you started this foolishness . . .'"

Monty seemed surprised Brando would take the trouble to come over and talk. He seemed quite moved. "I don't think either Marlon or I are imitators, which is why I guess we respect each other. Maybe because we both have delusions of grandeur."

Years later Brando told Maureen Stapleton he'd gone to see Monty after his accident and begged him to join Alcoholics Anonymous. He'd offered to go with him, "if you're afraid to go alone. I'll help you dry out." Monty kept drinking double vodkas and saying, "I'm all right, Marlon. I'll be all right," and Brando kept saying, "Don't you understand? You have got to stop this, you are killing yourself." Monty kept saying how moved he was Brando cared, but he did not have a drinking problem. "He said this while he was downing double vodkas," Brando told Stapleton. In the end he left. "Monty Clift is a lost cause," he said. He seemed enraged by the idea.

Larson said most of Monty's close friends periodically tried to get him to stop drinking. "Monty would always say he was terribly moved so many people cared, but he went right on drinking, always denying he had a drinking problem."

Sometime in the spring of 1957, Monty saw a private screening of *Raintree County*. He didn't like the picture, which he called "a monumental bore." Of his own performance he said, "excepting a couple of moments I'm horrific—wooden, frozen, walking through. In my beard I look like Jesus Christ in a union cap"; he predicted audiences would see the picture to guess "which is me before or after the accident."

He was, of course, right. It is still ghoulish to observe him in *Raintree County*. There are many spliced-together sequences which use both his old and new face; thus one sees close-ups of him before the car crash where the camera has caught his erotic promise, his sense of energy and risk; then in the very next shot he'll be on the screen in his postcrash face—in the same costume, same position, but looking stunned, exhausted. In most scenes his sexuality, magnetism, and spirit seem drained from his body, and the expression on his faintly bloated face is one of resignation.

Monty had always maintained being a sex symbol was "a lot of crap." However, he was well aware that his good looks had a great deal to do with his Hollywood success. In spite of what he'd said to Jack Larson about believing he still had a career, he was terrified he would not be able to survive as a movie star in films with such a visibly altered appearance.

Everywhere he went in Hollywood and New York, directors like William Wyler, friends such as Judy Balaban, reacted with shock or embarrassment when they saw his new face. Often he simply wasn't recognized. He grew used to saying, "Hey—it's Monty! Monty Clift!"

He visited his twin sister, Ethel, in Austin and talked about his fears. He had confidence in himself as a creative artist, but as a commodity—a damaged commodity in an era of handsome rebels (Brando, Paul Newman, Kirk Douglas, Richard Widmark)—he did not.

"He kept asking me—would his new face keep him from working, from being considered for parts? That's what he really cared about—working, fulfilling himself in his work."

In the past he'd had Fred Green hang mirrors all over the duplex because he loved catching glimpses of himself at different angles. "He'd been so spectacularly handsome," his lawyer, Jack Clareman, said. "People used to gasp when they met him. Now they gasped for a different reason." "Montgomery Clift looks strange," one of the fan magazines wrote. He became very self-conscious about his new face for a while, and he took down most of the mirrors in his home. He also hated being photographed. "He'd enjoyed being beautiful," Jeanne Green said. "It was one less thing to worry about."

Losing his looks sobered him. Some of his friends believed it made him grow up. "He'd gotten away with a lot of shit because he was so gorgeous," Bill Gunn said. "And he knew it. He knew it's easier to be beautiful in this life. We even talked about it once. 'God, what I missed out on,' he said. 'I'm catching up on the pain.'"

To the world, however, he insisted he didn't look any different. What he meant was he didn't feel different. The irony of the situation never failed to amuse him; he was still the same person with the same sense of isolation, acute perceptions and dreams under that broken, rearranged face.

For a while he imagined he was faceless, like a blank piece of paper or a block of unmarked clay. In Italy he had seen the statues of Roman soldiers and emperors dug up from the ruins of dead cities and set out on pedestals in the Borghese Gardens or the Doge's Palace. Their scarred profiles contained *life*—even without noses and only holes for eyes. "It has something to do with dominating space," he said, and he set out to achieve that in his acting.

For his next film role, Noah Akerman in *The Young Lions,* he went about perfecting his gift of stillness—his technique for projecting a power deep within himself. He still had his magnificent eyes and he used them to phenomenal advantage. Then, while his battered face remained immobile (he couldn't move his upper lip easily, and there were no muscles in his left cheek), he conjured up a myriad of brooding, soul-searching feelings, and they transformed his expression.

"But only after I've found my ladder of truth," he would say. "There has to be a ladder of truth in a character, so even if the dialogue doesn't work you can change that, but the basic truth is there."

The story in *The Young Lions* follows the lives of three soldiers during the Second World War—Christian, a Nazi officer, to be played by Brando; Michael, a frustrated Hollywood draft dodger, to be played by Dean Martin; and Noah Akerman, a sensitive Jew who becomes one of the war's minor heroes in spite of himself.

Monty had always admired what he called "the Jewish genius for survival," a quality he saw in Noah as he did in the Jews he admired personally, like Barney Balaban, Lew Wasserman, and Billy Silverberg, men who clung passionately to life. To Monty, Noah was an unsung hero "in the sense that he's *persistent*." He related to his persistence, to his deep, private suffering, his lofty aspirations, his conviction that he was a drab, unappealing man, a loner who wanted to be accepted as "one of the boys," yet on his own terms.

He would suggest the fact that Noah was a clerk at Macy's before the war, he decided, by wearing baggy, too-big uniforms; by distending his ears and building his nose up with putty; by losing weight, dropping from 150 to 130 pounds.

"With all the accoutrements and mannerisms I'm trying for the essence of something," he said. "Acting is an accumulation of subtleties—like shaking the ash from a cigarette when a character is supposed to be completely absorbed in a conversation."

Noah the nonconformist, the young proud father who gets into absurd fights to defend his manhood, his Jewishness—Noah became an artistic expression of faith for Monty. It was his favorite role—the performance he wrought most painfully and carefully from his own experience, his own observations.

Throughout January of 1957 Monty lived with Libby Holman at Treetops, struggling with *The Young Lions* and trying to recuperate from the accident.

He would spend entire afternoons making notes in his script while Ella Fitzgerald played on the hi-fi. Every so often Gerald Cook, Holman's accompanist, would pass through the all-white living room and see him staring out the window watching the snowflakes cover the lawn.

From time to time he left Treetops to be driven into New York to work with his physical therapist, Cora Alice Winter, in the hopes he could strengthen his back. He also would see his mother. Sunny was always the same. Energetic, strong, sometimes wild, sometimes venomous, usually triumphant in any situation, she never discussed the changes in Monty's face. During the first weeks of his return East she went out of her way in an agony of trying to please him, to do everything for him although he begged her not to. She began coming too often to the duplex unannounced; she tried to insinuate herself into his life and run it again.

She was virtually raising one of Brooks's daughters, Cathy, and she also went regularly to Boston to visit Suzanne, Brooks's oldest daughter, a shy withdrawn girl who wanted to be a ballet dancer. Sunny was concerned, she told Monty, because Suzanne had no interest in being presented to Boston society; Sunny couldn't understand why—"she's a thoroughbred!"

Monty would listen to Sunny's extravagant plans for Suzanne, which included a debut at Versailles, then would lose patience and they would begin to quarrel.

She criticized his friends, his drinking; she raged against the pills. And all of a sudden the terrible guilt he felt whenever he was with her returned. "Sunny can kick you in the balls and make *you* feel guilty," a friend of the family said.

Monty's adolescent revolt culminated in one horrendous confrontation in the Clift apartment, as witnessed by Bill Le Massena who had been invited to dinner.

During the meal Monty announced loudly that he was going to play "The Jew Noah Akerman" in the movie *The Young Lions*. "I was picked because I look so Jewish," he said. "Everybody *thinks* I'm Jewish," he added, knowing this would infuriate his father, who was anti-Semitic.

While his father stared at him aghast, Monty repeated, "Everybody thinks I'm Jewish, Pa," and then he began hooting with laughter until Sunny interrupted gently, *"Monty, dear, why are you doing this to me?"*

The sound of that question brought back memories of his boyhood when every time he attempted to be independent, to make choices, decisions, she told him he was wrong and she was right; and when he disobeyed her anyway she would cry, *"Why are you doing this to me?"* Her obsessive domination furthered his tendencies for self-destruction and self-inflicted humiliation. Always near the surface, in spite of his achievements, were gnawing self-doubt and withdrawal.

Sunny continued lecturing. Finally Monty lay down on the floor and began rolling back and forth and crying, "Oh, Ma! You are such a cunt, such a cunt!"

He tried not to see so much of her after that night. "One thing that used to irritate Monty terribly about me was he couldn't get me upset about anything," Sunny recalled years later. "Whenever we argued I always remained calm."

35

Monty talked obsessively to his friends about playing Noah Akerman in *The Young Lions*. Hope Lange would be playing his wife, Eddie Dmytryk was to direct. Exteriors were being planned for Paris and Alsace-Lorraine. He arranged to stay at the Palais Royale along with the rest of the cast, and thought he also might fly to London on weekends to catch up on theater.

But as the day approached to leave New York for filming he fell into a depression. *Raintree County* was opening around the country, receiving bad reviews. *Newsweek* dismissed the movie as "an opulent emotional circus."

Monty was upset about this, but he was more upset about his unrelieved feelings of panic. He was terrified of going in front of the cameras again, terrified that because of his new face he wouldn't be able to play the part of Noah the way he wanted to. "I wish I could get somebody else to act it for me—I'm going to have to dredge—yes, dredge it out of me."

He began roaming through New York, visiting bars, pacing through Central Park. After hours of strenuous walking he would return to his duplex and collapse in a stupor. Neither action, withdrawal, nor Dr. Silverberg seemed to help. The stage fright kept coming back, in waves of nausea.

"And Billy can't solve it," he would laugh; nevertheless, he seemed more attached to his analyst than ever; their relationship continued to be an emotional one and more powerful than he ever acknowledged. He still saw him every day when he wasn't working. He spoke of his great wisdom and kindness.

However, friends sensed that Silverberg had set him an impossible goal: to accept his homosexuality and live with it. "Monty never accepted his homosexuality; he hated it, was horrified by it," Josh said.

When he talked about being gay, one had the feeling he was repeating what Silverberg had told him. "There is a deep-seated prejudice against homosexuality," he would mumble as if by rote. "While there may be tolerance for it privately, it will never be accepted in even the most liberated circles."

Monty's sexual guilt, coupled with the anxiety he felt about *The Young Lions,* made his days and nights unbearable. Instead of showing up in Paris to start filming in May of 1957, he vanished. When he couldn't be found the producers organized a search. He was discovered in a third-rate brothel in southern Italy, dead drunk. "Nobody got mad at him," said a press agent. "We were just glad he was alive. Spencer Tracy used to do that before a picture. Get bugged and disappear somewhere with a bottle."

Once Monty began working he was fine, Dmytryk says. He'd never seen anybody work as hard. He recalls coming to his hotel room to pick him up for dinner and finding him working out a drowning scene. "Sweat was running off his forehead. He looked exactly like a man who had rescued himself from death."

He kept pestering Dmytryk about *The Young Lions* script. "It bears no resemblance to Irwin's novel!" he cried.* He insisted on reinstating as much of Shaw's original dialogue as possible, and he and Hope Lange worked for hours improvising on the scenes they had together.

"Monty cut his own lines to a bare minimum," Miss Lange said. One of their most emotional scenes, in an army prison meeting room, is done almost entirely in pantomime.

During filming, Monty became friendly with Dean Martin and did everything he could to help the singer in his first dramatic role, just as he had with Sinatra during *Eternity.* They would run lines together; when he saw Martin was nervous he would break him up. During a party sequence he hid under a piano on the set and tickled Martin's leg until he had a laughing fit. In the evenings, they would go off and have drinking contests. Martin nicknamed him "Spider" because of the extravagant gestures he used when he talked.

He and Brando barely spoke. Monty was incensed when he discovered Brando wanted his role of the Nazi officer idealized. He tried

---

* Irwin Shaw recalls Monty "was bitter as I was at the deformation of the book. But he was superb—the best and truest to the character I'd written."

to convince him that the toning down of Christian would make him less striking.

Monty later confronted Dmytryk. The director admitted agreeing to the character changes so that Brando would star in the film—he confided that Brando also wanted to die very dramatically at the end of the picture, rolling down a hill with his arms outstretched like a Christ figure. "He does that, I'll walk off the picture," Monty said. Brando was ultimately shot in the head by Dean Martin.

They had no scenes together, but in spite of their differences Brando often sneaked onto the set to watch Monty work, concealing himself behind a camera. One afternoon Monty caught sight of him and whispered to Dmytryk, "Tell Marlon he doesn't have to hide his face when he watches me act."

As for himself, he only observed Brando shoot two takes. In both he improvised; he hadn't even bothered to memorize his lines. Afterwards Monty snorted, "Marlon is sloppy—he's using about one-tenth of his talent."

Later he said, "One must know a bad performance to know a good one. You can't be middle-of-the-road about it, just as you can't be middle-of-the-road about life. I mean, you can't say about Hitler, I can take him or leave him. Well, I can't be middle-of-the-road about a performance, especially my own. I feel that if I can vomit at seeing a bad performance, I'm ahead of the game."

Near the end of the shooting in Paris, he ran into Alfred Lunt and the two dined together. Nervous and overjoyed at seeing his idol, Monty had too many martinis, and after their meal, going down in an elevator, he fell drunkenly on top of the elder actor. He was full of extreme apologies, but Lunt could not accept them; he never saw Monty again. "Alfred cannot tolerate drinkers," said an old friend of Lunt's. "He was bitterly disappointed in Monty because he felt he hadn't lived up to his potential as a stage actor. Naturally Monty picked this up—it devastated him."

After that night, Monty worked more intensely than ever on *The Young Lions,* but as soon as filming was over for the day, he would often drink himself into oblivion.

One evening a crew member saw him go "momentarily berserk." He hadn't had that much to drink, but suddenly he crawled on top of a car right outside the Georges V Hotel. He stood on top of it and did a little dance—jiggling and twitching like a paralytic. Then he collapsed on the hood. He had to be lifted off.

When he returned to Hollywood to complete the picture, he filmed his big fight scene. As usual he went into strict training beforehand and was coached by ex-prizefighter Johnny Indrisano. It took four days to film, and he refused to use a double. He was completely exhausted afterwards and began suffering from leg cramps.

A doctor told him he had phlebitis and advised wearing an elastic bandage. Could he still play tennis, Monty asked. The doctor assured him he could and prescribed Benadryl for his cramps, and asked if there was anything else bothering him? Monty confided he often vomited in the mornings, he guessed from too much smoking and drinking. The doctor gave him a supply of Miltown and he also prescribed belladonna for his "stuffy nose."

Later in the 20th Century-Fox makeup department, he happened to open up his bag of pills. "I've never seen anyone who was on so many drugs," a cast member said. "And yet he survived, he created, it was quite extraordinary."

The close of the picture fell on Monty's birthday. He was given a big party on the set. "He got an enormous charge out of it," Dmytryk said. "He couldn't believe anyone would want to go to the trouble."

36

Monty had been back in New York a week when he got to know the woman who would sustain him as his dearest friend for the rest of his life. A tiny (four-foot-ten) flat-footed brunette with a perpetually disgusted expression, Nancy Walker had spent most of her thirty-five years in show business. "So I never was star struck, stage struck or anything else struck. What I was, was hostile, unhappy and basically very shy when I knew Monty, and he understood."

They both agreed that life was a kind of grotesque comic strip, and that most of the time people play roles and wear masks, but the masks sometimes don't fit. "That's the beauty part. Monty and I never played roles with each other, or let's say, hardly ever—and we didn't wear masks. Speaking of masks, I used to tell Monty if you hadn't been in that car crash you'd just be another aging pretty face. I liked his face better after the accident; his strength *shone* through."

Nancy Walker was born Anna Myrtle Barto (Nancy Walker was a name she picked out of a hat—literally). Her parents Dewey and Myrtle were vaudevillians—she grew up in theaters and music halls touring across America and Europe in the company of comics like W. C. Fields and Burns and Allen. "I took my first toddling steps on a stage."

When she was eight her mother died, but Nancy went on touring with her father. "I never had a home. I stayed in different hotels every week. We lived out of suitcases. I took school courses by mail."

She always had a subliminal feeling of abandonment—something else that drew her to Monty. "He'd had a dislocated childhood too, and we both felt embarrassed by what we felt was our lack of formal education."

She met Monty in 1948. "I walked into Gregory's Bar to make a phone call—it was so dark I couldn't find the phone—Monty helped me." But their real friendship didn't start until ten years later when he came backstage to congratulate her on her performance in *Wonderful Town,* and to ask her to supper. She told him she'd love to but her husband, David Craig, was ill. "With that, Monty started climbing the walls practically. 'What can I do?' and 'How terrible!' and 'What is the matter?' He was always dramatic and exaggerated in his reactions; some people thought he was nuts. I thought it was grand, his carrying on. Didn't bother me one bit."

After that night, "he was on the phone every day asking if there was anything to do to help—he seemed genuinely concerned about David and about me and how his illness was affecting me."

Eventually Monty and Nancy developed the habit of phoning each other several times a day no matter where they were in the world (this habit continued until the day of Monty's death). "We would talk for hours—on heavy subjects like old age or stuff like whether Sid Caesar's latest comedy routine had worked on the 'Show of Shows.'"

They lunched and dined together at least twice a week "often at his favorite restaurant, Voisin." They also went to movies and the theater together and haunted Monty's favorite stores—Hammacher-Schlemmer, Jensen's, and Bulgari jewelers. Every so often Monty would have Nancy help him pick out presents for the people he cared about; as a surprise, he once gave her a delicate pearl necklace from Bulgari after pretending it was for Mrs. Fred Zinnemann. Nancy burst into tears, then worried her husband might be upset. "But why, Nancy?" Monty demanded. "It's just a string of beads."

Nancy says some of Monty's friends were jealous of them because they were so close. "At his parties we'd often go off in a corner and gab, and we shut everybody else out. Our friendship was extremely emotional—a responsibility—a treasure to both of us. It was on a level I've never experienced before or since. I wouldn't want a friendship like that again. I couldn't take it. But I realize now I used to tell him much more than he ever told me. He never discussed himself."

Nancy ignored his drinking. "Sure he drank. Don't we all? Sometimes he'd act terrible and I'd throw him out of our apartment. He often wanted to see how much he could get away with." Sometimes he pretended to be drunk so he wouldn't have to deal with certain social situations. Sometimes he drank out of boredom or because he was very nervous or shy about something. Nancy understood because she drank out of boredom and nervousness too.

Nancy thought Monty was strong, but that many of the people surrounding him (his mother, his analyst, his agents, some of his friends) made him feel weak. "People wouldn't let him be strong. He'd been raised to believe he was weak. I used to get so mad at his secretary. We'd be going out to dinner, and she'd say, 'Now you be sure Monty eats,' and I'd snap, 'Isn't that what you're supposed to do when you go out to dinner?' and she'd cluck, 'But poor Monty is so frail—cha-cha-cha,' and I'd say, 'You are crazy. Monty is as strong as an ox.' He had arms like iron—hands like a musician . . . whenever I got bugged, I'd phone him and I'd say, 'I need you. I don't care whether you need me, I need you,' and he'd cry, 'Nanny, what is it? Tell me!' He needed to be needed."

On March 23, 1958, Mike Todd was killed in a plane crash. Monty, in New York, called Elizabeth Taylor immediately. Her doctor, Rex Kennamer, now her physician as well as Monty's, answered the phone and told him she was under heavy sedation and couldn't be disturbed.

Two days later on March 25, Kennamer was at the Chicago Hilton with Elizabeth and the rest of the funeral party. The phone rang again. "It was Monty," Kennamer recalls. "He said he was in Chicago in a hotel down the block. He just wanted Elizabeth to know he was nearby. He wasn't going to see her unless she wanted to see him, but he would attend the funeral, and he would be there in the crowd if she needed him."

Later, unrecognized in baggy raincoat and crewcut, Monty drove out to the Jewish Waldheim Cemetery in Zurich, Illinois, outside Chicago. Thousands of fans lined the sidewalk, road, crowds double-parked along the road; teenagers and housewives were scrambling up on tombstones to try and get a look at Liz.

Monty managed to get inside the tent which was stretched over Todd's open grave, and he attempted to hear the services, which were almost drowned out by cries of "Liz! Liz!"

When she finally appeared the throng rushed at her with a roar, and her black veil was torn from her face. Police helped her into her limousine. The car was almost overturned by the noisy crowds pressing against it trying to get a look at her tear-stained cheeks.

Monty could not believe the ugliness of the mob. "It was noisy,

vengeful," he said. "I saw envy in their faces, envy and hatred and
bleakness." There was another detail he never forgot—and once he
and Elizabeth talked about it: hundreds of people in that crowd
seemed to be munching on potato chips.

37

On April 2, 1958 Monty, in ruffled tux, escorted Libby Holman to the New York premiere of *The Young Lions* at the Paramount Theater on Broadway. He told several friends he expected the reception of his performance to be nothing short of superlative. "I've already written my Oscar acceptance speech," he confided jauntily to press agent John Springer.

Privately, however, he was nervous. He believed his future career now hinged on whether his portrayal of Noah was critically and commercially accepted. It would be the test as to whether he went on to become a major actor or forgotten as a "flash-in-the-pan movie star."

He knew he was not the same man who had startled audiences with his talent and beauty as the cowboy in *Red River*. The accident had changed and darkened his sensibility. He had *A Place in the Sun* and *From Here to Eternity* to his credit, yes, but what he'd tried to do in *The Young Lions* was riskier. In a medium where the close-up is all-important, he had attempted to develop his character with a minimum of tight shots. His Noah, the tender, disagreeable, proud soldier, is often seen obliquely—from an angle—a distance—yet one can understand him from his presence and the way he shapes his experiences.

When the lights went down in the Paramount Theater that night the all-star audience (it was an Actors Studio benefit) broke into applause as the name "Montgomery Clift" swam in under the title. But after he made his first appearance on screen a girl in the balcony screamed and fainted, and there were shocked murmurs of "Is *that* him?"

One of Monty's guests saw him tense visibly but he didn't move. He just continued to stare straight and unblinking at the unrolling film. Every so often he cursed Brando's performance. "Marlon has turned Christian into a fucking Nazi pacifist."

When the movie was over three hours later, there were cheers and bravos and dozens of actors crowded up the main aisle to congratulate him.

Maureen Stapleton, also in the orchestra, remained in her seat. "I thought Monty was extraordinary, but I couldn't stop thinking 'that poor destroyed face.' "

Afterwards in the lobby reporters approached him for his reaction to the woman who'd screamed. He ignored the question, but reporters kept at him about the effects of the accident. What kind of adjustments had he made? How did he cope? Was he still in pain? Finally exasperated, Monty said, "Look, guys, I've managed to forget the whole thing, but my movie studio hasn't, so will you lay off? Can't you just say Montgomery Clift now bears a striking resemblance to Gregory Peck?"

With that he went on to the party at the Waldorf with Libby Holman, Hope Lange, and her husband, Don Murray. Throughout the evening actors kept coming over to congratulate him—actors like Paul Newman, Anne Bancroft, Geraldine Page, and Marilyn Monroe. He was beside himself. He kept repeating over and over, "What a beautiful night. *Fan*tastic!"

After the Waldorf party broke up, Monty, still elated by all the compliments from his peers, took Libby to Reuben's for a nightcap. They were joined by Hope Lange and Don Murray. Hope had the *Times* review of *The Young Lions,* and she was crying; Monty snatched the newspaper out of her hand and read out aloud, "Clift's performance is strangely hollow and lackluster as the sensitive Jew. He acts throughout the picture as if he were in a glassy-eyed daze. . . ."

There was an embarrassed silence at the table. Monty spent the rest of the evening trying in vain to cheer Hope up. He clowned, he joked, he punctuated his talk with hoots of laughter. "It was very depressing," John Springer said. "He was in obvious torment and he kept trying to be funny."

Much later—around three in the morning—Springer drove back in the limousine to Libby Holman's townhouse. He and Monty wandered into the antique-filled living room decorated with photographs of Clifton Webb, Josh White, and Bea Lillie. Libby mixed everybody drinks. She seemed exhausted under her tan.

"Nobody could think of anything to say," Springer recalls. "We stood around without saying a word." Finally after about twenty minutes had gone by, Monty started to sob. "Noah was the best performance of my life," he told them, "I couldn't have given more of myself. I'll never be able to do it again. Never."

Actually the reception of his performance in *The Young Lions,* though mixed, was mainly favorable. *Newsweek* called him "virtually flawless"; *Time* said, "Clift is wonderfully funny and touching," and Beckley in the *Tribune* said, "Montgomery Clift is superb in his inarticulate anguish as he walks with his girl's father who has never met a Jew."

But as the weeks went by Monty exaggerated the bad reviews. "They are all terrible!" he told his friends. He never talked about the letters and phone calls he received from people who praised his acting as Noah and who called him a truly great and tragic actor.

While *The Young Lions* was not Monty's most successful film (it did not sweep the country as had *The Search* or *A Place in the Sun*) it did moderately well. However, there was not even a mention of the Academy Award nomination he wanted so much. He even alluded to it in an interview. "I've been nominated three times. . . . I do feel that the awards pay too much attention to popularity and not enough to merit. . . . It's a funny thing about awards. You know neither Chaplin or Garbo *ever* got one. The ones that really merit it haven't got the Oscar."

Shortly after *The Young Lions* opened, Maria Schell came to New York to star in the TV special *For Whom the Bell Tolls.* Monty devoted most of his time to her, coming each day to rehearsals so he could—as he put it—"study her radiant, madonna face."

"After rehearsals most of the cast would go back to Monty's duplex," Miss Schell recalls. "Jason Robards, Christopher Plummer, Maureen Stapleton, and myself. Monty had a German cook of whom he was very proud. She cooked marvelous German dishes."

After dinner they would sit around drinking and talking till dawn. "Everything that happened on those nights seemed *heightened,*" Miss Schell said. "None of us seemed to have any limits—the world was filled with infinite possibilities. Monty and Christopher and Jason would argue about poetry and life and death, and sometimes the conversation would get so furious Maureen and I would think the roof's going to fly off and the sky will tumble in on us. I remember once Christopher playing the piano wildly and then we were all on the street hailing cabs and then we were at Jason's apartment . . . .

"And Monty never stopped. Never stopped talking or drinking. He was always in motion performing little jigs, mimicking, curling his body around chairs. He seemed alternately charming, ludicrous, disagreeable, shifting, teetering into his own private abyss."

Miss Schell said, "I was too young to see his torment. All I knew was we had complete rapport. We were very much alike in that we were both obsessed with our work. We both had a passion for detail."

Schell wrote copious notes in the margins of her scripts—she said in the handwriting of the character she was playing. Monty loved that touch. "I drove to the center of the being I was trying to become until I knew it as my own. So did Monty. I loved him very much and he loved me."

They were inseparable until she went off to Europe to do another film, but they kept in touch by transatlantic phone.

After Maria Schell left New York, Monty became increasingly antisocial; sometimes he acted stupid. When he did accept an invitation the evening turned out unpleasantly. Once at Dinty Moore's, as Myrna Loy was starting to tell a funny story about Clark Gable to Maureen Stapleton, Monty suddenly crawled on top of their table and began shouting nonsense.

Later he took Nancy Walker to dinner at Arthur Miller and Marilyn Monroe's, and he behaved frenetically—grimacing, stumbling, talking in half-finished sentences. Monroe, who admired Monty more than any other actor, commented, "He's the only person I know who's in worse shape than I am."

The drugs he took that made him behave so strangely were "the same drugs we all took right through the 1960s," Tennessee Williams said. "Nembutal, Doriden, Luminal, Seconal, phenobarbital." These same drugs provided Monty with some escape, but since he took them indiscriminately, and usually mixed them with liquor, they were also poisoning and maddening him; he grew increasingly isolated that year.

Bill Gunn recalls that in the early summer of 1958 he was appearing somewhere "in the wilds of Massachusetts playing in *Member of the Wedding* with Ethel Waters. One night during intermission between the first and second acts, I got this call on the pay phone backstage from Monty in New York. He begged me to come back to the city *immediately*—it's urgent, he says. I told him I'm doing a show, but he wouldn't take no for an answer, so finally I asked him to tell me what the trouble was, realizing he was terribly upset. He said he'd been to dinner at Libby's, and afterwards as he walked home he realized he'd had too much to drink so he sat down on the sidewalk, afraid he was going to pass out. A stranger came up to him and said, 'I know you're Montgomery Clift. Let me take you home.' He allowed him to, he was in no condition to do otherwise, but as soon as he got inside the duplex he panicked. 'I am sure this stranger is still in the house with me about to rob me blind. You have got to come and help me, Billy—now.'"

Gunn told him he couldn't, he was in the middle of a performance—call the police, he said, and he hung up the phone. Monty called back three more times before the curtain came down, and when Gunn returned to his dressing room he found a chauffeur waiting there. "I've been sent by Mr. Clift," he said. "I'm to take you by limousine to the airport. There's a special plane waiting to fly you back to New York."

Gunn says, "I thought, Okay, Monty, okay—if you've gone this far I'll go along with you. I threw some stuff into a bag and ran out to the limo. Sure enough, after a half hour drive we get to this rinky-dink airport, and there's a plane revving up on the runway just for me. We eventually land in Newark, New Jersey where another limousine is waiting to pick me up and drive me to Monty's. I arrived at the duplex about 3 A.M. I rang the bell and rang and rang. No answer. So I went to the corner—to Daly's bar—and used the pay phone. No answer. I let it ring, oh, maybe fifty or sixty times. Finally Monty answered sounding very groggy. I said, 'Hey, Monty, it's Bill Gunn. I'm here.' And he shouted back happily, 'Billy! What the fuck are you doing in New York? I thought you were touring in Massachusetts!' And I said, 'Monty, you jerk, you sent for me, you hired a limousine and a private plane and another limousine to get me down here because you were afraid you were being robbed.' And there was a long silence and then Monty said, 'Did I do all that? I don't remember. I don't remember anything.'"

Gunn subsequently searched the duplex for the mysterious stranger. The apartment, of course, was empty. "Everything's okay," Gunn told him, and Monty gave a sigh of relief.

The following day he arranged to have Gunn flown back to

Massachusetts for his next performance, "but the plane I was supposed to take from La Guardia took off without me. I was stranded. I phoned Monty frantically and told him I'd probably be fired now, since I couldn't make the show in time. Monty said not to worry, to wait in the phone booth—I did—and minutes later a guy runs over to me and says, 'Mr. Clift asked me to helicopter you to your theater.' Which he did."

In late 1958, Monty began filming *Lonelyhearts* for Dore Schary on the coast. Nancy Walker remained in New York. "I was flipping—about my life—my career. I had this anger in me I didn't know what to do with. I knew I was being childish because I wanted everything to go my way—anyhow I told my husband David, 'I gotta talk to Monty.' There were certain things I told Monty about myself that I never told anybody else. So anyhow I phoned him and I told him I was miserable and he said, 'What plane are you coming out on tonight?' "

By the time she arrived in Los Angeles, he'd juggled his schedule so he had free time, and he was there to meet her at the airport in his limousine. "We drove to some restaurant and talked till the place closed. About how performers live out of proportion and how that hurts and how I wanted to be able to take everything in my stride. Monty helped me see I had to focus my concentration on things other than my work—when I wasn't working. The next day Rudi, Monty's driver, appeared at my hotel and said, 'Mr. Clift said I'm to take care of you—if you want to go shopping or anything, and if not come out to the studio and be with him.' It was Monty's way of making sure I wasn't alone. He pulled me through that dreadful period. He got so involved in my problems that Dore Schary phoned me and said, 'Nanny, cool it, will you? Monty's so concerned about you he's forgetting about the picture.' "

Nothing could have been further from the truth. Monty was not only extremely involved with *Lonelyhearts,* he was very worried about it. He'd originally agreed to do the movie assuming it would be as comic and as savage an exploration of the grotesque as the Nathanael West novel on which it was based.

Unfortunately the Dore Schary screenplay had none of West's agony—the horrors of American aloneness superimposed against a backdrop of garish pop culture. Nor did it have the element which attracted Monty initially—the element he wanted to drown in—that is, the obsession of the Christ-figure hero for the miseries of humanity.

Monty had always identified with guilt-ridden dualistic characters. When it came to suffering he had acute perceptions. Like *Lonelyhearts,* he spent a great deal of time hearing the confessions of his friends, often solving their money or job problems. Like *Lonelyhearts,* he was usually silent and inarticulate about himself.

In the movie version, Lonelyhearts is renamed Adam White, and he is no longer a man divided by love and hate and literally destroyed by his inability to solve the conflict. He is a decent boy-next-door who works on a newspaper batting out a lonelyhearts column, giving advice to cripples, dwarfs and madmen. When he begins caring too much about their problems his evil editor, Shrike (Robert Ryan), bullies him into meeting one of his correspondents (Maureen Stapleton), the crying, kvetching wife of a cripple. She ultimately seduces him. Afterwards, he gets drunk, repents, and inexplicably goes off into the sunset with his girl (Dolores Hart). He does not get killed by the cripple, as happens in the West novel. Director Vincent Donahue explained, "Dore didn't believe the Christ figure needed to be crucified."

Monty spent long hours discussing the production faults with co-star Robert Ryan. "Even with liquor on his breath he was meticulous in his criticism," Ryan recalled.

Lonelyhearts was being filmed in what looked like chiaroscuro—everything had a brownish tint; "Monty felt we all looked slickly unreal. He respected and liked Dore Schary—he believed he was sincere and an idealist, but he thought the *Lonelyhearts* script sucked. 'Where's the corruption? the misery? the evil? the disease? Hysteria has been replaced by blandness,' he said. 'Miss Lonelyhearts, meet Andy Hardy.'"

Every so often he would joke about his tenuous connection with "the new Hollywood." "Louis B. Mayer is dead. Long live TV!" Wasn't it the beginning of a new era of independent producers like Schary and Hecht-Hill-Lancaster? The Breen office was no longer so powerful, "so now I'm asked to star in *Sons and Lovers* adapted by Jerry Wald." They chuckled bitterly over Stanley Kubrick's remark to Dwight MacDonald: "The reason movies are so bad out here isn't because people are cynical money hacks. Most of them are doing the best they can. They really want to make good films. The trouble is with their heads, not their hearts."

Monty had hoped *Lonelyhearts* would be a very special film. There was a deadness and a violence in him now that coincided powerfully with West's hero. He had read all of West's novels in an effort to understand his vision.

At one point he showed Ryan a paragraph from West's *The Dream Life of Balso Snell* which he said was a perfect description of a fractured personality. "I was going to use it as my image for *Lonelyhearts*."

The paragraph went "when you think of me think of two men—myself and the chauffeur within me . . . from within he governs the sensations I receive through my fingers, eyes, tongue, and ears . . . imagine having this man inside you fumbling and fingering your tender organs with stumbling soiled feet. . . ."

Ryan believed that description fit Monty. "He was a man of such vast contradictions. Sober, he deluded himself with fantasies—drunk, he became savage and scornful of any illusions."

Ryan, a heavy drinker himself, recognized that Monty had reached a crisis—a turning point with his alcoholism. He had not got the help he needed—his illness was now chronic. He worked best in the mornings; after lunch he was often high on speed or spaced-out on drugs. He told Ryan he occasionally suffered from shivering fits, cold sweats, hallucinations. "I had this dream where I smelled nothing but strawberry jam." Still he denied he was an alcoholic.

Throughout filming of *Lonelyhearts* at the Sam Goldwyn studio, anecdotes proliferated about Monty's bizarre behavior. How he climbed around the set in big boots when he wasn't being used "to attract attention," how he would jump on Dore Schary's lap when they were watching rushes, how he occasionally ran nude from his bungalow at the Bel Air.

Then there was his emotional outburst after filming the big fight scene between himself, Bob Ryan, and Mike Kellin. "Bob and I rehearsed with him for hours," Kellin said. "Monty was having a hard time coordinating his movements. My last line was 'son of a bitch' as Monty hits me. Well, finally after dozens of takes Monty hauls off and socks me so hard I'm reeling and I really yell 'son of a bitch!' and stagger back in shock. Vinnie kept the cameras rolling—it was a great take. When he called "Cut!" Monty burst into tears. He hadn't meant to hurt me, Jesus, God, he couldn't help it—I told him *I* should have been crying, I was the one who was hurt, but he kept on bawling. When we tried to shoot the close-up it was impossible. Monty couldn't do it. He was sent back to the Bel Air. Bob Ryan ended up putting on Monty's shirt and jacket. It's Bob's arm and fist you see in that close-up."

"But," Kellin continued, "as anguished as Monty was, and I sometimes felt there was an actual physical presence hovering in the room that he was terrified of—when he acted a scene it was sculpted forever. There was a solidness about the work—a rocklike quality. There was nothing casual about his acting. If he had genius it was that he revealed himself so totally as an actor—he stripped himself naked. He hid his real life—nobody was as mysterious or remote as Monty except I guess to a few friends. But in his acting he revealed himself as powerfully as a scream."

Maureen Stapleton, working for the first time in films, had all her big dramatic scenes with Monty. "He was so *there* half my work was done when I acted with him." Sometimes between setups she would go back to his dressing room, and he would fall asleep in her arms. "He had such terrible insomnia I knew it would help if he could doze off, and also asleep some of his torment would disappear. I would hold him very still."

Once she happened to look down at his feet. "They were bare and very fragile—the blue veins stood out and his toes seemed tiny—minute—curled like a baby's. Tears filled my eyes." Then he woke up and he seemed refreshed and at peace. He didn't seem to notice she'd been crying.

The other female stars of the movie—Dolores Hart and Myrna Loy—gathered in Monty's dressing room for lunch, along with Stapleton and Nancy Walker, who remained in Hollywood for the duration of the shooting.

Surrounded by women who cared about him, Monty could be funny and charming. His conversation was the kind women delight in —wicked little jokes, emotional analyses of people and places, and he could beat a woman at her own game of intuition and tell secrets about them.

"Myrna Loy responded to him almost visibly," an observer said. "There were sparks. He had this kind of cosmic thing. She is a very private person—very calm—contained. He seemed to understand everything about her—even her hangups."

Miss Loy had been discovered by Rudolf Valentino, who'd been looking for someone to play an Oriental siren in *What Price Beauty*. After her part in that 1925 production she was type-cast as a femme fatale; for the next seven years the red-haired, freckled Miss Loy appeared exclusively as Chinese and Japanese seductresses. When talking pictures arrived, she delivered her lines in pidgin English.

Then in 1934 she created the role of Nora Charles in Dashiell Hammett's *Thin Man* series, with William Powell. Witty, sophisticated, calm in every situation, she came to personify "the perfect wife" for American audiences in over thirty films. By 1938 she was one of the ten most popular movie stars in the world. Later, in pictures like *The Best Years of Our Lives* and *Lonelyhearts* (where she played Shrike's long-suffering wife), she was no longer funny, but she remained the good, not the fallen, angel.

In 1947 she joined her first political group when she and other actors formed the Committee for the First Amendment to Fight for the Abolition of HUAC. Later, former Secretary of State Dean Acheson invited Miss Loy to work with UNESCO, organizing a Hollywood film committee which would act as a liaison with the industry, supplying it with material for films promoting international brotherhood.

Monty was impressed with Loy—by her wit, her compassion, her commitment to liberal causes.

Over the next few years she became entangled in his romantic life. They saw each other frequently and traveled together to the Caribbean. S. J. Perelman recalls dining with them in New York. "Monty was staying with Myrna. Or at least he wanted to give that impression."

Not long after they met, Miss Loy tried to persuade him to stop drinking. She stopped drinking herself in an effort to keep him on the wagon. Many of her friends thought she was deeply in love with him and wanted to marry him.

As always, Monty managed to keep her separate from his other close emotional involvements. Myrna, Libby, Nancy, Elizabeth Taylor were compartmentalized as was everyone else he cared about. Any man or woman who got close to Monty fell into a trap. They all thought he or she was the most important person in his life—but nobody knew how *Monty* felt—because he never really committed himself.

That summer Brooks, out of work, was living in El Paso, Texas with his third wife, Dorothy, and their new baby, Patti; he became so despondent he wrote Monty saying he was thinking of taking L.S.D. as an antidote to his guilt and pain.

Monty sent back a letter enclosing a check for $1,000. "I hope this will be of some help to you," he wrote. "I'd like to volunteer something you conceivably already know. About lysergic acid. It artificially creates schizophrenia. If I were paid $500 I wouldn't take lysergic acid. You are dealing with a terrible unknown and I say this caring for your life. Love, Monty."

The two brothers began corresponding periodically again after an article appeared in *McCall's,* which quoted Monty as condemning Brooks's erratic life-style, his three marriages. In answer Monty wrote back, "It has taken me months to make my peace with quotes that were never uttered. Those words were never said by me to anybody. I must tell you I feel no criticism of your life, the way you lead it, or the way it works out. Although I recognize a vindictive side to my nature it would never show itself at your expense. This letter is meant in no sense as a palliative. The sad thing I feel is that the fourth estate writes irresponsibly and they couldn't care less about the damage they inflict by slinging around untruths . . . my love to you, Monty."

After Brooks decided to move to California, Monty set up appointments for him with various people, including Lew Wasserman. Later, still out of work, Brooks returned to New York. He was now separated from his wife and so broke he went on NBC TV's "Tonight Show." He was paid $350 for revealing he was Montgomery Clift's brother.

Monty, embarrassed, and angry, phoned him. They met and Brooks said, "We had a long talk about his celebrity and how it may have destroyed me to some extent and he was upset about that. I kept assuring him that being Montgomery Clift's brother had nothing to do with my problems."

Shortly thereafter Brooks was offered a job at an advertising agency producing radio and TV commercials.

He saw Monty frequently, and they talked of Sunny; she remained a constant subject of conversation. She was still obsessed with her identity, still trying to get the Andersons and the Blairs to acknowledge her as blood kin. She had recently sent Brooks some Anderson memorabilia which she said he could throw away if he wanted, but she added she hoped he and his children would behave in such a way that it would be unnecessary for them to proclaim "we're thoroughbreds!" She added bitterly that most people are either sheep or goats and then there are those (meaning the Andersons) who will only acknowledge you if you pay enough money. "I have never had enough money," she said.

For a while, in 1958, Monty talked about going into directing. Every so often he attended Actors Studio sessions where he usually sat unrecognized. He came the morning Marilyn Monroe did *Anna Christie* with Maureen Stapleton. Norman Mailer saw him and asked him to a reading of his play *Deer Park*. Monty agreed.

He had always admired the crafty, bullying novelist, imagining he could float in and out of the fires of hell and escape unsinged. "Norman thinks playing it safe is the worst violation in life," he said.

Monty joined guests Gore Vidal, Elaine Dundy, and others in Mailer's Brooklyn Heights apartment, and "Norman proceeded to read the entire play himself—*all* the parts in a very ponderous voice," Dundy recalls. "Monty lounged on the floor smoking, frowning; he was cold sober. The reading went on for hours—interminably. Finally, Monty shouted, 'Norman, for Christ's sake! Let *me* read it well.' Then he rose to his feet and wrestled the script away from him."

Everyone expected a great reading. But after scanning the dialogue for a few moments, Monty threw the manuscript into the air and shouted, "Aahh this is such crap!" Mailer, hurt because *Deer Park* was (and is) his favorite work about love and disgrace in Hollywood, said nothing. Eventually Gore Vidal collected the pages and he finished reading the play to the assembled guests. Monty meanwhile lay back on the floor and lit a cigarette as if nothing had happened.

In March of 1959, *Lonelyhearts* opened at the Victoria Theater in New York to almost universally bad reviews. The *Times* said, "Clift is remarkably affecting, but there is no redemption for the sad sacks in *Lonelyhearts* and the basic weakness of this picture is to pretend that there is." Berkley in the *Herald Tribune* maintained, "*Lonelyhearts* is a bit hard to take even though Montgomery Clift works every hesitant eyeball rolling moment to the bone," and Dwight MacDonald wrote a devastating essay about it in *Esquire* stating bluntly that "all the film has in common with the book is the names of the characters."

Monty, of course, was extremely upset by the reception of the movie, but he talked to few people about it. He was too busy trying to decide what to do next; he seemed unaware that much of Hollywood had grown tired of his endless problems. Now that he was becoming known as a "crazy drunk," a pillhead, confused, quarrelsome, most of the film community wanted nothing more to do with him. Humanity was not involved. He was no longer a hot property—he was considered simply a bad risk.

"It was hard enough dealing with Gable and Tracy, but at least they worked diligently within the star system; they were big moneymakers for their studios, superstars who kept their drinking and grief off the set," said a former MGM story editor. "Monty's ordeal was so naked it disgusted and frightened a lot of people."

But friends rallied. Elia Kazan signed him for his movie *Wild River,* a picture about the New Deal and TVA which was to be shot on location in Tennessee that fall. "Monty is the perfect combination for the part; that's why I cast him. He's intellectual, but he's vulnerable too."

Before that, at Elizabeth Taylor's urging, and because she was also going to be in it, Monty agreed to costar in *Suddenly Last Summer,* Tennessee Williams's one-act play dealing with two subjects ordinarily considered taboo; homosexuality and cannibalism. Gore Vidal shaped the screenplay about a skeptical brain surgeon (Monty) who has to find out why a wealthy southern lady (Katharine Hepburn) insists her beautiful but hysterical niece (Elizabeth Taylor) can only be helped by having a frontal lobotomy.

Monty told friends he was glad he was finally playing a doctor. "I'll have a chance to put my bedside manner into practice," he joked. But friends worried he was in no condition to work.

In July, there was a flash fire in his brownstone. Police and firetrucks arrived along with the *Daily News* just as Monty appeared, followed by a group of young men, all of whom vanished into the grey dawn.

The duplex had been badly damaged by the fire—the bedroom was a blackened shell. Monty phoned Curt Behrens, who'd repainted the apartment in 1954. "We talked about repairing the place—it would cost a fortune. Monty said he didn't like the apartment anymore, he was fixing to move." Behrens asked him what had caused the fire, and Monty replied, "Smoking in bed."

Later a story got around that the fire had started during a cocaine party. There was much talk of wild parties, since Monty handed out so many keys to the duplex.

One friend recalls, "I had a key and I decided to spend the night since I'd sublet my place because I was moving to the Coast. Anyhow, I came by without phoning, barged into the master bedroom—it was about four in the afternoon, Monty was sitting up in bed like a princess with three other guys. When he saw me he bolted into a closet. I backed out of there fast, and I left my key in the living room." Later he phoned to apologize, and Monty was very cool to him and pretended he didn't know what he was talking about.

As a precaution, his secretary, Marge Stengel, accompanied Monty to London, where *Suddenly Last Summer* started filming in late July. "Marge was supposed to see to it that he was sober on the job," a press agent said.

They reserved two suites at the Savoy Hotel and traveled to and from Shepperton Studios in a rented Rolls-Royce. Monty's back was giving him a lot of pain, so he went to the osteopath three times a week in Portland Place. "He washed down his codeine pills with brandy," Tennessee Williams said.

Throughout the filming of *Suddenly Last Summer* Monty was consistently late on the set, and he had trouble remembering his lines. Katharine Hepburn became concerned. "He used to have the most peculiar expression on his face. Whenever we'd shoot a scene, big beads of sweat would pop out on his forehead."

She became so worried about his health she took him with her to her country place outside London on weekends and tried to convince him to get off liquor and pills. "None of my arguments did any good. I thought he was weak. Simpatico but weak."

His condition got so bad, director Joseph Mankiewicz threatened to cancel the picture, but Elizabeth Taylor fought him on it. She was in a foul mood. The English newspapers had been full of stories ridiculing her current marriage to Eddie Fisher.

If she was disappointed in Monty she never showed it. Instead she was unfailingly loyal, affectionate, teasing. Producer Sam Spiegel wanted to get rid of him after seeing some early rushes. Elizabeth snapped, "Over my dead body." Monty stayed.

But Spiegel, who'd been extremely friendly before the picture started (they often shared caviar) no longer would speak to Monty, and Mankiewicz, worried about going over the budget, was short-tempered with Hepburn and baited Monty cruelly whenever he was inaudible or had a memory lapse. He would often sit doing a crossword puzzle while they struggled to rehearse a scene.

By the end of filming Hepburn was so furious at both men that as soon as she completed her last take she spat—first in Mankiewicz's face, then on the floor of Sam Spiegel's office.

She was incensed by their brutality, their lack of compassion for Monty. (However, years later she told an interviewer, "I didn't spit just for Monty Clift! I spit at them for the way they treated *me*.")

Monty, meanwhile, never appeared bothered by the verbal beatings he received from both director and producer. The pills he was on relaxed his muscles, soothed his nerves, and pushed back panic. "I'm fine," he would mumble, "fantastic."

Between takes he would wander back to his portable dressing

room which was stocked with fresh shirts, orange juice, and books, and he would listen to his Ella Fitzgerald tapes or answer his mail with Marge Stengel.

Before the accident Monty had drifted into countless affairs with men and women. It suited his personality to have sex with a variety of partners. It was also a way of meeting different kinds of people, exploring different worlds, searching, always searching for the right person with whom he could develop a lasting relationship.

After the accident and as his drug addiction became more serious, Monty was often impotent, and sex became less important to him. His deepest commitments were emotional rather than sexual anyway, and reserved for old friends; he was unflinchingly loyal to men like Bill Le Massena and women like Elizabeth Taylor, Libby Holman and Ann Lincoln.

He still saw Ann; she would come to the duplex and they would get drunk together and reminisce about *Foxhole in the Parlor,* the play they'd been in on Broadway eighteen years earlier.

Sometimes at the duplex, Ann ran into a young Frenchman named Giles. Monty had met Giles after filming *The Young Lions.* He was twenty-six; slightly built, he had charming manners and slanting inquisitive eyes, and his dark curly hair covered his well-shaped head like a cap. Although he was high-strung and cried a lot, he could make people laugh when he told jokes in his pronounced French accent.

Monty thought he had a very distinctive style: the way he wore his snug Italian jersey, or sometimes knotted a scarf around his neck; he used expensive cologne. Monty told Brooks that Giles had spent his boyhood growing up in a chateau somewhere in the wine country outside Paris. His family was wealthy. They ran a prosperous import-export business with offices all over Europe.

Originally, Giles had wanted to be in fashion, and he had apprenticed with one of the most famous haute couturiers in France before coming to New York and moving in with an older man, a dress manufacturer who kept him for several years while he tried to establish himself as a designer on his own. He met Monty while he was working for a Seventh Avenue dress firm, and he wrote him dozens of love letters. After Giles quit designing, Monty started giving him money regularly, although he often complained to Brooks, "I can never give him enough dough." He would scold the young Frenchman when he stole his jewelry or his luggage, and then Giles would cry.

Monty needed someone to take care of him and love him and Giles pursued him relentlessly, making himself useful and even taking abuse. By 1958 he was secretly ensconced as bed partner and errand boy.

None of Monty's friends knew of Giles's existence, however. Then Jack Larson had a bizarre introduction to him. "Monty had lent me his duplex while he was making *Suddenly Last Summer*. I was putting the key into the lock when the door suddenly opened and a hand reached out and grabbed my wrist and a voice asked 'Is that you, Jack?' and I said 'yes'—terrified—and the voice said 'I'm Giles and Monty has told me all about you.' With that he began describing details about me and about my friend Jim Bridges." Larson and Bridges finally entered the apartment and Giles became hysterical, crying, " 'If Monty ever finds out I've met you he'll never speak to me again!' and he started throwing furniture around—he eventually tore up the entire bedroom."

Larson said he later learned that Giles had stayed with Monty the entire time Monty was filming *Lonelyhearts* and seeing so much of Myrna Loy. "But Giles was secreted away in a room at the Bel Air Hotel and never allowed to come out. He had to wait and be available for Monty."

When Monty came back from filming *Suddenly Last Summer* he talked about buying a brownstone. He said he wanted to create a real home. He discussed it with his lawyer and he began phoning real estate agents. "I want to buy a house because I may get married and have kids some day," was the way he put it.

He subsequently invited Larson and Bridges to have dinner with Giles "and we all pretended we'd never met."

Monty's relationship with Giles was now out in the open, but the young Frenchman's presence in the duplex caused tension between Monty and Marge Stengel, who'd been Monty's secretary-confidante for five years. Marge thought Giles was an opportunist, weak, and potentially dangerous. Monty then began complaining, "Marge is trying to take over my life." For a while he threatened to take Giles with him as his secretary-assistant when he went to Tennessee to film *Wild River*.

"Apparently Marge made a terrible fuss," said Jack Larson. "Monty got ugly and Giles burst into tears, a ploy he frequently used to get people's sympathy."

In the end neither Marge nor Giles went along; instead an ambitious young actress named Donna Carnegie traveled with Monty. "She served as secretary, answering his mail, reading scripts," said an MCA agent. "But she was also there to make sure Monty didn't drink or take pills."

To complicate matters, Donna told Brooks she had fallen in love with Monty.

During the filming of *Wild River,* Monty ignored Donna's advances. They had necked a couple of times the previous summer at Treetops, and now she was telling people she was in love with Montgomery Clift.

Monty didn't believe her. "She's using me to get into Actors Studio," he confided to his brother. "She wants to know Kazan." He was frankly more concerned about his bald spot. He worried continually, he worried about looking old. He would get up early every morning and sneak into makeup so that the spot could be concealed with black dye before anyone else noticed it. However, Jo Van Fleet would already be seated in front of the lighted mirrors getting her hands wrinkled. She was playing a ninety-year-old woman and she was only forty-three.

Sometimes after breakfast, Monty would walk down the main street of the little town of Cleveland, Tennessee, where most of the movie was shot. He crunched through the piles of dead leaves like a marionette—moving stiffly, as if pulled by strings. Sometimes he leaned to one side or stumbled, and the townspeople, watching curiously from the diner, thought he was drunk.

He was not drunk. He'd promised Kazan he would not touch a drop of liquor or take pills, and he didn't. He knew how important *Wild River* was; Kazan had been working on nine variations of the screenplay since 1955; "It's my love affair with the New Deal," he said.

Still, without liquor Monty felt very fragile, so he reached out to members of the company for support. He hung around cameraman Ellsworth Fredericks, a bluff, friendly man who talked about wanting to "embrace the entire world." And whenever Molly Kazan visited from New York he had long heart-to-heart conversations with her about his future plans, which included starring in *The Disenchanted* (in which he would play F. Scott Fitzgerald) and *The Labor Story,* which centered around the Centuria Mine disaster.

He liked to stay in his room in the ramshackle Hotel Cherokee playing his Ella Fitzgerald records and marking up his script. From his window he could see the rolling Tennessee countryside aflame with autumn colors; the Cumberland Mountains were blue with frost.

He wanted to be very good in *Wild River*. He believed in the story—a fundamental one, almost biblical in its implications, inspired by Kazan's gut feeling about Roosevelt's New Deal, that whenever history changes something wonderful is lost.

Monty was playing the part of Chuck Glover, who in 1935 is sent by the U.S. Department of Agriculture to the wilds of Tennessee. He must convince a rugged old pioneer named Ella Garth (Jo Van Fleet) to move off her farm so that her land can be flooded as part of the TVA project to harness the Tennessee River. As the story progresses Monty's Glover emerges as a rather peculiar, enigmatic man, often tactless with the rednecks he's dealing with; he gets into fights with Ella Garth's sons; he falls in love with Garth's granddaughter Carol (Lee Remick). Their romance is fumbling, passionate; but Monty's unsettling presence dominates the movie.

During filming Monty got close to Lee Remick, the beautiful and talented actress who'd created such an impact as the sexy drum majorette in *A Face in the Crowd*. Lee was a warm, vibrant woman, already married and the mother of two young children. She and Monty had many talks about raising kids; he wanted to know what it felt like to be a parent. Later Monty phoned his twin sister, Ethel, in Texas to extol Lee Remick's virtues. "He was extremely impressed with her balance, her maturity—he couldn't get over it."

The scenes they have together in *Wild River* are extremely rewarding to watch—full of gestures, looks, rich in implications. Before going in front of the camera they rehearsed in great detail. Kazan often sat with them on the banks of Lake Chickamauga, where so much of the movie's action takes place, and he would listen to them run their lines, smoking a cigar, spectacles on his nose.

"I wanted their scenes to show ambivalence—attraction, repulsion, fear, love," said Kazan. "I'd literally stop the action time and time again and just zero in on the intensity of their feeling." In the car when they suddenly embrace. Walking through the woods. As they float across the river on the raft. One is meant to get the feeling, although they never express it verbally, that part of them wants to stay on that slippery drifting raft forever, and another part of them wants to break the moment and leap off.

The movie took over two and a half months to shoot. During most of that time Monty stayed sober. "He became increasingly strong and more sure of himself," Kazan said. And in some of the rushes he was "exactly as I wanted him to be—earnest, simple, sincere." In other scenes, however, his face appeared frozen, holloweyed, and off camera with Donna he was hostile, lashing out angrily when he discovered her searching his room for liquor. He denied he had any; he denied too that he had ever said he cared about her.

When his relatives, the Clifts from Chattanooga, came on location bearing a huge basket of fruit and champagne, he stood in the shower until they left. He also refused to stay up late with Libby Holman, who visited early on in the filming.

He was interested in doing the best possible job in *Wild River*. He would phone Bill Le Massena in New York to tell him how he hoped this would be his comeback film after the failures of *Lonelyhearts* and *Suddenly Last Summer*.

"The company became very much like a family, which Monty enjoyed," Kazan said. "We filmed in that little town for twelve weeks —we were all in the same hotel, sharing our meals together, arguing, talking together. And there's something very lonely about being out in the deep country. Anyhow, we all got very close."

Just before Christmas Lee Remick's husband, TV director Bill Colleran, was badly hurt in a car crash in Hollywood. Lee flew out to be with him, and Monty went abruptly off the wagon. He knew what it was like to be in a car crash. He still had nightmares about his own.

"He came on the set," Kazan recalls, "and he fell on his face in front of me right in the mud. Drunk. I picked him up and he apologized. I told him it was all right because it was all right—up until then he'd done a wonderful job. I knew how rough it had been for him to boom—stop drinking. He didn't taper off—he just stopped."

The picture finished in subdued fashion. When Lee Remick returned from California she made hourly calls to her husband in the hospital. Monty was irritable, hung over, furious at Donna because she had discovered his hiding place for vodka. He had kept the liquor concealed in a bottle marked terpin hydrate codeine.

38

It was freezing cold when Monty came back to New York. Over the holidays he went back to his physical therapist, Cora Alice Winter, and began to exercise to build up his strength. Mrs. Winter recalls, "I confided to Monty I always felt blue around Christmas and didn't feel up to buying presents for my relatives in Texas. Next thing I knew Monty arranged to have his limousine take us around to all the department stores where he helped me pick out gifts for my entire family!"

After the New Year Monty purchased a brownstone from Serge Obolensky on East Sixty-first Street. It was only a block away from his duplex, but he saw no reason to move to another part of Manhattan. He loved this particular street—it was quiet and lined almost exclusively with old homes.

He bragged about his new house, a spacious four-story building with seven rooms, six fireplaces, six baths, and a huge tree-filled garden. "President Teddy Roosevelt gave the house to Alice Longworth as a wedding present," he said. In the 1940s Clifton Fadiman had lived there. All in all, distinguished company; he was pleased.

He moved in late January and spent the next months attempting to decorate. But unlike the duplex, where every bit of space was utilized, entire rooms in the brownstone remained unused and in disarray, including the spectacular sixty-foot living room-study on the second floor. Heaped in one corner were cartons and cartons of Monty's books. They weren't unpacked until early 1966.

He did not star in *The Disenchanted* or *The Labor Story* as he thought he might. Instead, late in the spring of 1960, he signed to co-star in *The Misfits,* a much-touted movie which Arthur Miller had written for Marilyn Monroe.

The plot focused on three aging cowboys (Clark Gable, Eli Wallach, Monty) who drive wild horses out of the mountains near Reno to frighten them with airplanes, and then rope the horses from a fast-moving truck and sell them for dog food. Monroe would be playing a recent divorcée who meets this trio of "misfits" in a Reno casino and begins flirting with all of them.

Monty decided to play the part of Perce, the punch-drunk cowboy, after reading only one page of the script. He was attracted by the scene where Perce hangs on the phone with his mother: his imagination was caught by "what he says to his mother, what he shows—what she means to him, and doesn't mean to him. I phoned Arthur immediately and said I'd do it." He had nothing but praise for the screenplay ("Arthur is wildly aware of the ambivalent relationship between men and women!") and he was very excited about working with John Huston for the first time.

Shortly after signing for *The Misfits* he invited Bobby Lewis over to see the new brownstone. The director arrived in the front hall just as Monty appeared to throw himself down the stairs from the second floor. "It was as if he were trying to destroy himself."

He refused to discuss the incident. After picking himself up he walked into the huge unfurnished living room and attempted to have a conversation.

As a result of the fall he injured his arm, and he had to go to a specialist for treatment. He wanted to be in good condition for *The Misfits,* in which he would be riding and roping horses.

The specialist suggested he have a complete physical, which he did a few days later. During the consultation he confided he'd been having a hard time keeping his balance, particularly when sober, and he kept suffering memory loss.

He said he'd actually forget he was walking down the stairs and suddenly he'd find he was falling. "It's like my brain's being short-circuited." He also complained of twitching and such bad vision he could no longer keep a driver's license. His physician, Dr. Arthur Ludwig, had his eyes examined and found he had premature cataracts, very unusual in such a young man. (He was only thirty-nine.)

After further testing it turned out he was suffering from a rare form of metabolic disorder called spontaneous hypothyroidism:* His

---

* In 1957, Libby Holman's doctor in Stamford had told him he had a thyroid deficiency which was supposedly corrected by taking thyroid medication. It's possible his

parathyroid glands, which normally control calcium metabolism, were not producing enough of their specific hormone. The low calcium levels were causing muscle spasms and cramps, making him lose his balance, develop premature cataracts and suffer memory loss.

He was given vitamin D and extra calcium, with some improvement, "but he never really returned to normal," Dr. Ludwig said. He continued to have trouble keeping his balance, and as time went on he suffered greater and greater memory loss. He never connected his hypothyroid condition with his swift changes of mood.

Although he was warned not to, he continued to drink so heavily that by May of 1960 he came down with alcoholic hepatitis, and his doctor sent him to Mt. Sinai Hospital for ten days. A resident recalls, "He didn't seem to know who or what he was. He seemed to be subject to free-floating anxiety—he was afraid of sex, of authority." He was in such an agony drying out that a friend sneaked in bottles of vodka to him. The resident found out and gave the friend hell.

That same month *Wild River* opened in New York and was dismissed by critics as "strangely disturbing but not smashing . . . Clift a mite more animated than usual . . . but the story wanders aimlessly into the backwaters of violence, sex, segregation and anti-Semitism . . ."

It would be more than fifteen years before *Wild River* would be reevaluated by the British Film Institute as a major cinematic achievement and directors like Truffaut would call the movie "the accomplished work of mature artists."

A great many people came to visit *The Misfits* on location in and around Reno, Nevada. Clifford Odets came, and Frank Sinatra, Lady Marietta Tree, comic Mort Sahl, and scores of reporters posing as barflies. They hoped to ferret out the reason for the rumored breakup of the marriage of Arthur Miller and Marilyn Monroe.

Everyone gave parties while John Huston won and lost up to $15,000 a night at the dice tables. High in the Sierras there were forest fires. Some of the cast watched the Kennedy-Nixon TV debates.

Nobody would talk about the script trouble—Arthur Miller was already doing frantic rewrites. Producer Frank Taylor kept insisting *The Misfits* was the ultimate movie.

---

hypothyroid problems started as far back as 1928 when he was held under water in the *Isle de France* swimming pool and got an infected gland which had to be cut open in Munich. "He always had trouble with his balance, but when I knew him he seemed hypertense," Jeanne Green said.

Near the start of filming, Magnum photographer Elliot Erwitt gathered Monty, Gable, Monroe, Eli Wallach, Arthur Miller, John Huston, and Frank Taylor for a group portrait against the wall of a sunbaked Nevada saloon. It was a hundred degrees, and Marilyn became sweaty and agitated. To relieve the tension Monty burlesqued his passion for her. He was standing on a box and he fell from it onto the ground where he lay briefly, hooting with laughter.

His reputation as "pillhead" and "drunk" had preceded him so the company, with the exception of Marilyn, was apprehensive. Frank Taylor arranged to have him driven in an air-conditioned limousine to and from the desert locations. He told the chauffeur if any emergency arose he should call his hotel immediately. "I had a hotline telephone by my bed. I was on call twenty-four hours a day for both Marilyn and Monty—I tried to coddle and protect both of them."

Such precautions were unnecessary except on one occasion, when Monty got drunk and obstreperous at a lesbian bar near the Truckee River. Taylor was phoned. He went over personally to escort Monty out of the bar and take him back to his hotel suite.

Taylor said he got Monty into bed and later he fell asleep on the couch. Around five in the morning Taylor was awakened by Monty's naked form sleepwalking into the hall and towards the elevator. Taylor vaulted after him and managed to sling him over his shoulder just as the elevator door opened and "hordes of tourists poured out. I panicked. Here I was holding Montgomery Clift bare-assed in my arms, but nobody blinked an eye."

Monty prepared for his role by riding up to six hours a day in the desert with his stunt double, Dick Pascoe, who was also teaching him to rope a calf. He accompanied Pascoe to a rodeo in Pocatello, Idaho one weekend so he could hang around the stables and watch the cowboys exercise their ponies and rub grease onto their leather chaps.

He discovered the best place to get the feel of a rodeo was behind the chutes, those rectangular enclosures from which cowboy and bucking bulls emerge in frenzied hoof-pounding explosions. "It's like being backstage," he said, "so much nervous energy, so much tension."

During the rodeo, bending over a chute to help another cowboy climb on the back of a Brahma bull, Monty was cut badly on the bridge of the nose by the bull's horn. Paradoxically, in the Miller script, Monty as Perce is cut in the same place in a fall from a bucking horse.

Later, when the script called for him to be led to an ambulance in a semiconscious state after a fall from a horse, he threw himself violently to the ground over and over again to prepare for the scene.

His very first appearance in *The Misfits* (the two-minute phone call Perce makes to his mother to tell her she won't recognize his badly beaten face) is one of his very best pieces of acting. He doesn't seem to be doing anything more than shrugging and uttering a few half-swallowed words in that phone booth, but his behavior in that scene and others, the secret of all great film acting, has so much weight and urgency and conviction it enlarges the meaning of the movie.

Later he spoke to reporter Jim Goode about the actor's problem of remaining vulnerable. "Perce is a wonderful part, and if I don't do it justice I'll shoot myself. . . . I wish I were more thin-skinned. The problem is how to remain sensitive to all kinds of things without letting them pull you down."

During filming he had dinner quietly most nights with his makeup man, Frank Larue, and press agent Harry Mines. He insisted on sharing his very generous per diem with Mines. "I couldn't possibly spend it all myself." He was not very talkative, Mines recalls. He spent long periods in frowning silence, as if he were trying hard to remember something.

He did not seek out Kevin McCarthy at all. Kevin had been hired to play a small part so that, Taylor said, "Monty would have an old friend around."

But they were no longer close. They were pleasant enough together, but any feeling of intimacy was gone. Privately, Monty told friends he felt Kevin had used him to get ahead in his career. They never saw each other after *The Misfits;* it was almost as if their relationship had never existed.

Toward the middle of filming, Libby Holman came to Reno. Monty had looked forward to seeing her, but they fought almost continuously in his hotel room at the Mapes. She cued him on his lines and teased him unmercifully about his memory loss. He never told her or anyone about his hypothyroid condition, but he did phone Josh in New York; "I just want a little peace, mon vieux—a tiny little peace."

He said he was refusing to take sides in the ongoing feud between the Arthur Miller camp (which included Huston, Eli Wallach, Taylor) and Marilyn Monroe's entourage, which was headed by her drama coach, Paula Strasberg, and joined by her hairdresser, Whitey Snyder, and her masseur, Ralph Roberts.

"It mainly has to do with script revisions and who's upstaging whom," Monty said.

Actually, it was far more serious than that. Marilyn Monroe had become so addicted to pills she could barely function. When she did work, she was paranoid, unreasoning with Huston and Miller, feuding with Eli Wallach, causing endless delays.

Her marriage to the playwright was over. They tried to keep their rift a secret by sharing a suite at the Mapes Hotel, but they were barely speaking. Once she shut the door of her limousine in his face in front of the entire crew. When she appeared on location she often seemed somnambulistic; she was suffering from acute insomnia and took up to four Nembutals a night, but even breaking open the capsules and licking the powder from the palm of her hand did no good. She could not sleep.

Monty understood. Barbiturates didn't help his insomnia either. He was now so terrified of being unable to fall asleep he'd had his own bed shipped out from New York and put in his Mapes Hotel suite along with especially thick black curtains for the windows. But he remained wide awake until dawn.

"Monty and Marilyn were psychic twins," Frank Taylor said. "They were on the same wavelength. They recognized disaster in each other's faces and giggled about it."

This was peculiarly evident the day they shot their biggest scene together, a five-minute love scene outside a Dayton, Nevada saloon. There were flies buzzing around; black tarps were everywhere, as they were filming it "day for night." Before each setup Marilyn drank water from a paper cup. Monty took swigs of grapefruit juice laced with vodka from his thermos.

Once the cameras began rolling they responded to each other like children—tender, zonked out, a little desperate. They both fluffed their lines repeatedly. The scene took all day to shoot.

Between takes they would huddle together, comparing notes on how to cope with their insomnia. Marilyn said Ralph Roberts could massage her into drowsiness. Monty retorted the best way to exhaust himself was talking most of the night on long-distance phone.

He phoned Nancy Walker regularly. "I can't remember our conversations," Miss Walker said, "but he never talked about anything unpleasant. He didn't want to upset me."

He also phoned his former secretary, Marge Stengel, and begged her to come back and work for him again. Miss Stengel refused. She left him in early 1960, unable to cope with his heavy drinking and his dependence on pills. At one of their last meetings Monty had angrily rammed his head into Miss Stengel's stomach.

Clark Gable spent his time between takes tinkering with his new Mercedes or racing it 135 miles per hour around the desert. He never complained, but Monroe's lateness unnerved him, and the constant rewrites of the script and Huston's casualness bothered him (the director went duck hunting every weekend while Miller labored over new dialogue). Worst of all, the expected "chemistry" between Gable and Monroe wasn't happening on film. As shooting progressed, he began to drink heavily.

Still, he tried to be sympathetic to everybody, particularly to Monty, whom he found "awful hung-up." He thought he understood Monty's need to drink as being the same as his: masculinity and strength meant holding a lot of alcohol and not showing its effects.

One afternoon, Monty and Gable were shooting a particularly difficult scene in the desert with Marilyn, and "she was screaming during the scene and it was Marilyn screaming, not the character," Frank Taylor said. "Right in the middle of the scene, before Gable said his key line, Monty sauntered up behind him and lit a cigarette. I could tell Gable was very upset but he finished the speech and the scene was over. It was a perfect take."

Then Taylor hurried to Gable's dressing room and found the actor angrily pacing up and down. "That goddamn fag stole the scene from me by lighting that cigarette!" he exclaimed. Taylor defended Monty—said he would never do such a thing. The following morning he had Gable watch rushes—something Gable ordinarily never did— and he admitted he was wrong: "That faggot is a hell of an actor!"

Afterwards he helped Monty when the crew moved to the rodeo grounds for shots of Perce mounting a bucking horse. The horse was nervous; Monty was equally so. According to Jim Goode's book *The Story of the Misfits,* Gable held the animal while Monty got on, and seconds later the horse reared back and crushed Monty against a fence, tearing his shirt from top to bottom. Huston kept the cameras rolling; it was a terrific take.

Gable's enthusiasm for Monty's talent increased after they shot a bar scene, which occurs just after Perce is let out of the hospital after being thrown from his horse. According to Jim Goode's book *The Story of the Misfits,* Gable watched the rushes. When Monty says, "What was that they put in my arm?" he had a wild look in his eye, Gable told Jim Goode. "It could only come from morphine and booze. . . ."

Later Monty and Gable had another scene together where they're being driven in an open car through a rodeo parade. Along the way Monty kept punching Gable in the arm and Gable, who had arthritis, kept saying, "please stop!" Monty didn't. Finally, right in the middle of a take, Gable roared, "For Christ's sake, cut that out!" Monty immediately burst into tears. Shooting halted. With that Gable stared helplessly at John Huston and the entire crew and then he bellowed, "What in fuck is the world coming to?"

Marilyn Monroe's emotional problems shut down production on three different occasions. On one of them Monty flew back to New York to see Giles. On another, he and Eli Wallach went to Los Angeles to see an Ella Fitzgerald concert, and on an impulse while he was there he phoned the Greens and invited them to come along. "We did but it wasn't much fun," Jeanne said. "We met at the Beachcomber, but for some reason Monty didn't want to order dinner, so we just drank until it was time to go to the concert. None of us had a very good time."

The third time Monroe got sick, Monty asked *Misfits* press agent Harry Mines if he could go with him to San Francisco. They registered at the Mark Hopkins Hotel, and Mines said, "I was dying to walk around the city—we'd arrived in midafternoon. But Monty said, 'You know I'm an insomniac. I've got to have some sleep. You stay with me and wake me in an hour.' "

Mines remembered Monty bought a lot of magazines at the newsstand and gave Mines a script called *The Hustler,* which Robert Rossen had asked him to consider. Then, very carefully, he showed him how to wake him up. " 'Don't shake me or I'll fly right up to the ceiling,' he said. 'Just call out my name very softly: Monty? Monty?' and he insisted I rehearse it. Next thing I know I'm whispering in his ear, Monty? Monty? He said I did it fine."

After about an hour Mines woke him up and he seemed refreshed, and together they walked around San Francisco. There was fog rolling in from the Bay as they took a cable car, which Monty got a big kick out of, and later they strolled through Chinatown and over to the City Lights Bookstore. "We had dinner at Trader Vic's, and we ran into John Huston who came over to our table and sat for a while. The following day we went to stores like Gump's and had lunch at the Palace Hotel."

Possibly the most dramatic part of *The Misfits* was the filming of the wild horse chase on a fifteen-mile-long salt flat near Dayton, Nevada. There were frequent windstorms, and alkali dust covered the company trucks and trailers as well as Gable, Wallach, and Monty, who weren't using stunt doubles to catch the horses; instead they took turns roping an angry mare—first from the back of a pickup truck, then on foot.

According to Jim Goode: "The mare dragged Gable and Wallach along the dry lake floor. . . . For some unknown reason Monty had not been wearing gloves when the sequence began so he could not put them on without raising the question as to where the gloves had come from. He was forced to throw the mare barehanded, with his single rope running around in back of her, and pulling her legs out from under in the process."

His hands were lacerated and bleeding, but there was nothing anyone could do about it. The air was full of advice from Gable and Huston shouting commands: "Come again, Monty, run for it. Pull, Monty." "Huh?" "Pull hard." "I am." (Wallach) "Perce, look at your hands. Stop being a Christ figure." Gable later asked Huston, "Did you see the color of him?" (Huston) "Monty?" (Gable) "Grey."

There were parties right up to the last day of shooting in Nevada. Huston gave a very noisy drunken birthday party for Monty and Arthur Miller at the Christmas Tree Inn outside of Reno. There was another, grander one at the Mapes Ballroom, in honor of Huston's stepmother, Nan. She took a particular fancy to Monty, and they started seeing a great deal of each other.

Then *The Misfits* finished shooting November 5 in Hollywood. It was forty days behind schedule and a half million over budget. Arthur Miller was so exhausted he fell asleep during the last take. Huston meanwhile was already talking to reporters about his next picture, *Freud,* which he hoped to make with Monty and which had a screenplay by Jean-Paul Sartre.

After *The Misfits* was over, Monty remained in Hollywood for a few days at the Bel Air Hotel. He agreed to be interviewed by Joe Hyams.

Sprawled on a couch or pacing the floor of his suite, he talked animatedly about the fortieth birthday party Huston had given him in Reno. "I feel my life is just beginning," he said. He spoke of having a short supply of initiative these days, but aside from acting he still hoped to direct, as Marlon Brando and Karl Malden had done.

There was a small silence and Hyams asked him why he rarely attended any Hollywood parties.

"Because they don't ask me," he blurted. "I don't know why that is exactly. Someone once said, have you any friends? I said I had seven very dear friends. They said nobody has more than two friends, how come you have seven?"

Monty laughed. "That reminds me—four, five years ago I sent out sixty Christmas cards and got sixty back. Next year I figured what the heck, you know, it's like you give me a bottle of Scotch, I give you a bottle of gin; nobody gives anything away.

"So the next year I posted seven cards to my friends—simple little cards, just blue paper on which I'd drawn a little message in red crayon.

"That year I got my usual sixty Christmas cards but next year I got five. See what I mean? I didn't hand out the Scotch; I didn't get the gin."

In April 1961, Monty got a lot of publicity when he worked in Stanley Kramer's *Judgment at Nuremberg* for no salary. He'd originally been asked to consider the role of prosecuting attorney (subsequently played by Richard Widmark) but instead he chose the bit part of Peterson, a feeble-minded Jew who is sterilized by the Nazis, because the role intrigued him.

"To be an actor is to play any part—large or small—that has something important to say," he told columnist Sidney Skolsky. When Stanley Kramer phoned him in Puerto Rico where he was vacationing in January 1961 and offered him $100,000, he said he'd do the part for nothing—just expenses.

"Since it's only a single scene and can be filmed in one day, I strongly disapproved of taking an astronomical salary," he told the *New York Times* later. "But in the business I felt it was more practical to do it for nothing rather than reduce my price or to refuse a role I wanted to play."

He got two weeks at the Bel Air Hotel plus two first-class plane tickets for himself and Giles. Before leaving for the Coast that April he packed his little photograph of Kafka and he told Nancy Walker he was going to get a "very bad haircut." "Monty believed the poor slob he was playing would get a special haircut before testifying against war criminals."

He spent the first day rehearsing with Spencer Tracy at Revue studios in Hollywood. They rehearsed on a complete replica of the Nuremberg courtroom, built on rollers so the cameras could move in at any angle. Monty's scene, which ran seven minutes, was to be done mostly in close-up. He was worried about remembering his lines.

When time came to shoot the sequence he panicked—and he fluffed in take after take. Finally Tracy ambled over and said, "Fuck the lines—just play to me." Kramer recalled, "Spencer was the greatest reactor in the business. Monty did play to him, and the words poured out of his mouth—the results were shattering."

He spoke in a whisper, full of terror and unhealed suffering; his eyes were like those of a ten-year-old child. He recited his entire story to Tracy very simply, only rising to hysteria when he held out a photograph of his mother who'd been murdered in a concentration camp.

As soon as the highly charged scene was over, Tracy ran from the judges' bench, threw his arms around him, and praised him in glowing terms for his powerful, sensitive playing; he was nominated for an Academy Award for best supporting actor for his performance.

Afterwards Monty hung around on the set for a few days watching other sequences being shot, including one with Judy Garland. Garland, who was playing a German housewife, "was in terrible shape and big as a house," Kramer recalled. "It was her first film part in seven years and she was excruciatingly nervous. But I thought she came across magnificently on film."

Monty huddled in a corner watching her film the scene. Tears streamed down his face. After Kramer called cut, he wandered over to the director who asked expectantly, "Wasn't Judy magnificent?"

Monty wiped his cheeks. "Awwww Stanley," he replied, "she did it all *wrong!*"

39

On almost every one of his movies John Huston chose a victim. Or so the legend went. After he signed to work with him as *Freud* in late spring of 1961, Monty was warned repeatedly about the director's sadism with actors. Friends would phone from Hollywood to cry, "Be careful or John will get his ice pick into you," and Monty would answer, "I know, dear, I know."

In *The Misfits* he'd watched Huston slyly insult Marilyn Monroe and bait Arthur Miller cruelly about his "pedestrian" script revisions. In some quarters, the director was blamed for Gable's fatal heart attack because he'd goaded the sixty-year-old star into roping the wild horses without using a double. ("But Clark didn't have to do it," Monty would argue. He told people he wasn't afraid of working with Huston—he could take care of himself, he said. He'd spent many pleasant evenings in Reno drinking and talking with the man; he disliked his game playing, his false heartiness; but he admired his relish for life.)

Freud, of course, would be unlike any movie Huston had ever made, but then Huston, Monty knew, had an eclectic unpredictability which appealed to him. His *Maltese Falcon, Treasure of the Sierra Madre* and *African Queen* demonstrate a general truth about Huston films, which is that the circumstances of their making are often as dramatic and memorable as the movies themselves.

Certainly this was true of *Freud,* which began as a 2,000-page screenplay by Jean-Paul Sartre and ended on a claustrophobic set in Munich with cast and crew in an hysterical uproar.

The genesis of the movie went back to 1943 when Huston directed a documentary called *Let There Be Light* about soldiers who'd had mental breakdowns in battle—their rehabilitation, their return to normal life. "A wounded psyche is hard to watch," Huston wrote later, "almost too personal. Making that film was like having a religious experience."

Huston never forgot his brief cinematic exploration into man's unconscious; he couldn't stop thinking about it. In 1955 he began formulating a movie about Freud. "But not a biography—a motion picture which would dramatize the experiments that led to his discoveries."

He visualized Freud's career as "a kind of thriller, a mystery of a special sort." He chose the years 1885–1890 when Freud was at a crucial stage in his development, about to marry his long-time fiancée, Martha Bernays, about to leave neurology and concentrate on his theories regarding man's unconscious. He hoped to cap the picture with Freud's struggle to have his amazing concepts—particularly the Oedipus complex—recognized and accepted.

Montgomery Clift was his first and only choice to play Freud, but he had to fight for him. Universal told Huston he was a drunk and unreliable, citing his erratic behavior on *Lonelyhearts* and *Suddenly Last Summer* as examples.

Huston stood firm. He argued for Monty's extraordinary sensitivity and intelligence, and for the peculiar enigmatic quality he had that all great stars have. "He was mysterious. He always held something back."

As soon as Monty signed for the film he began reading Ernest Jones's biography of Freud, and during his analytic sessions he worked on his characterization with Dr. Silverberg, pummeling him with questions. How would Freud behave toward a patient? How would he move, react? Wouldn't he feel an overwhelming responsibility to someone whose life he was trying to shape? "Montgomery Clift's Freud was done in tribute to Billy Silverberg," Dr. Lily Ottenheimer said.

Genius, Monty decided, was what set Freud apart—he became the quintessential loner, disconnected from everyone, including his family, because he was forced to transcend them as he labored to create and justify his own world. And Monty was most concerned with how one plays a genius.

Freud was self-centered, Monty said. "If I'd known him I wouldn't have liked him." Freud had terrible anxiety attacks. He felt more guilt than the average man because he felt more alone. He studied himself as relentlessly as he studied everyone else.

"There is somebody who is living my life and I know nothing

about him," Pirandello wrote in his journal. Monty repeated that thought to Pat Collinge. The image of another self inside us who breathes the same air we breathe, walks the same streets, was an image that had given him nightmares for years. He was sure Freud felt the same way.

Monty and John Huston began their talks about the movie at St. Clarens, Huston's remodeled Irish castle, in the summer of 1961. Sir Stafford Clark, one of England's greatest psychiatrists and an expert on Freud, joined them. Monty seemed edgy but full of ideas. His hypothyroid condition had worsened; he had to steel himself whenever he crossed a room, and one reason he embraced people so fiercely was to keep from falling.

Huston, of course, had no knowledge of his condition, so Monty's behavior annoyed him. He was also concerned about his consumption of liquor. "Our discussions about Freud were academic, specific, and Monty would put forth an opinion or an idea—some of which were very good—but as soon as he got drunk he sounded absurd. He would rant and rave and he would weep if we disagreed with him."

At one point an English journalist came to St. Clarens to interview Monty; they all had dinner together. The following morning Huston said he realized the journalist had spent the night in Monty's room. "The incident seemed trashy—I felt Monty had insulted me. It was messy. I wish he'd considered my family and how I felt about it. I can't say I'm able to deal with homosexuals."

Shooting began in Munich September 11. Monty had a suite at the Continental Hotel but on weekends he stayed at Maria Schell's comfortable pretty white villa on the fashionable Pienzenauerstrasse. Miss Schell recalls, "I knew he was ill, but I didn't know with what. He kept dropping things. A cup of coffee. Lighted cigarettes." Still he worked on the script. He and Susan Kohner, who was playing Freud's wife, Martha, rehearsed their early scenes together. "Monty figured out all sorts of details for us in the scenes," Miss Kohner said. "He also took the time and trouble to help me find things in myself which made my part come alive for me. He did it quite humbly. He had great humility about his talent."

Giles had come to Munich too; he was always introduced as Montgomery Clift's secretary. He used Monty's car and chauffeur during the day to tool around the city to various shops and cafes. He also brought a succession of muscular working-class German boys on the set. They loitered around Monty's dressing room, making everybody very uncomfortable until finally, they were asked to leave.

At the start of filming, Huston presented Monty with three versions of the cut-down Sartre script. Monty tried to work with all three —he found much of the dialogue forced and pedantic, and he told Huston so, adding he didn't want to sound like "Don Ameche discovering the telephone." He had no idea Huston had rewritten much of the dialogue.

They had their first open disagreement filming a short scene between Freud and his then fiancée, Martha. Monty wanted to show some tenderness, some love, but Huston, who disliked any open show of affection between men and women on film, forbade it. They argued; finally, rather than hold up shooting, Monty went along with what Huston wanted. But he was so upset by the argument he kept fluffing his lines, and there were constant retakes.

Not long after that Monty began rehearsing one of the most important scenes in the picture, a sequence in which Freud enrages his colleagues by elaborating on his theories of the unconscious.

The set, an old-fashioned amphitheater, was crowded with press, with over a hundred extras as doctors, and with the crew: prop master, electrician, sound man, key grips, hairdresser, makeup man, Gladys Hill, Huston's long-time secretary, Doc Erickson, Huston's production manager, set decorator Steven Grimes, cameraman Douglas Slocombe, as well as principal actors Larry Parks and Eric Portman.

Monty, in beard and frock coat, was visibly nervous as he walked stiffly out on stage and began one of his long speeches; he occasionally glanced at notes.

Suddenly Huston interrupted him, saying he must speak extemporaneously. Monty replied that he would not, that Freud always spoke from notes. Huston contradicted him. They bickered back and forth. The director insisted he couldn't see his expression or shoot a proper close-up if his head was bent over notes. Finally Monty tried the speech staring straight into the camera. He fluffed repeatedly; there were endless takes.

During lunch break, Monty phoned Nancy Walker in New York to complain about Huston. "John is misbehaving, Nanny," he said.

"And what about you, sweetheart, are you misbehaving?"

Monty assured her he was not. The same afternoon he strode back into the amphitheater and played the scene word-perfectly.

But he continued to criticize the script. "I'm being forced to think out loud," he told Josh in another transatlantic call. "It's 'Eureka, I've found it!' type stuff. It sucks." He balked at certain scenes, was unable to memorize others.

Sometime in midshooting a Dr. Black, a hypnotist, came on the set as one of Huston's advisors, presumably to coach Susannah York, who was playing the hysterically repressed Cecily, the first patient Freud hypnotizes. Dr. Black remained in Munich for several weeks—he attended rushes where he made frequent suggestions and criticisms. He also stayed uncomfortably close to Monty, lunching with him, dining with him; he made an unsuccessful attempt to hypnotize him. Monty told people he thought Black was treating him like a patient and he didn't like it. Later a story got around Hollywood that Monty had been hypnotized into memorizing his lines by Black. When he angrily confronted Huston with the story the director shrugged, "You're paranoid, boy."

Meanwhile, the Sartre script was being endlessly revised by Huston and his producer, Wolfgang Reinhardt, the rotund son of Max Reinhardt, who had earlier worked on Huston's disastrous *Red Badge of Courage*. There were delays as they struggled to dramatize the experiments and personal conflicts of Dr. Freud.

Still, rushes looked promising. Monty was giving a remarkable performance (even Huston, in his fury, agreed), all the more remarkable considering that he was struggling with a debilitating condition which hampered his movements as well as his memory.

Since he could no longer move his body with ease (he walked more and more like a marionette) he chose to express emotions through his hands. During the picture his hands are prominent, in close-ups and longshot, fingers laced together when he's thinking; they cut through the air to make points, they clench, they ball into fists, they fold in his lap when he's in repose. Monty believed that the body reveals character; in this film the vocabulary of his hands is explicit and intricate, but so subtle one barely notices when he makes a gesture to punctuate a speech or fill a silence.

Gossip about the chaotic filming of *Freud* and Montgomery Clift's "strange behavior" popped up regularly in the European press and the Hollywood trade papers. By the end of October, it was noted in *Daily Variety* that the picture was not going to be finished on time and might go a million over budget.

It was said that insurance claims were going to be made by Universal, and the delays would be attributed to Monty's inability to memorize lines, although it was common knowledge that Huston's extravagances were as much to blame for the delays. He had a penchant for costuming hundreds of extras and then not using them, of okaying one outfit for a principal, changing his mind, making another. He once threw out an entire set and insisted on a new one at tremendous expense. Often he would keep cast and crew waiting while he had an extended conversation with a visitor.

Monty was bewildered by Huston's behavior. "He acts as if he's lost interest in the production," he told Josh over the phone. He implied that Huston was treating him "like two cents," forcing him to do take after take without letup, making him say every line "as if it's precious writ!" He was upset because a spate of ugly stories had appeared about him in the German press. He had played Jews in his last two pictures; he was now playing "the Jew Freud." Wasn't it about time Montgomery Clift admitted he was Jewish himself, or was he ashamed? Monty felt the stories were anti-Semitic and wondered why Huston didn't put a stop to them.

Then there came a point where, as Monty told his physician later, "John earned his reputation as the laughing sadist." This particular incident occurred during the filming of a dream sequence in which Freud dreams he's being pulled by a rope down a long dark tunnel towards his mother.

The scene had no dialogue, but because of the eerie visual effects, the scene had to be shot again and again. Huston forced Monty to pass the rope through his hands without stopping, until by the ninth take his palms were raw and bleeding and he was in obvious pain.

A few days later director and star were guests at some public function in Munich. Huston noticed Monty's bandaged hands. "Did I do that to you?" he called out in his warm, mellifluous voice. "Son of a bitch!"

Soon after this incident, Sir Stafford Clark arrived in Germany, presumably to act as another advisor on the film. Several of the actors met with him to complain of Huston's treatment of Monty and to ask him to do something about it.

The famous analyst stayed in Munich long enough to dine separately with Huston and Monty and to watch the filming of a sequence. Clark had an intriguing theory which he confided to several people in the company—during *Misfits,* Huston had imagined himself a father to Monty. When Monty transformed himself from a confused cowboy into the bearded genius Freud, he no longer had any need for the director's advice, and Huston developed a love/hate relationship to Monty.

Monty ridiculed this theory. "I could never become emotionally connected to John on any level, least of all as a father figure." When he was asked why, he said, "because his eyes are empty—they have no feeling in them at all, even when he's his most charming. And that makes me very uncomfortable."

Once the company arrived in Vienna there were more production delays. The original plan had been to complete locations in two weeks. Huston filmed in parks, by the Danube, and in the Franz Josef train station, hoping to capture the shadowy baroque essence of the Austrian capital. Whenever he thought the rushes lacked authenticity he would add more costumed extras, more carriages with drivers in period dress.

During the last week in Vienna, while Monty was filming a scene with a group of extras, his hat was knocked into his eye. He complained that something had happened to his vision. Huston sent him to a doctor who could find nothing wrong, but Monty insisted on flying to London to consult with a specialist. Huston was furious at this delay. He remained furious until a telegram came from Monty announcing he was suffering from cataracts.

"Now he'll have to use a seeing-eye dog," Huston joked. When she heard that remark Susannah York burst into tears. Huston admitted later the remark was in bad taste.

A week later the company moved back to the Munich studios and Monty returned from London. He did not discuss his eyes, but he did phone his brother and told him he was terrified of going blind.

For a while Huston left him alone, presumably because accountants had arrived from Hollywood and were trying to exercise some control over the vast amounts of money that were still being spent on *Freud*.

Days and nights wore on. Discussion and rehearsal were now impossible. Monty carried his thermos of grapefruit juice and vodka and resisted the ever-changing script, maintaining there were lines he simply couldn't say—"they made no sense." Nobody could ever agree on one version or reading. He would be handed new scenes at the end of the day and was expected to know them by five the following morning. He said he simply could not memorize lines, he did not have enough time.

"We had dialogue written all over the set, on the backs of doors, walls, on boards, in front of the camera," Huston recalled. "But it soon became obvious that on top of everything else Monty really *couldn't* see—it was macabre."

Huston became so undone by "the infernal memory lapses, his secret drinking," he decided to stage a fight to frighten him into shaping up. "I even considered using physical violence. I wasn't trying to destroy him. I wanted to save my movie!"

They met in an empty room, a few chairs by the door, a phone. "All we did was glare at each other," Huston recalled. Finally Monty asked him, "Are you going to kill me?" Huston ended up saying nothing to him.

By the middle of December, production delays had skyrocketed to over $600,000 and tension became unbearable on the set. Just before Christmas, Universal tried to persuade Monty to make a claim for his cataract condition against the Fireman's Fund* which held a million-dollar policy for the company. Monty refused. Between takes he would place calls to Lew Wasserman at MCA, yelling about betrayal, about being destroyed.

He told friends afterwards he was accosted at his hotel by Universal executives insisting he make the insurance claim "or else." "The pressure is lunatic," he cried. He found it impossible to study his lines in peace so he escaped to Maria Schell's house and tried to relax there. "He was ill. He'd be talking to me and he'd drop a lighted cigarette on the carpet and not remember. I had my doctors come and see him, but they could never find out what was the matter with him." He did not tell anyone about the hypothyroid condition. He was devastated by Huston's treatment of him. And Huston expressed indifference about the insurance claims. Later he would say he had "not wanted anything like this to happen."

According to Monty's lawyer, some people would benefit if Monty were blamed for the overexpenditures. "There were guys in Huston's entourage who had brought their girlfriends over to Munich and put them on the payroll. It was a terribly corrupt, amoral situation, particularly disgusting because they were making Monty the scapegoat. He knew it. He told me some of Huston's people were openly jubilant when the news came out that he had cataracts!"

* Fireman's Fund Insurance Company insures performers. They paid $320,725 to cover production losses incurred when Monty had his car accident during the filming of *Raintree County*.

By the end of filming the entire company had divided into two camps—most of the actors were pro Monty, the production crew pro Huston. As one of the crews said, "I knew which side my bread was buttered on."

40

Monty's suitcases lay unpacked in his brownstone for months after he returned from Munich in January of 1962. He went almost directly into Mt. Sinai Hospital for a hernia operation. He'd begun to suffer from very bad varicose veins in his legs; they were operated on as well. When he was released from Mt. Sinai, his jaw was still giving him pain, so he began going to his Brooklyn dentist for treatment.

The *Freud* litigation had started. Lawyers on both sides were drawing up copious briefs. Universal was getting depositions from everyone in the cast. Monty was furious because he and Susannah York were being accused of "collusion," "simply" he said, "because we often felt it necessary to rehearse our lines till 4 A.M."

For reasons yet to be established legally, *Freud* had cost $4 million to complete in five and one-half months instead of the budgeted $2 million for three months. Huston was blaming Monty for holding up production. He claimed he'd been drinking and had an "anxiety neurosis." Now an attempt was being made to collect more than half a million dollars from the Fireman's Fund, which had insured Monty. If this failed, he would be personally sued for the money.

He laughed at the idea of anyone trying to collect "that much dough" from him, but he was well aware the suit could have a devastating effect on his career. Until it was settled he would not be able to work; no major studio would touch him.

He hoped the case could be settled out of court; he was considering starring in a movie about Dr. Tom Dooley. He wanted to have his cataracts removed as soon as possible. But the operations (he would have to have two) were being put off until the clouding on the eyes had thickened sufficiently. He was having more and more difficulty seeing. He continued to have nightmares about going blind. His doctors said this would not happen.

Nancy Walker became concerned about Monty's spirits; she dropped by the brownstone every day to regale him with stories about her childhood in show business. "Nanny is a fantastically rich person," Monty would say.

And he was touched at Giles's attempts to make him stop drinking. "He actually seems to care," he told Bill Le Massena. Giles wanted Monty to stop seeing Silverberg because every time he came back from a session he would be drunk. For a while Monty tried to break with the analyst, but Silverberg phoned the brownstone repeatedly until Monty returned to his therapy.

On an impulse, he took the analyst to a special screening of *Freud;* together they discovered that for several seconds during the dream sequence close-up they could actually see the cataracts forming over the pupils of his eyes.

While Monty was in Munich, Libby Holman impulsively married Lou Shanker, a jovial, cigar-smoking painter who wore a beret. She'd confided she wanted to "lead a normal life with a man her own age," but soon after the marriage she told her accompanist, Gerald Cook, she'd made "another terrible mistake." She and Shanker couldn't communicate.

Meanwhile Monty would talk to her on the phone, telling her about his cataracts and his dinners with Marilyn Monroe. He was also seeing Nan Huston (Walter Huston's widow). Nan was in her early sixties, a former actress with tiny hands, fluttery, unstable, very feminine. She lived in an enormous apartment on Sutton Place. During the spring of 1962, Monty came there often, sometimes with Susan Kohner, who'd just become engaged to designer John Weitz.

Then there was the Baroness, a plump middle-aged German lady with pale eyes and mysterious wealth, who could be seen going in and out of Monty's brownstone at odd hours. To anyone who listened she talked nonstop about her great passion for Montgomery Clift, whom she'd loved for ten years, she said, and for ten years she had roamed the world hoping by chance they would meet, and he would ask her to marry him.

Wherever she went she covered her hotel walls with stills from *Red River* and *A Place in the Sun,* and she filled journal after journal with her impressions of Monty. She believed she was the only woman who could make him happy.

Eventually her fantasies propelled her to Hollywood. By now

she was determined to meet Monty face to face. She had written Warner Brothers, MGM and 20th Century-Fox asking for his address, but they had never answered. One afternoon shortly after her arrival in California, she called out to Burt Lancaster during a press conference he was holding at the Beverly Hills Hotel and asked him, "Where does Montgomery Clift live?"

Lancaster was very respectful. "I think Montgomery Clift is a great actor, lady, but I don't have a clue as to where he lives."

After eight months of taking cabs and driving around in circles through Beverly Hills, Malibu, and up and down Sunset Boulevard, the Baroness flew to New York. She managed to track down Monty's brownstone on East Sixty-first Street sometime in 1962, knocked on the door, which had recently been sanded and rubbed, the brass trim and coach light lovingly polished. Giles answered. Monty happened to be coming down the stairs. When she saw him she let out a cry and threw herself at his feet, sobbing in German that she loved him, had always loved him, and to please not send her away.

He invited her inside. She showed him her stack of journals which she carried everywhere. When he realized they were dedicated to his life, he asked if he might read them. She said yes. He read them several times, reportedly telling her later, "I never knew anyone could love me that much."

Monty saw the Baroness periodically until his death. Occasionally, he allowed her to come in for breakfast unannounced. She could not always wait to be invited. She was impatient to see him, listen to him. They would have long conversations in German sitting in the living room of his brownstone while *Der Rosenkavalier* played on the hi-fi. Sometimes she would stay for dinner with Bill Le Massena, who said, "She was about as looney a dame as I've ever met. She'd convinced herself that Monty was madly in love with her. Of course, Monty was clinically interested in her facial expressions, her gestures, her walk."

When the Baroness met Sunny, she informed her she would someday be Monty's wife. She sent her great bunches of flowers with cards signed "Your future daughter-in-law." She managed to steal one of Monty's silk shirts and she slept in it until the shirt became ragged. When her brother came to New York, she offered him to Monty as a present "because he is young and handsome—and he will be very, very kind."

In August 1962, Marilyn Monroe died from an overdose of

sleeping pills. Monty reminded friends of the famous photograph Elliot Erwitt had taken of the *Misfits* cast—himself, Miller, Huston, Wallach, Frank Taylor, Gable and Marilyn—all posing jauntily in the hot Nevada sun. He remembered "deaths always come in threes in show business." First Gable. Now Marilyn. Who would be next?

He didn't want to think about it; instead he flew up to Maine to see Silverberg, whose long-time companion Ed Shipley was dying. "Billy is inconsolable," Monty said, when he returned. It was obvious he was upset.

By now the *Freud* litigation had been dragging on for six months with Universal asking Monty to concede his emotional upset over his cataracts caused undue delay in the production. Monty refused to concede this, and late that summer he and his lawyer Jack Clareman met with the lawyers from Universal at the Waldorf and he gave lengthy testimony (as did the entire cast and crew) describing everything that had gone on during filming, including Huston's treatment of him.

At the end of the summer Roddy McDowall came back from Rome full of stories about the filming of *Cleopatra*. Monty was both amused and flabbergasted at the amount of publicity the Burton–Taylor scandal had generated. "It's lunatic," he cried. "Bessie Mae is now the most famous woman in the world!" However, he told friends he suspected Burton was behind the promotion of the romance. "Richard wants to be famous at any cost," he said.

In Boston in October of 1962, Brooks's oldest daughter, single and pregnant, murdered her lover after he'd refused to marry her, and flew abruptly to South America. She only stayed a few days, however, during which time she contemplated jumping out her hotel window. She decided against it—she was pregnant and wanted her baby. She then returned to Boston and gave herself up to the police, subsequently confessing to the murder.

The *Daily News* headlines screamed: "Montgomery Clift's niece shoots a man . . . the deb who killed. . . ." Monty knew his niece had been miserably unhappy for most of her life and had attempted suicide on several occasions.

Throughout the autumn the phone rang incessantly with calls from reporters from all over the world wanting to hear his reaction to the murder. ("Perfect!" was his private sarcastic response.) He remembered his niece as having a haunted quality, hunched shoulders, and glittering eyes under swooping dark brows. She seemed hunted, furtive; occasionally she spoke in an unintelligible accent. He had Giles tell reporters, "no comment."

Nor would he speak to his mother when she called to discuss the tragedy. He found out she'd gone to Boston and arranged the best legal and psychiatric aid for her granddaughter.

He was too agitated about the *Freud* litigation and his approaching cataract operations; he talked of nothing else. He was positive he would go blind. He hung on the phone with Brooks talking for hours about how he'd always taken his sight for granted.

"He didn't seem bitter—he seemed astonished at this latest turn of events," Brooks said. "He'd always been accident-prone, falling down, burning himself with cigarettes, slipping—it was part of his nature. But going blind was something else."

On December 6, 1962, he went into Mt. Sinai for his first operation. Giles accompanied him. Sunny had been phoning, but he refused to speak with her despite Giles's entreaties: "She's your *mother*," he kept saying. She came to the hospital anyway and stood outside the door of his room the morning of his operation conferring with the doctors.

"She looked formidable," a doctor recalls. "She was a tiny slender woman, around seventy-four I'd guess. Snow white hair. Brilliant eyes exactly like Monty's. I remember she took everything we said *personally*. She said things like, 'The operation is scheduled for ten? I could have been here at eight.' She trembled with pent-up energy, but she was in perfect control. She hadn't seen her son in months; she was determined to see him now."

Giles eventually led her into the room and he remained in the door while she tiptoed over to the bed where Monty lay half sedated. "Hello, dear," she said.

He turned his face to the wall, so she sat down beside him. She stayed as long as the nurses would allow, talking exhaustively, reassuringly in her liquid, melodious voice.

Every family has phrases and words of their own—the Clifts had a special language thick with dark prophecies, secrets, evasions, references to the past, and Sunny knew the language by heart. Now she reminisced about their travels in Europe when he was a boy—skiing in Saint Moritz, learning gymnastics on the Riviera with Boof and Sister, tennis lessons in Vevey. "Didn't we have fun? Weren't you happy?" When he couldn't answer she moved swiftly into the present, describing her latest job, evaluating antiques at the Metropolitan Museum, talking about her recent involvement with the Quaker Meeting House down on East Twentieth Street.

Finally, Monty took a long breath and held it deep in his chest. "Oh Ma," he cried, "give me your strength. I need your strength."

After Monty got out of the hospital in January, he seemed—for a brief period—quite happy. The operations had gone smoothly. Although he no longer had peripheral vision he could still see—with thick-lensed glasses. He talked about the meaning of life to friends like Brother Thomas, who came down from his monastery to visit him. He talked about "coming close to the nadir . . . the closer we come to the negative, to death, the more we blossom. People who are deaf and blind are the people who are most tuned to life."

Freud was playing to capacity crowds at Cinema I and II, within walking distance of his brownstone. The film had opened in December and got for the most part good reviews: "Montgomery Clift gives an eerily illuminating performance. . . ." *Freud* was subsequently selected to represent the United States at the Berlin Film Festival.

However, in spite of the accolades and good box office, the legal wrangles between Universal and Monty continued. An entire year had gone by and nothing was settled. He kept asking his lawyers, "When will this be over so I can go back to work?" and they kept answering, "Soon, soon."

In February, he flew down to St. Thomas in the Virgin Islands and stayed with Nancy Walker and her family.

They were a curious pair, the broken movie star and the pint-sized comedienne. Nancy describes herself as "grabby with friends. I never want to let go with anyone I like." At this point, in his state of frailty and eclipse, Monty needed Nancy's vitality, her interference, her humor.

They spent most of their time sitting on the beach playing with her daughter or talking. "We'd scream with laughter about all sorts of things, we'd gripe and bitch and then Monty would say, 'Let's stop being pains in the ass and get on with the business of living.'"

He could be very cryptic about his acting. No artist likes to talk about his work, but every so often they would get on "that cliché subject, the connection between suffering and creation." Neither one of them would ever dare say, is it worth it? "But," she said, "we both sensed we had to keep on delivering." It was the only way Monty could justify his existence.

41

He started planning a garden as soon as he got back to New York
—"white birches in honor of Chekov"—and he also agreed to see
writer Lyn Tornabene, who'd been assigned to do a major profile on
him for *Cosmopolitan* magazine.

Mrs. Tornabene remembers his brownstone as "all texture, no
color." Upholstered pieces were beige—there were nine-foot beige
couches in the sitting room, decorated with biege throw pillows
hand stitched in black, which he said he'd ordered in Switzerland.
Exquisite silver objects were everywhere; the crystal ashtrays
gleamed like jewels. But the house was underfurnished; entire rooms
on the third and fourth floors stood vacant.

For the interview, a thickly bespectacled Monty wore grey
slacks, white shirt, grey cashmere cardigan. He was boyishly thin,
clean shaven. His shoulders hunched. "He made me feel it would not
only be rude but sinful to say anything that would offend him," Mrs.
Tornabene said.

Throughout their talk he smoked Reyno Filter cigarettes in a
holder. He prefaced most of his answers with "Listen, *honey*."

She told him she was surprised to see him—she'd heard he was
hostile to the press. With that he sat down in a chair behind her so
she couldn't see his face. "I give my time for an interview and a reporter comes in with an angle into which everything has to fit." He
then gave a cruel but funny imitation of a writer typing away, then he
jumped to his feet and moved to another chair. "A writer writes
'Montgomery Clift hates money'—the next person who says that I'm
going to sue!" He paced the room angrily, "I have a reputation for
being hostile and yet I've given countless interviews except when I'm
working—can you blame me?" He sat down in another chair, and

Tornabene moved near him, asking if this was where he would finally settle. He looked as if he'd been scolded. "I'm sorry," he said. "We'll sit on the couch." He did not pace again.

From then on he rambled, expressing himself in half-finished sentences, in waves of his hand. He talked of the movie *Sundays and Cybèle*. He'd met with the director, Serge Bourgion, and had been very impressed with him. "He's nice, and it's wonderful to meet somebody with talent who's nice." He talked about Marilyn Monroe. "She gave so much as an actress; working with her was like going up and down on an escalator. No, Hollywood didn't kill her—she had many deep-seated problems. . . ." As he spoke, he unconsciously emptied one ashtray into another, and handed the full one to Giles to be emptied. He called Giles "Gillie."

At one point he left the room to make a phone call. When he returned he was chuckling, "I thought of a description of me borrowed from E. B. White. 'He drinks wine from older years and uses Kleenex from the old box.'"

Mrs. Tornabene says, for reasons she can't remember, she and Giles "broke up about that."

When he began discussing actors his voice sounded contemptuous. He refused to name ones he admired. "I never do that." He put most of his peers into three categories: "whores," talented actors who accept roles only to make money; "bathroom actors," actors who get a script, check it in the bathroom, and emerge ready to go on camera; and "self-strokers," actors with their own trampolines who act only for themselves without giving. He was proud that in his own estimation he was none of these—"Looking back on my career I can honestly say I've done nothing in theater or movies that I'm ashamed of."

Several times during their talk he called himself "a bottom neurotic. That's when you're at the bottom and you're working your way up to being a top neurotic."

During the cocktail hour, one of his doctors, with his wife and two children, came over to "give him a vitamin shot." Afterwards Monty sat in rapt attention with the little girl and boy, laughing, chuckling, emitting small, delighted moans. When the family left he told Tornabene the little boy reminded him of himself as a child, "never caring where the scars fell, slamming into things, finding ways to crawl up ladders, pull out plugs, always falling down, not caring about the black and blue marks. . . ."

The brownstone was silent. Giles put on more Ella Fitzgerald tapes. "You see how quiet it is here?" he demanded. "I lead a pheno-barbital existence. That's why I don't have to take it. I have it."

Monty waited a year and a half for the *Freud* suit to be settled. He waited a year and a half to be paid the $131,000 due him in over-time. In June 1963, he sued Universal for services rendered for his portrayal of *Freud*. In a counteraction filed in New York Supreme Court, the movie company claimed that "Montgomery Clift owes $686,364.74 for causing production delays in the filming."

A voluminous brief filed in Monty's behalf disclosed that while the movie was being shot in Munich in 1961 he'd discovered he'd had cataracts in both eyes.

"Since my return to the United States," Monty's brief stated, "I have had these cataracts successfully removed, and my doctors assure me there will be no recurrence and that my eyesight is as good as it was before this condition developed."

Monty's eye condition was one of the main points in Universal's suit. The company claimed that his illness forced additional expendi-tures for the movie. But it also charged that production was delayed because Monty repeatedly failed to memorize his lines properly.

Monty said he'd been contracted to make the picture for $200,000 and he'd never received the balance he was now asking. "The movie opened last December and has played to capacity busi-ness in New York and other cities," he pointed out.

"I mention all the foregoing as proof of the fact that no reason-able person can quarrel with the quality of my services, and I am confident that the defendant itself will not deny the excellence of the film and my portrayal of the role of Sigmund Freud."

Monty charged that when the cataract condition was discovered Universal tried to persuade him to make a claim for his illness against the Fireman's Fund Insurance Company.

"I do not deny that I was upset when I discovered I was a vic-tim of cataracts," Monty went on, "but I refused to accede to the de-fendant's demand that this condition created a disability which was responsible for delays in the production of the picture."

After a hearing before Supreme Court Justice Greenberg, Monty won his claim and was subsequently paid $131,000. But the public-ity, coupled with the talk in Hollywood about his drinking, his inabil-ity to memorize lines, made him virtually unemployable.

He didn't believe his career was ruined until Tom Ryan sent him his screenplay of Carson McCullers' *The Heart Is a Lonely*

Hunter and suggested he might want to play the part of the deaf-mute Singer, to whom everybody tells their troubles.

Monty read the script and instantly agreed. He had been moving closer and closer to this kind of characterization. He wanted to act a person whose life and adventures are carried on in total silence. He thought it would be the supreme challenge for him as an actor to portray a vivid being who never utters a sound; he had experienced what it was like to exist in semidarkness when he was recuperating from his cataract operation. He was also going slightly deaf. "Just because you lose your sight or your hearing doesn't mean you lose your mind," he said.

Monty's physical therapist, Cora Alice Winter, arranged for him to start working with friends who taught at Gallaudet College of the Deaf in Washington, D.C.; he had long talks with Tom Ryan and his new agent, Robbie Lantz, whom he'd signed with after MCA broke up. Lantz ultimately tried to make a deal with 20th Century-Fox, the studio that owned the McCullers story. But 20th turned thumbs down on Montgomery Clift as the star. When he demanded to know why, he was told he was uninsurable.

The money people in Hollywood and Europe considered him finished. His behavior on *Freud* remained the talk of the industry—how he'd stumbled and cried and had such frequent memory lapses he'd delayed production. When it was argued these accusations were exaggerated, that he was a four-time Academy Award nominee who'd starred in fifteen movies before *Freud* and never caused any production delays, the answer to that was, "He caused delays in one movie. That's enough—he can no longer be insured."

At first Monty continued to meet with the few directors willing to gamble on him, and he would discuss projects for hours, but whenever Lantz tried to negotiate with the producer involved, the response was invariably, "Clift is uninsurable."

He began drinking heavily again and fighting with Giles. Work had always held him together; work had been his salvation, his emotional support, his reason for being. He couldn't bear the idea of waiting on other people to give him the opportunity to create. In despair he began wandering the streets at odd hours.

Meanwhile *Freud* was still playing around the country, and his old movies like *The Search* and *I Confess* were popping up on TV. In art houses *Red River* and *A Place in the Sun* had become cult films.

His drug dealer, "Bird," saw him come into a bar in Harlem very late, about three-thirty in the morning. "Monty looked terrible.

Unshaven, dirty—he asked if he could buy heroin from me for some friends. I was going to go out and get it for him, when all of a sudden there's a fuckin' murder at the bar. One guy shoots another guy in the gut—blood spurts out, there's all sorts of screamin' and yellin'—the murdered guy was a pimp. His girl starts keenin' over him. Monty just stands there in the midst of the noise, the confusion, watching the whole scene. He's hanging there like a ghost, and then he glides out the door into the night . . . Now I'm not sure he was ever there. . . ."

42

Until the outcome of the *Freud* suits Monty had, to a large extent, hidden his fragmented private life. In the past only his intimates knew he often cruised on Forty-second Street before going to bed with Libby Holman; he never discussed the beatings he suffered at the hands of some of the male hustlers, or the robberies in his brownstone that he allowed to happen because he was too drunk to care. The threats of blackmail were handled discreetly by his lawyer. The dirty phone calls were eliminated periodically by changing his unlisted phone number.

If at forty-one he was sick that he had wasted so much time, trapped in a macho age, unable to relate genuinely to so many people who mattered to him, he still believed he must keep his sexual identity concealed from the public. Otherwise his career would be finished, his life discredited.

"He never admitted being homosexual to me, and I'd been his lover," Josh said. "This may sound strange, but I'm not sure he was ever exclusively homosexual, since he was capable of affectionate erotic relationships with either sex."

Sometimes he talked vaguely of unisex being a wave of the future, but mainly he kept his thoughts about sex to himself. However, by the fall of 1963, unable to work, his career in a shambles, Monty began behaving as if "he didn't give a shit about anything," Josh said. "He'd call out to guys—you know, solicit them from his brownstone window—a couple of times he cruised up Third Avenue."

He also stopped hiding his dark side. "I'm morally ambivalent," he used to say. He admired achievers like Alfred Lunt and Thornton Wilder, but he was fascinated with women like Libby Holman—the sensualists who could hurt and destroy him if he allowed them to. Long ago he'd been involved with a famous male dancer, "a cold cruel man" who introduced him to the gay orgy scene. Now he was attracted to Giles's brand of corruption.

Giles's scene was drugs and kept men—young Europeans who slept with both men and women for money, but who were often paid for companionship as well. Giles organized parties in the brownstone; chorus boys, male models, hustlers wandered through Monty's living room drinking his liquor and eating the Beluga caviar he still ordered by the pound.

"Monty kept saying he wanted to walk through the fires of hell and come out unsinged," Josh said. "Well, in a sense with Giles he did, because in spite of all the ugliness he remained pure—untouched. It was as if the sordid goings-on passed *through* him and then disappeared into the air."

Occasionally Giles brought back strangers to spend the night. For a few weeks there was a young soldier living on the top floor of the brownstone. He caught the flu and Monty phoned one of his doctors to give him some antibiotics.

The doctor came over. "Here's this freckle-faced kid, not more than eighteen—a buck private from somewhere in the Ozarks," the doctor said. "He's lying in bed with a temperature but he seemed very happy. I mean, he'd caught the flu in a movie star's house!"

Not long after that Bill Clift dropped by the brownstone unannounced and found a couple of male hustlers fixing their breakfast in the kitchen. As soon as he introduced himself as Montgomery Clift's father they tried to serve him coffee. Then Monty came downstairs, arms outstretched, "Oh, Pa, dear, fantastic to see you!" Mr. Clift left, quite agitated.

Later Bill Clift made an appointment to see one of Monty's doctors—a specialist who'd been treating his back. "He came into my office," the doctor said, "and he asked me point blank what is going on in his son's life? I felt I couldn't discuss it with him so I changed the subject. And he said, 'Can't you please get Monty to be nicer to Sunny?'"

Many of Monty's friends shied away from him now. "He was impossible to take in public," Dore Schary recalled. "At the theater he'd hoot and laugh in the midst of performances; during intermissions he'd embrace you with such violence you were almost knocked over."

Producer Frank Taylor was one friend who remained loyal to

Monty. "We would commiserate about the box office failure of *The Misfits*—Monty gave me a pair of antique sconces, to ease the pain," he said.

Afternoon drinks at Monty's became a ritual for Taylor throughout the spring of 1963. "I'd come by for a martini around five once or twice a week before going home on the train to Connecticut." Sometimes, according to Taylor, Monty and Giles were civilized and entertaining. "They drank martinis out of silver goblets." Sometimes they quarreled. Once when Monty was out of the room, Giles showed Taylor track marks on his arm and said Monty had got him addicted to heroin. Taylor didn't believe it.

As the months went by, Taylor notice their relationship increasingly seemed punctuated by violent arguments over minor details. Giles had forgotten to replace a dead bulb in a lamp—Monty had neglected to put more money into Giles's account.

Even with these disturbances there seemed an attempt on Monty's part to lead his life as he always had, lunching on oysters with Nancy Walker almost daily at Voisin, talking to director John Cassavetes, who wanted him to star in a movie of his in spite of everything. He was announced to play opposite Sophia Loren in a film. Meanwhile Giles looked for jobs on Seventh Avenue designing clothes, which he'd done before. He was unable to find work. In May of 1963 Giles slashed his wrists; no one knew of the suicide attempt except Monty's doctor.

Taylor recalls: "The last time I saw Monty was the summer of 1963. I got loaded. We talked and drank until it was very late. Finally the Carey Cadillac—the limousine Monty always traveled in around New York—pulled up outside and Giles said they were going out. He suggested they drop me off at Grand Central. I said fine. I was in no condition to get myself into a cab. . . ."

"We all piled into the limo—I fell back on the seat and closed my eyes. The next thing I knew we were speeding past the train station, and from what I could see we were now over on the West Side near the Hudson River piers. . . ."

They stopped at a place that Taylor thinks was probably "Dirty Dick's" at the foot of Christopher Street. It was a rather sinister little bar that was then popular with male hustlers, sailors, dock workers, the beautiful people who came slumming . . . .

Monty and Giles staggered out of the limousine and disappeared inside. Taylor attempted to get out, too, telling the chauffeur he wanted to catch a cab uptown, but he was advised against it—the neighborhood was dangerous. There had been robberies, knifings. They were still arguing when a squad car pulled up beside the limousine and a cop poked his head out the window and asked Taylor, "Are you a friend of Montgomery Clift's?"

Taylor nodded and the cop advised him "to get Clift out of that bar. We've had enough trouble with him already. He comes almost every night—we don't want to arrest him, but if we have to we will. . . . We've got a lot of complaints."

Taylor asked, "What am I supposed to do?" The cop told him simply "go in and get him out of there. We can't enter without a warrant. He's in the back room behind a leather curtain—that's where the rough trade hang out."

Taylor continues, "I was scared shitless, but I finally walked into the bar. It was a nondescript little place, almost empty, with a lighted juke box standing silent in one corner." He ordered a drink—straight Scotch—which he gulped down, and then he moved to the end of the room and pulled back the leather curtain.

He was practically knocked down by a blast of music, the smell of urine and beer. His feet crunched on melting ice. Directly ahead of him was a circle of about thirty people. They appeared to be observing some sort of performance. "My first thought was they're watching an illegal cock fight," but as he moved closer and stood at the edge of the circle he saw they were watching Monty, who was stretched out on a table, passed out fully clothed in his grey flannel suit while butch dykes, drag queens, transvestites, guys in leather jackets crawled all over him humming like insects.

"Some were kissing his neck, others were fondling his crotch. I thought I was going to vomit. It was the most debauched scene I've ever witnessed—like some Dionysian rite. I half expected a wall of fire to shoot up in front of us, to see the devil himself appear and laugh derisively.

"Some force stronger than myself made me push my way through the circle and pick Monty up off the table. The instant I did that the crowd erupted into a spasm of anger and hostility. 'No—No! Don't take him away—you can't take him away!' they screamed. Some of them were salivating.

"Luckily Monty was terribly thin—he weighed no more than 135 pounds; he felt like a fragile bird in my arms. I stumbled back through the bar—it was as if I was running on my knees out the door. The crowd roared at my heels.

"I threw Monty into the limousine, got in after him, and shouted to the driver, 'Take him home!' The whole thing had been like a nightmare, an apocalyptic nightmare. . . ."

After Taylor got Monty inside the brownstone, he never saw him again.

By mid-1963 Monty's relationship with Giles had totally disintegrated, and they began plotting against each other, devising all sorts of ways to torture each other. Monty resented Giles for taking advantage of him; "He wants my money and my celebrity." He hated Giles for being afraid of him, he hated him for *his* drinking, *his* drug taking. He accused Giles of bringing disreputables into the house and driving his real friends away.

"I used to come into the brownstone and watch them go at each other. It was like a prelude to Virginia Woolf," said a screenwriter. "Giles was a tormenter, but Monty was no slouch. He could be very sadistic. He'd pretend to sympathize with Giles's problem—Giles was a pathological thief and liar, and then he'd rub his nose in it."

Finally, Giles attempted suicide again. One morning Monty discovered him unconscious on the living room floor. He phoned Bill Le Massena hysterically.

Le Massena called Monty's personal physician, Dr. Ludwig, who rushed Giles to Gracie Square Hospital. "We barely pulled him through," the doctor said. "After I got his stomach pumped out he began babbling about his victim-victimizer relationship with Monty. How Monty had got him hooked on drugs—how he retaliated by getting him dead drunk and dragging him into gay bars where he was tormented for his sexual inadequacies."

Later Sunny and Bill Clift arrived at the hospital and conferred with Dr. Ludwig. They decided Giles and Monty should be separated permanently for their own good. When he left the hospital Giles stayed at Bill Le Massena's apartment until he could get settled elsewhere.

After Giles's near-suicide, Monty's main drive seemed to be an anguish so acute it threatened to topple him into insanity. He never left the brownstone. His doctor came by regularly to check up on him and make sure he was taking his calcium. He found him stumbling, losing his balance: "He always seemed to be drunk."

He actually drank little, but one vodka could get him tipsy. His body had lost the ability to burn up alcohol. He couldn't understand this; it made him all the more hostile and despairing.

"He was unwilling or unable to talk about anything that was

bothering him," the doctor said, "but he was suffering terribly. He seemed absolutely dazed with misery."

The doctor decided he must get him into the Menninger Clinic immediately. He knew he would never sit home and dry out; he needed detoxification in a hospital situation. He also needed to be treated for his many levels of depression.

Dr. Ludwig phoned Dr. Silverberg, telling him he thought Monty was having a breakdown and should be put into a hospital right away. The analyst retorted, "I disagree. His drinking is merely a symptom of a far more deep-seated problem; Menninger's is not the answer."

Exasperated, the doctor went to Monty's lawyer, Jack Clareman, and his agent, Robbie Lantz. They decided they should go to Monty together and discuss his "life-and-death situation" with him frankly.

The meeting was set for three in the afternoon. Monty insisted they gather at Dr. Silverberg's office on East Sixty-sixth Street, or he wouldn't attend. He came in late; the minute he got in the door he and Silverberg embraced, hugging and kissing each other on the cheek. Then Monty lounged on a couch while his lawyer, agent, and personal physician explained why they felt it imperative he enter the Menninger Clinic for psychiatric observation.

He listened very seriously, and then he said, "If Billy wants me to go I'll go."

Everybody turned apprehensively to Silverberg, who shook his head.

Monty shrugged. There was nothing more to be said. Later the three supplicants gathered at a Schrafft's for coffee. "We all had the feeling that Monty would have sold us down the river for Billy Silverberg," Dr. Ludwig said. "There was a tremendous attachment between the two men, which was obvious the moment you saw them together."

Shortly after that Bill Clift was urged to confront Silverberg about Monty's condition, which he did over the phone. The psychiatrist told Bill: "My dear sir, if that man gets out of my control he'll die within three months."

Desperate, Sunny went to Monty and told him he must commit himself into a hospital. "The liquor is making you crazy," she told him, to which Monty retorted, "If you let them put me into a hospital, Ma, I'll jump out a window and it'll be all your fault."

So the problem remained: who could take care of Monty? In

this condition he could not be left alone. For a few days Sunny debated about whether she should move into the brownstone, but she was argued out of it. Then Dr. Ludwig, the physician who'd recommended Menninger's, suggested hiring a companion, someone who was discreet and sympathetic and strong enough to cope with Monty's various problems but who didn't behave like a "nurse or a jailor."

Ultimately such a companion was found. His name was Lorenzo James. He was black, of indeterminate age, and a graduate of both Howard University and the Parsons School of Design. He had been both actor and singer for a number of years. When he couldn't get work in show business he took care of heart attack victims who were well enough to be recuperating at home. He came highly recommended.

43

When he first entered it, "Monty's brownstone was in chaos," Lorenzo said. The front door, half broken down by burglars, had been left that way. Strangers wandered in and out; friends of Giles, they kept asking for him and for Monty, who stayed in seclusion in his third-floor bedroom.

Lorenzo had the door repaired immediately and the lock changed, and he refused to let anyone in unless the person was cleared by Monty. He even kept old friend Bill Gunn waiting in the downstairs hall. Gunn was infuriated. "I had to," Lorenzo argued, "I had to get the house running smoothly and peacefully again."

One of the first things Monty told him was, "No more strangers." He only wanted to see certain people at certain times. Otherwise he wanted to be left alone.

Giles kept on returning: first to pick up his clothes, then later hoping Monty would take him back. Their meetings were harsh and unpleasant; on two occasions Lorenzo had to throw Giles out bodily. During the fights Monty vanished onto the third floor. He seemed to have no interest in seeing or talking to Giles again.

For a while he seemed to have no interest in anything. He didn't even want to take a bath. Lorenzo finally gave him steaming hot towels to put on his face. He liked that, and eventually Lorenzo persuaded him to get into a warm tub. That was the beginning of a new and healthy regime.

Lorenzo made Monty get up early and watch the *Today Show* while sipping hot tea with lime. Then he exercised, either with a man from Klein's gym or with Lorenzo himself. He also took his medication for calcium deficiency, and he cut down on the pills. He had hidden his liquor supply, but Lorenzo found it and told him calmly to put it out in the open. From then on he kept his vodka and aquavit in full view in his bedroom, and he began drinking less. He also started eating regularly, nutritious foods like shell steaks and yogurt mixed with fresh peaches.

Almost every day he went to the movies, always the noon show. Lorenzo would phone ahead and tell the box office, "Montgomery Clift is coming," so they could slip in unnoticed. Usually this precaution was unnecessary; the theaters were half empty. They would sit at the back of the orchestra so Monty could talk back to the screen. Once, during *The Servant,* a movie he saw innumerable times, he shouted to Dirk Bogarde, "Oh, get on with it!"

Aside from the movies he didn't go out much, except to see Silverberg. Occasionally, Lorenzo sat in on the sessions. "They would just talk," he recalled. "They were very close friends. The situation had been reversed; Silverberg told Monty his problems; his companion Ed Shipley had died and he was lonely. Monty would tell him how he enjoyed being a hermit. His house was his cocoon," Lorenzo said. "The minute we'd get in the door he'd cry out, 'Oh, God, isn't it good to be home again?'"

In the evenings he'd read "like a vulture," Lorenzo said. The *Times,* the *Trib,* the *London Observer.* Often he'd play a record he'd had made specially in 1952 called "Potpourri Montgomery." On it were his favorite songs. He was also very interested in keeping up with his astrological sign, Libra. "They say it's the most balanced sign." He had his chart read regularly by Maria Crummere, and *Freud* costume designer Doris Langly Moore sent him his daily horoscope from a London newspaper. He often compared the Libra predictions to Elizabeth Taylor's sign, Pisces—she had her chart done regularly too. "Bessie is a real Pisces—dreamy, sentimental, all female."

At the end of five months, Monty's health and spirits improved so much he began writing Lorenzo little notes which he'd leave on the stairs: "Thank you for everything, sincerely yours in 2B" or "Don't wake me I'm smoking. M." At the end of five months Lorenzo not only got a raise but a title. He became Montgomery Clift's secretary, and he moved into one of the spare bedrooms on the fourth floor of the brownstone.

Lorenzo tried to get all of Monty's old friends to come to the brownstone and visit him. "I wanted Monty to start seeing his peers again." Nancy Walker came. So did Bill Le Massena and Blaine

Waller, but Thornton Wilder* refused, and Kevin never was available; many other old friends didn't seem to have the time.

"Monty was very bitter about being abandoned by so many of his friends," Blaine Waller said. "He thought everybody had used him. I'd be sitting with him alone in that big brownstone and I'd think, 'Where is everybody now that he's down?' He'd been good to a lot of people, giving them money, his friendship, listening to their troubles; now he was forgotten and almost totally alone."

On an impulse, in early 1964, Sunny Clift phoned Ned Smith and told him she thought Monty would like to see him, so Ned began driving down regularly from Connecticut to the brownstone. "He talked a lot about his operations and his health and how life was really going too fast for him. When I told him I was happily married, he said 'My God, Smythe! You're happy? I didn't know anybody could be happy. There's something wrong with everybody. How can you be happy, Smythe?'" Later Ned visited Sunny, and they discussed Monty and the shape he was in and Sunny confided, "Some mothers lose their sons in the war. I have to watch mine killing himself day by day before my eyes."

She had started visiting Monty regularly too, after a long period when they hadn't spoken. At Lorenzo's urging they would have dinner at the brownstone together.

They often began their evenings in total silence. Language for them had never been a way of expressing or changing their realities; they were too absorbed in their own dilemmas—he with his complicated illness and sense of failed promise—she still searching, searching for identity, recognition, roots. They were very much alike and yet they had little in common. Bound together by ties of love and suffering they still didn't know each other very well.

Sunny persisted in treating Monty like an eighteen-year-old. At these dinners she would refer wistfully to the elegant manners he'd had when he was working with the Lunts in *There Shall Be No Night*.

Invariably they would start sparring with each other and their conversation would disintegrate into old arguments, old guilts. Sometimes Sunny would bring up the subject of the Andersons and the Blairs and the fact that she had never been recognized, and Monty would curse at "those sons of bitches." But then he would get drunk

* Years later Wilder wrote: "Monty was an extraordinarily gifted actor and until his drinking became excessive, delightful company."

and hurl insults at his mother, calling her "whore" or "bastard"; Sunny would sit there very stiffly, nodding, "Yes, dear, of course I am." Later when Brooks asked Sunny, "Do you think Monty loves anybody?" Sunny snapped, "He loves one person—himself."

Finally Lorenzo suggested, "For once be nice, be sober when your mother visits. Show her you are strong."

The next time Monty did just that. He was considerate, kind, and he didn't drink at all. Sunny was stunned. She phoned Lorenzo the next day to ask, "Is Monty all right?"

Her question was unusual; she rarely confided in Lorenzo; she disliked him too intensely. Once when he attempted to take her arm when they were crossing the street, she drew away as if he were poison. "She could barely be civil to me. I understood. She was jealous because I was taking care of her son better than she could."

As time went on Sunny made it clear she preferred having Monty visit at her apartment on Seventy-ninth Street.

"We would usually just talk," Sunny recalled. "Monty was such a marvelous actor—on stage and off. He would tell me he adored me and admired me and later I'd hear he'd called me a bitch."

In February of 1964, Bill Clift suffered a heart attack and was rushed to the hospital. Monty wanted to see him, but Sunny kept him as well as Ethel and Brooks out of the room until Bill died. Nobody questioned her. If Monty was upset about his father's death he never revealed it.

"They were such a queer family," Lorenzo said. "Isolated. Closed off. Remote, suspicious of each other—except for Monty and his twin sister."

After Bill Clift's funeral, Monty became concerned his mother didn't have money to live on; he and his lawyer, Jack Clareman, met with her at the brownstone to discuss her financial future. Monty was living off the money he'd earned on *Freud*. Universal was paying him what they owed him ($131,000) in $25,000 yearly installments.

Sunny was working off and on for a literary appraiser, organizing and listing the papers of Brooks Atkinson, Tennessee Williams and Elia Kazan, among others, but she did so using a pseudonym. "I didn't want anyone aware that Montgomery Clift's mother needed money," she said. She knew Monty's financial situation was tight so she fought him when he offered to give her an allowance. Monty got so angry she finally agreed to a weekly sum.

Once she was gone he did a very precise imitation of her vocal intonation, the way she tugged at her widow's veil. "He got a tremendous kick out of it," Lorenzo said. "I told him Mrs. Clift could have been a great actress," and Monty laughed. "Yeah, she would have played all the parts Helen Hayes turned down."

He was trying very hard to understand his mother. He told Lorenzo, "Brooks was the love child. Sister and I were black caraculs." Then he repeated a story he'd heard from nurse Wilke: Sunny was in labor a long painful time with the twins. After fifteen hours Ethel popped out, and Sunny gave a sigh of relief and lay back on the pillows. "It's over," she said. But the doctor said, "No, it isn't. Mrs. Clift, there's another baby in there." And Sunny screamed and cried, "Oh, no—I don't want another baby, not now—not ever again!" and she kept fighting as the labor pains started and Monty struggled to get out of her womb, and another fifteen hours passed and he was born.

During the summer of 1964, Monty got involved with decorating the brownstone. Lorenzo painted all the rooms off-white, and record producer Ben Bagley hung bright orange awnings on the outside of the house.

Nancy Pinkerton, a young actress Monty had met in Ogunquit, came by for a drink, and the minute she arrived she asked, "Monty, where did you get those psychedelic awnings? They're terrible.

"And he said, 'But look!' He was sitting on the stairs as he often did. 'But look!' he repeated, and then he came down and walked me into the living room library which was still not completely furnished. 'Look at that light!' he said, and sure enough, the light filtering through the orange awnings and into the room was the most beautiful light I'd ever seen. It was like being under an amber gel. Everybody who sat in that room would look like a million dollars. Monty said he didn't care how his house looked from the outside, he was creating his ambiance for himself inside, and it was pleasing to him aesthetically; everybody would have a scrim."

Nancy would occasionally have dinner with Monty downstairs on the bottom floor facing the garden. "One time he began talking about *The Misfits* and about how Gable and Monroe were gone and he was next," she said. "He said it very matter-of-factly. Then he told a little story about himself and Marilyn, how once on location he'd grabbed her bottom and she turned and gave him the most wonderful smile. Well, Monty could tell a story like that and the whole world was in that moment—you could see him recognize the loneliness in *her* smile. You could see her recognize the loneliness in *his* eyes. . . . The story had a luminosity the way Monty told it."

But other times blended together in Nancy's mind, "because we did the same thing over and over; the house was always silent except the ringing phone that he never answered, and Monty had a way of talking to me as if I knew what he was talking about—his conversations were full of oblique references, kaleidoscopic visions, themes that had no connection. Half the time I didn't know what he was talking about, but I didn't ask questions, I just listened. Monty was often on drugs for his pain. He gave himself injections of something. There were hundreds of disposable syringes in the bathroom. Some of the time I was with him at night he was in such a state of altered consciousness that his mind and his spirit seemed to be traveling very fast through space. On those nights he acted as if he had to talk to someone—it was imperative—the words came out in a violent hyped-up stream. . . ."

Once Nancy remembers him being "so whacked out he sat on the rug by his desk and he began lolling around on the floor. Then he got into the closet in the den on the top floor and out toppled marvelous photographs of him as Prewitt in *From Here to Eternity.*' "

Bill Le Massena was also with him on another occasion "when he was really zonked out. He told me, 'I'm melting away, mon vieux, I am disintegrating.' "

To Nancy Pinkerton he talked a lot about "Bessie Mae this and Bessie Mae that and how she once had been given five big syringes of Demerol by her doctor in Beverly Hills. Her back was killing her. Monty wouldn't let her take the Demerol. He took the syringes off her bedside table and threw them all away. Another time he went into a long rap about how Bessie Mae's entire life revolves around 'where's the dog's leash, baby?' "

He talked a lot about how so many people were taking advantage of him—"I'm being robbed blind," he said. He talked bitterly about his doctors—he had at least seven or eight he saw regularly—dentist, podiatrist, oculist, nerve specialist, heart surgeon, shrink—and he was beginning to think none of them had ever really cared about helping him—about relieving him of his agonizing pain.

Nancy finally sent him to her doctor, a young osteopath named Richard Bachrach, on Forty-first Street. "Monty was in agony," Bachrach recalled. "He had bursitis in both shoulders and arthritis in his neck; he had a slipped disc in his back. He asked me for a prescription for Demerol. That meant he gave himself injections, or somebody did. This is why so many people thought he was a heroin addict. Demerol is like codeine, very addictive. Combined with liquor it makes you feel almost unbearably floaty.

"Monty was in enormous pain—had been for almost ten years ever since his car accident. He was exhausted from the pain. 'It never lets up,' he said. 'I can't see well or hear much, can't move my arms. Can't anything be done?' "

Bachrach began by giving him injections of Aristocort forte in his shoulder. It worked well, gave him relief, but it was too strong—it ultimately would have disintegrated the shoulder bone. Later Bachrach suggested Monty try DMSO, which was a "great new pain killer. You just rubbed it into your skin like a lotion. It came out your lungs and your breath smelt like horse pee, but the stuff worked miraculously."

Monty used it, and for the first time in years he was completely without pain, and he stopped taking Demerol. He was so grateful to Bachrach he invited him to the house for dinner, and he brought him out to Fire Island, where he'd rented a place at The Pines.

Monty was able to use the DMSO for several months before the FDA took the drug off the market, labeling it unsafe. DMSO had been tested on rats' eyes and the female rats got pregnant; the males developed cataracts. Monty was furious. Bachrach told him "look, they're not sure what the side effects of this drug are on humans," to which Monty retorted, "I've had cataracts and I can't get pregnant—so what the fuck?"

Monty wanted the DMSO so much he managed to get it through a veterinarian (it could still be used on horses). When he was unable to obtain it any more he went back to Demerol.

Since the accident Monty had often considered plastic surgery for his slightly twisted upper lip and off-kilter nose. Privately he had never adjusted to his new face; he hated it, and not working he spent more and more time contemplating his rearranged features. He told Jack Larson, "When I look at myself in the mirror I'm repelled by what I see. I want to vomit."

One day Lorenzo confided he'd had his entire face redone by a plastic surgeon named Manfred Von Linde. As a kid, growing up in Florida, his lip and cheek had been severely slashed by a bulldog. "I was completely disfigured until Manfred performed eight operations on my face and made me look human again."

Monty was flabbergasted since Lorenzo didn't have a single

scar; ordinarily when black skin is deeply cut it heals leaving thick white marks on the flesh. Monty called Von Linde "a magician" and Lorenzo countered with, "If he'd been Satan himself, I'd still be eternally grateful to Manfred."

Some people considered Von Linde bizarre, even satanic. In 1962 he had been held on suspicion of murder after his socialite wife of two weeks, Lucille Rodgers, had died mysteriously on their honeymoon in Haiti. Von Linde had the body embalmed before an autopsy could be performed. His wife's family, suspecting foul play because he had just been made sole heir to her fortune, had him arrested.

He was held in jail for five days during which time the authorities discovered he was not a member of royalty, as he had claimed. He had been born plain Robert Dent in Birmingham, Alabama. (He'd changed his name legally to Von Linde in 1958.)

Since there was not enough evidence to indict him for murder in Haiti, he got off and returned to New York, where his friends bragged he'd used a mysterious poison to kill his wife, a poison that couldn't be detected in the blood stream.

Not long after Von Linde was served with a $500,000 malpractice suit by actress Joan Dixon. She maintained that after he performed corrective surgery on her breasts at St. Clare's Hospital she suffered infection and disfigurement.

Von Linde survived that scandal too, and since then had been practicing plastic surgery at Knickerbocker Hospital. He also had an office at Sixty-third and Park, which was always full of patients. (On the side he performed illegal abortions in New Jersey for $500 apiece.)

He'd rented John Barrymore's old house in Greenwich Village, where he was known as a "weird character," a man with a smirking, hairless face and cultivated manner who escorted society dowagers to charity balls but who on occasion supplied dead bodies to a notorious homosexual "funeral parlor" on Sixth Avenue. For fifty dollars one could go in and have sex with a corpse.

Lorenzo brought Von Linde to the brownstone to meet Monty. "They became good buddies," he said. Von Linde visited frequently, once or twice spending the night. Ned Smith described him as a "sinister little fellow." Jack Larson said he was "evil."

Monty remained fascinated by Von Linde, by his checkered past and by what he thought was a vast knowledge of medicine. They had long discussions about operations and diseases. Manfred gave Monty a medical dictionary which he pored over. Eventually they discussed the possibility of plastic surgery on Monty's face.

In the spring of 1964, Elizabeth Taylor came to New York to be with her new husband, Richard Burton, who was about to open on Broadway as Hamlet.

She invited Monty to the opening and when he ambled down the aisle and saw her resplendent in diamonds, black hair hanging down her back, he hooted, "Bessie Mae! Bessie Mae!" and she wasn't the least bit embarrassed. She got up from her seat and embraced him warmly. Afterwards he attended the party Alexander Cohen gave for the *Hamlet* cast in the Rainbow Room.

It was bedlam; hundreds of photographers and the curious pressing to catch a glimpse of the most publicized couple in the world. Monty left, disgusted, and met his brother for a drink. He told him he thought Burton was a phony actor and then proceeded to recite much of *Hamlet* from memory. "And that is the way the prince should be played," he said when he finished around four in the morning. "I may be prejudiced, but Monty was brilliant," Brooks said. "He played Hamlet as a totally split personality."

Monty never told Elizabeth how he felt about Burton. Instead, he invited her to the brownstone for dinner or he went to the Regency Hotel where she and Burton had a suite. Sometimes the three of them would have supper after the theater at Dinty Moore's. Once during a meal, Burton commented wryly, "Monty, Elizabeth likes me but she loves you."

She always behaved as if they'd never been separated, as if his success and failure and their mutual tragedies made no difference. ("Tragedies are not cathartic," he'd say. "They make life more mysterious.") They would laugh and tease each other. He would try to get her to read more books—he insisted she read Edna O'Brien. Invariably conversation focused on their ailments.

"Bessie Mae is the only person I know who has more wrong with her than I have," Monty would laugh, and he would list part of her medical history: ruptured spinal disc, bronchitis, phlebitis, ulcerated eye, tracheotomy . . . .

Elizabeth was then thirty-two, shrewd, immensely beautiful, and the biggest movie star in the world, commanding a million dollars a picture. She still considered Monty "her dearest friend," the first person to take her seriously as a thinking, feeling human being, and she was determined to do something constructive for him. She told one of her press agents, "If he doesn't work soon he'll die."

They began discussing the possibility of starring in the film version of *The Owl and the Pussycat,* since they had always wanted to do a comedy together. Elizabeth had already agreed to do the picture, so she gave Monty the script and they read the parts out loud together, but then Ray Stark, who was producing it for Seven Arts, became wary of insuring Monty. He said he would have to put up his brownstone as collateral.

Elizabeth wouldn't let him. Later that year, in between filming *The Sandpiper* and *Virginia Woolf,* she phoned frequently from California to discuss more projects. At one point Burton got on the extension to ask why didn't all three of them co-star in a remake of Hemingway's *The Macomber Affair.*

Then Robbie Lantz suggested *Reflections in a Golden Eye,* Carson McCullers's gothic horror story about American sexuality. Monty would play a latent homosexual Army officer obsessed with a young private who's in turn obsessed with Monty's beautiful wife (to be played by Elizabeth).

Monty read the script and agreed to do it, but when Elizabeth told him she wanted Burton to co-star and direct he got upset. He didn't like Burton's acting (he called it "reciting"), and he made Monty feel uneasy as a man. He and Roddy McDowall had often discussed "poor Richard," as he was called behind his back.

At one point he even tried writing a letter to Elizabeth saying just that, explaining why it would be impossible for him to ever work with Burton, and he dictated the letter to Nancy Pinkerton when he was high on Demerol. "I never sent the letter," Nancy said. "Of course, he never knew."

Eventually Burton decided not to do *Reflections.* He didn't like the part, that of a third banana, as an agent described it. In the interim, Elizabeth convinced John Huston to direct and he got his assistant, Gladys Hill, to start revamping the script. When Monty learned Huston had become involved, he seemed philosophic. "If John can stand it, I can." Elizabeth announced to the press that she and Monty were going to co-star in another film. But Ray Stark and Seven Arts reminded her: "Monty Clift is uninsurable," to which she retorted she would pay the bloody insurance, and she put up the bond with her own money.

Monty's agent, Robbie Lantz, wrote: "Miss Taylor was determined to have (Monty) in *Reflections* and to make another picture with an actor she admired greatly and loved as a friend, and her immense devotion to him was not only responsible for the acceptance of Clift by John Huston, (Taylor) also overcame certain insurance problems."

However, production kept getting postponed; no matter how much Elizabeth defended Monty, Seven Arts kept reminding her of his reputation for falling apart. Nobody was sure Montgomery Clift could act anymore.

Monty wondered himself. Sometimes he would phone Sunny at night. She told Brooks: "I'd be reading in bed and the phone would ring and it would be Monty and he'd order me to take a cab to his brownstone right away. He had to see me. So I'd do it and he'd be waiting on the sidewalk and he'd say, 'What in hell took you so long?' and I'd say, 'Do you want me to rent a room from you? For ten years you didn't want to see me and now I'm supposedly at your beck and call.'"

They would go inside and suddenly Monty would lie down on the floor and begin kicking his feet, "as if he was swimming." And he would cry out he was afriad he could no longer act and that work had been the only thing that made him feel he was functioning . . . .

Every so often he tried to divert himself with his relatives. He arranged little dinners for his niece Suzanne, who had pleaded guilty to manslaughter in the shooting death of her lover, but had been declared insane at the time of the murder. She'd been put on probation and had spent the last three years in a mental hospital raising her baby.

She would come to the brownstone and she and Monty would sit on the floor of the living room playing with the baby. And every so often she would refer to the lover she had murdered in a grand voice accented like Sunny's: "Wasn't he a handsome man?" And didn't their baby resemble him in more ways than one?

In December, Brooks told Monty he was getting married again, this time to Eleanor Roeloffs, a slender platinum blonde who is now White House correspondent for *Newsweek*. Brooks asked Monty if he would be best man and if the wedding could be in the brownstone. Monty agreed to both requests.

Eleanor recalls, "My parents ran a deli in Queens, and they didn't approve of me marrying Brooks Clift. So his brother was a movie star. He'd been married three times, had five kids, and he was much older than I was. The day of our wedding our minister phoned me to ask me if I'd please change my mind."

Meanwhile Monty and Lorenzo organized the entire ceremony, ordering the flowers from Christatos and the champagne from Sherry's. Sunny arranged tiny rows of sandwiches.

At the very last moment, Mrs. Roeloffs, Eleanor's mother, appeared and stood glowering throughout the ceremony. After the ceremony was over she was completely charmed by Monty, who served her champagne and teased her. Then he brought a gracious and courtly Sunny over to get acquainted; she received Mrs. Roeloffs rather like a monarch.

Eleanor and Brooks left the brownstone for their honeymoon but Mrs. Roeloffs stayed behind. After the wedding, Sunny took Mrs. Roeloffs to lunch every week.

"They had nothing in common," Eleanor said. "Except of course they now shared a mutual family. And family was the most important thing in Sunny Clift's life."

44

By mid-1965 *Reflections in a Golden Eye* still did not have a starting date. Monty had not worked for four straight years, and it looked as if he might never work again; other than *Reflections* he received virtually no offers with the exception of a couple of Italian westerns. He did narrate a TV documentary called *Faulkner's Mississippi,* and he also recorded *The Glass Menagerie* for Caedmon Records with Julie Harris. Afterwards Harris and Tennessee Williams listened to the playback in the control booth, and Harris cried.

He spent most days by himself in the brownstone, with brief excursions to Bloomingdale's or the theater. On Lorenzo's day off, Ben Bagley would take Monty to see Godard movies, and he and Ned Smith had lunch at Isle of Capri. Sometimes he went to Birdland with singer Johnny Mathis. Occasionally he'd be brought to an Andy Warhol party, and if he was pointed out, there would be merely a flicker of interest in his once-famous name.

He was defensive about being unemployed. He'd been asked to join the Actors Studio production of *The Three Sisters* in London, but he hadn't wanted to work with Lee Strasberg; the only movie he'd been offered was *John Goldfarb, Please Come Home,* a comedy which was to star Shirley MacLaine. "Twentieth thought Monty was so right for the lead they said to hell with his insurance problem," Jack Larson recalls. "But Monty loathed the script."

He never stopped believing he would work again. He never quite gave up hope about *Reflections.* He confided to Ned Smith, "I can't get a job, Smythe, but Elizabeth Taylor is the greatest friend. She keeps on trying to help—everybody else has deserted me."

On an impulse he started going regularly to his astrologist,

Maria Crummere, to see if she had any answers. He'd sit on the floor of her apartment on East Seventy-first Street while she drew his horoscope on a blackboard. Given the exact time, date, and place of his birth she would calculate his personality traits and talk about his particular sign, Libra: how its symbol is neither animal nor human, it is an inanimate scale; and he would keep interrupting, "Maria, how can you possibly remember all these things?"

After two hours' work on his chart she always predicted he would get a movie; that the *Reflections* business would be resolved. "When? When?" he'd demand. "I saw a movie in the stars for Monty," she said, "I saw other things in store for him, but I only told him the good stuff."

He still thought a great deal about the art of acting. He avidly followed the work of his contemporaries; he particularly admired Paul Newman and the young Robert Redford, whose performance he'd enjoyed in *Barefoot in the Park*. And Laurence Olivier remained his idol; he made special trips to London to see him in *Uncle Vanya* and *Othello;* afterwards they had supper in Olivier's dressing room.

As for Brando, who had floundered badly in recent years with movies like *Bedtime Story* and *Mutiny on the Bounty,* Monty scrutinized his career and likened him to "a force of nature." When Brando bought his island in Tahiti, when he joined the March on Washington, when he invited a tribe of Indians to live in his Beverly Hills mansion, Monty said, "Marlon isn't finished yet. He's just resting up. He'll be back—bigger than ever." (Eight years later Brando made *Last Tango in Paris* and *The Godfather*.)

Frail as he was now, it was still Monty's deepest instinct to watch. "Look! Look!" he told a young actress who came to him for advice. "If you look really hard at things you'll forget you're going to die."

He could not forget his own pain, however. "He was always in agony," Lorenzo said. "His legs were giving him more and more trouble—they'd knot into terrible cramps and I'd have to massage them—his back was hurting, too—he had never recovered from the accident."

In the early summer of 1965, Monty phoned Ned Smith in Stamford and said he wanted him to come to the brownstone "immediately"; he had a terrible problem.

Smith drove into New York, and as soon as he arrived, Monty began explaining very rapidly how he gave a lot of parties in the second-floor study, but when he went to mix drinks he had to mix them in a closet and "I can't hear anything and I don't like that."

He told Smith he'd decided to knock down one wall and put in a bar, but if he knocked down the wall, would the entire house collapse? It was a matter of vital importance.

Lorenzo argued it would be totally impractical, but Smith took Monty's side. "It's your house and if you want to knock the wall down, do it—just get a sledge hammer and break down the wall."

He did exactly that. He bought a big sledge hammer, and at three in the morning he began banging and bashing and knocking the entire wall down until the entire floor was covered with big chunks of plaster. When Smith came by the following day he found Lorenzo very upset: "Isn't this terrible?"

Smith said "No—no," and he subsequently designed the kind of bar Monty wanted "with posts here and traceries there—it was shaped like the prow of a ship."

They went to a lumber yard together where Monty chose the wood. "I love wood," he would say; a carpenter was hired to build the structure of teak and brass with a little stainless steel sink on the side. "It was magnificent," Smith said.

Just before it was completed Monty told Smith excitedly, "I'm going to have bourbon on one side, Scotches on another, there'll be vodka and apricot brandy and white wine, and if anybody wants something odd like anise it'll be in the deep freeze," and Smith joked, "Maybe you shouldn't have had this thing built." And Monty looked at him "sort of hurt" and said, "It's all right, Smythe, everything will be all right."

Sometime in early July the bar was finished and Smith was invited to come over to the brownstone to see it. Monty answered the door. "His face was ashen, his eyes were bulging from behind his thick glasses, and he had the most objectionable boil on his cheek, as big as a dollar. 'Who asked you co come?' he demanded sharply."

Smith told him, "You asked me to see the bar."

"Hokey," Monty said. "Hokey," and he allowed him inside. He smelt very strongly of anise.

In October of the same year, Salka Viertel, now living in Klosters, phoned Jack Larson to tell him that her old friend Raoul Levy had written a script which he also planned to direct and produce, a low-budget spy thriller called *The Defector,* about an American physicist who is blackmailed by the CIA into spying during a holiday in Germany.

She knew Monty was desperate for work so she'd suggested him for the part of the physicist; Levy was very excited by the idea—it didn't matter to him that Monty was uninsurable. Salka wanted to know if he was still drinking—or was he in control? Larson assured her he was fine, and *The Defector* was airmailed from Switzerland immediately.

Monty read it and called the screenplay atrocious, but agreed to star if only to prove to the industry that he was in good shape to act again.

There were endless calls back and forth to Levy in Europe, to Robbie Lantz in New York. Most of the talk centered around Monty's insurance problem. Weeks went by. Monty kept phoning Maria Crummere to ask, "Am I going to get this movie? Am I?" She kept telling him, "You're the only actor who can do the part."

Eventually Seven Arts, the distributor for *The Defector,* sent its doctors to the brownstone unannounced to examine Monty. He passed his physical but, in spite of this, he still could not be insured.

Then Leslie Caron agreed to co-star as the love interest. She thought the script was terrible too, but she said she'd do the movie "for Monty." Levy decided to go ahead with the production without insurance; a few days later Seven Arts and John Huston finalized an August shooting date for *Reflections in a Golden Eye.*

Monty was, of course, jubilant. *Defector* would be in a sense the dry run for *Reflections.* He was determined to do the best possible job to prove to Elizabeth he'd been worth the risk.

He wanted to photograph well, so shortly before Christmas he went secretly to a small clinic in Westchester and he had Von Linde "do" his eyes. He'd been worried about nonexistent bags and lines.

Von Linde botched the job, scarring Monty's cheek and infecting his eyelids. Monty's own doctor had to rush over to the brownstone and clean him up. "I gave him hell for letting Von Linde touch him, and I made him promise not to let him do anything else to his face."

Over the holidays Monty flew down to Austin, Texas, to spend the holidays with his twin sister and her family. "We went skiing in Red River, New Mexico, and we spent several days in Sante Fe," Ethel recalled. "Monty's back was bothering him a lot." He showed her the disposable syringes and the Demerol. He said he had to give himself injections to ease the terrible pain.

After New Year's Eve, Monty went to London, where he and Leslie Caron attempted to rewrite *The Defector* themselves, with Warren Beatty, who was then Caron's constant companion, looking on. However, just before the film began shooting, Caron bowed out, saying she would be unable to get along with director Levy. He had told her the rewrites of her part had distorted his screenplay. Frantic, Monty went to see Simone Signoret who happened to be in London, and he begged her to be in the movie with him. He was terrified the movie would not be made because Caron had decided to withdraw.

But Levy had no intention of canceling the production. The other principals, Hardy Kruger and Roddy McDowall, were on their way to Germany. He told Monty to stop worrying.

The Defector was filmed in and out of Munich through a rainy, chill February, March and April of 1966. Reporters on location recall how Monty seemed to be struggling to hold himself together. He never relaxed. "We all knew this wasn't the greatest movie in the world," said a cast member. "Any other actor would have zipped through it, but he was killing himself from the strain."

"He gave so much it was painful," said actress Marisa Mol, who replaced Leslie Caron. "His acting was torn from the inside . . . it's almost as if he was acting to destroy himself."

The script was melodramatic, muddled. Hardy Kruger (who played a Russian spy) and Roddy McDowall (a CIA agent) attempted to make sense out of their jumbled dialogue while Raoul Levy, who'd earlier gained fame for writing *And God Created Woman,* seemed more interested in resolving his love life. He pursued several women on and off the set—always unsuccessfully. (After the movie was over he shot himself through the head outside his estranged mistress's apartment.)

During filming, Monty did all his stunts himself including falling time and time again into the icy Elbe River. He refused to wear a waterproof suit under his clothes. Lorenzo became very concerned; "he was taking too many risks."

Mira Rostova, who'd come along as Monty's coach, sat in his limousine holding his contact lens case and script and watched the proceedings grief-stricken. "Monty was in severe pain but he pushed himself to the limit. He had to prove to the world, and to himself, he could still act."

In the evenings, Mira and Lorenzo would return to the Grand

Continental Hotel in Munich, seeing to it that the Baroness, who had followed Monty to Germany, did not get into Monty's suite.

Monty did not see the rushes every night, nor did Mira. "Neither one of us could bear to." The rushes showed for the most part a dispirited, weary actor with a gaunt, ravaged face and a body so emaciated the insides seemed boneless. In some close-ups his huge eyes glittered calm, unthinking.

As soon as the picture finished dubbing in Paris Monty and Lorenzo flew to London, seeing friends like Betsy Blair and Leslie Caron, who gave him a big party to which Sharon Tate, Roman Polanski, and Barbra Streisand came. Streisand had always wanted to meet Monty—they spent a long time talking together in a corner.

Just before he left for New York, Monty visited Fred Zinnemann on the set of *A Man for All Seasons*. "I was shocked by his appearance," Zinnemann said. "He looked like a dying man, but he was so sweet—and interested in everything that was going on. The cast was marvelous. They all wanted to meet and talk with him. Monty was still a legend to other actors. He knew that and I think it moved him."

He came back to New York and spent most of his time working on the brownstone, although he complained of being exhausted. He had Lorenzo scour the marble fireplaces until they were snowy, and Ben Bagley came over and helped arrange the thousand books alphabetically on the second floor. "Oh, gosh, isn't this marvelous?" Monty would cry, and Bagley decided he had never met a person "with such a spirit to live and to change. But he was an absolute physical wreck. Varicose veins all over his body—losing his hair, pain in his back." The hypothyroid condition was getting worse. His hands were very gnarled. He looked like an old man.

In the last weeks of Monty's life, Ben Bagley said, he often spoke of feeling "trapped" in the brownstone. He said he was becoming "afraid of Lorenzo." He would phone Bagley late at night at his home in Queens and beg him to come back to New York and stay with him. He would send a car, and when Bagley arrived at the brownstone Monty would be crouching by the door with money in his hand for the driver.

The repeated doses of Demerol were causing him to hallucinate, to become fearful and increasingly paranoid. Late at night, unable to sleep, in agony with his back and his legs cramped with pain, he was sure everyone including Lorenzo was out to get him.

He compared their relationship to Pinter's *The Servant,* a movie he continued to see whenever possible, Dirk Bogarde errors notwithstanding. Why does the servant take over the master's life? he would ask rhetorically, thickly. Must every relationship between two people be a power struggle?

In the last week of his life his moods went up and down depending on how much Demerol he injected into himself. Some days he would talk wildly of firing Lorenzo; on other days he would say he was so grateful to him he had put him into his will. Sometimes he would threaten to stop seeing Elizabeth Taylor; then the thought would make him burst into tears.

He was just as emotional with Bill Le Massena. "Oh, Billy," he would cry, "I'm sorry. I'm so sorry." He was very much aware that he had destroyed himself physically.

A few days before he died he phoned a woman friend and asked her to have breakfast with him. They met in Central Park. It was a lovely summer morning. He talked about *The Defector* and how he never could have finished it without Roddy McDowall's moral support. He talked about how much he looked forward to working with Elizabeth Taylor in *Reflections in a Golden Eye.*

Around noon they walked onto Fifth Avenue, past the Sherry-Netherland Hotel, and the F.A.O. Schwarz toy store. They went down Fifty-eighth Street and Monty insisted they stop at Maison Glass, where he bought a pound of caviar. They ate it a few minutes later in the huge booklined study on the second floor. "The sun streamed in on us," she remembered. "It was beautiful."

Monty spent July 22, 1966, the last day of his life, closed off in his bedroom. "We barely exchanged a word," Lorenzo said, "but this wasn't unusual. There were often days when he simply wanted to be all alone with his head."

He considered going to Fire Island—he had again rented the house at The Pines, but he hadn't used it at all—but he decided against going.

In the afternoon he ate a goose liver sandwich. He and Lorenzo talked briefly about the place he was going to rent in Italy. They planned to leave for Rome at the end of July. *Reflections in a Golden Eye* had an August shooting schedule.

Around one in the morning Lorenzo came up to the bedroom

again to say good night, asking him if he wanted to watch *The Misfits* which was about to go on the Late Late Show.

"Absolutely not!" Monty shouted. It was the last thing Lorenzo heard him say.

Lorenzo went to wake Monty up at six A.M. and he found his bedroom door locked. He thought this was odd since Monty never locked his door, so he knocked repeatedly; when he got no answer he tried to break the door down but this proved impossible. He finally ran down into the garden and climbed up on a ladder into the bedroom window.

He found Monty lying dead on top of his outsize bed. "I went into total shock," Lorenzo said, "but I did manage to phone Monty's doctor and his lawyer, Jack Clareman."

Monty's personal physician, Dr. Ludwig, was on vacation, and so one of his associates, Dr. Howard Klein, came over immediately to examine the body. As the New York Medical Examiner's official report stated, he found Monty "lying face up in bed, glasses on, no clothes on. Right arm flexed. Both fists clenched. No evidence of trauma. Rigor present. Underclothes and pants scattered about on floor of bedroom. Liquor cabinet in bedroom. No empty bottles lying about. No notes, weapons, etc. . . ."

Jack Clareman arrived at the brownstone not long after, as did the police. He, Lorenzo, and Dr. Klein were questioned, and as the medical investigator stated in the death report, Monty "had been hallucinating for a few days and had been trying to stop drinking to get in shape for his new movie."

The body was subsequently taken by private ambulance to the City Morgue at 520 First Avenue, where an autopsy was performed by Dr. Michael Baden, Associate Medical Examiner. In the results of the autopsy he indicated there was no evidence of foul play or suicide, and the following day in the *New York Times* obituary he stated, "Mr. Clift died of occlusive coronary artery disease." He added that he'd been suffering from a calcium deficiency in his body for four years.

For the next forty-eight hours Lorenzo remained in the brownstone tied to the phone. As soon as Monty's death was announced on the radio, there were calls from friends and journalists, all over the world. He talked for a long time to Elizabeth Taylor in Paris, who kept repeating, "I'm in a state of shock. I can barely accept it. I loved him. He was my brother—he was my dearest friend."

He spoke to Ethel, who gave him permission to start making funeral arrangements until she arrived from Austin. She insisted on Monty's being given a proper church ceremony; she stressed she did not want him to have the Quaker service her father had been given in a plain room at the Friends Society on Second Avenue.

Lorenzo phoned Campbell's, he phoned St. James Episcopal Church, and he kept phoning Sunny Clift, who was nowhere to be found. Finally he reached her. By then she'd been informed of Monty's death, so she was cool, controlled. "The first thing she told me was she wanted Monty to have a Quaker service at the Friends Society." He decided he would let Ethel and her mother fight that battle out between themselves.

At one point Monty's agent, Robbie Lantz, appeared at the door with some friends, a young couple who had three children, and said they were interested in buying Monty's house. They came inside and sat in the second floor study washed with its beautiful orange light, and Lantz began reminiscing about Monty.

The day of Monty's funeral was overcast. There were only 150 people in St. James Church; the funeral was private, Ethel decreed—invitations had been limited.

Outside, several hundred people, housewives, movie buffs, tourists, stood quietly on either side of the church entrance and watched while celebrities like Lauren Bacall, Nancy Walker, Libby Holman, Dore Schary entered the church.

Inside, the half-light cast by the stained glass windows dappled the mahogany coffin which stood at the foot of an altar banked with flowers. Nearby there were two huge bouquets of white chrysanthemums from Elizabeth Taylor, as well as flowers from Roddy McDowall, Myrna Loy, and Lew Wasserman of MCA.

Sunny Clift sat in the front row along with Ethel and Brooks. Behind her were friends like Ned Smith, Bill Le Massena, Nancy Pinkerton as well as Lorenzo James.

Donald Coats, the church organ master, played Bach's "Sinfonia," the "Cathedrale Prelude," and the Fugue in E Minor. Reverend Canon read from the Psalms and from an Epistle of St. Paul to the Corinthians that contained the phrase, "Whatever you are doing, whether you speak or act, do everything in the name of the Lord."

Prayers were recited by the congregation and Canon Chase gave a benediction ending the service.

In fifteen minutes it was over, and people filed quietly out of the church. Fans waited on the sidewalk until the pallbearers slid Monty's casket into the waiting hearse. A few roses dropped off from the blanket of roses on the casket. Nancy Pinkerton stooped down and picked up a handful of petals. The hearse drove off.

Afterwards some of Monty's oldest friends stopped to offer their condolences to Sunny. She accepted them with cool graciousness.

Monty was buried in a little Quaker cemetery which stands on a hill in Brooklyn. Nancy Walker planted two hundred crocuses there, and Sunny arranged for the simple buff granite marker designed by Ned Smith's nephew, John Benson, who designed John F. Kennedy's gravestone at Arlington.

Not long after his death Ethel sold Monty's brownstone to Robbie Lantz's friends—the young couple with three children. She had one stipulation before she agreed to sell. They must put a bronze plaque on the house which would read "Montgomery Clift lived here in 1960–1966." The couple agreed. Ethel supplied the plaque and saw it fastened securely to the house.

The couple have lived in Monty's brownstone on East Sixty-first Street ever since. They love the house and are very happy there. But at first they had problems.

People kept noticing the plaque, ringing the doorbell, knocking on the kitchen windows. Small crowds gathered and strangers came around: drug addicts, movie freaks, and one teenage boy who kept insisting he was Montgomery Clift's bastard son.

The couple decided their privacy was at stake; they planted a flowering bush in front of the plaque. Today they are no longer bothered by strangers at all hours of the day or night. The plaque is still there. However, it is completely hidden by a thicket of lush green leaves.

Appendix 1

THEATER CHRONOLOGY

AS HUSBANDS GO, a comedy by Rachel Crothers; a Sarasota, Florida amateur production, March 30, 1933.

FLY AWAY HOME, a comedy in three acts, by Dorothy Bennett and Irving White. Staged by Thomas Mitchell; setting by Raymond Sovey; produced by Theron Bamberger and Warner Brothers. Opened at the Forty-eighth Street Theater, New York, on January 15, 1935.

Harmer Masters	Montgomery Clift
Buff Masters	Georgette McKee
Linda Masters	Joan Tompkins
Corey Masters	Edwin Philips
Penny	Clare Woodbury
Tinka Collingsby	Lili Zehner
Johnny Heming	Philip Faversham
James Masters	Thomas Mitchell
Armand Sloan	Albert Van Dekker
Maria	Geraldine Kay
Gabriel	Sheldon Leonard
Taxi Driver	Elmer Brown
Nan Masters	Ann Mason

JUBILEE, a musical comedy in three acts and twenty-nine scenes. Book by Moss Hart. Music and lyrics by Cole Porter. Staged and lighted by Hassard Short; dialogue directed by Monty Wooley; costumes designed by Irene Sharaff and Connie DePinna; orchestra conducted by Frank Tours; orchestrations by Russell Bennett; dances arranged by Albertina Rasch; scenery by Jo Mielziner; produced by Sam H. Harris and Max Gordon. Opened at the Imperial Theater, New York, on October 12, 1935.

The King	Melville Cooper
The Queen	Mary Boland
Prince James	Charles Walters
Princess Diana	Margaret Adams
Prince Peter	Montgomery Clift
Prince Rudolph	Jackie Kelk
Lord Wyndham	Richie Ling
Eric Dare	Derek Williams
Karen O'Kane	June Knight
Evá Standing	May Boley
Charles Rausmiller (Mowgli)	Mark Plant
Mrs. Watkins	Jane Evans
Laura Fitzgerald	Olive Reeves-Smith
A Sandwich Man	Charles Brokaw
Professor Rexford	Ralph Sumpter
The Beach Widow	Dorothy Fox
Cabinet Minister	Leo Chalzel
Cabinet Minister	Charles Brokaw
Lifeguard	Don Douglas
Announcer	Albert Amato
Master of Ceremonies	Harold Murray
The Drunk	Jack Edwards
The Usher	Ted Fetter
Keeper of Zoo	Leo Chalzel

YR. OBEDIENT HUSBAND, a "sentimental comedy" in three acts, by Horace Jackson. Settings by Jo Mielziner; staged by John Cromwell; produced by Marwell Productions (Fredric March and John Cromwell). Opened on Broadway at the Broadhurst Theatre, New York, on January 10, 1938.

Mrs. Scurlock	Dame May Whitty
Mistress Binns	Brenda Forbes
Prue	Florence Eldridge
Podd	Frieda Altman
Richard Steele	Fredric March
Joseph Addison	J. W. Austin
Partridge	Martin Wolfson
Elizabeth	Marilyn Jolie

Patrick	Harold Thomas
Silas Pennyfield	Walter Jones
Lady Envil	Helena Glenn
Lord Envil	Leslie Austen
John Gay	John Pickard
Mrs. Howe	Ethel Morrison
Thomas Howe, M.P.	A. J. Herbert
Lady Warwick (Mrs. Addison)	Katherine Stewart
Lord Finch	Montgomery Clift

EYE ON THE SPARROW, a comedy in three acts, by Maxwell Selser. Staged by "John M. Worth" (a pseudonym for Antoinette Perry, according to Burns Mantle), produced by Girvan G. Higginson. Opened on Broadway at the Vanderbilt Theatre, New York, on May 3, 1938.

Philip Thomas	Montgomery Clift
Nancy Thomas	Katherine Deane
Freeman	Edgar Stehli
Roger Sanford	Barry Sullivan
Ted Strong	Philip Ober
Barbara Thomas	Catharine Doucet
Fejac Strode	Leslie King
Jim Wright	Perce Benton
Rostican	Stiano Braggiotti
Florence Augden	Dorothy Francis
O'Mara	Francesca Lenni
Thomas Hosea	Edward Fielding
Rent Collector	Ernest Woodward
First Moving Man	Lester Damon
Rug Man	Sandy Strouse

THE WIND AND THE RAIN, a comedy in three acts, by Merton Hodge. Directed by Charles J. Parsons. At the Millbrook Theatre, Millbrook, New York, July 25-30, 1938.

Mrs. McPhe	Shirley DeMe
Gilbert Raymond	Lex Lindsay
John Williams	James Gregory
Charles Tritton	Montgomery Clift
Dr. Paul Duhamel	Allan Tower
Anne Hargreaves	Evelyn Evers
Jill Manning	Celeste Holm
Roger Cole	Jeffrey (William Clark)
Pete Morgan	Robin Clapp

DAME NATURE, a comedy in three acts, by André Birabeau, derived from the French by Patricia Collinge. Staged by Worthington Miner; settings by Norris Houghton; production under the supervision of Theresa Helburn, Lawrence Langner, and Worthington Miner; presented by the Theatre Guild as the first production of its twenty-first subscription season. Opened on Broadway at the Booth Theatre, New York, on September 26, 1938.

Max	Thomas Coffin Cooke
Beer, a Schoolboy	Charles Bellin
Second Schoolboy	Frederick Bradlee
Third Schoolboy	Edwin Mills
Concièrge	Edwin Cooper
Doctor Faridet	Harry Irvine
Leonie Perrot	Lois Hall
André Brisac	Montgomery Clift
Batton	Morgan James
Fourth Schoolboy	Peter Miner
Nanine	Kathryn Grill
Marie	Grace Matthews
Madame Brisac	Jessie Royce Landis
Monsieur Brisac	Onslow Stevens
Uncle Lucien	Forrest Orr
Paul Marachal	Wilton Graff

THE MOTHER, a play in three acts, by Paul Selver and Miles Malleson, adapted from the late Karel Capek's last play. Staged by Miles Malleson; setting by Lester Polakov; produced by Victor Payne-Jennings in association with Kathleen Robinson. Opened at the Lyceum Theatre, New York, on April 25, 1939.

The Mother	Nazimova
The Father	Reginald Bach
Andrew	Stephen Ker Appleby
George	Carl Norval
Christopher	Alan Brixley
Peter	Tom Palmer
Tony	Montgomery Clift
The Old Man	Edward Broadley

THERE SHALL BE NO NIGHT, a play in three acts, by Robert E. Sherwood. Staged by Alfred Lunt; settings by Richard Whorf; costumes by Valentina; produced by the Playwrights Company and the Theatre Guild Opened on Broadway at the Alvin Theatre, New York, on April 29, 1940.

Dr. Kaarlo Valkonen	Alfred Lunt
Miranda Valkonen	Lynn Fontanne
Dave Corween	Richard Whorf
Uncle Waldemar	Sydney Greenstreet
Gus Shuman	Brooks West
Erik Valkonen	Montgomery Clift
Kaatri Alquist	Elisabeth Fraser
Dr. Ziemssen	Maurice Colbourne
Major Rutkowski	Edward Raquello
Joe Burnett	Charles Ansley
Ben Gichner	Thomas Gomez
Frank Olmstead	William Le Massena
Sergeant Gosden	Claude Horton
Lempi	Phyllis Thaxter
Ilma	Charva Chester
Photographer	Ralph Nelson
Photographer	Robert Downing

MEXICAN MURAL, a play in "four panels," by Ramon Naya. Staged and produced by Robert Lewis; scenery by Herbert Andrews; lighted by Wil Washcoe. Opened at the Chanin Auditorium, 122 East Forty-second Street, New York, on April 26, 1942.

First Panel: Vera Cruz Interior

Rumbero	Wallace House
Comparsas	Priscilla Newton,
	Robert Lander
Didi Ruiz	Perry Wilson
Dona Alex	Kathryn Grill
Lalo Brito	Montgomery Clift
Luisa	Eda Reiss

Second Panel: Miracle Painting

Celestina Ruiz	Libby Holman
Chelina	Terry Dicks
Doctor Brito	Spencer James
Morena	Gertrude Gilpin
Petra	Henrietta Lovelace
Verbena	Mira Rosovskaya
	(Mira Rostova)
A Lady	Norma Chambers

Third Panel: Moonlight Scene

Mariano Ruiz	Kevin McCarthy
Miguel Ruiz	Owen Jordon

Troubadours	Wallace House,
	Spencer James
Mata Hari	David Opatoshu
Gold Shirts	Larry Hugo,
	William Le Massena,
	Morton Amster
People of Vera Cruz	Tom Barry, Viola Kates,
	Priscilla Newton,
	Robert Lander, and
	others

Fourth Panel: Patio with Flamingo

The Redhead	Kenneth Tobey
Juliana	Norma Chambers
Maria Chris	Viola Kates

THE SKIN OF OUR TEETH, a "new comedy" in three acts, by Thornton Wilder. Staged by Elia Kazan; settings by Albert Johnson; costumes by Mary Perry Schenck; produced by Michael Myerberg. Opened on Broadway at the Plymouth Theater, New York, on November 18, 1942.

Announcer	Morton Da Costa
Sabina	Tallulah Bankhead
Mr. Fitzpatrick	E. G. Marshall
Mrs. Antrobus	Florence Eldridge
Dinosaur	Remo Buffano
Mammoth	Andrew Ratousheff
Telegraph Boy	Dickie Van Patten
Gladys	Frances Heflin
Henry	Montgomery Clift
Mr. Antrobus	Fredric March
Doctor	Arthur Griffin
Professor	Ralph Kellard
Judge	Joseph Smiley
Homer	Ralph Cullinan
Miss E. Muse	Edith Faversham
Miss T. Muse	Emily Lorraine
Miss M. Muse	Eva Mudge Nelson
Usher	Stanley Prager
Usher	Harry Clark
Girl	Elizabeth Scott
Girl	Patricia Riordan
Fortune Teller	Florence Reed
Chair Pusher	Earl Sydnor
Chair Pusher	Carroll Clark

Convener	Stanley Weede
Convener	Seumas Flynn
Convener	Aubrey Fasset
Convener	Stanley Prager
Convener	Harry Clark
Convener	Stephan Cole
Broadcast Official	Morton DaCosta
Defeated Candidate	Joseph Smiley
Mr. Tremayne	Ralph Kellard
Hester	Eulabelle Moore
Ivy	Viola Dean
Fred Bailey	Stanley Prager

OUR TOWN, a play, by Thornton Wilder. Staged by Jed Harris and Welsey McKee. Revived by Jed Harris. Opened at the City Center, New York, on January 10, 1944.

Stage Manager	Marc Connelly
Dr. Gibbs	Curtis Cooksey
Joe Crowell	Richard Dalton
Howie Newsome	Donald Keyes
Mrs. Gibbs	Evelyn Varden
Mrs. Webb	Ethel Remey
George Gibbs	Montgomery Clift
Rebecca Gibbs	Carolyn Hummel
Wally Webb	Teddy Rose
Emily Webb	Martha Scott
Professor Willard	Arthur Allen
Mr. Webb	Parker Fennelly
Woman in the Balcony	Alice Hill
Man in the Auditorium	John Paul
Lady in the box	Frederica Going
Simon Stimson	William Swetland
Mrs. Soames	Doro Merande
Constable Warren	Owen Coll
Si Crowell	Roy Robson
Baseball players	Alfred Porter, Charles Wiley, Jr., Henry Michaels
Sam Craig	Jay Velie
Joe Stoddard	John Ravold
Mr. Carter	Walter O. Hill

THE SEARCHING WIND, a play in two acts and six scenes, by Lillian Hellman. Staged by Herman Shumlin; settings by Howard Bay; costumes by Aline

Bernstein; produced by Herman Shumlin. Opened on Broadway at the Fulton Theatre, New York, on April 12, 1944.

Moses Taney	Dudley Digges
Samuel Hazen	Montgomery Clift
Ponette	Alfred Hesse
Sophronia	Mercedes Gilbert
Emily Hazen	Cornelia Otis Skinner
Alexander Hazen	Dennis King
Catherine Bowman	Barbara O'Neil
First Waiter	Edgar Andrews
Second Waiter	Joseph de Santis
Hotel Manager	Walter Kohler
Eppler	William F. Schoeller
Edward Halsey	Eric Latham
James Sears	Eugene Earl
Count Max von Stammer	Arnold Korff

FOXHOLE IN THE PARLOR, a "new" play in three acts and one scene, by Elsa Shelley. Directed by John Haggott; setting by Lee Simonson; produced by Harry Bloomfield. Opened on Broadway at the Booth Theatre, New York, on May 23, 1945.

Leroy	Reginald Beane
Tom Austen	Russell Hardie
Vicki King	Ann Lincoln
Ann Austen	Flora Campbell
Senator Bowen	Raymond Greenleaf
Dennis Patterson	Montgomery Clift
Kate Mitchell	Grace Coppin

YOU TOUCHED ME!, a romantic comedy in three acts and six scenes, by Tennessee Williams and Donald Windham, suggested by D. H. Lawrence's short story by the same name. Staged by Guthrie McClintic in association with Lee Shubert. Opened on Broadway at the Booth Theatre, New York, on September 25, 1945.

Matilda Rockley	Marianne Stewart
Emmie Rockley	Catherine Willard
Phoebe	Norah Howard
Hadrian	Montgomery Clift
Cornelius Rockley	Edmund Gwenn
Rev. Guilford Melton	Neil Fitzgerald
A Policeman	Freeman Hammond

THE SEAGULL, a play in two acts and four scenes, by Anton Chekov, adapted by Mira Rostova, Kevin McCarthy, and Montgomery Clift. Staged by Norris Houghton; incidental music by Max Marlin; scenery by Duane McKinney; costumes by Alvin Colt; lighting by Klaus Holm; revival opened at the Phoenix Theatre, New York, on May 11, 1954.

Mme. Irina Arkadina	Judith Evelyn
Constantin Treplev	Montgomery Clift
Peter Sorin	Sam Jaffe
Nina Zarechnaya	Mira Rostova
Shamrayev	Will Geer
Paulina	June Walker
Masha	Maureen Stapleton
Boris Trigorin	Kevin McCarthy
Dr. Dorn	George Voskovec
Medvedenko	Jon Fiedler
Yakov	Karl Light
Cook	Lou Polan
Housemaid	Sarah Marshall

Appendix 2

FILM CHRONOLOGY

THE SEARCH, original screenplay by Richard Schweizer in collaboration with David Wechsler, with additional dialogue by Paul Jarrico. Directed by Fred Zinnemann; produced by Lazar Wechsler for MGM. Opened on March 24, 1948.

Ralph Stevenson	Montgomery Clift
Mrs. Murray	Aline McMahon
Mrs. Malik	Jarmila Novotna
Jerry Fisher	Wendell Corey
Mrs. Fisher	Mary Patton
Mr. Crookes	Ewart G. Morrison
Tom Fisher	William Rogers
Karel Malik	Ivan Jandl
Joel Makowsky	Leopold Borkowski
Raoul Dubois	Claude Gambier

RED RIVER, screenplay by Borden Chase and Charles Schnee, based on a story by Borden Chase. Produced and directed by Howard Hawks; released through United Artists. Opened on September 30, 1948.

Thomas Dunson	John Wayne
Matthew Garth	Montgomery Clift
Tess Millay	Joanne Dru
Groot	Walter Brennan

Fen	Coleen Gray
Cherry	John Ireland
Buster	Noah Berry, Jr.
Quo	Chief Yowlachie
Melville	Harry Carey, Sr.
Dan Latimer	Harry Carey, Jr.
Matt (as a boy)	Mickey Kuhn
Teeler	Paul Fix
Sims	Hank Warden
Bunk Kenneally	Ivan Parry
Old Leather	Hal Taliaferro
Fernandez	Paul Fiero
Wounded Wrangler	Billie Self
Walt Jargens	Ray Hyke

THE HEIRESS, screenplay by Ruth and Augustus Goetz, from their play of the same name, suggested by Henry James's novel *Washington Square*. Directed and produced by William Wyler for Paramount. Opened on October 6, 1949.

Catherine Sloper	Olivia deHavilland
Morris Townsend	Montgomery Clift
Dr. Austin Sloper	Ralph Richardson
Lavinia Penniman	Miriam Hopkins
Maria	Vanessa Brown
Mirian Almond	Mona Freeman
Jefferson Almond	Ray Collins
Mrs. Montgomery	Betty Linley
Elizabeth Almond	Selma Royle

THE BIG LIFT, written and directed by George Seaton. Produced by William Perlberg for 20th Century-Fox. Opened on April 26, 1950.

Danny MacCullough	Montgomery Clift
Hank	Paul Douglas
Frederica	Cornell Borchers
Gerda	Bruni Lobel
Stieber	O. E. Hasse
Private	Danny Davenport
Gunther	Fritz Nichlisch
Himself	Capt. Dante V. Morel
Himself	Capt. John Mason
Himself	Capt. Gail Plush

A PLACE IN THE SUN, screenplay by Michael Wilson and Harry Brown, based on the novel *An American Tragedy* by Theodore Dreiser, and on the

Patrick Kearny play adapted from the novel. Produced and directed by George Stevens for Paramount. Opened on August 28, 1951.

George Eastman	Montgomery Clift
Angela Vickers	Elizabeth Taylor
Alice Tripp	Shelley Winters
Hannah Eastman	Anne Revere
Marlowe	Raymond Burr
Charles Eastman	Herbert Heyes
Earl Eastman	Keefe Brasselle
Anthony Vickers	Shepperd Strudwick
Mrs. Vickers	Frieda Inescort
Dr. Wyeland	Ian Wolfe
Marcia Eastman	Lois Chartrand
Bellows (Defense Attorney)	Fred Clark
Jansan	Walter Sande
Boatkeeper	Douglas Spencer
Coroner	John Ridgley
Mrs. Louise Eastman	Kathryn Givney
Judge	Ted de Corsia
Kelly	Charles Dayton
Rev. Morrison	Paul Frees
Mrs. Whiting	William R. Murphy

I CONFESS, screenplay by George Tabori and William Archibald, from the play *Our Two Consciences* by Paul Anthelme. Produced and directed by Alfred Hitchcock for Warner Brothers. Opened on March 22, 1953.

Father Michael Logan	Montgomery Clift
Ruth Grandfort	Anne Baxter
Inspector Larrue	Karl Malden
Willy Robertson	Brian Aherne
Otto Keller	O. E. Hasse
Alma Keller	Dolly Haas
Pierre Grandfort	Roger Dann
Father Millais	Charles André
Murphy	Judson Pratt
Vilette	Ovila Legare
Father Benoit	Gilles Pelletier

FROM HERE TO ETERNITY, screenplay by Daniel Taradash, based on the novel by James Jones. Directed by Fred Zinnemann; produced by Buddy Adler for Columbia Pictures. Opened August 5, 1953.

Sgt. Milton Warden	Burt Lancaster
Robert E. Lee Prewitt	Montgomery Clift
Karen Holmes	Deborah Kerr
Angelo Maggio	Frank Sinatra
Alma (Lorene)	Donna Reed
Capt. Dana Holmes	Philip Ober
Sgt. Leva	Mickey Shaughnessy
Mazzioli	Harry Bellaver
Sgt. Fatso Judson	Ernest Borgnine
Cpl. Buckley	Jack Warden
Sgt. Ike Galovitch	John Dennis
Sgt. Maylon Stark	George Reeves
Sgt. Pete Karelsen	Tim Ryan
Mrs. Kipfer	Barbara Morrison
Georgette	Kristine Miller
Annette	Jean Willes
Sgt. Anderson	Merle Travis
Treadwell	Arthur Keegan
Sgt. Baldy Dhom	Claude Akins
Sgt. Turp Thornhill	Robert Karnes
Sgt. Henderson	Robert Wilke
Cpl. Champ Wilson	Douglas Henderson
Friday Clark	Don Dubbins
Cpl. Paluso	John Cason
Capt. Ross	John Bryant

INDISCRETION OF AN AMERICAN WIFE, screenplay by Cesare Zavattini, Luigi Chiarini, and Giorgio Presperi, with dialogue by Truman Capote, from a story by Cesare Zavattini. Directed and produced by Vittorio De Sica. Released by Columbia Pictures. Opened on June 25, 1954.

Mary	Jennifer Jones
Giovanni	Montgomery Clift
Commissioner	Gino Cervi
Paul	Dick Beymer

RAINTREE COUNTY, screenplay by Millard Kaufman, based on the novel by Ross Lockridge, Jr. Directed by Edward Dmytryk; produced by David Lewis for MGM. Opened on December 20, 1957.

John Shawnessy	Montgomery Clift
Susanna Drake	Elizabeth Taylor
Nell Gaither	Eva Marie Saint

Jerusalem Stiles	Nigel Patrick
"Flash" Perkins	Lee Marvin
Garwood B. Jones	Rod Taylor
Ellen Shawnessy	Agnes Moorehead
T. D. Shawnessy	Walter Abel
Barbara Drake	Jarma Lewis
Bobby Drake	Tom Drake
Ezra Gray	Rhys Williams
Niles Foster	Russell Collins
Southern Officer	DeForrest Kelley

THE YOUNG LIONS, screenplay by Edward Anhalt, based on the novel by Irwin Shaw. Directed by Edward Dmytryk; produced by Al Dichtman for 20th Century-Fox. Opened on April 2, 1958.

Christian	Marlon Brando
Noah	Montgomery Clift
Michael Whiteacre	Dean Martin
Hope Plowman	Hope Lange
Margaret Freemantle	Barbara Rush
Gretchen Hardenberg	May Britt
Hardenberg	Maximilian Schell
Simone	Dora Doll
Sgt. Rickett	Lee Van Cleef
Françoise	Liliane Montevecchi
Brant	Parley Baer
Lt. Green	Arthur Franz
Pvt. Burnecker	Hal Baylor
Pvt. Cowley	Richard Gardner
Capt. Colclough	Herbert Rudley
Corp. Kraus	John Alderson
Pvt. Faber	Sam Gilman
Pvt. Donnelly	L. Q. Jones
Pvt. Brailsford	Julien Burton

LONELYHEARTS, screenplay by Dore Schary; based on Nathanael West's novel *Miss Lonelyhearts* and the play by Howard Teichman. Directed by Vincent J. Donahue; produced by Dore Schary; released by United Artists. Opened on March 4, 1959.

Adam White	Montgomery Clift
William Shrike	Robert Ryan
Florence Shrike	Myrna Loy
Justy Sargent	Dolores Hart

Fay Doyle	Maureen Stapleton
Pat Doyle	Frank Maxwell
Gates	Jackie Coogan
Goldsmith	Mike Kellin
Mr. Sargent	Frank Overton
Older Brother	Don Washbrook
Younger Brother	John Washbrook
Mr. Lassiter	Onslow Stevens
Edna	Mary Alan Hokanson
Bartender	John Galludet
Jerry	Lee Zimmer

SUDDENLY LAST SUMMER, screenplay by Tennessee Williams and Gore Vidal; adapted from the play by Tennessee Williams. Directed by Joseph Mankiewicz; produced by Sam Spiegel for Columbia Pictures. Opened on December 22, 1959.

Catherine Holly	Elizabeth Taylor
Mrs. Venable	Katharine Hepburn
Dr. Cukrowicz	Montgomery Clift
Dr. Hockstader	Albert Dekker
Mrs. Holly	Mercedes McCambridge
George Holly	Gary Raymond
Miss Foxhill	Mavis Villiers
Nurse Benson	Patricia Marmont
Sister Felicity	Joan Young
Lucy	Marie Britneva
Medical Secretary	Sheila Robbins
Young Blond Intern	David Cameron

WILD RIVER, screenplay by Paul Osborn, based on the novels by William Bradford Huie and Bordon Deal. Directed and produced by Elia Kazan; presented by 20th Century-Fox. Opened on May 26, 1960.

Chuck Glover	Montgomery Clift
Carol	Lee Remick
Ella Garth	Jo Van Fleet
Hank Bailey	Albert Salmi
Hamilton Garth	J. C. Flippen
Cal Garth	James Westerfield
Betty Jackson	Barbara Loden
Walter Clark	Frank Overton
Sy Moore	Malcolm Atterbury

Ben	Robert Earl Jones
Jack Roper	Bruce Dern
Sam Johnson	Robert Earl Jones

THE MISFITS, screenplay by Arthur Miller. Directed by John Huston; produced by Frank E. Taylor; released by United Artists. Opened on February 1, 1961.

Gay Langland	Clark Gable
Roslyn Taber	Marilyn Monroe
Perce Howland	Montgomery Clift
Isabelle Steers	Thelma Ritter
Guido	Eli Wallach
Old Man	James Barton
Church Lady	Estelle Winwood
Raymond Taber	Kevin McCarthy
Young Boy	Dennis Shaw

JUDGMENT AT NUREMBERG, screenplay by Abby Mann. Directed and produced by Stanley Kramer; a Roxlon production released through United Artists. Opened on December 19, 1961.

Judge Dan Haywood	Spencer Tracy
Ernst Janning	Burt Lancaster
Col. Tad Lawson	Richard Widmark
Mme. Bertholt	Marlene Dietrich
Hans Rolfe	Maximilian Schell
Irene Hoffman	Judy Garland
Rudolph Peterson	Montgomery Clift
Capt. Byers	William Shatner
Senator Burkette	Ed Binns
Judge Kenneth Norris	Kenneth Mackenna
Emil Hahn	Werner Klemperer
General Merrin	Alan Baxter
Werner Lammpe	Torben Meyer
Judge Curtiss Ives	Ray Teal
Friedrich Hofstetter	Martin Brandt
Mrs. Halbestadt	Virginia Christine
Halbestadt	Ben Wright
Maj. Abe Radnitz	Joseph Bernard
Dr. Wieck	John Wengraf

FREUD, screenplay by Charles Kaufman and Wolfgang Reinhardt, from a story by Charles Kaufman. Directed by John Huston; produced by Wolfgang Reinhardt for Universal. Opened on December 12, 1962.

Sigmund Freud	Montgomery Clift
Cecil Koertner	Susannah York
Dr. Joseph Breuer	Larry Parks
Martha Freud	Susan Kohner
Frau Ida Koertner	Eileen Herly
Dr. Theodore Meynert	Eric Portman
Professor Charcot	Ferdinand Ledeux
Carl von Schlosser	David McCallum
Frau Freud	Rosalie Crutchley
Jacob Freud	David Kosoff
Jacob Koertner	Joseph Furft
Babinsky	Alexander Mango
Brouhardier	Leonard Sachs

THE DEFECTOR, screenplay by Robert Guenette and Raoul Levy, based on the novel *The Spy* by Paul Thomas. Produced and directed by Raoul Levy; presented by Seven Arts Pictures. Opened on November 16, 1966.

Professor James Bower	Montgomery Clift
Counsellor Peter Heinzman	Hardy Kruger
C.I.A. Agent Adam	Roddy McDowall
Frieda Hoffman	Macha Meril
Orlovsky	David Opatoshu
Ingrid	Christine Delaroche
Doctor Saltzer	Hannes Messemer
The Major	Karl Lieffen

Index